Arnulfo L. Oliveira Memorial Library

# MASTER
## of WAR

**THE LIFE OF GENERAL GEORGE H. THOMAS**

Benson Bobrick

*Simon & Schuster*

NEW YORK LONDON TORONTO SYDNEY

Simon & Schuster
1230 Avenue of the Americas
New York, NY 10020

Copyright © 2009 by Benson Bobrick

First Simon & Schuster hardcover edition February 2009

SIMON & SCHUSTER and colophon are registered trademarks of
Simon & Schuster, Inc.

For information about special discounts for bulk purchases,
please contact Simon & Schuster Special Sales at
1-800-456-6798 or business@simonandschuster.com

Designed by Paul Dippolito
Maps by Paul J. Pugliese

Manufactured in the United States of America

1    3    5    7    9    10    8    6    4    2

Library of Congress Cataloging-in-Publication Data

Bobrick, Benson, date.
Master of war: the life of General George H. Thomas / Benson Bobrick.
      p.        cm.
Includes bibliographical references and index.
1. Thomas, George Henry, 1816–1870.   2. Thomas, George Henry, 1816–1870—
Military leadership.   3. Generals—United States—Biography.   4. United States.
Army—Biography.   5. United States—History—Civil War, 1861–1865—
Campaigns.   6. Unionists (United States Civil War)—Virginia—Biography.   I. Title.
E467.1.T4B63      2009
973.7092—dc22
[B]                    2008031843
ISBN-13: 978-0-7432-9025-8
ISBN-10:      0-7432-9025-9

All photographs courtesy of the Library of Congress.

*To*
*Hagop Missak Merjian,*
*one of the great teachers of my youth*
*&*
*Marvin and Evelyn Farbman,*
*beloved friends*

# CONTENTS

*"Time and history will do me justice."*
—MAJOR GENERAL GEORGE H. THOMAS


*"It takes time for jealousy and ambition, spewing out calumny, to gnash, gnaw, and consume themselves. But time is long, and justice never dies."*
—MAJOR GENERAL OLIVER O. HOWARD, "A SKETCH OF THE LIFE OF GENERAL GEORGE H. THOMAS"

# MASTER
## *of* WAR

# 1. AN END TO INNOCENCE

On April 8, 1870, the remains of the man were deposited in a metal casket, twined around with a ribbon of ivy and mounted on a dais in the chancel of St. Paul's Church in Troy, New York. An elegant crown of evergreens and roses was placed at the head, surmounted by a cross of immortelles; a wreath of japonica and lilies at the feet. The president of the United States, Ulysses S. Grant, was in attendance, as were Generals William Tecumseh Sherman, Joseph Hooker, Philip Sheridan, George Gordon Meade, and other notables of rank among the vast concourse of mourners and admirers who had come to pay their respects. The special train that had carried his body eastward from the Pacific just a few days before had been met by silent crowds at every station, and flags across the nation were hung at half-mast. The casket itself, however, bore only a simple silver plate inscribed with the name of the deceased and the dates of his birth and death. At the special request of his widow, no panegyric or eulogy was pronounced over his grave. After a brief service, the casket was conveyed to Oakwood Cemetery where it was interred in a vault; and after an honor guard of soldiers fired their customary burial salute, the procession departed, "each portion wheeling out of the lines on the return, as it reached its appropriate place."

In this exquisitely modest yet majestic fashion, typical in all ways of the man, General George H. Thomas passed from the scene. Even then he was considered by some the greatest general the Civil War had produced, but Grant and Sherman would both outlive him by many years and successfully promote their own reputations, often at his expense. Both would also glorify each other, write popular memoirs

1

that at times revised the facts, and by accident or design ensure that Thomas would be placed third or last in the acknowledged triumvirate of Union commanders who had determined the outcome of the war. For a century or so, history seemed to follow their lead and to adopt that judgment, which also became the popular verdict.

That judgment has since been slowly reversed. In recent years, a kind of consensus has emerged among many close students of the war that Thomas surpassed not only Grant and Sherman but even Lee. While historians continue to debate the painful and embarrassed question as to which of these worthies was more reckless in his tactics or more wasteful of his men, they have increasingly come to marvel at the skill, imagination, and humane economy with which Thomas fought his battles, winning every one. No one has ever asked why Thomas sent his men to pointless slaughter, because he never did. In a war distinguished by mind-boggling carnage, he was notably free of the promiscuous or chronic blunders that often stained the major clashes of the war. He poured his men into battle only when it counted; and when it counted, he prevailed.

All this would be little more than academic praise if his battles had been minor, or his role peripheral as the war played out. But the opposite was true. He gave the Union its first major victory at Mill Springs, Kentucky (January 19, 1862), which helped save Kentucky for the Union and opened the way to Tennessee; rendered service at the siege of Corinth (where he practically superseded Grant); held the center at Stones River where, on a wooded knoll known afterward as "Hell's Half Acre," he snatched victory from defeat, and, in consequence, secured Middle Tennessee; took charge of the most important part of the maneuvering from Decherd to Chattanooga during the Tullahoma campaign (June 22–July 3, 1863), with its great victory at Hoover's Gap; once more saved the day, at Chickamauga, where, on the crest of Horseshoe Ridge with three-fifths of the Union army streaming to the rear along with its commander, Thomas planted himself and a decimated array of broken regiments, brigades, and divisions, and held his ground long enough to permit the army to make an orderly retreat; routed the Confederates at Missionary Ridge in the Battle of Chattanooga, which won that engagement for Grant; par-ried John Bell Hood's all-out attack at Peachtree Creek in the Atlanta campaign; and destroyed Hood's army at Nashville to end the war in the West. Then, despite Grant's interference, he built a cavalry force that neutralized the industrial hubs of Selma and Montgomery, Alabama; overcame the supposedly invincible Nathan Bedford Forrest; and helped to capture Jefferson Davis in Georgia with his network of spies. In the end, it could be said of him uniquely that whereas Sherman never won a battle and Grant often battered his way to victory with overwhelming force, Thomas was the only Union general to destroy two Confederate armies, and the only one, besides, to save two Union armies from annihilation by his personal valor and skill.

William Swinton, in his classic book, *The Twelve Decisive Battles of the War*, published in 1867, while memories were still fresh, wrote: "The figure of Thomas looms up, in many respects without a superior, in most instances without a rival even, among the Union generals created by the war." As one fellow officer declared: "The incidents of his life lie like massive facts upon the face of our national history."

Historians have been intrigued by Sherman's neurotic personality, and Grant's rise from drunkard to commander-in-chief. They might be more justified if both men had mastered themselves. But neither did. "He stood by me when I was crazy," said Sherman, in a famous assessment of their friendship, "and I stood by him when he was drunk." But Sherman remained unstable throughout his career; and Grant, however capable in some respects, remained small-minded, devious, and (with interludes) a heavy drinker to the end. In an unpublished manuscript, entitled "Heroes of the Great Rebellion," General James H. Wilson, Grant's own favorite cavalry commander, concluded sadly that Grant in the end owed much of his military stature from the war to John A. Rawlins, his able chief of staff. Only Thomas, in his judgment, emerged as the towering figure that he was: "The peer of any other general in the army . . . full of dignity and authority . . . a proud, self-respecting, honorable man."

One fellow officer (Major Donn Piatt, judge advocate in the celebrated treason trial of General Don Carlos Buell) wrote: "Grant felt uneasy and ashamed in the presence of Thomas, and both Grant and Sherman were troubled with the thought that truth and justice would award to their subordinate in office the higher position on the honor roll."

Thomas himself once said that Time and History would do him justice. General Oliver O. Howard, in a biographical tribute declared: "It takes time for jealousy and ambition, spewing out calumny, to gnash, gnaw, and consume themselves. But time is long, and justice never dies."

Born on July 31, 1816, at Newsom's Depot in Southampton County, Virginia, not far from the famed site of the Battle of Yorktown, which sealed the fate of the Revolutionary War, George Henry Thomas came from sturdy frontier stock. His father, John Thomas, was of Welsh lineage, and his mother, Elizabeth Rochelle, of French Huguenot descent. When George was twelve, his father died of a farm accident, leaving a wife and nine children behind. Almost nothing is known of his siblings. His two older brothers, John and Benjamin, and two sisters, Judith Elvira and Fanny, figure only briefly in his recorded life.

The family was relatively well-to-do, owning a farm in the Tidewater district with twelve to fifteen slaves, and his father, though not a member of the planter aristocracy, was "a prosperous farmer with spreading acres of tobacco, cotton and corn." The home Thomas grew up in was a large, two-storied white house set in a beautiful clearing among a stand of ancient oaks. One particularly large oak tree of "almost perfect symmetry" shaded the front yard.

On the whole, the country was a richly productive one, with a good balance of Piedmont and Tidewater soil types, with creeks and small streams coursing to the Nottoway and Meherrin Rivers, forming valleys and rolling plains. The wetlands were well suited for cattle and hogs; the sandy loam for tobacco and most crops. Luxuriant forests of cypress, gum, and loblolly pine furnished all the county's lumber needs. Here and there farms, plantations, and crossroad villages had been carved out of the woods. Part of Tidewater Virginia had given up on tobacco, which impoverished the soil, and many old tobacco fields were overgrown with trees and shrubs. The Thomas property, like many others, was dotted by haystacks and corn and cotton patches, with various satellite sheds, slave cabins, and a barn. Dogs, chickens, pigs, cows, mules, and horses were all kept as pets or livestock. The apple orchard provided an apple brandy "potent enough to make a sailor reel." The Thomas farm was not exceptional in this, for no homestead was considered complete without a brandy still.

At fall harvest time, peas and beans were gathered in; livestock slaughtered; leaves of tobacco stripped from their stalks; potato vines scalloped from their roots. These were packed into hogsheads, along with shocks of corn. As the cotton leaves turned russet and fell to earth, "the gently rolling fields were draped in angel-white."

Some twenty miles east of the Thomas farm lay the outermost margins of the Great Dismal Swamp, an immense, 300-square-mile quagmire, which had long served as a sanctuary for wildcats, deer, and possum, and a haven for outlaws and runaway slaves. Half-inundated with standing pools and divided by creeks and veinlike streams, its spongy, saturated soil—composed entirely of decayed plant fiber—quaked underfoot. Like a number of smaller swamps, known as the Little Dismal, Alligator, Catfish, Green, and so on, along other county lines, the Great Dismal was overgrown with shrubs and creepers, forming a dense brake or jungle that could be crossed only by log or corduroy roads. The children of many a runaway slave were born, bred, lived, and died there. Some lived in huts in "back places" hidden by bushes, and difficult to reach. Occasionally an inquisitive explorer would come upon a skeleton intertwined with vines and briars.

Some of the waterways (like the Nottoway and Meherrin Rivers) were also "minefields of submerged cypress trees and fallen timbers and could only be negotiated by flatboats and canoes." All this gave to the area a lagoonlike grandeur that must have fascinated young Thomas as much as later generations were spellbound by the winding recesses of the Mississippi Delta in the stories of Mark Twain.

Though the county (named for the third earl of Southampton, a favorite of James I) had a noble provenance, the county seat of Jerusalem (called Courtland now), on the Nottoway River, was scarcely grand, with a population of 175, and "a smoky cluster of buildings where pigs rooted in the streets and old-timers spat tobacco juice in the shade." Two-thirds of the county population of 16,000 was made up of slaves, and at nearly every courthouse, tavern, and post office could be seen handbills offering rewards for those who had run away. Conditions of their servitude varied from farm to farm, as they did from state to state, with those in Virginia on the whole better than those in Georgia, Alabama, Mississippi, and other parts of the Deep South. There, on large cotton plantations, they toiled in the hundreds under the lash like beasts of burden almost around the clock.

In Virginia, on the other hand, the population of freed blacks had been on the rise. The emancipation spirit in Southampton County (fostered chiefly by Quakers) was unusually strong, but freed blacks were said to be subversive by example—"seducing [the slave], if possible, from allegiance to his master, and instilling, as far as practicable, into his mind false and fallacious notions of liberty and equality, wholly incompatible with the relations of master and slave." That placed them in a kind of limbo, and most found it hard going, as they tried to adapt to a society tacitly hostile to their needs. Some, grown helplessly abject, even asked to be reenslaved, in accordance with legislation passed before the Civil War.

Yet the general segregation was loose. Black and white children often played together, black women carried black and white babies together in their arms, and though blacks were technically not supposed to be allowed in first-class trains, servants accompanied their masters everywhere. In larger towns, blacks also mingled, uneasily, with whites in the streets. Frederick Law Olmsted, on his famous tour of the South about this time, recalled:

> I saw a Virginian gentleman lift his walking-stick and push a woman aside with it. In the evening I saw three rowdies, arm-in-arm, taking the whole of the sidewalk, hustle a black man off it, giving him a blow, as they passed, that sent him staggering into the middle of the street. As he recovered himself he began to call out to, and threaten them. Perhaps he saw me stop, and thought I should support him, as I was certainly inclined to: "Can't you find anything else to do than to be knockin' quiet people round! You jus' come back here, will you? Here, you! Don't care if you is white. You jus'

come back here, and I'll teach you how to behave—knockin' people round!—don't care if I does hab to go to der watch-house." They passed on without noticing him further, only laughing jeeringly— and he continued: "You come back here, and I'll make you laugh; you is jus' three white nigger cowards, dat's what you be." Olmsted saw an amazing number of mulattos as well as blacks—"full half, I should think, are more or less of negro blood, and a very decent, civil people these seem, in general, to be; more so than the laboring class of whites, among which there are many very ruffianly-looking fellows."

Beyond the towns, homesteads were few and far between, and one could ride along rough roads for hours and not encounter a single house. When a mansion appeared, it was seldom grand, and to a Northerner accustomed to the great growing cities of the North, even Richmond was a comparatively shabby place. In 1830, it had a population of about 28,000, with a Grecian-style capitol building (designed by Thomas Jefferson) picturesquely set among some hills. But few other buildings had architectural merit; the streets were unpaved and lacked sidewalks except for dirt or gravel paths; and even the capitol, though imposing from a distance, was a "pretense of dignity," made of cheap stucco or imitation stone. Richmond's commercial bustle was also not unlike that of any other large rural town. Immense wagons, drawn by six mules each, crowded the streets; long, narrow canal boats loaded with tobacco, flour, and raw country produce plied the nearbly streams. Dens of iniquity abounded, with "at least as much vice," wrote Olmsted, "as in any Northern town of its size."

Though Thomas was born into the corrupted privilege of a slave-holding life, he seems to have been almost untouched by prejudice. We have a charming glimpse of him as a child from one of his black playmates named Artise, who was interviewed about him long after the Civil War. "George," said Artise, "was playful as a kitten" and often ran about with the slave children under the great spreading oak tree in the yard. He seemed to "love the Negro quarters more than he did

the great house" and would sneak sugar and other treats to his playmates as they went off to look for raccoons and possums in the woods.
That was not unheard of. But an uncommon decency showed itself in
him even then. Artise recalled that when Thomas was a bit older, he
secretly gathered the children of the family's slaves together each day
after his own schooling and "against his parents' wishes" taught them
how to read and write. He also gave them Bible lessons, and shared
with them at night what he learned each day in school. Perhaps he
passed on other kinds of knowledge, too. From a saddlemaker he
learned how to make his own saddles; from a cabinetmaker, fine furniture, in an early development of his mechanical skills.

On the whole, his life as a boy was an idyllic one, yet full, too, of
heroic models whose lives were mingled with state pride. Thomas
grew up at a time when Virginia was still the center of the American
political world. James Madison was president when he was born, followed by James Monroe, the fourth Virginian of the first five presidents during the first thirty-six years of the nation's life. John Marshall,
also from Virginia, was chief justice, and was to hold, unrivaled, that
position until Thomas was almost a young man. Most of the secretaries of state had been Virginian, and in Congress the influence of the
state was paramount. Soldiers who had served under George Washington had also "poured the stories of their hardships and the greatness of their leader into his youthful ears."

Then, when he was fifteen, he was nearly cut to pieces in Nat
Turner's great slave revolt.

For years, Nat had toiled away in apocalyptic rage in the fields of a
nearby farm. Rage had even shadowed his birth, for his mother—an
olive-skinned woman abducted in her teens from the Valley of the
Nile—had wanted to kill him rather than see him raised as a slave. To
make the catastrophe of his childhood complete, a few years later, his
father, also a slave, disappeared.

Nat led a fated life. When he was just "three or four," he seemed to
know things that only divine knowledge could impart, and his mother,
as well as others called to witness, were so "astonished," he recalled,
"that they said in my hearing, I surely would be a prophet, as the Lord
had shown me things that had happened before my birth." That made

an indelible impression on his mind. His parents also told him that he was "intended for some great purpose," and even his master, Benjamin Turner (whose given name he took), and members of Turner's Methodist church found Nat's "singularity of manners" and intelligence striking. It was said within his hearing that he "had too much sense" to be "of any service to any one as a slave," which sowed the seed of hope in him that he might one day be freed.

Political developments helped that seed to sprout. Nat had learned to read and write with remarkable ease, was aware of current events, and nineteen when the Missouri Compromise debate took place. As Congress hashed out the question as to whether Missouri should be admitted to the Union as a slave or a free state, an amendment was introduced in Congress to free slave children at the age of twenty-five. It failed to pass, but was widely publicized as indicating what the future might hold.

Nat attended the local slave church and went to "Negro praise meetings" held in forest clearings and tumbledown shacks, where a unique black culture thrived. He memorized whole books of the Bible and "grew to manhood with the words of the prophets roaring in his ears." One day while praying at his plow Nat thought he heard a voice in the wind—the Spirit called out to him—"Seek ye the kingdom of Heaven and all things shall be added unto you—as to the prophets of old." In response, he pondered the intricate promise of biblical teaching, with its Old Testament emphasis on justice and righteous indignation, its New Testament ambiguities of peace brought with a sword.

That was his inner world. In a typical day, Nat rose before first light, ate a breakfast of cornpone and mush, milked the cows, fed the hogs, and toiled in the woods and fields until dusk. His spring was spent planting cotton; his summer, in hoeing and grubbing in the ground to make the crops grow. All summer long, he battled swarms of mosquitoes and gnats. By summer's end, he was stripping leaves of tobacco from their stalks, until (without intermission) it came time to pick cotton in the fall. That painstaking, backbreaking chore had to be done with machinelike diligence to get the bolls of cotton in before the first frost. After that, Nat had to harvest the corn and pull and stack the hay. In between—and among—all these tasks, he repaired fences, cleared new fields, chopped firewood, and did a variety of other chores.

A short, powerfully built but wiry man, with a medium-black complexion and bright, deep eyes, Nat bore it all for the most part with stoic fortitude. He was upright, honest, and diligent, never smoked or drank, had an alert, restless manner, and walked with a brisk, springing step. In 1821 he had run away when an overseer beat him and hid out in the woods for thirty days. But then to everyone's surprise he returned of his own free will. "The Spirit appeared to me," Nat explained, "and said I had my wishes directed to the things of this world, and not to the kingdom of heaven, and that I should return."

Despite a rough-and-tumble life—his "distinguishing marks" included a large knot on one of the bones of his right arm from a blow, and a scar on one of his temples from a mule's kick—he was manifestly thoughtful, brilliant, and astute. He had "a mind capable of attaining anything," wrote one white lawyer who got to know him. "For natural intelligence and quickness of apprehension, he was surpassed by few men."

That earned him no relief, as the promise of his future dimmed. In his twenties, he married a slave girl named Cherry, but not long after that he was auctioned off with the livestock to another farm. There his new tasks were even more exhausting than the old. From time to time, Nat began to have dramatic visions as he worked even harder in the corn and cotton patches, battling weeds and weevils and "struggled through the damp fields behind a mule-drawn plow." On one occasion he saw "white spirits and black spirits engaged in battle, and the sun was darkened—the thunder rolled in the Heavens, and blood flowed in streams—and I heard a voice saying, 'Such is your luck, such you are called to see, and let it come rough or smooth, you must surely bear it.'" Nat withdrew himself as much as he could from normal social contact to "serve the Spirit more fully," and it revealed to him occult truths—"the knowledge of the elements, the revolution of the planets, the change of seasons, and the operation of the tides." This was about 1825. Convinced that the end of the world was near, he strove to purify himself before the Judgment Day arrived. In time, he felt qualified to preach the word of God: "The Holy Ghost was with me and said, 'Behold me as I stand in the Heavens'—and I looked and saw there were lights in the sky to which the children of darkness gave other names than what they really were—for they were the lights of the Savior's hands, stretched forth from east to west, even as they were extended on the cross."

Nat's natural eloquence impressed those around him (white as well as black) and overawed his fellow slaves. "And they believed and said my wisdom came from God." Nat did not disclaim it, but "having soon discovered to be great," he recalled, "I must appear so, and wrapped myself in mystery, devoting myself to fasting and prayer." He became known as Preacher Nat, and in the role of a slave preacher was allowed to move about the county almost without restraint. In this way, he became familiar with all the byways, homesteads, ponds, swamps, and streams within the county line.

One day, he discovered drops of blood like dew on the corn. In the woods he found leaves with hieroglyphic characters and numbers etched on them, and figures drawn in blood like those he had seen in the sky. The Holy Spirit revealed their meaning. "For as the blood of Christ had been shed on this earth, and had ascended to heaven for the salvation of sinners, and was now returning to earth again in the form of dew—and as the leaves on the trees bore the impression of the figures I had seen in the heavens, it was plain to me that the Saviour was about to lay down the yoke he had borne for the sins of men, and the great day of judgment was at hand."

The idea of a great slave uprising took hold in his mind.

Though America had thus far escaped any organized revolt, everyone was keenly aware of the full-scale revolution that had taken place in the 1790s on the French island of Santo Domingo, in which the independent black republic of Haiti was born. Now and then a local scheme had also been exposed. In 1799, a group of slaves bound from Maryland for Georgia had rebelled and killed two whites. In 1800, a conspiracy to burn Richmond was unmasked. Rumors of insurrection often filled the air. Meanwhile, beginning in the spring of 1831, there had been slave revolts in Martinique, Antigua, Santiago, Caracas, and the Tortugas.

As always, Nat looked for confirming signs. An eclipse of the sun on February 12, 1831, seemed to give it—a message, he believed, from the Holy Spirit that he should "arise and prepare" himself and "slay" his overlords. He assumed the title of "General," assembled a handful of confidants, and "pored over a crude map of Southampton County which he had drawn with berry juice." He waited for a second divine confirmation of his plans. On Saturday August 13, 1831, it came. Residents along the entire Eastern Seaboard of the United States awoke that morning to a sun that seemed to be in its last stages of extinction. As it dimmed remarkably, it grew so pale that "it could be looked at directly." Then changing hues, it went from green to blue to white. Finally a black spot appeared on its surface "like a black hand." In Virginia and elsewhere, it was seen as an omen of some earth-shaking deed. Alarm gripped residents from South Carolina to New York. To those on Manhattan Island, the sky seemed ablaze, and the whole of Newark appeared on fire. One journal in Raleigh, North Carolina, scornfully invoked "the absurd predictions of the ancient Astrologers," who "view such events as portending some direful catastrophe, and think that the world is coming to an end, or a bloody war is near."

And yet, mutatis mutandis—were they not right?

Nat had kept his plans close, and set the rising for Sunday, August 21. The night before he met with six confederates deep in the woods at a place called Cabin Pond. One brought a pig, another some brandy for a feast, and "in the glare of pine-knot torches" they hammered out their plans. Nat fully expected other slaves and freed blacks alike to rally to his band. Shortly after midnight, they set out through the woods toward their first farm. In the beginning, everything went more or less as planned. From farm to farm, they overpowered and killed their victims with knives, axes, clubs, and hoes. Other slaves joined and by dawn there were fifteen in Nat's "army"—nine on horses, also armed with guns. There was little to slow them. The isolated families could scarcely comprehend their peril, and the widely scattered farms were unsuited for joint defense. Apple orchards abounded, and corn, cotton, and tobacco fields provided a wide screen for events transpiring nearby.

The company of insurgents increased from house to house—from fifteen, to twenty, to thirty. Their plan was then for "an advanced guard of horsemen to approach each house at a gallop, and surround it till the others came up." When their numbers grew to sixty or so, Nat hoped to strike at the county seat of Jerusalem, and loot the local arsenal of arms before the whites could send to Richmond for aid. This scheme was forestalled only by an accidental encounter with a posse of eighteen whites, which briefly scattered his band.

The Thomas house was near the center of the rising. On the afternoon of August 22, as Nat's men drew near, a neighbor, James Gurley, "rode into the yard to give warning that sixty drunk and blood-stained black farm hands were approaching by a back road." Mrs. Thomas and her children piled into a carriage, as the mounted slaves pursued. George, then fifteen, drove the horses. But Nat's band gained ground. When it appeared the slaves would overtake them, they abandoned the carriage and took to the woods. "In and out of gloomy Mill Swamp, across Cypress Bridge and the bottomlands of the Nottoway River," they escaped in their hectic flight to the county seat of Jerusalem, ten miles from home. Meanwhile, the family slaves refused to join the revolt. Forced at first to ride with the band, they deserted at the earliest opportunity, and finding their way to Jerusalem, were lodged for safekeeping overnight in the jail.

Nat and his little army camped in the woods that night, hoping for more recruits in the coming day. That hope was soon dashed, for word of the rising had now spread, and local militia were assembling with their arms. Over the next two days, the insurgents drifted off and one by one were captured. Nat, however, eluding all pursuit, hid out for six weeks in a dugout under some fence rails in the woods. At night he took his water from a nearby stream, and food by stealth from neighboring farms. "Alone with the fox's bark, the rabbit's rustle, and the screech-owl's scream," as one writer put it, he brooded in despair.

Then one day a dog sniffed out the provisions he had hidden in a cave. Nat fled through the woods with 500 or 600 men in pursuit, but with "a more than Indian adroitness" again escaped and for ten days more concealed himself among the wheat stacks in a field. On Sunday, October 30, he was finally spotted by an armed farmer as he emerged from a hole in the ground. Exhausted, Nat gave himself up and was imprisoned, tried, and hanged. Before he died, he dictated his remarkable "Confessions"—a classic of their kind. Nothing about Nat was prosaic. Asked by the counsel assigned to defend him, whether, as a condemned captive, he still believed in his own providential fate, he answered sharply, "Was not Christ crucified?"

When it was all over, some sixty whites and 200 blacks (most by reprisal killings) lost their lives.

In the winter of 1832, in the aftermath of the revolt, slavery itself was subjected to a stormy debate. "The seals are broken which have been put upon it for fifty years," the *Richmond Enquirer* declared. Many in the South (including Virginia's governor John B. Floyd) thought emancipation was the only way to prevent more violence; but others thought deporting blacks to Africa—in keeping with a long-standing, if somewhat covert, scheme—made more sense. The upshot of the deliberations, however, was the enactment of stricter laws enforcing servitude.

Thomas had lost a number of neighbors and schoolmates in the rising; but he had also learned a different lesson from that adopted by his state. To Thomas the calamity proved "in terms of blood and death" that the desire for human freedom could not be suppressed. It also evidently convinced him that the institution of slavery was "intolerable to the enslaved," and that the idea of the contented slave under the care of a benevolent overlord was a sentimental myth.

In the years after the insurrection, Thomas attended Southampton Academy, "a private school of the higher grade." Upon his graduation he entered the law office of his maternal uncle, James Rochelle, county clerk at Jerusalem, and served there as his deputy for two years. As county clerk, Rochelle was the chief executive officer of the county and a man of social stature whose daughter would later marry President John Tyler's son. He had also been one of those present when Nat Turner's "Confessions" were transcribed. For young Thomas, the position was an excellent training ground, and kindled an interest in the law that would endure.

One day in the spring of 1836, Congressman John Y. Mason called at Rochelle's office and let it be known that he had a West Point appointment to fill. He had heard good things of Thomas, sized him up, and upon returning to Washington, commended Thomas to the secretary of war for admission to the school. The secretary sent the appointment on to President Andrew Jackson, who promptly signed it, in one of those seemingly incidental acts on which the future of a nation turns. That May, as Thomas was about to set out for West Point, his oldest brother, John, gave him some advice: "Having done what you conscientiously believe to be right, you may regret, but should never be annoyed, by a want of approbation on the part of others." That was high-minded advice to give a youth of nineteen, and suggests (where other evidence is scant) an extremely elevated level of family discourse. Indeed, Thomas took it to heart—so much so, it could almost serve as a motto of his life.

A few days later, Thomas stopped off at Washington, D.C., to pay his respects and thank Mason. But the congressman was sternly brusque: "No cadet from my district has ever graduated at the Military Academy. If you do not, I never want to see your face again." With that admonition, Thomas entered West Point on June 1, 1836.

But by today's standards, the entrance exam was not demanding, and as long as the prospective plebe could read, write, and do a little arithmetic, he usually passed. Once admitted, however, only about a third of the cadets made it through. Richard S. Ewell and Bushrod Johnson (both later Confederate generals) were classmates. Ulysses S. Grant entered the Academy in Thomas's last year. William Tecumseh Sherman was his roommate, along with Stewart Van Vliet, later a distinguished soldier from Vermont.

By all accounts, Thomas was a handsome young man, about six feet tall, strong and stout, with fair skin, light brown hair, deep blue eyes, and a square jaw. A year or two older than most plebes, he was "reticent and introspective, serious, dignified," and mature beyond his years. According to William S. Rosecrans, later a major general, he "bore a remarkable resemblance to [Gilbert] Stuart's portrait of [George] Washington," and other cadets sometimes called him "Washington," respectfully, or "Old Tom."

From the beginning, he made his mark. He got through the usual harassment to which newcomers were subjected, but as an upperclassman refused to participate in hazing new cadets. More boldly, he had rebuffed attempts at hazing when he was just a plebe. Stewart Van Vliet recalled: "Sherman, Thomas and I arrived at West Point the same day and all three of us were assigned to the same room, on the southside of the Old South Barracks. One evening a cadet came into our room and commenced to give us orders. 'Old Tom,' as we always called him, stepped up to him and said, 'Leave this room immediately or I will throw you through the window.'" The cadet fled; and that put a stop to all harassment, at least in the barracks where they lived. Oliver O. Howard, the famed Civil War general and civil rights crusader (for whom Howard University is named) remarked, upon hearing this story: "If anybody could bring good out of evil, Thomas could. You couldn't place him where he would not be a friend of the insulted, the outraged, the oppressed."

At West Point, Thomas learned to live in spartan simplicity in a sparsely furnished room with a rolled mattress, a table, a workstand, and a straight-backed chair. The bed had blankets on it that reeked of rancid lanolin; for daily upkeep, he had a tin washbasin, a scrub brush, a bucket, and a broom. The room, small for three, was about twelve feet square, poorly ventilated, hot in summer, cold in winter, with heat provided by coal-burning grates. Cadets had to carry water to their rooms in buckets from an old-fashioned well worked with a wooden pump. Lighting was provided by candles and whale oil lamps. (Gaslight did not come in until just prior to the Civil War.)

After reveille, each cadet had a half-hour to spruce up his room. "We then march to the mess hall," one plebe wrote home, "& if one speaks, raises his hand, looks to the right or left . . . we are reported, indeed we are reported for everything. . . . When we arrive at the tables, the command is given 'take seats' & then such a scrambling you never saw. . . . We have to eat as fast as we can, & before we get enough the command is given 'Squad rise.'" Thereafter, except for two more breaks for meals, study, drills, and parades consumed the day. "It was heads up, eyes to the front, and one seldom saw one's boots," recalled one plebe.

Life was superimposed on a grid of regulations, with even the storage of clothing and equipment governed by pedantic rules. Trunks had to be placed in corners, dress caps behind the door, clothes on pegs over bedsteads, muskets in gun racks with locks sprung, and books on the shelf farthest from the door. Cadets were forbidden to receive money or supplies from outside and were barred from smoking, drinking, or playing checkers, chess, or cards. Demerits were given for disobedience of any kind, and a cadet who accumulated 200 in a single year was dismissed. In Thomas's plebe year, he had only twenty for such minor crimes as improperly blacked shoes, dust on the floor of his room, and "a dull speck on a button of his uniform."

The cuisine at West Point was meager, and typically consisted of boiled potatoes, meat, pudding, and bread. That led to strenuous efforts at improving (or at least expanding) their fare. "We stole boiled potatoes in handkerchiefs and thrust them under our vests," William S. Rosecrans remembered. "We poked butter into our gloves and fastened them with forks to the under side of the table until we could smuggle them out of the dining room . . . We stole bread and when we got together at night . . . would mix everything into hash and cook it in a stewpan over the fire. We ate it hot on toasted bread." Sherman, who "usually had a grease spot on his pants" from such feasts, was said to be "the best hash-maker at West Point." Some cadets even risked expulsion by going down to Benny Haven's tavern in nearby Highland Falls to feast on oysters and ale.

The students got to eat their fill only once a year, at a Fourth of July dinner, and were only then allowed to drink wine. "We had glorious times on the fourth getting drunk," wrote one cadet, and "were quite patriotick."

In their regular studies, cadets learned all about the science of permanent and field fortifications, batteries and entrenchments, battle order, reconnaissance, outpost duty, the elements of strategy, and the tactics of attack and defense. Artillery instruction included not only the duties of the gun crew and the art of firing (grapeshot, rockets, grenades, night firing, the effects of rifling, and so on) but the manufacture of powder and projectiles, the construction, testing, and inspection of weapons; the characteristics of various kinds of ordnance, coastal artillery, and the composition of siege trains. Field training included line, company, and battalion drill; artillery, infantry, and cavalry tactics; and horsemanship (all cadets had to know how to ride). In addition, cadets were expected to acquire some knowledge of French, drawing, geography, history, natural and experimental philosophy (i.e., physics), chemistry, ethics, political science, and geology. The Academy Library contained about 14,000 volumes, most on military subjects, but quite a few on the sciences (chemistry, mineralogy, geology, botany), with a sprinkling of history, biography, poetry, and fiction. The library also subscribed to several literary periodicals, such as the *American Register* and the *North American Review*.

To afford practice in command, the corps of cadets was organized as a battalion of infantry divided into four companies each.

All this might seem a full and proper training for a soldier, but the Academy was often criticized for emphasizing mathematics, science, and engineering over military skills. West Point, in fact, was the child of the Corps of Engineers and its superintendent was invariably an officer of that branch. The Academy was as much an engineering as a military school. Almost 75 percent of classroom time was devoted to engineering and its ancillary disciplines, mathematics and physics, with all other subjects, including military history and tactics, compressed into the remaining hours. How a student fared in mathematics, science, and engineering also determined class rank, which in turn determined the branch of service to which he was assigned. So the top students entered various branches of the Engineering Corps. New offerings in Spanish, history, and law were only added in 1854 (when Robert E. Lee became superintendent, and Thomas was one of West Point's famed instructors) and more classroom time given to the science of war.

Thomas was a dedicated, if not obviously brilliant, student but fairly mastered all his subjects, which, as one colleague put it, he stored away "in the recesses of his great brain." Though he struggled a bit in his first year with French, he took to subjects like astronomy, mineralogy, geology, botany, mechanics, chemistry, topography, and optics. Botany, indeed, was a lifelong love. In time, he also proved to have a better grasp of the science of fortifications, and of infantry, cavalry, and artillery tactics than most if not all of his peers.

One of his teachers (Albert E. Church, the famed educator, who helped make mathematics a fixed feature of American public schools) later recalled that Thomas "never allowed any thing to escape a thorough examination, and left nothing behind that he did not fully comprehend." Some of West Point's more incandescent academic stars (like Sherman) did not hold on as well to what they learned. Thomas, on the other hand, "never forgot anything," wrote R. W. Johnson, one of the Union's best cavalry generals. "His mind was a storehouse filled with useful and valuable information on all subjects" and long after he left West Point "he could solve difficult mathematic problems with such ease that one might have thought he had just been teaching the principles in school." In the battalion organization at West Point he also rose from corporal to sergeant to lieutenant (outshining both Sherman and Grant).

At West Point, Thomas heard now and then from his family (in the main, from two older brothers, John and Benjamin) and kept track of friends. In a letter to John from his junior year, we learn that Thomas wasn't worried about his course work, longed for a break ("A furlough is the last thing thought of at night and the first thing in the morning"), was glad to hear that John was "in love with farming again," regarded farming as the "most noble and independent life a man can follow," and would "quit soldiering upon the spot" himself if he had a farm of his own. He told John that he had had a letter from Benjamin, too, who "as usual writes of marriage and money, but in such a way that no one can understand what he means." In other news, General Winfield Scott had just come through and had told everyone at the Academy that he did not think there would be a war with England despite the expectation of it that then gripped Maine and other New England states. Even so, Scott had decided to establish a large training camp near Elizabethtown, New Jersey, just in case.

Though West Point was a Northern school, it was dominated as the Federal Government itself had been for some time by the Southern aristocracy. "A strong southern feeling" overall was "prevalent," as Rebel general J. E. B. Stuart later wrote. West Point would even be accused (by Senator Benjamin F. Wade of Ohio) of being "the hotbed in which rebellion was hatched." Moreover, its standard curriculum included a subversive textbook—William Rawle's *A View of the Constitution of the United States of America*—which taught secession as an option for any state in conflict with Federal authority. No one reading Rawle can doubt it. He wrote:

> The principle of representation, although certainly the wisest and best, is not essential to the being of a republic . . . It depends on the state itself to retain or abolish the principle of representation, because it depends on itself whether it will continue a member of the Union. To deny this right would be inconsistent with the principle on which all our political systems are founded, which is, that the people have in all cases, a right to determine how they will be governed. . . . The states then may wholly withdraw from the Union. . . . The secession of a state from the Union depends on the will of the people of such state.

A number of Southern officers—including Robert E. Lee—claimed after the Civil War that it was this teaching which gave them the legal and ethical basis for taking up arms. Lee apparently told Bishop William Holland Wilmer of Louisiana: "If it had not been for the instruction I got from Rawle's textbook at West Point I would not have left the Old Army and joined the South." However, since others came to a different conclusion, despite the same teaching, Lee seemed to be saying that he had failed to reason the matter out rightly for himself.

Not so Thomas. In later years, pressed by an aide as to whether there had ever been any constitutional basis for secession, Thomas was asked, " 'Supposing that arrangements were being made for a peaceable dissolution of the Union by the Government, the North from the South, and that it was in progress, what would you have done?' Thomas replied promptly, 'That is not a supposable case; the

Government cannot dissolve itself; it is the creature of the people, and until they had agreed by their votes to dissolve it, and it was accomplished in accordance therewith, the Government to which they had sworn allegiance remained, and as long as it did exist, I should have adhered to it.' "

That showed a rigorous logic no artful dodging could match.

# 2. A WIDER WORLD

In 1840, Thomas graduated twelfth in a class of forty-two, Sherman sixth, Van Vliet ninth. Paul O. Hebert, a future governor of Louisiana, stood first. Assigned as a second lieutenant to the 3rd Artillery Regiment, Thomas joined it at Fort Columbus, in New York Harbor, in September, drilled recruits there for a month, but was soon dispatched to Florida to serve in the Seminole Wars.

Most of the fighting took place in the Everglades, "a swampy land of water and hummocks, given over to alligators, miasma, moccasins, mosquitoes and ticks." There was hard soldiering and little glory in such service, but before setting out, Thomas examined a book he found in the Academy Library, *The Territory of Florida* by John Lee Williams, which gave him some idea of what to expect. Williams had explored many of Florida's rivers, bays, and lagoons, "traced ancient Indian works and scattered ruins," studied the local snakes, birds, fish, and other wildlife "up to black bear and panther," and the luxuriant, exotic flora that imparted a lush brilliance to its semitropical world. Tales of the aborigines also "stimulated his curiosity concerning Indian life." To round out its account, the book provided a careful chronological review of Florida's known history—from 1497, when Sebastian Cabot first sailed along its eastern shore—and described with disgust the early treachery of white Europeans in the dealings with natives. This was followed by a brief sketch of the lives of some Seminole chiefs, with a handy glossary of Indian words at the end.

The Seminole Wars were long, drawn-out affairs—lasting from 1817 to 1858—between the government and a number of Indian tribes. Most of the tribes were Creek, but collectively they were known as the Seminoles. The war went through various stages, but the most important fighting took place between 1835 and 1842 when Thomas was there. At the time, part of Florida still belonged to the Spanish empire, and its Everglades (like the swamps of Virginia) had become a haven for fugitive convicts and escaped slaves. Some of these slaves eventually became members of the tribal communities and joined war parties in attacking the encroaching whites. After the Federal government in 1812 attempted to take over West Florida from the Spanish, the conflict intensified, and the United States became involved in its first guerrilla war. Andrew Jackson and subsequent presidents failed to subdue the natives, or persuade them to resettle in what became known as the Indian Territory (now Oklahoma) to the west. The government thought it had an agreement in 1832, but the great chief Osceola rejected it, vowing to fight on until "the last drop of Seminole blood had moistened the dust of their hunting ground."

When the government made it a crime to furnish the Indians with guns or ammunition, Osceola declared that that made the Seminoles no better than slaves. "The white man shall not make me black," he declared. "I will make the white man red with blood; and then blacken him in the sun and rain . . . and the buzzard shall live upon his flesh." For years the natives outwitted and outfought the army, burned settlements, sugar plantations, and even overran forts. In 1836, a new U.S. general came in with a "surge" approach but failed to turn things around. After a truce was reached in 1837, the government arrested Osceola—even though he had arrived to parley at the president's invitation under a white flag. New Indian leaders stepped forward to take his place. Meanwhile, the Seminoles were supplied with weapons, ammunition, and other goods by Cuban and Bahamian traders, and the ongoing cost to the government in blood and treasure was high. A "Mosquito Fleet" of schooners and barges stationed offshore tried to intercept the smuggling; search and destroy missions were launched; and tens of thousands of dollars offered as bribes to chiefs to persuade them to give up. The Indians were even tracked with bloodhounds, but the dogs lost their scent in the watery glades. By 1841, when Colonel W. J. Worth took charge, thousands of U.S. soldiers had been wounded, almost 2,000 killed, and public patience for the war had pretty much run out. It had cost too much, gone on for too long, and been marked by too many mistakes. Finally, in August 1842 Congress passed the Armed Occupation Act, which provided free land to settlers willing to defend it. Attrition worked its will. Over time, the valiant Seminoles began to disappear.

When Thomas was there, however, they were still a redoubtable force. His company sailed to Florida by way of Savannah, Georgia, in November 1840, and proceeded to its station at Fort Lauderdale, the rest of the regiment being scattered from St. Augustine to Key Biscayne.

As Thomas disembarked, he discovered

a cluster of weather-beaten cane-built huts and a few Indian wigwams, all very dirty and overrun with cockroaches. The shabby little settlement stood about two hundred feet from the ocean, and behind it ran a deep and slow-moving river. Farther back lay the jungle of tropical growth where thorn-clad vines tangled thickly about the swamp cypress, each limb hanging heavy with Spanish moss. Fires from Indian encampments lit up the far horizon. It was a picturesque scene at twilight, but troops enjoyed little sleep the first few nights. The buzzing of mosquitoes and other winged insects was almost continuous, and an army of fleas infested every cot. From the upland and swampy jungle came the scream of the panther, the hoarse bellow of the alligator, the shrill call of the whippoorwill, and the dismal cry of the loon. Foxes yelped and owls hooted, and the single solace of the evening was the nightingale's sweet song. The soldiers soon learned to fish for pompano, redfish, snappers, and green turtles with net and line.

In Florida, the food was dreadful and creature comforts scarce. Even the commanding officer at the fort was forced to settle at breakfast for muddy coffee, tough buckwheat cakes, and "semifluid rancid butter floating in a cracked cup." Thomas (who had a taste for good food) was placed in charge of feeding the detachment and "discovered he could stretch green-turtle steaks just so far." He promptly set about getting together a decent bill of fare and devoted much of his time to the quest for supplies, venturing into the woods for wild game.

The book by Williams proved useful to him here, for it not only described where to find (and how to best grow) rice, sweet potatoes, pumpkins, peas, and corn, but what to watch out for in the cane-brakes and swamps. For anyone who had never seen an alligator be-fore, he conjured it up: "Floating in the water he resembles a log. On land he looks like a huge snake, with the addition of thick short legs and sprawling claws. But it is in his wallow, a large mud hole among the rushes, that the alligator is most at home, surrounded by a hun-dred young, all barking like pups."

Thomas would have preferred more soldierly duties, but his broad competence worked against him. He was given so many bu-reaucratic tasks—as commissary, quartermaster, ordnance officer, and adjutant—that, he wrote to a former classmate, he had scarcely enough time for his own meals. After nearly a year of wrestling with problems of supply, Thomas finally joined Captain Richard D. A. Wade, who with sixty other troops set out on a mission from Fort Lauderdale in twelve canoes. Within hours, they surprised an In-dian quietly fishing at the northern point of an inlet, and induced him to lead them to his village, about fifteen miles to the west. There on the morning of the 6th they captured twenty Indians, six rifles, de-stroyed fourteen canoes and a stock of supplies. Eight other Indians were killed attempting to escape. Leaving their prisoners behind under guard, the troops tramped through pine barrens, bogs, saw grass, and hummocks for two days to a cypress swamp thirty miles to the north. There on the 8th they surrounded another village, sur-prised and captured twenty-seven more Seminoles, took another six rifles and one shotgun, and destroyed more provisions and canoes. On the 9th they came to the shores of a lake where they destroyed more boats and a hut.

As Indian expeditions went, this was accounted a success. Thomas himself had also done well. Captain Wade's report thanked him for his "valuable and efficient aid," and Colonel Worth, commanding, recommended his promotion to first lieutenant, "for gallantry and good conduct," which in time would be conferred.

In December 1841, Thomas's stint in Florida came to an end when his company sailed around the peninsula to army headquarters at the head of Tampa Bay. In early February 1842, it proceeded up the Mississippi River to New Orleans to refit. As his army transport drew near, he could make out "the pile-built, broad levee, its wharves crowded with ships and laden with cotton bales, molasses casks, and hogsheads of sugar and tobacco. The old French forts within the city limits were deserted and crumbling, but farther out from the town were the modern bastions named for heroes of the War of 1812." From New Orleans, he sailed for Charleston, South Carolina, on July 1, and took service at Fort Moultrie. The fort, on Sullivan's Island, was a historical landmark on a par with Bunker Hill. During the Revolutionary War, it had withstood a withering twelve-hour cannonade from British warships, as its soft, spongy palmetto logs absorbed the British shot. With each barrage, the fort had actually grown stronger, for the shot became embedded in its walls. By the battle's end, they were veritable walls of iron.

Despite its storied past, when Thomas arrived the area was more widely known for its "bowers of roses and fine summer homes." Prominent Charleston families who sojourned on the island in summer were honored guests at dinner parties at the fort, and Thomas, who had just "won his spurs" by gallant conduct, was evidently a great favorite at society events. As a young officer, he was noble and dashing, with a regal bearing, and looked (one colleague said) like "a patrician of ancient Rome." Captain Erasmus Darwin Keyes, his company commander and later a major general, thought him exceptional in every respect. Though striking, he was self-effacing, and there seemed to be no trace of envy or malice in him, arrogance, or spite. He "received and gave orders with equal serenity, did his duty, and was never hurried, impatient, or late. A long acquaintance with him invariably led to affection and respect." His close friends found him amusing, even hilarious at times, with a deadpan wit.

At Fort Moultrie, Thomas was in the company of a number of familiar companions, including Captain Keyes, Sherman (now also a first lieutenant), Van Vliet, Lieutenant Braxton Bragg, and Captain Robert Anderson, one of Thomas's former instructors at West Point. The Union, united as it was, was well represented by this coterie of talent—Keyes from Massachusetts and Maine, Thomas from Virginia, Sherman from Ohio, Anderson from Kentucky, Bragg from North

Carolina, and Van Vliet from Vermont. All but Van Vliet would achieve fame in the Civil War. The garrison lived on terms as intimate as those "of a family," Thomas later recalled fondly. Even Braxton Bragg, despite his own abrasive disposition, found the others congenial and, curiously enough, "argued bitterly against the possibility of Secession" at the time. Later, as a member of the Confederate high command, he would face Thomas in three of the most momentous battles of the war. Meanwhile, a site of future conflict was taking shape before their eyes. The War of 1812 (with its crowning indignity the burning of Washington, D.C.) had shown the gross inadequacy of American coastal defenses. On the advice of Napoleon's famed military engineer, General Simon Bernard, a shoal opposite Fort Moultrie had been selected for a new harbor installation, and there the officers could watch tens of thousands of tons of rock and granite (some from as far away as Penobscot, Maine) being dumped, as the foundations of Fort Sumter were laid. Over time, the five-sided brick masonry fort, with five-foot-thick outer walls towering fifty feet above low water, would rise into view. When it was not yet complete, Robert Anderson would find himself in charge of its hopeless defense in the opening scene of the war.

Thomas remained at Fort Moultrie until December 1843, when he was ordered to duty with Company C, 3rd Light Artillery, then stationed at Fort McHenry, Maryland, on Whetstone Point near Baltimore. Once again he moved in high social circles for a season, as "many delicately inscribed invitations to parties and masquerade balls found their way to the fort." If there was any romance in his life at this time, however, the evidence for it has vanished. More likely, the social mixing was a formal affair. Meanwhile, on May 17, 1843, he had been promoted to first lieutenant of artillery. In the spring of 1844 he returned to Fort Moultrie where he remained, except for a tour of recruiting duty in New York, until the outbreak of the Mexican War.

The Mexican War grew out of the annexation of Texas and the dispute with Mexico over the boundary line. In 1836, Texas (a Mexican province) had declared its independence and soon afterward applied for admission to the United States. This was enabled by an act of Congress in March 1845. In response, Mexico began to muster an army along the Rio Grande. Zachary Taylor, a hero of the War of 1812, was dispatched to Corpus Christi, at the mouth of the Nueces River, where the entire Regular Army of the United States as it then existed—about 4,000 men—assembled for the fight. Mexico had a larger army, but was in the midst of a political revolution, and its force was subverted by factions from within.

The territory in most dispute—between the Nueces River and the Rio Grande, about 130 miles wide along the coast—was low and flat, covered with prairie grass, chaparral, or thickets of cactus and mesquite. South of the Rio Grande, westward to the slopes of the Sierra Madre, it was more densely covered with trees and vegetation; and the climate fiercely hot.

The war broke out for many reasons. America wanted to add New Mexico (which included the future state of Arizona) and California as well as Texas to the Union; the South wanted another slave state. Taylor's instructions were "to defend Texas from invasion . . . and should Mexico invade it . . . [to] employ all his forces to repulse the invaders, and drive all Mexican troops beyond the Rio Grande." Mexico's plan was to assemble as large a force as practicable at Matamoros, near the mouth of the Rio Grande, on the South Side, and drive all American troops beyond the Nueces to the north.

On June 26, 1845, Thomas's Company E of the 3rd Artillery was ordered to the Texas front. He reached New Orleans on July 19 and five days later, with the 3rd and 4th Infantry Regiments, sailed for Corpus Christi under Taylor's command.

The U.S. Army, with its baggage and supplies, was transferred slowly and methodically from Corpus Christi to the Texas bank of the Rio Grande. The Mexicans made no attempt to oppose it. As soon as Taylor's forces arrived, they began to construct within sight of Matamoros a stronghold afterward known as Fort Brown. Its garrison included the artillery unit to which Thomas belonged. The nature of the country and the dense coverts of the chaparral favored ambushes and surprises, and U.S. foraging parties began to have a hard time. Supplies, running short, had to be fetched from the port of Point Isabel, twenty-five miles away. Taylor, marching to the port, took charge of the task.

Meanwhile, the garrison at Fort Brown was cut off. On March 7, 1846, Taylor set out to relieve it and, expecting to be intercepted and attacked, took up a position in an old dry bed of the Rio Grande. Dotted with pools and bordered by timber, the channels offered a good barrier behind which to post his troops. There, at a place called Palo Alto, or "High Woods" (from a lofty stand of timber), the opposing armies clashed. The outnumbered Americans immediately found themselves on the defensive, and the battle turned into an artillery duel. At dawn the next day, the Mexicans withdrew and reestablished their line in a "resaca," or swale, which passed through thickets of mesquite. On May 9 the Battle of Resaca de la Palma was fought, and after a furious fight, the Mexicans were driven back across the Rio Grande.

The victories of Palo Alto and Resaca de la Palma gave the United States control of the Rio Grande; but for lack of troops, especially cavalry, Taylor was unable at once to improve on his gains. Moreover, due to logistical failures, his army had to lie idle for three months.

The Sierra Madre range became the new Mexican line of defense. Taylor established his advanced base at Camargo (on the San Juan River, three miles from its junction with the Rio Grande) in August, and there Thomas and part of his battery joined him, by way of Reynosa, for an advance on Monterrey.

Most of the houses in Camargo had been wrecked by recent freshets and were overrun by scorpions, tarantulas, centipedes, and frogs. The water of the river was contaminated; the heat of the day fierce. "The mortality in our camp was appalling," wrote one fellow soldier. "The dead march was ever wailing in our ears." Thomas, encamped with his battery in the plaza, avoided both the tainted water and the commissary whiskey, and slaked his thirst on ripening peaches, which grew in abundance nearby.

The next major battle took place at Monterrey, a fortified town guarding the way to Mexico City from the north, at the mouth of a mountain pass. On August 19, Taylor began his advance, taking the infantry, except for one brigade, up the Rio Grande on steamers, while

cavalry and artillery proceeded overland. Thomas commanded a section of light artillery in this march. In late September, Taylor's army of
about 6,500 came to Walnut Springs, three miles from their goal.
Monterrey was well defended, enclosed on the west and south by high
mountain walls, and on the north and east by channels of the San
Juan River and tributary streams. Within the town itself, there was a
masonry citadel north of the main plaza and several small forts and
stone buildings covering the roads. South of the town lay a steep
gorge; to the west, the stone wall of a cemetery and stone parapets.
Behind these defenses, the Mexican commander, Pedro de Ampudia,
had about 10,000 men.

On Sunday, September 20, the siege began. Fighting reached the
city streets the next day and Thomas was in the thick of it. In command now of part of the battery under Braxton Bragg (one of his former associates at Fort Moultrie), he found himself pent up in a narrow
alley where bullets showered down. In its exposed position, his battery was hit pretty hard. A number of men and more than a dozen
horses went down "making the ground about the guns slippery with
their gasped foam and blood." The men remaining worked to strip
the harnesses from the fallen animals "determined that not a buckle
or strap should be lost." At length, ordered to retreat, Thomas paused
to reload his guns, and in the midst of heavy fire, retired slowly and
coolly gave the enemy a farewell shot.

On Tuesday, September 22, the bishop's palace was taken after a
prolonged and bloody struggle, but the cathedral in the central plaza
and most of the city itself remained in enemy hands. On the 23rd in
house-to-house fighting the Mexicans were finally driven from the
plaza and the housetops, as Thomas's guns helped clear the barri-
caded streets. "Old Tom," as he had been known at West Point, had
become "Old Reliable," as his grateful comrades dubbed him from the
fight.

In the aftermath of the battle, the American troops attended services in the cathedral, where an organist "interspersed sacred music
with operatic airs." Other troops explored the bishop's palace, and the
luxurious gardens and baths of Ampudia's palace, "its corridors and
marble-paved halls now crowded with the wounded and the dead."

Thomas was promoted to captain for gallant and meritorious conduct by Zachary Taylor, while a number of other generals took note of him, too. One wrote that Thomas and his fellow gunners deserved "the highest praise for their skill and good conduct"; another commended him "for the bold advance and efficient management of the force under his charge."

For political reasons—chiefly as a restraint on Taylor's presidential ambitions—General Winfield Scott now took control of the American campaign. The upshot at first was a military mess. In Taylor's subordinate command, regular troops were replaced by volunteers, and Scott received only about half the men he had been promised to carry out his plans. But the two made the most of what they had.

As Taylor advanced on Buena Vista, Scott prepared to advance on Vera Cruz. Scott drew away much of Taylor's force, including all the regular troops, for his own army, thus leaving Taylor with only 5,000 men. Mexican general Antonio López de Santa Anna opposed him with an army 20,000 strong. Early in November, Taylor selected General John A. Quitman to lead the advance toward Tampico, with Thomas providing Quitman artillery support. Christmas Day 1846 "found the expedition on a hilly road near Villa Gran, a village surrounded by groves of orange trees and vast sugar estates." One fellow officer went into the mountains to try to bag a holiday turkey; Thomas and another obtained some eggs and other ingredients for eggnog, and coaxed the army physician into yielding up a bottle of rum to make the elixir complete. A few days later, the men marched into the great square at Victoria, capital of the state of Tamaulipas ("High Mountains"), on formal parade.

Taylor soon arrived with reinforcements and turned about again for Monterrey, where with Thomas he went into his old camp at Walnut Springs. In early February 1847, Taylor marched south to reinforce the garrison at Saltillo, where he learned that Santa Anna was approaching in force. Taylor beat a quick retreat, and took up a defensive position at Buena Vista, where a high flat plateau was cut into narrow tables by ravines. Deep gorges ran back to the mountains, with gullies on the right. There on February 21, the bloody and decisive Battle of Buena Vista was fought. The Americans had 4,757 men and sixteen guns. All the troops—except the artillery and two companies of cavalry—were volunteers. Santa Anna, on the other hand, had 20,000. For the Americans, the chances of victory appeared slight.

It was Taylor's plan to protect his base at Saltillo by blocking the road and carrying the fight beyond. A battery of five field pieces and two companies of infantry guarded a narrow defile. Six more infantry companies took positions in advance. Other troops were arranged en echelon on a high plateau extending toward the heights. Thomas commanded a field gun on the right near the front line. As the American soldiers filed into place, they caught sight of spiral clouds of dust rising lazily aloft to the south. The banners of the Mexican cavalry soon came into view, then thousands of troops, some hauling heavy guns, with bands playing national airs. Enemy uniforms "of every color of the sunset" shone on the plain; even the horses were clad "in gorgeous tassels and silks." Several hours were consumed in field evolutions, until Santa Anna, in the belief that Taylor might be overawed by this demonstrated power, invited him to surrender. "I wish to save you from a catastrophe," Santa Anna proposed gallantly, adding that his force numbered 20,000 men.

Taylor curtly refused.

That night his men slept on their arms. The battle began at daybreak, but the Americans had to defend a position too extensive for their strength. The American left was turned, and the whole American line was forced back. Bragg's battery was posted on the right. A Mississippi rifle regiment, under Jefferson Davis, then a colonel, was also on the field. Over the course of the next few hours, the center of the action revolved about the artillery position where Thomas was ensconced. Before him, the Mexicans were arrayed in a huge semicircle in overwhelming force. But the broken nature of the ground prevented them from operating en masse. As they tried to advance in staggered lines, Thomas replied with rapid vollies of round and hollow shot. When Santa Anna resumed the offensive, the American infantry (mostly volunteers) ran head-on into thousands of enemy soldiers coming out of a ravine. In the face of this advance, upon the broad plateau, the battery under Thomas, "without infantry to support it," in Taylor's words, "and at the imminent risk of losing its guns, came rapidly into action, the Mexican line being but a few yards from the muzzles of the guns. The first discharge of cannister caused the enemy to hesitate, the second and third drove them back in disorder and saved the day."

It was at Buena Vista that Taylor acquired his nickname, "Rough and Ready," which helped make him the next president of the United States. According to Taylor, the artillery "was always in action at the right place and the right time." But for the support of the guns, declared another officer, "we would not have maintained our position a single hour." "Thomas more than sustained the reputation he has long enjoyed in his regiment as an accurate and scientific artillerist," his immediate superior wrote. Bragg's own comparable expertise was celebrated in a famous anecote of the fight. For in the thick of it all, Taylor rode up on his white horse and called out, "A little more grape, Captain Bragg," which became a popular slogan in his subsequent Presidential campaign.

In his own account of the battle twelve years later, Thomas made no mention of his own distinction, only that he had been under fire for ten straight hours, from six o'clock in the morning to 4 P.M.

For his gallant conduct, Thomas was brevetted major on February 23—his third brevet in seven years. He was rising as fast on his own merits as anyone in the service—faster than William Tecumseh Sherman, Stonewall Jackson, or Ulysses S. Grant. Robert E. Lee would end the Mexican War as a lieutenant colonel; George B. McClellan and George Gordon Meade as captains. But all three had graduated well before Thomas from West Point.

By the victories of Palo Alto, Resaca de la Palma, Monterrey, and Buena Vista, Mexican authority was wholly and forever expelled from the soil of Texas, and American troops gained a morale and a prestige they would not lose until the Vietnam War. Up to the time of the Mexican War, as one military historian writes, "American troops had seldom known what it was to go after an enemy and defeat him. All their offensive campaigns—excepting Yorktown, where they had the moral and physical support of the French—in fact had been failures. All their strategic successes had also been achieved in retreats, and nearly all their tactical victories had been gained by standing on the defensive," even in the Seminole Wars.

Meanwhile, in subsequent actions in the war, General Winfield Scott scrapped the idea of attacking Mexico City from the north, and set his sights once more on the port of Vera Cruz. In early March 1847, some 12,000 troops disembarked in rough surf from a fleet of army transports a few miles to the south; but instead of taking the city by storm, Scott's general in charge, Robert Patterson, opted for a more humane and scientific, if less spectacular, siege, which succeeded with a minimum of casualties—something Thomas took note of and admired. Patterson told his chief engineer: "Vera Cruz must be taken with a loss not to exceed 100 men; for every one over that number I shall regard myself as his murderer." He did this by the skillful use of cannon fire. After a targeted bombardment of eighteen days, the city surrendered on March 29. American losses were just sixty-seven in wounded and killed.

From Vera Cruz, two roads led to Mexico City, both cutting through the Sierra Madre to join in the plain beyond. Scott took the route that went by way of Jalapa and Perote. Fifty miles from Vera Cruz, the Americans faced a large Mexican army entrenched at Cerro Gordo, along a steep mountain road marked by fortified plateaus. Scott wisely declined to assail these defenses directly, and called upon his elite engineering corps (which included P. T. G. Beauregard, McClellan, and Lee) to find a way by which they could be flanked. In three days, his engineers scouted and cut a rough road that brought Scott's army to the enemy rear. When the news of Scott's advance first reached Europe, the Duke of Wellington had said: "Scott is lost. He has been carried away by success. He can't take the city, and he can't fall back upon his base." But on September 15, he victoriously entered the city's gates.

In the humiliating negotiations that followed, the Americans not only demanded Texas, but California, New Mexico, and most of the current American Southwest. The Mexicans balked, and more battles followed—at Molino del Rey, Chapultepec, and elsewhere—ending in the formal Treaty of Guadalupe Hidalgo, signed on February 2, 1848.

The Mexican War was the one open-field conflict in which officers who would one day fight in the Civil War learned how battles might be won. Thomas seems to have absorbed its lessons better than most—perhaps all. He learned the importance of a pontoon train in pursuit (Resaca de la Palma); the trap of holing up too long in a fortified town (Monterrey); the decisive power of artillery when used with timely skill (Buena Vista and Vera Cruz); and, from the Mexican defeat at Buena Vista, two more things: the importance of drill and preparation, whether the troops were new or old; and the loss of advantage to even a large army without a disciplined, orderly plan of concerted attack.

Thomas remained in Mexico on duty until August 20, 1848, when his company recrossed the Rio Grande into Texas, making it among the last to leave, as it had been among the first to arrive. About the 1st of September he was ordered to Brazos Santiago, to take charge of the commissary depot at that place, and remained there until December, when his company was ordered to Fort Adams, Rhode Island. After a six-month leave of absence, he was placed in command of Company B, 3rd Artillery, on July 31, 1849.

In the interim, Thomas had come home to Virginia a hero of the late war. On July 19, 1847, a public meeting had been held at the Jerusalem Court House where speeches rang out in his praise and the community voted to present him with a ceremonial sword. The sum for it was raised by subscription and in due time it was fashioned in Philadelphia by noted metal craftsmen Horstman & Sons with a solid silver scabbard, enriched with engraved scroll work, and inscribed with the names of the places where he had fought. The grip was also made of silver, and the pommel of gold, grasping an amethyst. Included, too, was an engraved vignette of the Battle of Monterrey.

Thomas prized the sword for the honor it represented, but was profoundly embarrassed by the fanfare of the gift—indeed, dreaded going home to the waiting accolades. He even tried to find some way to postpone his visit for a couple of years, but upon reflection decided to go as soon as he could, to get it over with, as he put it, "and have the thing off my Mind. . . . If I could get off with a dinner only I should have great cause to congratulate myself."

He didn't quite succeed, but for other reasons, too, his homecoming was not a happy one. Though he welcomed the embrace of his family and old friends, he felt estranged from Virginia after more than a decade away. He brought with him new suits and shoes for all the black hands, but his two unmarried sisters seemed to him "to lead a lonely life" with "no associations which are more than barely tolerable" in their cloistered world. He wondered how they could stand it much longer, and thought they might be happier in Norfolk or some other large town. Every passing year seemed to take him emotionally further away from his boyhood ties. Family tensions also came to the fore. The family farm was struggling, and his sisters evidently resented his absence—and perhaps the wider world to which he now belonged. Nothing seemed to him more "horrible," as he put it, than family friction, but he hoped that time would tamp down the discord and their home "become as happy as it had been." However, the strains on the Thomas family "paralleled those of the nation," as one writer observed, and it would be a long time before the United States itself would recover the unity it had known.

Thomas remained in Virginia for six months, from February until August 1849, when he rejoined his regiment at Fort Adams, Newport, Rhode Island. Early in September, he was transferred to Florida again when the Seminole Wars flared anew. As he went from one outpost to another, taking charge of local problems of supply, he also collected rare mineral fragments and flowers. One of his companions was George Meade (then a captain, later the triumphant general at Gettysburg) who was surveying the ground for a chain of forts to extend from the Indian River to Tampa Bay. Their tasks on the whole were routine, but Thomas squirmed under the thumb of General David E. Twiggs, who had praised Thomas after the Battle of Monterrey but later clashed with him on a point of protocol. During the Mexican War, Twiggs had demanded a mule team Thomas needed for his guns. Thomas deemed the mules of greater service to the artillery than attending the comforts of a general's camp, and enraged Twiggs by appealing to higher authority to keep his team intact. Twiggs, who was something of a martinet, would take revenge on Thomas for this petty grievance every chance he could.

After an onerous year in Florida, Thomas embarked for New Orleans, and from there in November 1850 for Fort Independence, in Boston Harbor, where he served from January 1, 1851, until March 28. Meanwhile, in November 1848, Braxton Bragg had been offered the post of artillery instructor at West Point. He declined, but in a letter to former Congressman John Mason, now serving as secretary of the navy under President James K. Polk, he recommended Thomas in his place. "The vacancy, I think," wrote Bragg, "would suit your young friend Brevet Major George H. Thomas 3rd Artillery and it is one for which he is eminently qualified. . . . No officer of the army has been so long in the field without relief, and to my personal knowledge no one has rendered more arduous, faithful and brilliant service." The position, however, went to another artillery officer who outranked Thomas; but a few years later, about the time Thomas was sent to Boston Harbor, the post again became available and Thomas got the job. Its requirements were enlarged to take advantage of his skills, which included cavalry as well as artillery tactics, and over the next three years, beginning in April 1851, he would train some of the leading figures of the coming Civil War.

His star pupils included Philip Sheridan and J. E. B. Stuart (who learned their cavalry maneuvers under his direction), James B. McPherson, David S. Stanley, Stephen D. Lee, Alexander McD. McCook, John M. Schofield, Oliver Howard, and John Bell Hood. Howard, just entering the Academy then, remembered Thomas as "tall, perfectly well-proportioned and strongly built, with a large head, short brown hair, short mustache, and a firm walk." Though fair-skinned, his complexion was "bronzed by much exposure," and despite his grave demeanor, he had an "easy, kind manner" and "a warm and winning smile." Several years later, when Howard served under Thomas as a general in the advance on Atlanta, he recalled that there was something so warm and welcoming about the man that "his words and confidence drew toward him my whole heart."

Thomas was very popular at West Point because of his eminent fair dealing, for he was never known to punish or penalize a cadet without just cause. As a cavalry instructor, he was affectionately dubbed "Old Slow Trot"—not because he was "slow" (as later slander would have it, started by Grant)—but because of the wise direction he would give his cadets as they readied for a charge. During exercises on the Academy Plain, after the command to trot had been given and the cadets began to anticipate a gallop, "the deep and sonorous voice of Thomas would check their ardor with the order 'slow trot!' "

He won their respect all the more because he was exemplary in the subjects he taught. The artillery maneuvers he directed amid the rattle of gun carriages during exercises in the highlands were sometimes dazzling; and his horsemanship when jumping hurdles or leading a cavalry charge "caught every eye."

During his tenure at West Point, Thomas also established a firm friendship with Robert E. Lee, who became superintendent of the Academy in September 1852. Later they would serve together in Texas, where Lee often sought out Thomas as a companion on his circuit rides.

While at West Point, Thomas married Frances Lucretia Kellogg (a handsome woman, it is said, of charm and culture), the daughter of Warren Kellogg, a hardware merchant of Troy, New York. They had met in 1851 at the West Point Hotel, where Frances and her younger sister Julia often stayed with their mother during the summer months. At the time, Frances was thirty-one, Thomas thirty-six. Both were alike in temperament, congenial, with a certain dignified reserve. Both, perhaps notably, had also lost their fathers when they were twelve. Their marriage vows were taken at the home of the bride's uncle, Daniel Southwick of Troy, on November 17, 1852, and on this one occasion only Thomas wore his splendid ceremonial sword. After they were wed, they lived with Robert E. Lee and his family in the married officers quarters at West Point, and on Christmas Eve of the following year (1853), Thomas was promoted to captain in the 3rd Artillery, in addition to holding a brevet major's rank.

Though Thomas was a career soldier, the records of the Academy Library show that during his time as an instructor his reading was broad. Aside from a predictable array of books on military matters—artillery; gunpowder; the military operations of Antoine-Henri Jomini, a Napoleonic general and famed writer on the art of war (all in French); biographies of Napoleon; Louis XIV, and Frederick II—Thomas read an encyclopedic book on chemistry; the poems of Oliver Wendell Holmes; Nathaniel Hawthorne's *Twice-Told Tales*; the novels of James Fenimore Cooper; the works of Jonathan Swift; and various accounts of journeys through Germany, Syria, and Palestine. Some of these books were doubtless shared with his wife, who had been taught for seven years by the famed educator Emma Willard at her own elite school for girls in Troy.

At West Point, Thomas did much to upgrade the two departments in which he taught. He obtained new equipment, refurbished various facilities, improved the conditions in which the horses were kept, and expanded the role of cavalry and artillery tactics in the curriculum of the school. Robert E. Lee lobbied strenuously against his transfer, insisting there was "no more capable officer" in the service and should be kept where he was, where he could do the most good. But after only a year and a half of marriage, Thomas was called away to duty, and on May 1, 1854, placed in command of a battalion of the 3rd Artillery and ordered to Benicia, California, by way of the Isthmus of Panama. Wives sometimes accompanied officers on assignments, but this was one on which his wife could scarcely go.

The jungle march itself was a hard one, though not as hard as what lay ahead, and a number of his men became sick. At Benicia Barracks, the hospital facilities were inadequate, and Thomas successfully pushed the War Department to allow him to turn unused army quarters at the Spanish-built presidio into a medical ward. From Benicia, he continued on to San Francisco, where he was assigned to Fort Yuma, a desolate command near the junction of the Colorado and Gila Rivers on the Arizona line. A coastal steamer took Thomas and his troops (two companies of light artillery) to San Diego; from there Fort Yuma was reached by crossing the Imperial Valley, an overland trek of nearly 200 miles. The rugged pass separating the coastal plain from the interior desert was but the gateway to a barren land. The march, made in July, proved one of unnecessary hardship that nearly killed his men.

Thomas was irate. In his report to Pacific Division headquarters, he declared that troops should never be marched across the desert when the heat was fierce (and water so scarce), unless the purpose was simply to burn them up. For "the six days we were on the Desert," he noted, "the Thermometer ranged from 115 to 130 degrees." They had made it through only by caching their heavier stores for later transport, and by marching at night, with each day given over to a hunt for shade. If they hadn't done that, he said, "I doubt if I should have succeeded in getting half the command here."

Fort Yuma occupied land on both sides of the Colorado River separating California from Arizona and most of its indispensable supplies were brought up the river by chartered steamboats from the Gulf of California. These were managed by private firms, which proved unreliable. The river run was tricky, as the river overflowed in April but "dwindled to a sluggish brick-red stream during the summer," when steamers often got stuck in the mud. Thomas thought it foolish to contract out such work, and urged the government to take over everything having to do with the fort's needs. Scurvy was also a constant scourge, and a large graveyard testified to the risks of inadequate supply.

By any standard, Fort Yuma was a hardship post. "The hills around the garrison seemed to concentrate the rays of the sun upon the parade-ground," wrote one soldier, and it was not unusual for the thermometer to show 116 degrees in the shade. The nights were so hot and oppressive that sleep was out of the question until after midnight, and then only on the housetops, where one could hope for a soft breeze. Some of the men lived in quarters built of sun-dried bricks, but most took refuge in tents covered with improvised sheds made of branches to protect them from the sun. The surgeon at the fort remarked glumly that the watch in his pocket "felt like a hot boiled egg." In summer, the parade ground itself was almost a pretense, too exposed to be used.

Not surprisingly, as post commander Thomas found it hard to settle in. Before long the scorched air made "his skin dry and harsh, his hair crisp. Furniture brought in from the north would fall apart. A leather trunk would contract so the tray could not be lifted out. Ink would dry so fast that the nib of the pen would have to be washed off every few moments. Soap would lose one-sixth of its weight by evaporation and eggs their watery content." Round about were lizards, scorpions, and rattlesnakes, which constantly found their way into blankets, trunks, or clothes. Nevertheless, determined to leave things in better shape than he had found them, he put up new adobe buildings and, mindful always of any new technological advance, in March 1855 obtained new model long-range rifles for his men.

In other respects, he made the most of his time. While others "gambled, drank, or messed with the cashbox," Thomas enriched his desert world. Between reconnaissance patrols and the humdrum duty of garrison life, he explored the reaches of the Colorado River, gathered plant and mineral specimens (which he sent to the Smithsonian Institution in Washington), discovered a singular variety of leaf-nosed bat, and with the help of Indian interpreters learned to speak and write, according to his own system, the language of the local Yuma tribe. He was also instrumental in rescuing a little Mormon girl named Olive Oatman, whom some Apaches had kidnapped some years before.

Even so, he longed for his desert posting to end. Relief was in sight. In July 1855, Thomas learned that he had been appointed major of the 2nd Cavalry, a new, elite regiment created by Secretary of War Jefferson Davis and authorized by congressional act on March 3, 1855. This was "a mounted force of the highest grade," and Thomas later observed that Davis had almost certainly organized it as a cadre for a future Southern army in the event of Civil War. Indeed, one need only read the list of its field officers, every one of them future stars: Colonel Albert Sidney Johnston, Lieutenant Colonel Robert E. Lee, Major William J. Hardee, Major George H. Thomas, Captains Earl Van Dorn and Kirby Smith, and Lieutenants Fitzhugh Lee and John Bell Hood. Braxton Bragg might have belonged to it, too, but had commended Thomas in his stead. His letter to Davis was as generous as it had been to John Mason seven and a half years before. Thomas, he wrote, was "a solid, sound man; an honest, high-toned gentleman, above all deception and guile, and I know him to be an excellent and gallant soldier." Davis didn't need much persuading. He knew and admired Thomas since they had met in Zachary Taylor's Mexican War campaign, and had "kept a watchful eye on him ever since that day at Buena Vista when he brought his Mississippi Rifles to the all-but-lost field and found Thomas and other young artillerymen still holding it with the enemy swarming around the muzzles of their guns."

The 2nd Cavalry, in fact, would supply more officers to high command than any other such unit in military history. In putting it together, Davis knew exactly what he was about. Sixteen Civil War generals would come from its rolls—eleven fighting for the South. As if to stress its special character, even its uniforms were dashing, and featured a close-fitting blue jacket trimmed with yellow braid, a silken sash, and a large black Stetson hat, looped with an eagle and trailing ostrich plumes. The firearms it sported (Colt revolvers and rifle carbines) were of the latest make, and its thoroughbred mounts covered with handwrought saddles that "gleamed with shining brass."

Leaving Fort Yuma without regrets on July 21, 1855, Thomas again crossed the Imperial Valley in burning heat and on the last day of the month was at San Diego ready to sail. It look him a little more than a month to reach New Orleans, where he boarded a Mississippi River steamboat, to join his regiment on September 25 at Jefferson Barracks near St. Louis, Missouri. A month later, the 2nd Cavalry was detailed for duty in Texas, its various units to be strung out over hundreds of miles of Indian country at a dozen forts, posts, and towns. This was in partial fulfillment of the terms of the treaty that had ended the war between Mexico and the United States, which required the American army to protect Mexico from bands of raiding Indians (mostly Comanches) who slipped across the Rio Grande.

At Fort Washita, however, Thomas was detached for court-martial duties, which kept him occupied until sometime in January 1856. He was then sent to New York City on recruiting service and did not rejoin his regiment (at Fort Mason, 100 miles northwest of San Antonio) until May 1, 1856. He sent for his wife and two black servants, but upon his arrival, he discovered (to his dismay) that General Twiggs was in command of the department, which of course portended ill. Meanwhile, Robert E. Lee was a neighbor of sorts at Camp Cooper, 170 miles to the north, and after he had made a sweep in search of hostile Comanches that spring, set out for court-martial duties at Ringgold Barracks, 700 miles away on the Rio Grande. Lee had to pass through San Antonio going and returning and decided to pick up Thomas in September as a traveling companion all the way. Lee, notes one writer, "had a marked fondness for his fellow Virginian, a calm and silent man, shy and modest as a maiden," in whom he had total trust.

It was now September of 1856. On overnight stops the officers pitched their tents by the roadside, cooking their meals over an open fire. On September 13, they came to the town of Castroville, a picturesque Alsatian settlement and improbable oasis that seemed like a desert mirage. Established near a bend of the Medina River in a park-like area surrounded by pecan trees, it had quaint tile-roofed cottages, an old-fashioned European mill, and narrow lanes. Here, in the midst of the Texas prairie, French and German settlers had re-created a bit of their native land.

Both Thomas and Lee had a taste for good living, and after days of hardtack, bacon, and coffee, sleeping nights beside the trail, they reveled in the choice cuisine of the town's M. Tarde Hotel. There they were served by elegantly attired French waiters, dined on white bread, sweetmeats, and potatoes, and slept on soft French beds. A week later, after crossing an area beautifully enlivened by oak, mountain laurel, and mesquite, they passed through another small European hamlet called D'Hanis, before coming to Ringgold Barracks, where they assumed their court-martial tasks. Both were bored to death, as Lee wrote home to his wife, and relied on the skill of Lee's cook to divert them from their chores. "Neither Major [Thomas] nor I," he said, "can stand these long sessions of the court without eating." The land around Ringgold was also arid and harsh, and every leaf and branch seemed "armed with a point" designed "to poison the flesh." After Lee pricked the joint of one of his fingers on a plant known as "the Spanish bayonet," it swelled up so much he could scarcely write.

Early in November, with Ringgold behind them, a steamer took Lee and Thomas to Brownsville for another trial. It wasn't until March 1857 that Thomas was back at San Antonio, where his wife and a black cook joined him and where Lee and Thomas continued to dine together when they could. Mrs. Thomas often did the cooking herself and provided "waffles, eggs and wild turkey for breakfast," and "wild turkey, tomatoes, French peas, snap beans and potatoes followed by plum pudding, jellies and preserved peaches" for evening meals.

Then in May it was off together for another court-martial hearing at Camp Cooper with Lee now serving as host. In his letters home, Lee expressed some uncertainty about meeting Mrs. Thomas's needs. "The Major can fare as I do," Lee confided to his wife, "but I fear that she will fare badly as my man Kremer [his cook] is both awkward and unskilled." Yet again, in July 1857, they sat at a hearing at Fort Mason, with Colonel Albert Sidney Johnston presiding. When Johnston and Lee had to depart for various reasons, Thomas was left to pronounce a verdict, which led to another altercation with General Twiggs. The case involved a young lieutenant named Wood whom some settlers had charged with theft. The charge was evidently false and Thomas ruled in Wood's favor. Twiggs, however, who wished to curry favor with the local population, set aside the opinion, retried the case himself, and endorsed the charge. Thomas at once reported the facts to the secretary of war, John B. Floyd, who upheld the original verdict, much to Twiggs's ire.

In the fall, Twiggs ordered the 2nd Cavalry to Fort Belknap, Texas, to prepare for an expedition to maintain order among the Mormons in Utah. That plan was soon abandoned in favor of a couple of improvised assignments, which allowed him to break up the regiment. Two companies were ordered to Camp Cooper on the Clear Fork of the Brazos River; eight others on an expedition to the Wichita Mountains against some restive Indian tribes. Meanwhile, Lee had returned home for a family funeral and had assigned command of the 2nd Cavalry to Thomas at Fort Mason, where he lodged. By rights, Thomas, as ranking officer, should have been given command of the Indian expedition with Lee on leave. Instead, in another instance of petty spite, Twiggs gave it to his favorite, Earl Van Dorn. Thomas was further demeaned by being ordered "to stay at Fort Belknap in command of the regimental musicians, a few quartermaster's men, and the men on sick call." Once more, Thomas appealed to the secretary of war, who, after some delay, again ruled in his favor and told Thomas to take command. In a formal reprimand, Twiggs assailed Thomas for going over his head. Thomas, in reply, found fault with the general's grammar and declared that Lee would have "recognized his rights had he been there." In the meantime, Van Dorn had engaged the Indians in battle, which only served to stir up more trouble on the Texas border with Mexico, where Indian raids intensified.

Once more, Thomas was eager to move on. In a Christmas letter to his sister Fanny in Virginia, he wrote: "I have been waiting to learn if Col. Lee will [re]join the regiment before answering [your letter], as I had previously written that we would go on leave when he did. A few days ago I learned that his leave had been extended until the first of May next. So we will have to wait until that time . . . This place continues as wretchedly dull as ever, and we have had one or two as cold spells as I have ever experienced in New York even at this season of the year." He added that he wished he could have been part of a recent family reunion, and promised to send $100 to his sister Judith, who was trying to help finance the building of a local church. Should the project fall through, he wanted her to dispense the money to the poor.

When Lee returned, Thomas remained on duty, even though his mother had died in the interim when he had been unable to go home. Lee himself was restive and asked Thomas to take over at Camp Cooper, where good judgment was needed to curb rising tensions between some white settlers and peaceful Comanches on the reservation nearby. When he arrived, he found the area threatened with a border war. The commissioner of Indian affairs, however, decided on drastic action and ordered the Texas Reserve Indians (as they were called) removed en masse. It fell to Thomas in the late summer of 1859 to escort them to the Indian Territory, where they were to have new hunting grounds.

Returning to Camp Cooper on August 21, Thomas was obliged to declare all other Kiowas and Comanches discovered off their reservations hostile. To enforce the edict, he mobilized five cavalry companies and set out on a reconnaissance sweep. He picked up an Indian trail near the Cimarron River, then circled eastward to the headwaters of the Wichita River, before returning to Camp Cooper after fifty-three days in the field. The following summer, toward the end of July, he set out to explore the headwaters of the Colorado and Concho Rivers. On August 25, 1860, as he came back onto the stage road to return to his post, he caught sight of eleven mounted Comanches and gave chase. For a day and a half he persevered, in a stretch of hard riding over forty miles. Finally, as his company gained ground, "one old Comanche dropped off his horse and flattened out, unslinging his bow." Before he could be killed, he managed to wound at least three soldiers, including Thomas, who was struck in the chest when an arrow glanced off his chin. Thomas promptly pulled it out but the wound was an ugly one and left a wedge-shaped scar.

Upon his return to Camp Cooper, Thomas obtained a leave of absence and left his command on November 12, 1860, to rejoin his wife, who some months before had returned to New York. As he sped north by rail—with farms and plantations, marked by clusters of slaves, streaming by—he learned of Abraham Lincoln's momentous election as president of the United States.

# 3. "A HOUSE DIVIDED"

In the years leading up to the Civil War, the main parties were the Whigs and Democrats. (The Republican Party of Abraham Lincoln was formed from the Whig Party in 1856.) Democrats favored strict construction of the Constitution and states' rights; the Whigs (who had inherited the Federalists' mantle) preferred a broad construction of the Constitution in favor of the central government, the expenditure of national money on internal improvements, and a national bank. Generally speaking, the Whigs, like the Federalists, were strongest in the North and favored by intellectuals and large Midwestern farmers; the Democrats drew their strength among the struggling populace of great cities and the South.

At the nation's founding, several agreements had been forged between the states to give the new union traction, among them, the adoption of a Senate and a House of Representatives to mediate between the claims of federal and state authority; related to this was a clause in the Constitution that allowed the South, in the apportionment of its representation, to count each slave as three-fifths of a man. These, together with the Fugitive Slave Law of 1793, which provided for the return between states of escaped slaves, had helped keep North and South together, while (it was hoped) slavery succumbed to a natural death. But in the intervening years, two things occurred to dash that hope to the ground. First, the economic (or plantation) conditions that had long fostered slavery in the South were reinforced by a new dependence on cotton; second, instead of consenting to the national and international trend toward abolition, the South not only clung to slavery but sought to enlarge its domain for its own survival.

Since 1789, free and slave states had been admitted in pairs to ensure parity between the two interests, but in 1817 the demand of Missouri to be admitted as a slave state had threatened to tilt the scales. A compromise was reached in 1820 that allowed Missouri to come in as a slave state in conjunction with the free state of Maine, but it also prohibited slavery from all territory (Missouri excepted) north of the parallel 36° 30', that is, from the Great Northwest.

As the years passed, the population of the free states increased faster than that of the slave, giving them a numerical advantage in the House. That seemed to ensure that by a wholly constitutional, democratic means, slavery had been set on a course of extinction from the nation's life. That expectation, however, was upended by the territorial gains of the Mexican War. Texas being large enough to make four states, the North was now threatened with the spread of slavery in an exponential way. New Mexico, Arizona, and California were also at stake. A desperate struggle between both interests in Congress began. That led to the Compromise of 1850. Thanks to the mediating wisdom of Henry Clay, Texas, though given over to slavery, was left a single state. California was admitted as a free state; and New Mexico and Arizona left to go their own way—slave or free. Being unsuited for slave labor, their choice was not in doubt. However, in a concession to the South, a more stringent Fugitive Slave Law was passed.

The Whig Party, which had tried to keep the slavery question out of the political arena and to build its platform on such planks as a protective tariff, internal improvements, the cultivation of national spirit, and devotion to the Union, lost its base by not addressing the issue of slavery directly, as the times required. New parties moved into the gap. First, a Free Soil Party emerged; then the national Republican Party with the issue of slavery at its core.

The die would soon be cast. In short, though slavery as a social institution was more or less confined to the South, it had come to dominate the nation's political life. In one blunt synopsis: "It elected the Presidents, it filled the offices, it swayed the Senate, it cowed the House of Representatives and the nation generally by threats of breaking up the Union, the idol of the American heart. . . . It held the Northern merchants by the bonds of a vast commercial interest. . . . Catholics and High Church Anglicans were not intolerant of slavery; the Protestant churches were fearful of a rupture with their Southern wings."

Those who acquiesced to all this took comfort in the fact that the Constitution allowed for slavery and that their own arrangements therefore fell within the dignified compass of the "law."

Nevertheless, abolition societies multiplied. Harriet Beecher Stowe's *Uncle Tom's Cabin*, which depicted the plight of slaves in the most abject light, swept America by storm, and crusaders such as William Lloyd Garrison, who published *The Liberator*, an anti-slavery journal, commanded huge followings that crossed party lines. Under the new Fugitive Slave Law, "the people in the North saw with their own eyes the slave-hunter plying his trade in their cities, and innocent men and women dragged from their habitations and borne off in chains." An underground railway, as it was called (a system of safe houses and hideouts), was organized to forward slaves to Canada, and some of the states passed Liberty Bills in defiance of Federal law. About this time, the new American, or Know-Nothing Party—which appealed to settled Americans fearful of the power of the new immigrant vote—arose in reaction to the great influx of Irish Catholic immigrants from their famine-stricken land.

In spite of all this turmoil, the country had been advancing with mighty strides. Since the Union had been formed, the number of states had more than doubled, the population tripled, swollen by great waves of immigration—not only Irish, but German and Scandinavian—as settlements, once confined to the Atlantic seaboard, crossed the Alleghenies, entered the valley of the Mississippi, and passed on to the Pacific coast. Steamboats plied the waterways; railways had begun to knit the Midwest together with the North and South. A transcontinental railway had been surveyed by a young Northern topographical engineer named George McClellan at the behest of the Mississippi-born Jefferson Davis, then secretary of war under Franklin Pierce. The agrarian economy of the South seemed to be thriving; manufactures on a large scale expanded in the North; the mineral resources of the country were being mined. Not even a flurry of wildcat banks, frauds, bankruptcy, and crashes could subvert the hectic pace of this advance.

Yet one great issue, that of slavery, kept gnawing at the nation's heart.

If the Southern aristocracy fancied itself a bastion of gentility and refinement, outside observers, such as Charles Dickens, who visited Richmond in the early 1840s, saw that whites raised in an environment where slavery flourished had been fundamentally coarsened by the system they condoned. Almost every thoughtful politician, North and South, knew that the institution of slavery, with its misbegotten fruits, might one day drag the nation down. "While the union lasts, we have high, exciting, gratifying prospects spread out before us," declared Daniel Webster. "Beyond that I seek not to penetrate the veil. God grant that, in my day at least, that curtain may not rise . . . on the broken and dishonored fragments of a once glorious union; on States dissevered, discordant, belligerent; on a land rent with civil feuds, or drenched, it may be, in fraternal blood!"

With the passage of the Kansas-Nebraska Act in 1854, the nation had been set on its fateful course. Based on the idea of "popular sovereignty," that act had proposed to leave open to the settlers of each new state whether it would enter the Union as slave or free. It therefore expressly repealed the Missouri Compromise of 1820, nullified the Compromise of 1850, and reopened the struggle between freedom and slavery in the new territories of the West.

In the furor that followed, party lines were obliterated, as those opposed to slavery among Democrats, Whigs, and Free Soilers combined. The general drift of the parties, however, was on regional or sectional lines. In 1854, the Whig Party dissolved; the power base of the Democratic Party shifted to the South; and two years later the new Republican Party was organized in the Midwest and North around opposition to the spread of slavery.

As their candidate in 1856, the Republicans chose John C. Frémont; the Democrats, James Buchanan. Buchanan won, and a few days after he took his oath of office on March 4, 1857, the fateful *Dred Scott* decision of the Supreme Court was handed down. That decision, which denied freedom to a fugitive black, also ruled that bans against the extension of slavery were unconstitutional, as contrary to Fifth Amendment rights. In other words, the court decided that slaves were movable property that could be taken anywhere their owners wished. By extension, it was feared, even free states might be denied the right to prohibit slavery in their midst. This was the first time since *Marbury v. Madison*, in fact, that an act of Congress had been declared unconstitutional by the court. In the end, it was not so much agitation in the North for the abolition of slavery, but aggressive measures for its extension that brought on the war.

Madness was in the air. On October 16, 1859, the abolitionist John Brown, crazed by the recent murder of his son, attacked Harpers Ferry at the mouth of the Shenandoah Valley, and with a small armed band captured the Federal armory and arsenal, seized the bridge across the Potomac, cut the telegraph wires, and took possession of the town. His idea was to establish a stronghold in the mountains of Virginia, and by raising a slave revolt, establish an army of liberated slaves that would sweep through the South. His scheme failed and he was captured—by Robert E. Lee—and hanged. In the South, he was viewed as a criminal fanatic; in the North, by some, as a martyred saint.

In his race for the Senate in Illinois in 1858, Lincoln had framed the issue facing the nation in stark terms.

A house divided against itself cannot stand. I believe this government cannot endure permanently half slave and half free. I do not expect the Union to be dissolved. I do not expect the house to fall—but I do expect it will cease to be divided. It will become all one thing or all the other. Either the opponents of slavery will arrest the further spread of it, and place it where the public mind shall rest in the belief that it is in the course of ultimate extinction; or its advocates will push it forward till it shall become alike lawful in all the states, old as well as new—North as well as South.

Though Lincoln lost the Senate contest to Stephen A. Douglas (author of the Kansas-Nebraska Act) by a narrow margin, he emerged two years later as the Republican candidate for president. Meanwhile, the Democratic Party had split in two. Its Southern, pro-slavery wing nominated John C. Breckinridge of Kentucky; its Northern, Douglas. Yet another political faction, known as the Constitutional Union Party, put forth John Bell of Tennessee.

Southern leaders threatened to secede if Lincoln were elected. Most in the North doubted they would. "The love of Union and the orderly obedience to constituted authority had been so well established among our people," wrote Ohio senator John Sherman, "that few really believed that war, of which they knew nothing," would result. Moreover, many Southern voters also viewed the Union's preservation as next to sacrosanct. Some voted for Douglas (who cast himself as a Unionist); others, for Bell. George Thomas favored Bell, whose moderate, if cautious, program advocated adherence to the Constitution, continuing union of the states, and enforcement of the laws.

In the end, Bell emerged as the leading candidate of the Upper South, in Virginia, Kentucky, and Tennessee; Breckinridge, in all the slaveholding states except Missouri; Lincoln, in all the free states but one. When all the votes were tallied, Lincoln fell well short of a popular majority, but his electoral margin was clear. That, however, made him a minority president, which opened the door still wider to revolt.

A few months before, Alexander H. Stephens, a Georgia Representative, (soon to be vice president of the Confederate States), had predicted that "men will be cutting one another's throats in a little while. In less than a year, there will be war."

He was right.

After the election, Lincoln sought to downplay the extent of the crisis. Some of his statements were so offhand and congenial as to suggest that he failed to grasp the trend of events. "There is no crisis but an artificial one," he said on one occasion. On another, "There is nothing going wrong. . . . There is nothing that really hurts anyone," which was scarcely true. But of course he was just trying to ease the public alarm.

Yet even in private, Lincoln sounded oddly optimistic. In mid-November, he invited two of his Ohio supporters, Donn Piatt and Robert C. Schenck, to dinner in Springfield, Illinois. Piatt was a former judge and secretary to the Paris legation; Schenck had served with Lincoln in Congress and as ambassador to Brazil. Both had campaigned hard across Illinois for Lincoln as anti-slavery Democrats in the late election, and Lincoln wanted someone from Ohio in a cabinet post. If the leading candidate, Salmon P. Chase, then a senator, declined, either Schenck or Piatt might aptly fill that niche. At dinner, Piatt tried to impress upon Lincoln that war was almost certain. Lincoln thought not. Southern politicians, he said, would never give up their stake in the Federal government, which they had long controlled. He seemed to imply that a solution of some sort could still be found through backroom politics.

Toward the end of the month, Lincoln traveled to Chicago for consultation with other Republican leaders on the shape his cabinet might take. Since Piatt and Schenck were both relevant to the discussions, he invited them along. En route, the subject of the impending war once more came up. Piatt insisted that Lincoln not deceive himself in any way on that score. He even expressed doubt that in the gathering tempest Lincoln's inauguration would ever take place. Lincoln replied jokingly that the fall in pork prices in Cincinnati (hog capital of America) had affected his judgment. Piatt, now thoroughly annoyed, declared that "the countryside would soon be white with army tents." As often, Lincoln fell back on a homely expression to wrap the matter up. "Well, we won't jump that ditch until we come to it," he said.


As Thomas hurried north, he had a graver view of the nation's plight than Lincoln did. He even wondered if there would be a country left to serve by the time his leave expired. All the conflicting issues of national and state allegiance revolved with fury in his mind. At that moment, he embodied the full range of ambivalent emotions of an honorable man from a divided state—a man whose honor would be questioned no matter which side he chose. The strain of the moment (unlike any strain he would ever face in battle, where he was never thrown) tolled on him, and on his way through Virginia, he had an accident that almost disabled him for life. One evening, as the engine of his train was taking on water near Lynchburg, he stepped down onto what appeared in the moonlight to be solid ground; but instead of finding safe footing, he plunged down a steep embankment and seriously wrenched his spine. In great pain, he continued on to Norfolk, where he wired for his wife to join him. On December 15, they proceeded to the Thomas family farm in Southampton County, some thirty miles away. There Thomas convalesced for another three weeks, but he never fully recovered. To the end of his life, he remained in chronic, if intermittent, discomfort. His movements, always deliberate, were now sometimes ponderously slow. That physical carriage would later become a metaphor by which hostile rivals would critique his battle plans.

At his Virginia home, the political discussions were tense. His sisters were strong for the South; Thomas, somewhat torn. Meanwhile, on December 15, South Carolina voted to secede from the Union, followed by Mississippi on January 9, 1861, and Florida on the 10th. Instead of proceeding directly to New York, Thomas and his wife set out together for Washington. At the capital, Thomas went at once to see General-in-Chief Winfield Scott. He warned him that General Twiggs, who was close to the secessionist faction in Texas, would betray the government if hostilities broke out. Scott ordered Twiggs recalled, but the order was held up by President Buchanan, whose indecision on almost every matter of importance now paralyzed the ship of state.

For some Unionists, the secession of Texas was the bitterest pill of all. "Bound to the Federal government by the right of purchase," as one soldier put it, "admitted into the Union on terms of equality with the other States, and permitted to retain absolute control over her public lands, Texas should have been the last State in the Union to sever her connection, but when the treasonable tempest swept over the South, Texas . . . drifted from her moorings into the deep sea of revolt." Sam Houston, then governor, opposed the tide. A decade before, in a speech in support of the Compromise of 1850, he had said, "A nation divided against itself cannot stand." Lincoln, in his far more famous speech, had picked up the theme. But Texans now "rushed madly onward," passed the ordinance of secession, and called upon him to take the oath of allegiance to the South. He refused and was deposed.

Meanwhile, as Thomas had warned, Twiggs had capitulated to the Rebels with unseemly haste, even granting leaves of absence to all

Southern-born officers who wished to return to their native states and secure appointments in the Confederate army. On February 18, the Texas Rangers took control of army headquarters at San Antonio and raised the Lone Star flag. Thomas later said that had he been with his regiment he would have "marched the men north until we reached the loyal states, and the Rebels would not have taken a single prisoner or captured a cannon or a flag."

Reaching New York at last, Thomas took rooms at the New York Hotel on Broadway near 10th Street where, still in great pain, he was apparently "despondent over the prospects of any improvement" and wondered if he had come to the end of his career. Concerned for his livelihood (he was now forty-five years old), he began to look around for military work he could do. One morning his wife saw a notice in the *National Intelligencer* that the Virginia Military Institute was seeking a commandant of cadets. The position was not unlike the one that William Tecumseh Sherman, with less experience, then held in Louisiana and for which Thomas was clearly fit. On January 18, he wrote to the superintendent, Francis H. Smith, asking "what salary and allowances pertain[ed] to the situation," if it was not yet filled. A few days later, Thomas learned it had already gone to someone else.

On March 1, he wrote to the adjutant general in Washington asking to be made "Superintendent of the mounted recruiting service for the next two years," explaining that he was still too "lame" from his accident to attend to the normal duties of a field command. That position was not open either, but a week or so later, when the governor of Virginia, John Letcher, offered him the important post of chief of the state's ordnance, he declined, saying, "it is not my wish to leave the service of the United States as long as it is honorable for me to remain in it." There is no doubt that Thomas was furious that things had come to such a pass. Indeed, an acquaintance recalled that he was "strong and bitter in his denunciation against all parties North and South that seemed to him responsible for the condition of affairs." He thought it could have been avoided. At the same time, he "denounced the idea [of secession] and denied the necessity of dividing the country or destroying the Government."

Robert E. Lee's vacillations were more pronounced. In February (about the time Twiggs surrendered his command), Lee had been summoned to Washington by General Scott, in an ongoing effort to establish how much of the army might be kept intact. As he took the stagecoach at Fort Mason, Lee remarked: "I shall never bear arms against the United States but it may be necessary for me to carry a musket in defense of my native state." That implied that if Virginia seceded, the United States would no longer exist. In a technical sense, that was true. As late as March 30 (before Virginia formally seceded) Lee accepted command of the 1st Cavalry Regiment in Federal service, before undergoing his change of heart.

In the interim, secession had moved with tremendous speed. By February 1, Georgia and the five states bordering on the Gulf of Mexico had also joined. These took possession of all public property within their borders, such as mints, arsenals, navy yards, and forts; and wherever the United States flag was found it was torn down.

On February 4, 1861, representatives of the seceding states met at Montgomery, Alabama, to organize a provisional government and chose Jefferson Davis as their president on the 9th. In just five days, a rival republic had been born within the borders of the United States. The momentum did not abate. On February 28, the Confederate Congress directed Davis to assume control of all military operations in every state, and authorized him to accept as many volunteers as he might need. A week later, on March 6, he called for 100,000 men to take the field.

Neither side was really ready for war, but the South had done some things to prepare. During 1860, John Floyd of Virginia, Buchanan's secretary of war, had transferred from Northern to Southern arsenals at least 65,000 percussion muskets, 40,000 altered muskets, and 10,000 rifles. In late October, he had sent over seventy cannon to a fort at Galveston, Texas—even though the fort had yet to be built. At the same time, ships of the Federal navy (few in number as they were) had been dispersed by the secretary of the navy to distant ports, to forestall their use in the defense of Federal property. Ad hoc military units were also raised in the South—in Virginia's Southampton County, for example, where the company banner was inscribed with the words "Justice and Truth, Liberty or Death." That banner was decoratively stitched by Thomas's own two sisters, Judith and Fanny, and when the company was later mustered out, "There glowed from the eye [of each volunteer] a beam of content," reported one eyewitness, "and from the heart there seemed to leap an honest conviction that he was engaged in a noble, holy and patriotic cause."

In the North, on the other hand, military spirit seemed to have died away. On the eve of the war, most military organizations, wrote Senator John Sherman, "had fallen into disuse" and were even the object of "popular contempt." "Militia day" was often "a day of drunkenness and brawls," and the volunteers that assembled on town greens stumbled into line without order and were "hardly better than Falstaff's 'regiment'—without guns, uniform, or anything proper for a man of arms." Here and there Republicans had organized "Wide-Awake Clubs"—uniformed companies of volunteers (Ulysses Grant led one)—for torchlight and other processions. But they hardly filled the gap.

Throughout that winter and spring, according to the report of the Joint Committee on the Conduct of the War (created by the 37th Congress in December 1861), "There was treason in the Executive Mansion, treason in the Cabinet, treason in the Senate and the House of Representatives, treason in the Army and Navy, treason in every department, bureau and office connected with the Government." Senators from states like Kentucky and Virginia, which had not seceded, remained in the capital to defend secession in heated Senate debates, where their own sedition was manifest. One senator from Texas (Louis Trezevant Wigfall) was even allowed to attend executive sessions, where he acted as a spy. But Congress, still hoping for a reconciliation, was too timid to purge its own ranks. Instead, it panicked, and in a series of desperately proposed measures sought to appease the seceded states by extending the Missouri Compromise to the Pacific, admitting at least two new Western states as slave, and strengthening the Fugitive Slave Law still further until it was set with iron teeth. Congress even seemed willing to place slavery itself beyond the reach of constitutional amendment, enshrining it forever in the law.

In an atmosphere of crisis, Lincoln made his way to the capital, entered it by night under threat to his life, and on March 4, 1861, was inaugurated under military guard. On the day of his inauguration, Lincoln and Buchanan sat side by side in the presidential carriage that proceeded up Pennsylvania Avenue, lined with anxious throngs. They ascended the Capitol arm in arm, Buchanan looking "pale, sad, and nervous," his chest heaving with "audible sighs." Lincoln looked firm and grave. Lincoln then took his stand upon the platform of the Portico, with the Justices of the Supreme Court, senators, members of the House, foreign ministers, and other dignitaries filling every seat. In his inaugural address, he promised to do everything in his power to preserve the Union and pledged to maintain the authority of the Federal government with respect to its own property in every state. At the same time, he promised to do this without bloodshed or violence, unless these were forced upon him by the South:

> In your hands, my dissatisfied countrymen, and not in mine, is the momentous issue of civil war. The government will not assail you. You can have no conflict without being yourselves the aggressors. You have no oath registered in heaven to destroy the government; while I shall have the most solemn one to "preserve, protect, and defend it." I am loath to close. We are not enemies, but friends. We must not be enemies. Though passion may have strained, it must not break our bonds of affection. The mystic chords of memory, stretching from every battle-field and patriot grave, to every living heart and hearthstone, all over this broad land, will yet swell the chorus of the Union, when again touched, as surely they will be, by the better angels of our nature.

A week later Lincoln remarked to one senator, "I guess we will manage to keep house," but deep down he must have known that the divide could not be bridged. At the outset, even his own government was subverted from within. Upon assuming his duties as Lincoln's secretary of war, Simon Cameron recalled: "I found the nation without an army, destitute of all the means of defense. I found scarcely a man throughout the whole War Department in whom I could put my trust. The Adjutant General deserted. The Quartermaster General ran off. The Commissary General was on his death-bed. More than half the clerks [i.e., bureaucrats] were disloyal." Those who had sworn allegiance were tormented by broken friendships and other traumas from the break. On one occasion, General Winfield Scott came to Cameron in distress and said: "I have spent the most miserable day in my life; a friend of my boyhood has just told me I am disgracing myself by staying here, and serving this fragment of a government, in place of going to Virginia, and serving under the banner of my native state."

Meanwhile, Thomas awaited instructions in New York. After Texas had seceded, the 2nd Cavalry had gone to Indianola, Texas, where transports were waiting to take it north. The vessels steamed out of Matagorda Bay, and reached New York Harbor on April 13. Thomas, his leave canceled, was dispatched to meet the regiment as it disembarked. As he entrained with his men for Carlisle Barracks near Harrisburg, Pennsylvania, to reorganize and equip them for immediate service in the field, he learned that Fort Sumter was under siege.

For several months, all eyes had been turned toward the harbor of Charleston, South Carolina, where a tiny garrison of seventy-five men (two companies of artillery and a regimental band) had established themselves at Fort Sumter, the stout but still unfinished pentagular fortress on a shoal commanding the shipping lanes. The officer in charge was Robert Anderson, an artillery expert who had fought with distinction in the Seminole and Mexican Wars. A smart and courageous fighter, he was well suited to the post, but his appointment (like most war appointments) had its political side: he came from a border state (Kentucky), had married a Southern girl, and, until recently, owned slaves on his wife's Georgia estate. His father had taken part in the defense of Fort Moultrie in Charleston Harbor during the Revolutionary War, and Anderson himself had served there, too. If he was for the North, who in the South might not be as well?

Because of the delicate nature of the standoff, Anderson's instructions were carefully framed. The War Department had told him not to start any hostile action. Lincoln also didn't want "a useless waste of life. It will be your duty," Lincoln told him, through his secretary of war, "to yield to necessity and make the best terms in your power." At Sumter, Anderson had sixty-six heavy guns in three tiers, but only fifteen were mounted. He had close to 6,000 shot and shell, but lacked the friction primers he needed and the sights, quadrants, and levels with which to aim his guns. Most of his cartridge bags had to be stitched together out of flannel shirts and woolen socks. The barracks, quarters, and gun rooms of the fort were still under construction, and eight-foot-square openings yawned in place of gun embrasures on the second tier. Meanwhile, the Rebels had taken possession of all the other harbor defenses (including Moultrie) and seized the city arsenal with its 70,000 stand of arms. When the Federal government tried to resupply the fort with a merchant steamer, *The Star of the West*, the ship was turned back.

Then on March 6, General P. T. G. Beauregard (recently, if briefly, Lee's successor as superintendent of West Point) assumed command of the siege. Under his direction, a formidable system of shore and island batteries, variously mounted with mortars and heavy guns, was arrayed around the fort. Cannon were rushed to the scene from all over the South, and in all Beauregard had ninety-two ordnance with which to mount his assault. To prevent further attempts to relieve the fort by day or night, he blocked the main channel by sinking hulks loaded with stone on the bar, and placed powerful calcium lights in bombproof shelters on two harbor shoals. Stacks of dry timber were floated at the wide harbor entrance to be lit at the first alarm.

By the end of March, the garrison had run out of flour and there was scarcely a biscuit left to eat. When the last candle was burned, wicks were enclosed in tin tubes and floated on corks in cups of oil. Lincoln notified the Confederate authorities at Charleston that another attempt would be made to send provisions in. Without challenging the Confederates directly, or by any overt military action, that placed the burden of starting the conflict on the South. Anderson knew the fort must fall, and had already indicated to the besiegers that even without a bombardment he would soon be starved out. But on April 11, Beauregard demanded he yield.

The game was up. Anderson ordered the sentinels off the parapets, the posterns closed, and the flag, that had been lowered with the coming of night, "flung to the breeze." Then he sat down to await the coming shock. "It was a mild spring night," one contemporary wrote, "and not a sound disturbed the quiet that reigned over the peaceful waters of the bay." At half past four, on the morning of the 12th, there was a flash from a Rebel battery and an instant later a bombshell rose in a slow, high curve and fell upon the fort. "Sixty years and more of argument," as one writer put it, "of political facts and fictions, of expedients and unworkable panaceas were swept aside, like a cobweb, by a ten-inch shell." The bombardment thereafter was simultaneous from several directions. Solid shot crashed down on the little garrison huddled in their casemates, exploding everywhere, as Sumter's own cannon were thrown from their mountings, brick walls crumbled like powder, and red-hot shot set the wooden barracks on fire. From Fort Moultrie, Point Pleasant, Fort Johnson, Cummings Point, and Sullivan's Island, the Rebel batteries poured in concentric fire. Before long, nearly the whole interior of the fort was ablaze. For thirty-six hours, this terrific bombardment continued, almost without cease. To keep the powder magazines from exploding, the defenders threw a third of what they had into the sea. Anderson's guns now and then replied, but the Rebels had so cased their batteries at angles with greased iron that the balls flung from Sumter "glanced off like marbles thrown against the back of a tortoise by a child." In Charleston, people rushed to the wharves to observe the action and mounted the steeples and housetops as many a Southern belle, according to one Confederate, "stood, with palpitating heart and pallid face, watching the white smoke as it rose in wreaths, upon the soft twilight air."

About half past nine on the morning of the 14th, Anderson surrendered and the Stars-and-Stripes came down.

The attack on Fort Sumter fired the heart of the South, as it was meant to; but it also galvanized the North, where all talk of compromise disappeared. As the news flashed along the wires, people in every city, town, and hamlet were seized with indignation and amazement. Opposed political factions united into one common front. From then on, at least for a while, there were but two parties in the land—the Rebels, and those who upheld the Union cause.

In that respect, Fort Sumter was the Bunker Hill of the Civil War. Though its defenders met defeat, it rallied the North against the South as the colonists had been rallied against the British by that heroic stand. Lincoln, in his inaugural address, had said that if civil war was to come, the South would have to start it. Now they had done so, which absolved the North of all blame. The very next day, April 15, Lincoln called upon the people "to repossess the forts, places, and property which have been seized from the Union" and issued a call for 75,000 three-months' volunteers. Men stepped forth in abundance, but the price was high, as the states of the Upper South—Virginia, North Carolina, Tennessee, and Arkansas—joined the revolt. In the border states a desperate struggle developed at once between the opposing sides. Lincoln also ordered the blockade of all Southern ports and stationed armed steamships—the *Niagara, Minnesota,* and others—off Charleston Harbor, Chesapeake Bay, Old Point Comfort, the York and James Rivers, Savannah, New Orleans, and Mobile, where trade was effectively suspended by the force of their guns.

But the South was defiant, and the flames of rebellion kindled at Fort Sumter did not stop at the Potomac. On April 19, they burst out in Baltimore, where for several days the Rebels checked the advance of Union troops—the 6th Massachusetts and the 7th Pennsylvania Regiments—en route to Washington. On May 20, the seat of the Confederate government was moved to Richmond, while Confederate troops advanced to Fairfax and Alexandria, within view of the Capitol itself. As for Lincoln's call to arms, Confederate vice president Alexander Stephens scornfully boasted that it would require seventy-five times 75,000 soldiers to intimidate the South.

Outside Washington, railroads and telegraphs were cut; the capital itself was in a state of siege. To avert its fall, and to prevent the overthrow of the government, Lincoln assumed and exercised the war powers of Congress. By proclamation he began to increase the size of the army and navy, called for more volunteers, and by the time Congress assembled in special session on July 4, it found that its power to raise and support armies had already been exercised by the president to the extent of calling forth 230,000 men.

Ninety days after Fort Sumter was bombarded the roll of the regimental drum reverberated through America's far-flung forests and glens and the land, as Piatt had predicted, "was white with army tents." In both North and South, men were arming and falling into line to do battle and a whole generation of Americans was preparing to sacrifice itself with a benighted zeal to the God of War. They could hardly have imagined the horrific furnace into which they would be hurled. Indeed, Alexander McClure recalled that at the time it was thought Richmond could be taken—but at an unacceptable cost, which one Union general put at 10,000 men. At the very mention of that figure, his companion was "appalled to silence when compelled to consider so great a sacrifice."

Thomas was at Harrisburg, Pennsylvania, when word of the fall of Fort Sumter reached him and he immediately telegraphed his wife at New York, and his sisters in Virginia that he would cast his lot with the North. He had some of the same conflicting feelings Lee had, but his decision in the end was firm. He wrote his wife: "Whichever way I turned the matter over in my mind, my oath of allegiance to my Government always came uppermost." He then went at once to a magistrate to renew his oath of allegiance to the Federal government; three days later the legislature of his native state voted to secede.

In Thomas's Southampton home, his sisters turned his picture to the wall.

Even so, the notion that Thomas "went North" only because the South failed to offer him a high command took hold in some circles, and later gained credence among Southern partisans, such as General Fitzhugh Lee. The letter Thomas had written to the head of the Virginia Military Institute was claimed as evidence, even though he had simply been looking for a salaried job in his native state. Besides, at the time he wrote it (January 18), just two states of the Lower South had seceded, and the Upper South, including Virginia, had not, nor did it seem likely that it would. The fateful siege of Fort Sumter was also three months away. Like most Americans, he still hoped that secession, "which had gone up like a rocket, would come down like a stick."

Thomas told his longtime aide Colonel Alfred L. Hough (according to Hough's contemporaneous notes) that the charge was

an entire fabrication, not having an atom of foundation; not a line ever passed between him and the rebel authorities; they had no genuine letter of his, nor was a word spoken by him to any one that could even lead to such an inference. He defied any one to produce any testimony, written or oral, to sustain such an allegation; he never entertained such an idea, for his duty was clear from the beginning. These slanders were caused by men who knew they had done wrong, but were endeavoring to justify themselves by claiming their action to be a virtue which all men should have followed, and by blackening the character of those who had done right. It was evident they were determined that no Southern-born man, who had remained true to his country, should bear a reputable character, if continued and repeated abuse could effect a stain upon it.

Indeed, Thomas had already shown his allegiance in his December 1860 conference with General Scott about Twiggs; had rejected the position of head of ordnance for Virginia; and could surely have obtained a high command in the Confederate army if that had been his wish. After all, almost all of his most influential connections were in the Southern officer corps. Jefferson Davis admired him, and had picked him for his elite cavalry troop; Robert E. Lee valued him highly; Braxton Bragg's esteem for Thomas, before the war at least, was boundless ("No one has rendered more arduous, faithful, and brilliant service"), and so on. Had Thomas "gone South," he would have had extremely powerful friends in high places, and doubtless risen to the top. But he "went North" instead. And the bitter suspicion lingered long afterward that the South might actually have won the war if he had stayed.

In contrast to his Southern connections, Thomas had almost no one in the North to promote his career. Even his West Point sponsor, John Mason, was gone, having died the year before. Had he lived it is doubtful he would have done Thomas any good. Elected to the House of Delegates in 1823 and the state Senate in 1827, Mason had served three terms as an ardent pro-slavery Democrat in Congress, and as secretary of the navy and attorney general, respectively, in the cabinets of Tyler and Polk. It was Mason who had introduced the bill calling for recognition of Texas independence that led to the Mexican War. At the end of his life, as ambassador to France from 1853 to 1859, he had intrigued for the acquisition of Cuba as part of a Southern plot to create a Caribbean slave empire. When this unsavory scheme fell through, he collapsed, distraught, in the fall of 1860, and died of a stroke.

If Thomas was almost a political orphan, no one had better connections in Washington than did his old classmate William Tecumseh Sherman. His brother John was a powerful Ohio senator and former candidate for speaker of the house; another brother, Charles, was a Federal judge; and his father-in-law (and adoptive father), Thomas Ewing, had been secretary of the treasury under William Henry Harrison and the nation's first secretary of the interior (under Zachary Taylor, in 1849). Even so, when duty (and boundless opportunity) beckoned, Sherman lingered in Louisiana into 1861, while his brother John tried to lure him north with the promise of high office and power.

At the time of Lincoln's election, Sherman was president of the Louisiana State Military Academy. His last regular promotion—to captain—had come as a result of administrative duties in California during the Mexican War. After that, he had failed at both banking and the law. Though his military résumé was comparatively slight, John Sherman and Salmon P. Chase (Secretary of the Treasury as of March 6) both urged him in mid-April to go into the War Department where he would be "virtually Secretary of War, and could easily step into any military position that offers." As an alternative enticement, John told him that if he decided to rejoin the army, "I know that promotion and every facility for advancement will be cordially extended by the authorities. You . . . have great strength in political circles." Two days later, his brother wrote him again to urge him not to hang back. "You can't avoid taking . . . a part," he told him. "You can choose your own place. Some of your best friends here want you in the War Department. . . . If you want that place, with a sure prospect of promotion, you can have it."

Although Sherman regarded the impending war as a calamity and predicted the South would fail, "he was very conservative in his opinions in regard to slavery," his brother noted afterward, and was horrified at the possibility that anyone in his family might turn out to be an abolitionist. That may have been one factor in his caution. Another was his determination to hitch his wagon to a star. "I will bide my time," he replied to his brother. "I may miss the chance; if so, all right; but I cannot and will not mix myself in this present call. . . . The first movements of the government will fail and the leaders will be cast aside. A second or third set will rise, and among them I may be, but at present I will not volunteer as a soldier or anything else. If Congress meet, or if a national convention be called, and the regular army be put on a footing with the wants of the country, if I am offered a place that suits me, I may accept. But in the present call I will not volunteer." Sherman's patriotic ardor was certainly circumspect and governed by an overriding desire not to be associated with any fiasco at the war's start. He then went on (quite correctly) to criticize the call for 75,000 three-months' volunteers on the ground that the best of men could be made only indifferent soldiers in that time.

In mid-May, Sherman received a peremptory telegram from his brother Charles, the Federal judge, demanding that he come to Washington at once. He had been made a colonel. It soon became clear that he was also being seriously considered for a brigadier general's star.

Although America was already an enormous nation with a population of 31 million and a territory of more than three million square miles, the Federal government at the outset had almost no military power with which to enforce its will. The entire U.S. Army at the time consisted of 16,000 men, and most of these were on frontier duty in the West. The U.S. Navy consisted of ninety ships, and only forty-two of these were in active service. That was hardly enough to patrol the Confederate coastline, which contained hundreds of inlets, bays, and river openings and stretched for thousands of miles from Chesapeake Bay to the Gulf of Mexico. Nevertheless, at the beginning of the war, the North seemed to have the advantage: after all, twenty-three states (out of a total of thirty-four) had remained in the Union, including the border states of Maryland, Kentucky, and Missouri; and the western counties of Virginia formed their own pro-Union state, admitted to the Union as West Virginia in 1863.

Moreover, the North was much more industrialized. It had five times as many manufacturing plants. It also had more people—about 22 million as compared to nine million (including three million slaves) in the South. So in manpower the North had a preponderant edge. But it would need that to prevail. The South consisted of just eleven states, but together these made up a vast territory, as large as Portugal, France, and the British Isles combined. The South also didn't have to conquer the North, or win in a military sense. It only had to hold out long enough for the will of the North to fail. Indeed, though Northern whites outnumbered Southern whites by three to one, Southern whites had a domestic army of blacks to feed them and otherwise shore things up at home.

An effective blockade was essential. Lincoln's great secretary of the navy, Gideon Welles, worked nonstop to establish the North as a naval power. Lincoln, with quaint affection, called the navy the military's "webbed feet." Over time, ships were repaired and new ones constructed. Some steamboats were converted into warships by means of steel plating and deck guns. One new type of gunboat was the steel ram, a little ship with great speed and a heavy prow, which was used to sink another ship by poking a hole in its side. Eventually, the navy had 671 ships or vessels manned by 51,000 officers and men to make its blockade work.

For their part, the Confederates hoped the blockade would backfire by provoking the hostility of European states. In particular, Great Britain and France depended on Southern products like cotton for their own industry and trade. They also depended on Southern markets for their goods. Throughout the war, a skillful corps of Northern diplomats persuaded France and Britain not to intervene directly in the war, though both gave the South some covert aid. Meanwhile, the South sought to make the naval blockade ineffective and engaged pirates and smugglers to obtain needed goods. They also developed fast, blockade-running ships, and invented the first underwater mine and torpedo boat. The torpedo boat (or tactical submarine) was a small, cigar-shaped vessel, propelled by steam with a torpedo projecting from the bow. Both sides also constructed the first ironclad ships, which were covered with armor plate made from iron rails. In an epic battle at Hampton Roads, Virginia, the Confederate ironclad *Merrimack* and the Union *Monitor* would fight each other to a draw.

Politically, the war between the states was a civil war; but from a purely military point of view it was almost a war between two hostile nations, with the South regarding the North as invading its native soil. Railways were of paramount importance east and west, with three main lines running westward from the Atlantic Coast, and three others northward from the Gulf. But American territory had expanded much more quickly than lines of communication could be built across it, which also made it a country well suited for guerrilla warfare but awkward for organized armies with large baggage trains.

As it developed, the war took place in two general regions, or on two main fronts—the East, extending from the Atlantic Ocean to the Appalachian Mountains; and the West, from the Appalachian Mountains to the Mississippi River and beyond. The strategic objectives of the North were the great river systems of the Mississippi Valley (including the Mississippi itself, and the Cumberland and Tennessee Rivers); Chattanooga, and other positions in Tennessee, which commanded the railways that bound Confederate territory together, east to west; the Atlantic Coast, by blockade; and the valleys and mountain gaps that protected (or, alternatively, threatened) the Federal capital of Washington. In the East, the main political objective of the North was to capture the Confederate capital of Richmond.

Before it was over, there would be over 2,000 battles and well over half a million men killed. The new technology extended the field of war. Entrenched battlefields and colossal slaughter accompanied the development of the rifle. New and improved artillery also came in. Solid shot was used for striking an infantry column. Explosive shells and "spherical case" blanketed an area with what is known today as shrapnel. Canister, a shell filled with lead balls about the size of plums, was deadly for close action up to 300 yards. Similar to canister was grapeshot. This type of shell, filled with balls the size of oranges, was effective up to 700 yards. The Federals also made use of mortars—squat, heavy weapons that could lob large shells a great distance by high-angle fire, and were ideal for besieging forts or towns. Yet so much of the fighting was chaotic that the great German field marshal

Helmuth von Moltke would describe the four long years of war as presenting "two armed mobs chasing each other around the country, from which nothing could be learned."


There was lamentable merit to his charge. Lincoln was a man of great capacity and showed it in almost every area to which he turned his mind. But he had no personal military experience beyond a few weeks of campaigning in 1832 in the Blackhawk War. He had opposed the Mexican War as a war of aggression, and when someone once asked him if he remembered anything about the War of 1812, which took place when he was a child, he said, "I had been fishing one day and caught a little fish, which I was taking home. I met a soldier in the road, and, having always been told at home that we must be good to the soldiers, I gave him my fish."

Jefferson Davis, on the other hand, was a highly educated and accomplished military man. A graduate of West Point, he had served seven years in the Regular Army, first in the infantry, then in the cavalry; had led a regiment in the Mexican War; and had served as secretary of war under Franklin Pierce. He knew all about warfare and the proper structure of an army and everything that went into its equipment and supply. He also had "the trained soldier's horror of committing the lives of men, and the fortunes of the army and the country, in war," wrote one historian, "to the charge of men that knew nothing whatever of soldiering." Even before Lincoln's election, Davis had formed some elite fighting units, and had been secretly accumulating arms. Many of the higher officers were also known to him personally, and so among those who chose the South he knew at once whom to appoint to high commands. Davis made his share of grievous mistakes, but the South was able to organize itself more quickly for the fight ahead. Few important posts were entrusted to mere political appointees. "No citizen soldier," it is said, "without previous military education or training, was given a higher command than a brigade . . . until he had . . . proved his fitness."

In the army of the North, something like the opposite was true, where many senior appointments were the playthings of Congress and the partisan factions of each state. "Political generals" were the order of the day. Robert C. Schenck (Lincoln's former Congressional colleague) was a case in point. As Schenck himself recalled: "Lincoln sent for me and asked, 'Schenck, what can you do to help me?' I said, 'Anything you want me to. I am anxious to help you.' He asked, 'Can you fight?' I answered, 'I would try.' Lincoln said, 'Well, I want to make a general out of you.' I replied, 'I don't know about that Mr. President, you could appoint me as general but I might not prove to be one.' Then he did so and I went to war." Lincoln also failed to organize the nation for a long conflict and (in the early days at least) interfered too much with his commanders in the field. Later, he sometimes failed to monitor them enough. It is a terrible irony of the whole story of the conflict that he cared so much for the troops, yet gave a free hand to generals who were often reckless with their lives. Throughout the government, ignorance of military affairs was strangely rife. Almost every day, some new regiment from the North came in and marched along Pennsylvania Avenue past the White House in review. Politicians were often beguiled by these parades, though few of them really understood what an army was. John Sherman later recalled, with some amusement:

> Among the early arrivals in the spring of 1861 was a regiment from New Hampshire, much better equipped than our Western ones. My colleague, [Ohio senator] Ben Wade, and I went to the White House to see this noted regiment pass before Mr. Lincoln in review. As the head of the line turned around the north wing of the treasury department and came in sight, the eyes of Wade fell upon a tall soldier, wearing a gaudy uniform, a very high hat, and a still higher cockade. He carried a baton, which he swung right and left, up and down, with all the authority of a field marshal. Wade, much excited, asked me, pointing to the soldier: "Who is that?" I told him I thought that was the drum major. "Well," he said, "if the people could see him they would make him a general!"

On April 25, Robert E. Lee's rank and position in the 2nd Cavalry Regiment fell to Thomas, who, as lieutenant colonel, complied with the rule that every newly appointed officer renew his oath. He took it a third time ten days later when he was made a full colonel to fill the vacancy occasioned by the resignation of Albert Sidney Johnston. One fellow officer was surprised that Thomas was not annoyed at having to take the oath so many times. "I don't care a snap of my fingers about it," Thomas told him. "If they want me to take the oath before each meal I am ready to comply."

In camp at Carlisle, Thomas trained and equipped his men, forwarded six of his ten companies to Washington as soon as they were remounted, and made sure the North Central Railroad (which ran into Maryland) was secure. He also took charge of the First City Troop of Philadelphia (part of Pennsylvania's National Guard), and at the beginning of June, after five weeks in camp, reported with the rest of his men to General Robert Patterson at Chambersburg, where he was given command of Pennsylvania's 1st Brigade.

He had little time for social diversion, but after dinner one evening at the home of the publisher Alexander K. McClure, Thomas and some other officers, including Major Abner Doubleday (once thought to have been the inventor of baseball), debated the prospects for a short war. Most agreed that at least one battle would have to be fought before a compromise peace could be reached. McClure recalled:

> Thomas, with that modesty which always characterized him, was silent. Doubleday had met the Southerners in battle at Sumter and he knew how desperately earnest they were, and Thomas was a son of Virginia who knew that the Southern people were as heroic as any in the North . . . Doubleday surprised his fellow officers by declaring it would be one of the most desperate and bloody wars of modern history . . . and that they (the Rebels) meant to make it a fight to the death. He was the first to leave after the dinner, and when he was gone several leading officers ridiculed his ideas of a long and terrible war, and I well remember the remark of one of them that Doubleday was a Spiritualist and a little gone in the head.

But Thomas, added McClure, knew that Doubleday was right.

As the Civil War began, Thomas was as well rounded a soldier as the North could claim. He had fought with distinction in two wars; had experience with regular and guerrilla combat; a knowledge of garrison and frontier duty; and a grasp of artillery and cavalry tactics few of his compatriots could match. In the course of his promotions, from lieutenant to captain to major to colonel, he had "never leaped a grade." To his colleagues, he was a figure of commanding presence, with a thoughtful, deliberate manner and a grave, impassive face. Unaffected and manly, he had the air and bearing of a soldier, and seemed to embody living strength—"not a man of iron," wrote James A. Garfield, later president of the United States, "but of live oak." One army chaplain observed later that beyond his strength, there was a "reserve power which was to be the source of safety to great armies. He was destined to draw vast masses of men to him in reverence and love by the force of his personal character . . . and to hold them to duty and desperate daring by the subtle inspiration which emanated from the power which great emergencies called forth."

Though now a full colonel, Thomas continued to appear in camp as a major, since he gave no importance to a vain show of rank. All he cared about was that those below him knew he was in charge. (Later, he would continue to wear a colonel's uniform for five months after his promotion to brigadier general.) In this, as in everything else, he was a model for his men. "By their fruits shall ye know them." It was merit, and merit alone, that inspired his respect. That was the whole psychology of his command. In a letter to the adjutant general of the army five years before, he had remarked: "My experience teaches me that soldiers usually shape their conduct according to the characteristics of their officers and that the reputation of a command for efficiency and skill depends almost entirely upon the interest which their officers take in their instruction. I therefore do not think it advisable or even necessary to offer any inducements or rewards to acquire skill. It is sufficient for a soldier to be convinced that his officer takes pride in pointing him out as one of the most skillful and efficient of his command." In this instance, he was talking about marksmanship; but it applied to any attainment in the art of war.

Because of the reverence Thomas inspired, his men came to yearn for his approval, which brought out the best in them on and off the field. On every possible occasion he sought to instill lessons in discipline, self-reliance, and common sense. At Carlisle, one of his officers, Lieutenant Thomas M. Anderson, the nephew of Robert Anderson, the hero of Fort Sumter, wasn't sure how to handle a fellow officer who in a homicidal rage had threatened to kill another soldier. He asked Thomas what he should do. "In the last resort," said Thomas, looking out of the window, "death." From that, Anderson realized that Thomas expected him to figure out how to handle the matter short of that extreme. A little later, Anderson had to curb an illicit whiskey trade in the ranks. Thomas called him in to ask him what he had done. "I knocked in the head of the barrel," said Anderson, "and emptied it into the street." "Well," said Thomas, "I am glad you did not come to ask me this time what you should do."

As a career soldier, Thomas was naturally attuned to the niceties of protocol and expected to be deferred to in matters of seniority just as he himself deferred to rank. At the same time, he was prepared to challenge it, as in the case of General Twiggs, if he thought it was being abused. When a real emergency arose, no one was more apt to take charge. On one of his shuttles up from Charleston to New York for recruiting duty before the war, for example, he saved the ship and all on board from the besotted orders of a drunken captain in a violent storm. As the ship plunged and lurched in the tumultuous waves off Cape Hatteras, the first mate came to him and appealed for help. Thomas confined the captain to his stateroom, assumed overall responsibility for the ship, and with the first mate (who might otherwise have been charged with mutiny) rode out the storm.

Despite the smoldering contests that threatened to flare up in the border states, it became apparent that the main campaign at the start would be in Virginia or Maryland, somewhere between Richmond and Washington. The Federal government hurried its new troops and some regulars to the capital; the South comparable numbers to Virginia, and established its main camp at Manassas Junction, under General P. T. G. Beauregard. Toward the end of May, columns of Federal troops crossed the Potomac and seized Alexandria and Arlington

Heights. They established a camp on the south side of the river, and entrenched the line from the Chain Bridge, above Washington, to Alexandria, below. General Winfield Scott, then in command of the army of the United States, and a hero of two wars—"the only man in America," in fact, "who had ever actually commanded as many as 5,000 men"—was too old to take active command. So Brevet Major Irvin McDowell, a former artillery lieutenant, was made a brigadier general, and given command of the forces on the Potomac's south bank.

The Northern newspapers and public clamored for a prompt offensive, but General Scott doubted that the three-month levies could be counted upon for a campaign. On May 3, Lincoln had called for 42,000 three-year volunteers, but the public refused to wait for their training and Lincoln, in the first of many blunders, overruled the judgment of his lieutenant general, and ordered an advance.

Beauregard and McDowell each had about 30,000 men—the largest field armies ever assembled on the continent. About 12,000 Confederates under General Joseph E. Johnston were posted at Winchester, in the lower Shenandoah Valley; 18,000 Federals were assigned to oppose him under Robert Patterson's command. On the 12th of June, Thomas led the advance to the Potomac River at Williamsport, Maryland, where Patterson's troops went into camp.

Three days later, Thomas met with Sherman at a local inn, which served as a headquarters for senior army staff. It had been twenty-five years since they had roomed together as plebes at West Point, and Sherman, though just as rumpled and unkempt as he had been when a boy, was now a middle-aged man who talked nonstop with tremendous speed and wore a grizzled, short-cropped beard. His animated manner bordered on the manic, and he had an almost frantic gleam to his eyes. In the intervening years, their paths had crossed only once, when Thomas had stopped off to see Sherman in San Francisco en route to his desert post. Sherman now asked him how he felt about having to take sides. Thomas told him: "I have thought it all over and I shall stand firm in the service of the government." Then, as Sherman's brother John recalled years later in his memoirs: "They got out a big map of the United States, spread it on the floor, and on their hands and knees discussed the probably salient strategic places of the war. They singled out Richmond, Vicksburg, Nashville, Knoxville and Chattanooga. To me it has always appeared strange that they were able confidently and correctly to designate the lines of operations and strategic points of a war not yet commenced, and more strange still that they should be leading actors in great battles at the places specified."

The next day, Patterson ordered his vanguard, with Thomas in command, to cross the Potomac. Sherman and his brother sat on a boulder on the shore and "watched the cavalry splash through the waist-deep water where the ford angled sharply upstream to reach the Virginia shore." But within hours the order for the advance was countermanded by General Scott, in a sign of that fatal indecision which would mark the first major Union campaign.

In general, McDowell was to move against Beauregard while Patterson held Johnston in place. But Scott's instructions were unclear. Was Patterson to attack Johnston directly if he could? Or simply maneuver in such a way as to keep him from joining his forces to Beauregard's? On July 2, Patterson once more crossed the Potomac at Williamsport; had a running skirmish with the Rebels five miles in at Falling Waters, where troops under Thomas bested those of Stonewall Jackson; confronted Johnston at Martinsburg, and drove him back. But Johnston's movements were designed above all to buy time until he could join Beauregard by a forced march. On July 17, Patterson withdrew to Charles Town. That gave Johnston the chance to cut through a mountain gap to Piedmont, where his infantry entrained for Manassas. His movement was so completely masked by Stuart's cavalry that Patterson did not pick up on it until it was almost done.

Patterson thought he had managed to keep Johnston in place, and on the morning of July 18 wired the War Department to that effect. But shortly after midday, Thomas's scouts saw clouds of dust rising over the road leading from Winchester to the mountain pass. Racing to camp with the news, Lieutenant Thomas Anderson (the same officer Thomas had taken under his wing at Carlisle) informed Thomas, who rushed over to Patterson's tent "without stopping to put on his hat or button his coat. 'I know . . . that he told Patterson there was time even then to intercept Johnston,'" the lieutenant recalled. But Patterson wrongly supposed that McDowell must have already engaged—and beaten—Beauregard.

And so the stage was set for the First Battle of Bull Run. The battle, named for a stream that flowed near the little town of Manassas Junction, twenty-five miles south of Washington, was fought with misgiving by the opposing commanders, and by untried troops on either side. The Federals began their attack on the morning of July 21 by striking the Rebel left. They made good progress, but then Johnston's troops arrived. That changed the whole dynamic of the fight. Thomas Jackson's Virginia Brigade stood like a stone wall and kept the Rebel line intact. McDowell's flanking movement broke, and the Union cavalry panicked and ran. Hundreds of Union troops were captured and others trapped in the chaos by frantic civilians who had come down from the capital to picnic and watch the show. Many threw away their arms and knapsacks, abandoned their ordnance, cut the traces of their artillery horses, and mounted them in flight. On the narrow roads, private wagons and broken gun carriages all tumbled and crashed together, with injured horses plunging to and fro. The wounded were left to the mercies of the victors, as the turbulent stream rolled on.

After the battle, in which the Confederates lost about 2,000, the Federals 3,000, the Confederates entrenched on the heights at Centreville and pushed their outposts almost to the banks of the Potomac River, flaunting their flag.

In examining the defeat, several things became clear. First, an army animated by patriotism still needs discipline and training. Neither side yet had it, but the South at Bull Run had better generalship. General McDowell, in his later testimony before the Joint Committee on the Conduct of the War, dolefully noted:

I had no opportunity to test my machinery, to move it around and see whether it would work smoothly or not. In fact, such was the feeling, that when I had one body of eight regiments of troops reviewed together, the general censured me for it, as if I was trying to make some show. I did not think so. There was not a man there who had ever maneuvered troops in large bodies. There was not one in the Army. I did not believe there was one in the whole country. At least I knew there was no one there who had ever handled 30,000 troops. I had seen them handled abroad in reviews and marches, but I had never handled that number, and no one here had. I wanted very much a little time, all of us wanted it. We did not have a bit of it.

The huge blunder of three months' enlistments also ran through every complaint. Patterson had been reluctant to attack Johnston directly because some of his men were unwilling to fight on the eve of their discharge. In his official report, McDowell noted that a third of his army had crossed the Potomac in the same tenuous state. On the very eve of the battle, in fact, the 4th Pennsylvania Regiment of volunteers and the battery of the New York 8th Militia "had refused to remain one day more. All appeals to their patriotism were in vain—they insisted on their discharge that night; and the next morning when the army moved forward into battle, these troops moved to the rear to the sound of the enemy's guns."

Yet the plainest failing had been the lack of a sensible strategic plan. Patterson's two, related objectives had been to expel the Rebels under Johnston from Harpers Ferry (which Johnston burned when the operation began), and to prevent Johnston from marching to Beauregard at Manassas where their troops could unite. Military historians almost universally agree that he could have succeeded in both had Scott adopted the plan of operations proposed to him by Patterson, which Thomas had endorsed. That plan had been to cross the Potomac near Leesburg, where Patterson would have been in supporting distance of McDowell. But Scott had him cross at Williamsport, which placed the Union armies on exterior lines. That made it possible for the Confederate armies to combine. In a letter written some years later to Patterson, who was blamed for the defeat, Thomas offered balm for his wounds: "I have always believed, and have frequently so expressed myself, that your management of the three months' campaign was able and judicious, and was to the best interests of the service, considering the means at your disposal and the nature of the troops under your command."

Sherman had also taken part, leading a brigade of volunteers that crossed Bull Run after the attack on the enemy began. But then he got caught up in the rout. In Washington, his brother John anxiously awaited news. He spent the day with James Rollins, a member of Congress from Missouri; called on General Scott to find out how the battle was going (Scott thought well); rode to a new fort near Arlington to listen to the distant action; and returned to his lodgings on 15th Street in Washington. But "everywhere," he wrote, "there was an uneasy feeling. At eight o'clock in the evening I started for the residence of the Secretary of War to get information of the battle. As I approached I was seized by the arm, and, turning, saw Secretary Cameron. I asked about the battle, but, without answering, he hurried me into his house and said: 'Our army is defeated, and my brother [a colonel with McDowell] is killed.' He then gave way to passionate grief."

The defeat at Bull Run had a sobering effect on the North. Talk of a short war vanished. Congress authorized the calling up of half a million men for three years' service, and people settled down with grim determination to see the struggle through. The victories of Rich Mountain and Carrick's Ford (under George McClellan), which resulted early in July in the capture and dispersion of the enemy's forces in western Virginia, partly relieved the gloom that pervaded the North, but these triumphs were soon obscured by fresh tidings of disaster. On August 10, Union forces were defeated at Wilson's Creek, Missouri; on September 20, Lexington, Missouri, surrendered after a nine days' siege; on October 21, the Federals were repelled at Ball's Bluff, Virginia; and on November 7, the Battle of Belmont, which marked the debut of Ulysses Grant, ended in retreat.

Meanwhile, in mid-August, Robert Anderson, now a general, had been assigned to take a firm grip on the border states. Empowered to select four colonels for advancement to brigadier rank to serve under him in Kentucky, he chose Sherman, Ambrose Burnside (subsequently

replaced by O. M. Mitchel), Don Carlos Buell, and Thomas, whom he
had taught at West Point and knew from their service together at Fort
Moultrie. He sent his nomination to Lincoln, with the endorsement
of his nephew, Lieutenant Thomas M. Anderson, and Samuel J. Randall, a Pennsylvania congressman and future speaker of the house.
Randall had served under Thomas in the City Troop of Philadelphia
during the First Bull Run campaign. In his letter of August 3 to
Thomas A. Scott, assistant secretary of war, Randall wrote:

> I notice that the Government is now considering the appointment
> of proper persons to be brigadier-generals. In the name of God, let
> them be men fully competent to discharge the duties of the posi-
> tions to which they may be assigned. . . . Colonel George H. Thomas
> . . . is thoroughly competent to be a brigadier-general, and has the
> confidence of every man in his command for the reason that they
> recognize and appreciate capacity. . . . This appointment would
> give renewed vigor and courage to this section of the army. I am, as
> perhaps you know, a private in the First City Cavalry of Philadel-
> phia, and I never saw Colonel Thomas until I saw him on parade,
> and our intercourse has only been such as exists between a colonel
> and one of his soldiers; hence, you see my recommendation comes
> from pure motives, and entirely free from social or political consid-
> erations. . . . You will do the country a service by giving my letter a
> serious consideration.

Lincoln, who is said to have heeded some rumored doubts about
the loyalty of Thomas, supposedly conferred with Anderson and
Sherman at Willard's Hotel in Washington, where Sherman said he
vouched for Thomas and won Lincoln over to the idea of giving him
a command. "Mr. President, Old Tom is as loyal as I am," Sherman
said he said, "and as a soldier he is superior to all on your list." "Will
you be responsible for him?" asked Lincoln. "With the greatest of
pleasure," Sherman replied. In his memoirs, Sherman indicated that
Lincoln remained unsure "because so many Southern officers had already played false; but I was still more emphatic in my indorsement."
Sherman's account, however, was made up. He met Lincoln only

twice—in March 1861 and March 1865, and so not at this time. Else-where, he acknowledged that Anderson deserved the whole credit for the promotion; and the record shows simply that Lincoln wrote to Secretary of War Cameron: "At the request of Brigadier General An-derson, I have concluded to appoint George H. Thomas of the 2nd cavalry a Brigadier." Oliver Howard tells us that when Lincoln asked Anderson if Thomas's loyalty could be relied upon, Anderson replied: "Yes, I will guarantee it with my life." In his memoirs Sherman made Anderson's gallant gesture his own. On another occasion, he embel-lished the story further to cast more credit on himself.

Thomas learned of his appointment from Anderson in a personal letter dated August 19. That letter took a week to reach him, but on the 26th Thomas replied that it would give him "the greatest pleasure" to be under his command. He went at once to New Haven to visit his wife for a couple of days, where she was then staying with her mother and sister at the New Haven Hotel, and gave a colleague this appraisal of the situation in the East: "I may be mistaken, but I think the enemy are simply engaged now in stripping upper Virginia of all the stores and provisions in that region and will shortly retire to Richmond with their main force so as to be ready for any move which the government may make." Overall, he was "very much pleased with the appearance of things in and around Washington & now have some hopes that our new commanding general [McClellan] will prove equal to his task."

As Thomas took leave of his wife, it was a hard parting for them both—sadder, indeed, than either could have known for they would not see each other again for another three years.

On September 1, he entrained for the Western front.

# 4. MILL SPRINGS

*"Honor and shame from no condition rise—*
*Act well your part: there all the honor lies."*
—ALEXANDER POPE, *ESSAY ON*
*MAN*, EPISTLE IV, VI

From the beginning, Lincoln had seen clearly that the war would be won or lost in the border states. "Kentucky gone," he declared, "we cannot hold Missouri, nor, as I think, Maryland. These all against us, and the job on our hands is too large for us. We would as well consent to separation at once, including the surrender of this capital. . . . I think to lose Kentucky is nearly the same as to lose the whole game." By its strategic location, Kentucky controlled the east–west flow of industrial products such as iron and coal along the Ohio River; gave access to Louisville, Cincinnati, and other towns of industrial might; and was the gateway to Tennessee, rich in mineral ores—iron, saltpeter, copper, lead—and a breadbasket of the South. Great rail and river roads also extended by way of Kentucky and Tennessee through Alabama and Mississippi all the way to the Gulf of Mexico.

When the war began, Kentucky, though a slave state, had declared itself neutral, but that was sure to be short-lived. The governor was for secession, the legislature for the Union, though not with a whole heart. The legislature upheld the constitutional right of slavery to exist, but "denounced secession, and deprecated war." Before long, those favoring secession had armed themselves by joining State Guard units, those for the Union a rival militia called the Home Guards. On September 16, the Confederates seized Columbus on the Mississippi;

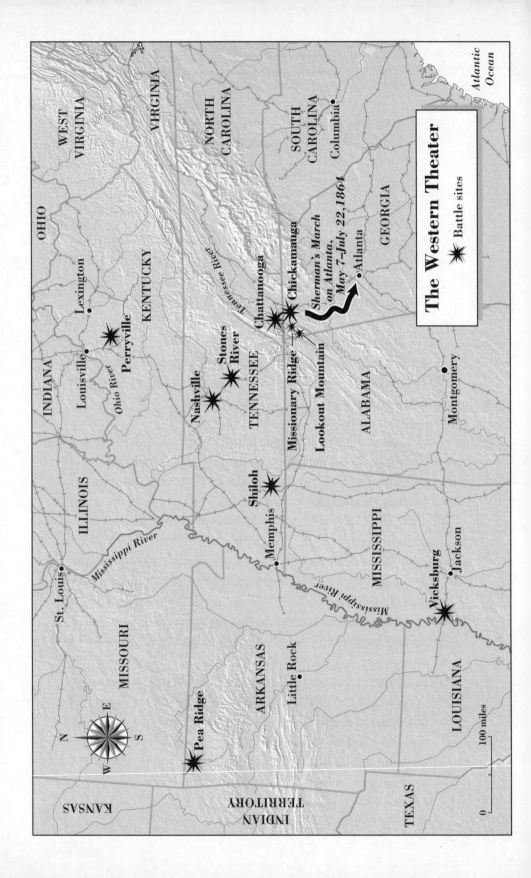

The Western Theater

* Battle sites

Sherman's March on Atlanta, May 7–July 22, 1864

Atlantic Ocean

OHIO
WEST VIRGINIA
VIRGINIA
NORTH CAROLINA
SOUTH CAROLINA
Columbia
GEORGIA
Atlanta
Chickamauga
Chattanooga
Missionary Ridge
Lookout Mountain
KENTUCKY
Lexington
Louisville
Ohio River
Perryville
Nashville
Stones River
TENNESSEE
Tennessee River
ALABAMA
Montgomery
INDIANA
ILLINOIS
Mississippi River
St. Louis
MISSOURI
Shiloh
Memphis
MISSISSIPPI
Jackson
Vicksburg
Mississippi River
ARKANSAS
Little Rock
Pea Ridge
LOUISIANA
KANSAS
INDIAN TERRITORY
TEXAS

N E W S

100 miles

0

the Federals, in response, took Paducah—and the contest for the state began.

Thomas arrived in Louisville just as these countermoves were made. No sooner had he disembarked than General Robert Anderson rushed him with a regiment toward Lexington to prevent Simon Bolivar Buckner's State Guard from seizing the arsenal at Frankfort and dispersing the legislature of the state.

Now grander strategies were laid. The overall command of Confederate forces in the West had fallen to General Albert Sidney Johnston, a former colonel of the elite cavalry unit to which Thomas had belonged. His Kentucky line was centered on Bowling Green—where Buckner had taken post on the Big Barren Branch of the Green River—and extended from Columbus on the left to Cumberland Gap on the right. Johnston had about 45,000 troops to man it, which he did not think enough, and the Federals had begun to turn Louisville into a hub for the Western war. At the same time, they had done little as yet to man their own lines. The loss of Kentucky (in conjunction with Missouri, which the Rebels hoped also to take) threatened to add 2.5 million people and a landmass the size of Italy to the Rebel states. That would also thrust the boundary of the rebellion right up to the Ohio River, from which its armies could strike into the heartland of Ohio, Indiana, and Illinois. Conversely, if Union troops could hold on to it, Kentucky offered a staging ground for striking south.

Anderson put Thomas in charge of the most important post in his command. This was the vital training center at Camp Dick Robinson, about twenty-five miles from Lexington and sixty miles north of Cumberland Gap. Named for the owner of the 3,000-acre estate on which it was placed, it was the first Union training and recruitment camp created south of the Ohio River, and since August 6 had served as a rallying point for Unionists from Kentucky and East Tennessee. En route, Thomas just barely escaped capture by some Rebels who hoped to kidnap him off his train. Forewarned, he changed trains to foil the plot, disembarked safely on the 15th and began to bring order out of the chaos he found.

Though the camp had been in existence for over a month, several thousand men were milling about without rifles, ammunition, artillery, wagons, uniforms, overcoats, shoes, adequate food and shelter, or even organized commissary stores. There was no staff to help with these shortages, or money to make them up. Most of the men had not yet been mustered into Union service, so he found himself in command of state levies over which he had no legal control. Moreover, the rolls were incomplete, so Thomas could only guess at the number of men he had. Not even incidental expenditures had been kept track of, which meant piles of back paperwork. As he tried to develop his own plans, obstacles of all kinds stood in his path. Local contractors would take nothing but cash, so he had to pledge his personal credit to obtain bank loans for supplies. He needed medical help to cope with a deadly outbreak of measles, and competent aides to handle raw recruits. Those recruits poured in, as the Confederate threat inspired new enlistments in Ohio, Indiana, and Illinois. Some of the men were wild mountaineers, resistant to all order and restraint.

Thomas gave himself up to his task with industry, wisdom, and determination, wearing all the hats he had worn in his long years of service, from drill sergeant to quartermaster to court-martial judge. Bull Run (and other clashes since) had shown him that undisciplined troops turned even a competent general into a bungler, since no well-thought-out plan could be carried out. As Thomas rolled up his sleeves, he discouraged anything that might waste his time. Even so, his day was often interrupted by curious visitors, journalists, politicians, and armchair generals eager to offer advice. Some even came to give speeches. Once, when calls were made for Thomas to make a speech, too, he said, "Damn this speech-making. I won't speak. What does a man want to make a speech for?" and abruptly left the stage.

By then, he had assembled a number of capable, dedicated aides. As the camp grew, Thomas attended dress parades; inspected clothing, arms, and accoutrements; and instructed the quartermaster, commissary, ordnance officer and provost marshal in their duties, as "step by step" one aide recalled, "ploughboys exchanged their slouching gait for an erect carriage, officers found more interest in studying tactics than in reading newspapers or talking politics, and on every side improvement was clear." Within three weeks, he could tell headquarters: "I am beginning to work some order out of the confusion which I found existed in every part of the camp when I arrived." Indeed, before long, Thomas had created the semblance of a small army, arranged into four brigades, with cavalry, artillery, and infantry contingents, of 8,000 men each. Comparatively modest as this was, it became the the nucleus of the great Army of the Cumberland that under Thomas never knew defeat. "Wherever and whenever Thomas was in command," wrote a colleague, it "swung its eagles through the smoke of battle to victory" through Kentucky, Georgia, and Tennessee.

While the Confederates set their sights on taking strategic towns like Somerset and Lebanon to their north, Thomas sought to occupy the same points as he pushed south toward Cumberland Gap. That stronghold was held by the Confederate general Felix Zollicoffer, a journalist turned politician who was popular in East Tennessee. Making his camp on the south side of the Cumberland River near Mill Springs, Zollicoffer had been told by Johnston to act in a defensive manner only, as part of a system of strategic postings that protected the vital line of supply that connected Virginia with Tennessee. Ambition seized him, however, and operating out of the fastness of his mountain camp, he seized the Cumberland Ford at Pineville, and carried out a series of highly effective hit-and-run raids against London, Barbourville, and other towns. At Manchester his men captured the Goose Creek Salt Works, raised their own flag, and carried off fifty wagonloads of salt. In response, Thomas sent troops to occupy a position at Rockcastle Hills northeast of London (to secure an important ford) where at a mountaintop base called Camp Wildcat they braced for a Rebel assault. Just in time, Thomas reinforced them and sent scouts to watch the foothills to warn of any Rebel move.

In the meantime, he had also developed a cogent plan to win the war in the West. With a force of 20,000 men properly armed, trained, and equipped, he thought he could strike through Cumberland Gap into East Tennessee; rescue its largely pro-Union population from Confederate rule; recruit among them; and cut the Virginia & Tennessee Railroad linking Chattanooga and Knoxville with the East. That would oust Zollicoffer from mountain passes, where he might also be trapped. On September 27, he sent Anderson his plan, which the latter embraced.

Less than two weeks later, however, on October 8, Anderson, worn out by his heroic defense of Fort Sumter and the strain of the Louisville command, relinquished his post. Sherman, as senior brigadier, took his place. Meanwhile, Anderson had submitted Thomas's plan to the War Department, which at first endorsed it, then in a political decision decided to entrust it to General O. M. Mitchel, commanding the Department of the Ohio, who had lobbied hard for the command. Mitchel informed Thomas that the War Department had ordered him to Camp Dick Robinson to prepare the troops for the campaign.

Thomas was not pleased. He asked to be relieved of his post; sent Mitchel an indignant note "since the Secretary of War thought it necessary to supersede me in command without, as I conceive, any just cause for so doing," and let Sherman know how mortified he was by this turn of events—"to have the execution of the very thing" he had been planning "taken from me when nearly prepared to take the field."

The change made no sense. Mitchel, a former West Pointer, had been out of uniform for some years teaching science and astronomy at Cincinnati College and had never seen action, having only an academic knowledge of war. Thomas, on the other hand, had field rank and standing, and had so far succeeded completely in all he had done. But that success was trumped by politics. Mitchel and Treasury Secretary Salmon Chase were allied, and Simon Cameron, then under fire for some procurement scandals, had turned to Chase as a shield. Mitchel had recently gone to Washington to talk about his own ambitions and had brought the governor of Ohio, another backer, along. He had also met with Andrew Johnson (the Tennessee governor-in-exile) and Horace Maynard, a Tennessee member of the House. Mitchel had written the War Department about "the necessity of placing in supreme command of this expedition to Kentucky and to Tennessee" a general "who will command the entire confidence of the government." He meant himself, of course (rather than, by implication, a Southern general like Thomas, of suspect allegiance), and on October 10, Cameron met with Mitchel in Cincinnati and approved the change in command. Cameron's support for Mitchel seems to have been an overt attempt to curry favor with Chase. Andrew Johnson had then come to Camp Dick Robinson on October 11 to present the letter from Mitchel to Thomas by hand.

Sherman, however, evidently saw Mitchel as a potential rival—both being Ohio men—and on October 13, told Thomas: "You are authorized to go on and prepare your command for active service. General Mitchel is subject to my orders, and I will, if possible, give you the opportunity to complete what you have begun. Of course I would do all I can to carry out your wishes, but feel that the affairs of Kentucky call for the united action of all engaged." (It says something about Sherman's political clout that he was able to ignore a directive from the secretary of war.)

Word of these machinations reached Robert Anderson, then recuperating in New York and he promptly wrote Sherman to urge that Mitchel "not be allowed to supersede" Thomas in the planned advance. Andrew Johnson then gave Thomas his support, and asked him for a written statement of what he needed to get the campaign underway. Thomas told him he needed four more regiments and two more batteries of artillery, all well drilled and fully equipped, money for food, forage, and winter clothing, and wagons and other means of transport to take them up through the mountains and ravines into the gaps.

Sherman's judgment now began to fail. He overinterpreted the implications of some Rebel raids, and in an irrational response to implausible rumors convinced himself that he was up against a veritable Rebel host. At a conference with Simon Cameron at Louisville on October 17, he asked for so many troops he was thought to be insane.

There is no doubt that Sherman was becoming unhinged. All his memoranda at this time verge on the hysterical, and on October 22, he complained to the War Department that veritable "miracles" were expected of his men.

Thomas, meanwhile, had a much better grip on the situation than Sherman did. He kept his own counsel, acquired all the supplies and reinforcements he could, posted a regiment at Rockcastle Hills, and on October 21 sent part of a brigade under General Albin Schoepf (an expatriate Austrian now in Federal service) toward Somerset to drive the enemy pickets back. At Camp Wildcat, a Rebel attack was also repulsed. While Sherman clamored for up to 200,000 men, Thomas, by his shrewd deployment of 8,000 to 10,000, had been consolidating ground along his projected route south.

Yet four days later, on October 25, 1861, Sherman sent Thomas the following dispatch:

*Louisville, Kentucky, October 25, 1861.*

*General George H. Thomas, Camp Dick Robinson:*

*Sir—Don't push too far. Your line is already long and weak. I cannot now reinforce you. An interruption of the railroads by an incursion from Prestonburgh would cut you off from that source of supply. Call to your assistance the regiment from train. The State Board is impressed with the necessity of energy in the organization of volunteers, but we are still embarrassed for want of clothing and arms. Promises are a poor substitute for them, but are all we have. I will again urge on the department the pressing necessity of more good officers and large reinforcements of men.*

Thomas read this anxious wire without alarm. His unwavering plan was to advance through the mountain gaps to Knoxville, destroy the Virginia & Tennessee Railroad, and pursue the Rebels to the hills. He told Sherman, as he had told Johnson: "With four more good regiments we could seize the railroad yet. With my headquarters at Somerset, I can easily seize the most favorable time for invading East Tennessee." Confident of succeeding, he moved his headquarters forward to Crab Orchard, then advanced to hold the roads by which the Rebels might thwart his march. Zollicoffer, who had been contemplating another Kentucky raid, retreated to Mill Springs.

At this point, there was another shake-up in the military high command. On November 1, General George McClellan, who had assumed charge of the Army of the Potomac after Bull Run, was called to Washington to succeed General Winfield Scott as commander-in-chief of all the armies in the field. He at once asked Sherman for a report;

Sherman, in an exasperated vein, once more detailed his plight. In sum, he described the enemy force he faced as so large that "the country never has and probably never will comprehend it." To make matters worse, he thought Lee might be on his way with reinforcements from the East.

The Confederates, in fact, had strained every resource to strengthen their line in Kentucky without weakening their army near Richmond. But at critical points, that line was still poorly manned. Zollicoffer, for example, had fewer than 15,000 men. Yet on November 5, Sherman wired Thomas: "I have done all in my power to provide men and materiel adequate to the importance of the crisis; but all things come disjointed—regiments without overcoats or wagons or horses, or those essentials to movement. I can hardly sleep to think what would be your fate in case the Kentucky River bridge should be destroyed or the railroad to your rear. I have again and again demanded a force adequate to all these vicissitudes." He thought Albert Sidney Johnston just then had put 45,000 men or more on the move. In response to a skeptical communiqué from the War Department, Sherman also notified the adjutant General on November 6:

> Our enemies have a terrible advantage in the fact that in our midst, in our camps, and along our avenues of travel, they have active partisans, farmers and business-men, who seemingly pursue their usual calling, but are in fact spies. They report all our movements and strength, while we can procure information only by circuitous and unreliable means. . . . With our present force it would be simple madness to cross Green River, and yet hesitation may be as fatal. In like manner the other columns are in peril, not so much in front as rear, the railroads over which our stores must pass being much exposed. I have the Nashville Railroad guarded by three regiments, yet it is far from being safe; and, the moment actual hostilities commence, these roads will be interrupted, and we will be in a dilemma. . . . Do not conclude, as before, that I exaggerate the facts. They are as stated, and the future looks as dark as possible. It would be better if some man of sanguine mind were here, for I am forced to order according to my convictions.

Sherman even sent an urgent wire to Lincoln, which closed in peremptory fashion with, "Answer." When Salmon Chase replied on Lincoln's behalf that the president thought Sherman had, despite his protests, an adequate force, Sherman was insolent: "I am sorry if I offended the President," he wrote, "but it would be better if all saw things as they are, rather than as we would they were."

If Sherman seemed paranoid and unable to act, Andrew Johnson, by contrast, was overzealous in pressing for a swift advance. On October 11, he had made a rousing speech at Camp Dick Robinson to refugees from his state in which he promised to lead them back to their homes in a victorious campaign. On the day Sherman sent his wire to the adjutant general, Johnson, then at London, Kentucky, with the troops under Albin Schoepf, wrote Thomas to ask why the intended advance into Tennessee had not yet begun. He had also heard rumors that Schoepf (in the advance) might be ordered to retreat.

Thomas counseled patience. He needed more men, but until they came could hold the line with what he had. The report of any retreat appalled him. "Have you heard by what authority the troops from London were to fall back? Because I have not, and shall not move any of them back, unless ordered, for if I am not interfered with, I can have them subsisted there as well as here." In the meantime, he noted, "some of our troops are not clothed, and it seems impossible to get clothing," a problem, by implication, he hoped Johnson would help address. He also urged him to follow through on his idea of getting men of influence to raise more regiments—so long as they met the mustering standards of the War Department's code. Thomas also wrote a note to General Schoepf with a copy of his reply to Johnson in which he stressed that any premature attempt to rescue the people of East Tennessee would be "culpable," especially when the Rebels were looking to take advantage of any ill-prepared movement made in haste. He was anxious, too, for "discontented persons . . . both in and out of service" to hold their tongues, at least for a while, adding, "We must learn to abide our time, or we will never succeed."

Nevertheless, Sherman thought Thomas was about to be cut off, or surrounded, and four days later, on November 11, ordered him to consolidate his forces and retreat. Thomas calmly replied: "I am sure the enemy is not moving between us. All my information is that they are moving south." Sherman insisted he was wrong. As the troops under Schoepf, in the advance, pulled back, they were filled with dismay. "Many were from East Tennessee and feared they would never return to liberate their homes. Clad in rags, their shoes almost gone, on November 13 "the disheartened soldiers gripped their rifles and faced about for a hurried and painful night march of fourteen miles over mud-filled roads." As they stumbled along, a regimental band played the "Dead March" from *Saul.* "We must have passed 200 Stragglers," related one Ohio soldier. "Some were lying prone on the ground sobbing, some stood on the highway swearing defiantly; others leaned against the fences sullenly," reluctant to decamp. The *Cincinnati Daily Commercial* described the retreat as "absurd" and "ruinous" and "enough to sicken the whole country," which it did.

Two days later, on November 15, General Don Carlos Buell (who had been one year behind Thomas at West Point) arrived to relieve Sherman, who left Kentucky in a near-demented state. The *Chicago Tribune*'s war correspondent wrote: "I know not whether it is insanity or not, but the General [Sherman] . . . despondingly said the rebels could never be whipped [and] talked of a Thirty Years' War." Transferred to the Department of the Missouri, now under General Henry W. Halleck, who in turn had replaced John Frémont (demoted for incompetence and graft), Sherman was given lighter duties to help him convalesce. Though his career was saved by the intervention of his brother and father-in-law (who both wrote Halleck to give him a second chance), his position in Missouri was tenuous at best. Newspapers all over the country were reporting that he was "crazy," and his effective authority was slight. Even lowly subordinates, he noted with dismay, looked upon him "with suspicion" and "askance."

Buell organized the Army of the Ohio, as his force was now called, into brigades and divisions. Thomas was assigned to the command of the 1st Division, made up of some cavalry and artillery units and four brigades. He united his forces at Crab Orchard and marched to Lebanon, midway between Lexington and Bowling Green. McClellan urged Buell to lose no time in pushing on toward Cumberland Gap, but Buell delayed. On January 5, 1862, Lincoln began to grow impatient and pointedly asked: "Have arms gone forward for East Tennessee?"

Meanwhile, in early December, Zollicoffer had crossed into eastern Kentucky to the north bank of the Cumberland River, where he hoped to take advantage of the recent Federal retreat. He fortified his winter camp in a loop of the river known as Beech Grove, opposite Mill Springs, and was joined there by Major General George B. Crittenden, who dolefully assessed the situation and took command. Thomas advanced to drive them back. On December 31, he had set out from Lebanon, his men pelted by snow and a cold, stinging rain. The going was slow, the roads knee-deep in mud. It was "like . . . pulling plows," one soldier recalled, while the ground seemed to quake like a bog beneath their feet.

Though troops under Thomas were forbidden to destroy private property along their route—or even tear down fence rails for firewood at night—the cold was so bitter that the rule was modified to allow them to use the top rail. Soon "cheerful fires were blazing," warming the troops at night. Farm animals were also off limits, but pigs and geese who strayed within reach were seized. It took two and a half weeks to march forty miles, but on January 17, 1862, Thomas came to a place called Logan's Crossroads, about midway between the Rebel camp (ten miles to the south) and Schoepf's posting at Somerset (nine miles to the east). Not including Schoepf's command, Thomas had only four infantry regiments near, or less than 7,000 men, to set against the 12,000 in the Rebel camp.

Thomas sent to Schoepf for reinforcements, but between them lay Fishing Creek, a substantial stream that surged through a deep gorge. The same tremendous, incessant rain that had swollen the Cumberland River and made the roads a fluid marsh had turned the creek into a torrent. So it was not at all clear that Schoepf could get his three infantry regiments and battery across. As he waited for Schoepf to come, he took diligent precautions to avoid being taken by surprise. He knew (as few others seemed to) that a surprise attack was especially hard for untried troops to bear; so on the night of the 18th, he threw out pickets and cavalry vedettes in a wide arc two miles to his front.

His picket system was more sophisticated than any yet tried. "The usual method," writes one historian, "was to string out hundreds of pickets at every conceivable bypath, bridge, clump of trees and wrinkle in the terrain." Thus dispersed, these troops could be scooped up before they could sound the alarm by an enemy advancing in force. Thomas, on the other hand, in addition to infantry pickets, "had strong patrols of cavalry out on the roads, able to fight a delaying action dismounted, then move back to prepared defenses" under the covering fire of their lines.

Crittenden didn't like Zollicoffer's defensive arrangements, which placed the river at his back, and, to preempt a rout, hoped to catch Thomas off guard early on the 19th before the Union forces could combine. Just before midnight, under a heavy winter rain, the Confederates set out with eight regiments, an artillery company, and a cavalry troop. The vedettes picked up the Rebel advance at dawn two miles in front of the Federal camp and fell back slowly on the infantry pickets, who fell back slowly in turn, as trained, to give the Union camp time to form into line. The long roll was immediately beat, and the regiments sprang to arms. Thomas had left little to chance. Meanwhile, he was able to keep the Somerset road open for Schoepf's brigade.

Though Thomas had now been a brigadier for almost five months, he had continued to wear his old uniform with its colonel's buff stripes. That was his way. But when the time came to show his rank to some positive purpose, he did. Now was the time. Resplendent in his new uniform, Thomas faced his men drawn up in double line and spoke a few calm words as each regiment filed into place. When an overeager Indiana colonel dashed up to him in a disheveled state to announce that his men were "ready," Thomas cut him short: "Go back to your command and fight!"

In just ten minutes, he had his men on the move. One regiment was ordered forward to the right. When Rebel cavalry tried to outflank it, another was advanced and spread out. Before long, the fighting covered a mile of broken ground. Sight lines were obscured by tangled brush, fallen logs, and fields of corn, which made the artillery hard to use. But as Thomas rode onto the field, he aligned the men as they came up. Soon the Federals had seized both sides of Mill Springs Road, reoccupied some ground a forward regiment had lost, and were moving through woods toward a hill the Rebels held.

Particularly heavy fighting took place around a log house, but after four hours, neither side had gained the upper hand. Time after time the Federal left and center advanced, fired, and fell back. Fog and smoke thickened the air. Some Rebels had good breech-loading rifles; others old flintlock muskets, dampened and made useless, which they smashed in rage against the trees. At one place the lines were so close that Federals and Rebels poked their rifles through the same fence. With no reserve to speak of, Thomas hammered away with all his men in one line. "Trees were flecked with bullets," wrote one Union soldier, "underbrush cut away as with a scythe. Dead and wounded lay along the fence, on the one side the Blue, on the other the Gray; enemy dead were everywhere scattered across the open field."

In the course of the battle, Zollicoffer mistook a Union colonel for a Confederate officer and rode up to him in the mist. He called out to the Kentuckians to stop firing, saying, "We must not shoot our own men." The colonel stood speechless for a moment, then Zollicoffer's aide realized his mistake. In a quick exchange of fire, Zollicoffer was shot through the heart.

The battle had been even. Then about eleven o'clock, reinforced by two regiments that had come up from Schoepf, Thomas made his move. He sent one against the enemy's right, and in concert with another, the 9th Ohio (a largely German troop), wheeled suddenly and charged the Rebel left with fixed bayonets. The horrified Rebels greeted the wall of steel with a feeble volley, then broke and fled. Panic spread, until it extended over the enemy's entire line. That decided the fortunes of the day. One wounded Confederate prisoner afterward told his captors: "We were doing pretty well until Old Thomas rose up in his stirrups and hollered 'Right wheel!' Then we knew you had us, and it was no time to carry weight."

The Rebels were pursued to within a mile of their fortified camp, which Thomas shelled for an hour as night fell. Meanwhile, his wearied infantry reposed on their arms, hoping to carry the position at dawn. During the night, however, the enemy fled across the river, and burned the boats they used to prevent a quick pursuit. The next morning Thomas's men swept into the camp, scooping up all the abandoned provisions, 150 wagons, piles of small arms, entrenching tools, camp and garrison equipment, a thousand or more horses and mules, and an artillery train of twelve guns. Thomas sent Schoepf's brigade after the Rebels, but they had scattered far and wide.

Crittenden wrote afterward that his men were so frightened they stole horses and mules to hasten their flight, which carried them past Knoxville and Nashville to the heart of Tennessee. The sight of a defeated and demoralized army is sometimes more disheartening to its side than their outright capture, as Thomas noted in a dispatch from Somerset on the 31st. And so it proved. Albert Sidney Johnston reported that two of Crittenden's regiments, "whose homes were in that neighborhood, almost entirely abandoned their organization, and went every man to his own house. A multitude deserted, and the tide of fugitives filled the country with dismay."

The Rebels had also left their dead and wounded behind. The body of General Zollicoffer, his face "marked by an expression of deep dejection," was embalmed at Lebanon and in a typical act of decent respect (which Thomas always showed opposing troops in the aftermath of a battle) returned to his Tennessee home under a flag.

In a war that would ultimately involve unspeakably large losses, some momentous victories were notably free of wanton carnage—as in this case. Thomas, with 7,000 men, had beaten a force of 12,000, and in killed and wounded, despite close fighting, had lost just 246 men. There had been "no tactical mistakes to be remedied by desperate countercharges," as one writer put it, no headlong assaults that would have wasted lives. Yet the Battle of Mill Springs checked the first Confederate attempt to take eastern Kentucky; restored morale to the beleaguered state made despondent by Sherman's erratic behavior; cracked the right flank of the enemy's long strategic line; and was the first significant Union victory of the war. The Rebel forces at Bowling Green evaporated without a fight, their flank having been uncovered by Thomas's win. The battle also set the stage for a Union advance into Middle Tennessee. That advance was delayed (to the great frustration of Thomas) but fear of its advent forced the Confederates to divert precious resources in an effort to prevent it, even before the effort was made.

In a sense, the battle had also "created a general." Civil wars toss up all kinds of adventurers, and when a government flails about (somewhat blindly, as Lincoln's did) in search of military talent, many dubious men are raised. Some were made generals before they had even fought a battle; others, promoted for negligible deeds. Conversely, some came out of nowhere, yet proved their mettle. Albin Schoepf was one. He had long since left the Austrian army and was working as a hotel porter when the war began. But as second in command to Thomas, he served well. In the larger sense, however, as one fellow officer noted later:

> Up to this time we had no generals; the Government was making experiments. Many men who had never commanded anything, but were clever politicians, were sent into the field to demonstrate their incapacity. . . . But here, on the contrary, was disclosed to the view of the country a real general, who had commanded and held well in hand ten thousand men [counting Schoepf's brigade], and with a portion of them had defeated in fair battle a force of the enemy nearly double his own. Thomas was literally the first general in point of time developed by the war, and equal . . . in the course of the war, to any which it brought forth.

Buell congratulated Thomas on his "brilliant victory" (the first triumph of magnitude for the North since the Union disaster at Bull Run), and the Ohio legislature passed a resolution in his praise; but Lincoln's communiqué announcing the triumph through his new secretary of war, Edwin M. Stanton, in the first of a series of prejudicial slights failed to acknowledge him by name. Nor was Thomas promoted promptly, though others who had done nothing as yet were already moving up. Stanton had not been secretary of war a week when the glad tidings reached him. In an exuberant order, he promised that, when the official reports were received, "the military and personal valor displayed in battle will be acknowledged and rewarded in a fitting manner." But that promise was not fulfilled.

When Thomas was mentioned for higher command, Lincoln demurred. Perhaps he was misled by intriguing voices. Or chafed at the idea that a Southern-born general should get credit for restoring prestige to Union arms. No one seems to know—or know how to make sense of his mistake. In the end, by depriving Thomas of due advancement, he may have exacted from his own side an awful price. For if Thomas had been advanced to major general after Mill Springs, as one historian points out, "he would have outranked Buell and Grant, and been given an independent command early in the war." That in turn might have saved the Union much blood and treasure "lost by the blunderings of men who passed ahead of him in rank."

Lincoln eventually nominated Thomas for the commission of major general of volunteers, but his promotion was not confirmed until April 25, and then not backdated to the day of battle, according to the usual protocol. By then, the euphoria of the North had subsided, and was no longer linked in the public mind to his success.

After Mill Springs, Thomas had wanted to seize opportunity by the forelock and advance into East Tennessee. The timing for it was all the more propitious because of the swift developments that now took place in the "river war," for which the victory at Mill Springs helped prepare the way. With 20,000 men, Thomas thought he could seal off Knoxville as a Rebel base. Albert Sidney Johnston thought so, too. He was at Bowling Green when he first learned the outcome of the battle and wrote to Richmond: "If my right is thus broken, as stated, East Tennessee is open to invasion, or if the plan of the enemy be a combined movement upon Nashville, it is in jeopardy. . . . The country must now be roused to make the greatest effort they will be called on to make during the contest. . . . Our people," he added in despair, "do not comprehend the magnitude of the danger they are in."

McClellan had readily embraced the campaign expounded by Thomas, for he saw that any army operating against Knoxville and Chattanooga must draw Confederate forces from the East. Under

Buell, however, the plan was discarded, after Andrew Johnson insisted to the War Department that instead of going through the Cumberland Gap to Chattanooga, the Federals should march to Nashville, where he could be formally reinstalled. That went against the better judgment not only of Thomas and McClellan, but of Lincoln himself. Generally speaking, Lincoln's overall view of the strategic situation was right. In a letter dated January 13, 1862, he wrote to Buell:

> I state my general idea of this war to be that we have the greater numbers, and the enemy has the greater facility of concentrating forces upon points of collision; that we must fail unless we can find some way of making our advantage an overmatch for his; and that this can only be done by menacing him with superior forces at different points at the same time, so that we can safely attack one or both, if he makes no changes; and if he weakens one to strengthen the other, forbear to attack the strengthened one, but seize and hold the weakened one, gaining so much.

Here was a chance, found and lost, to "hold the weakened one" which held the key to Kentucky and Tennessee. "If," as one writer put it, "it is a wise maxim in war to do what the enemy fears to be done," the East Tennessee campaign conceived by Thomas would have struck a dagger into the rebellion's heart. Instead, for the next three years Tennessee and much of Kentucky would be traversed by large, opposing armies, clashing from time to time without conclusive result. One hundred thousand men would fall on the Union side alone in that contest, which might well have been settled by 20,000 in January 1862.

Meanwhile, North and South had begun their struggle to control the great rivers of the West. They formed the natural route of Union advance into the South and were defended by strongholds like Columbus on the Mississippi, Fort Donelson on the Cumberland, and Fort Henry on the Tennessee. Johnston had about 12,000 men at Columbus, 11,000 at the river forts, and 22,000 entrenched at Bowling Green. Some of his men were poorly armed with flintlock muskets, fowling pieces, or squirrel guns. Others were well equipped. But so long as his communications remained unbroken, he had the advantage of interior lines and, as needed, could rapidly concentrate his troops. On the Union side, Buell and Halleck had about the same number of troops in Kentucky and Missouri, as well as a fleet of ironclad gunboats under Commodore Andrew Foote in southern Illinois. So long as he could hold his line from Bowling Green to Columbus, Johnston not only blocked the rivers against the advance of Union troops, but secured his entire interlocking system of track.

The Union hero of the river war as it developed was Ulysses Grant. The son of an Ohio tanner, he had done poorly at West Point in a number of subjects, including military tactics, and, except for horsemanship, "ranked near the bottom of an exceptionally weak class." But mathematics "came to him," as he put it, and his one ambition at the time was to teach it to the upper grades. He remained in the army for a time, distinguished himself in the Mexican War at Molino del Rey, Chapultepec, Monterrey, and other battles, and was promoted to captain. After that, he started on a downward career. Oppressed by the dreary monotony of frontier service, he sought solace in drink, finally resigning to escape a court-martial in 1854 on the charge of drunkenness. He failed at every kind of work he tried, sank into destitution, for a time sold firewood on the street in St. Louis, and when the Civil War began was holding a clerkship in the family leather store at Galena, Illinois.

After his first requests for an army appointment were ignored at Springfield and Washington, he gained command of an Illinois volunteer regiment and whipped it into shape. By September 1861 he had seen some action, showed a fighting spirit, and chiefly through the political influence of his local congressman, Elihu Washburne, who had helped Lincoln secure his party's nomination, had been made a brigadier general of volunteers. In the contest for Kentucky, he had occupied Paducah, but his one real battle (for Belmont, Missouri, fought on November 7, 1861) had ended in retreat.

By January 1862, when the Battle of Mill Springs was fought, the mouths of the Tennessee and Cumberland Rivers were held by Union troops under General C. F. Smith, and the district containing them had been added by Halleck to Grant's command. It was now called the District of Cairo, based in Southern Illinois. Farther upstream, where the two rivers approached by sweeping curves within a dozen miles of each other, the outworks of the two main Confederate forts, Henry and Donelson, were only seven miles apart. All the navigable water above them was closed to the gunboats and transports of Union troops. Early in February, Grant left Cairo with 15,000 men and in a campaign coordinated with the Union gunboat fleet under Commodore Foote set out to take the forts. Fort Henry, on the Tennessee, was the weaker of the two and Grant attacked it first. The Confederates saw at once that they were overmatched. On February 6, while Grant was still moving his troops into place, Foote's gunboats blasted the fort into submission, its commanding general having but ninety men with him when he surrendered all his guns, ammunition, and stores. Several thousand Rebels, however, whom Grant was supposed to attack from behind, escaped before he arrived. The Federals then seized an important railroad bridge above the fort, and moved on to Fort Donelson, which Grant rashly promised in a dispatch to Halleck would fall on the 8th. But it wasn't until the 13th that the Federal assault began with bombardments from Foote's fleet, and after two days of equal fighting, Grant on the 15th threw his men against the breastworks without any tactical plan. The Rebels responded with a deluge of grapeshot and canister that stopped the assailants in their tracks.

As night once more fell, the issue remained in doubt, and Grant began to fear he might have to entrench his army, build winter huts, and begin a regular siege. Luck was on his side. The defenders, supposing their plight to be worse than it was, made an ill-advised sortie that cost them nearly 2,000 men. The Federals took advantage of their shaken state, charged, and carried the fort's outer line. This charge was made by General C. F. Smith, a former commandant at West Point. He had once taught Grant but was now his subordinate, and his action won the day.

The Confederate position was now in fact as bad as it had seemed. General John Floyd, the fort's commander, who had been secretary of war under President Buchanan, did not wish to be made a prisoner, and turned command of the fort over to General Gideon Pillow. Pillow decided he was too important to be captured, too. So he turned it over to General Simon Bolivar Buckner, who accepted his fate. A number of white flags appeared on the battlements. Then an emissary arrived with a letter from Buckner under a flag of truce. In the parley that followed Grant demanded unconditional and immediate surrender, threatening otherwise to take the fort by storm. Buckner denounced Grant's terms but yielded, as he felt he must.

Grant was promoted to major general and was thereafter known as "Unconditional Surrender" (U.S.) Grant. Floyd and Pillow escaped, with about 3,000 men, on steamers lying in the river above the fort; and 1,000 cavalry under General Nathan Bedford Forrest eluded capture by fording a narrow creek to Grant's right.

In combination, the fall of the river forts and the victory at Mill Springs dealt a major blow to Rebel hopes in the West. Three weeks later, Union general Samuel R. Curtis advanced into Arkansas and on March 7 and 8, defeated the combined forces of Earl Van Dorn and Benjamin McCullough at Pea Ridge. At the same time, John Pope's Federal Army of the Mississippi embarked on an amphibious operation to clear upper Mississippi of Confederate posts. By April 8, gunboats and troopships had taken New Madrid, Missouri, and Island Number Ten near the northwestern tip of Tennessee. Pope's forces captured both strongholds, as well as 5,000 prisoners, a number of artillery pieces, and large amounts of ammunition and supplies. Meanwhile, the day after Donelson fell, Bowling Green, Kentucky, had been evacuated by the Rebels, and three days after that Nashville passed into Federal hands.

Nashville was the first of the Southern state capitals to fall. Unfortified at the time, it had no way of contesting the Union gunboats that steamed up the Cumberland River as Buell's army advanced from Louisville to force the Rebels out. The flight of Rebel troops through the city (which happened on a Sunday) so alarmed the inhabitants that "congregations were dismissed without the usual benediction," and men, women, and children could be heard yelling, "The Yankees are coming!" as they rushed madly through the streets. Johnston's troops joined the exodus, cutting the cables of the great suspension bridge over the Cumberland, which collapsed and fell to the bottom of the river "in a shapeless mass." The rear of the Confederate column was scarcely out of view when Buell arrived. Soon thereafter, Thomas, having brought his troops up the river by transport, disembarked and with Buell occupied Nashville until about mid-March. Before long, the city became a fortified supply base for Union operations in the West. Goods manufactured or warehoused in Louisville and Cincinnati were transported down the Ohio to the Cumberland River, then to Nashville as steamboats unloaded tons of cargo at the city's three wharves. The suspension bridge was rebuilt, with guard turrets at both ends, and local arsenals began to churn out gun carriages, muskets, percussion caps, swords, and shot. No sooner was Andrew Johnson installed as governor, however, fulfilling his fondest hopes, than word came from Grant on the Tennessee River that the Confederates were massing to his front.

Though Grant had seized the headlines with his "Unconditional Surrender" demand, C. F. Smith's decisive role at Donelson had also been recognized by his own promotion to major general of volunteers. He was given chief command of the expedition up the Tennessee River to assess the strength of the Rebel buildup in the area and to oversee the Federal concentration at Pittsburg Landing for a new offensive Halleck had planned. That now made him Grant's superior. But in a momentous twist of fate, he was mortally injured in early March by a fall, and Grant hurried to Savannah, Tennessee, to take his place.

# 5. FROM SHILOH
# TO PERRYVILLE

In the East, in the spring of 1862, the Confederate army had its right near Aquia Creek, blockading the Potomac; its left in the Shenandoah Valley; and its center at Manassas near Bull Run. Richmond was secure. The Rebels also held Norfolk, where the Confederate ironclad *Merrimac* had its haven and on March 8 proceeded to Hampton Roads and sank a Federal frigate and a sloop-of-war. The next day the *Merrimac* was met by the Union ironclad *Monitor* and forced to withdraw. But neither could destroy the other, and the stalemate between the two seemed emblematic of the stasis on the Eastern front. It was at this time that "All quiet on the Potomac" was coined as an ironic phrase to describe the suspended animation of McClellan's Army of the Potomac encamped near Washington.

Yet with McClellan in command in the East, Union hopes had been raised. Those hopes were not unwarranted. "Little Mac" (who stood just five feet six inches tall) had a Napoleonic aura, reinforced by his meteoric rise from retired captain to major general almost in a single bound. Thus far his career had been brilliant. He had entered West Point at sixteen; ranked second in a stellar class of fifty-nine (from which twenty generals emerged); had excelled as Winfield Scott's engineer-in-chief in the Mexican War; returned to West Point to teach (where he prepared the army's standard manual for use of the bayonet); superintended the building of Fort Delaware; explored the Red River; surveyed the Cascade Mountains on the Pacific for transcontinental track; and in 1855 was dispatched to study military establishments abroad. This led to his historic report, published in 1857, which provided an eye-opening account of the Crimean War, and described

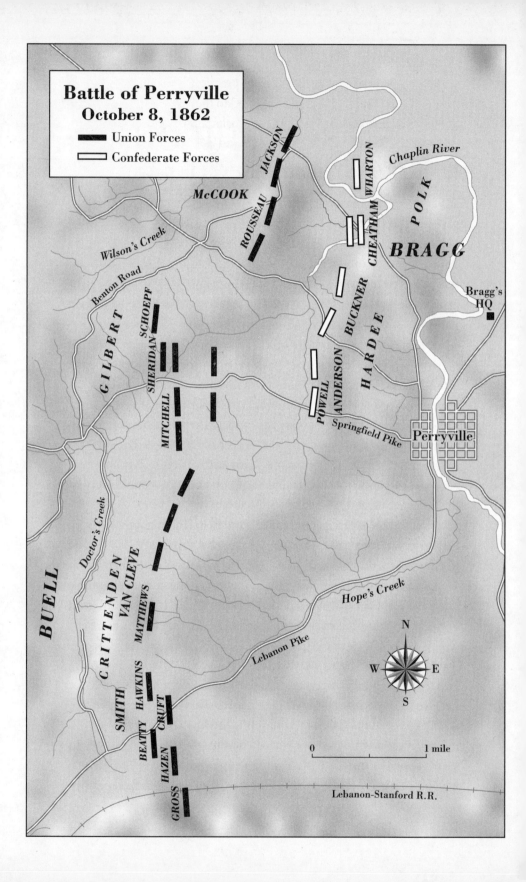

**Battle of Perryville**
October 8, 1862

■ Union Forces
□ Confederate Forces

JACKSON

McCOOK

ROUSSEAU

Wilson's Creek

Benton Road

GILBERT

SCHOEPF

SHERIDAN

MITCHELL

Doctor's Creek

BUELL

CRITTENDEN

VAN CLEVE

MATTHEWS

SMITH

HAWKINS

BEATTY

CRUFT

HAZEN

GROSS

WHARTON

Chaplin River

POLK

CHEATHAM

BRAGG

BUCKNER

Bragg's HQ

ANDERSON

HARDEE

POWELL

Springfield Pike

Perryville

Hope's Creek

Lebanon Pike

N
W        E
S

0        1 mile

Lebanon-Stanford R.R.

varying aspects of European military practice in detail. "Nothing of interest," it was said, "which appertained to the organization of troops and camps, the construction of field works, approved methods of reducing fortified positions, the merits and defects of the various national military systems was left out."

In peacetime service, there seemed nothing left for him to do. In 1857, he therefore resigned to become a railroad executive and was president of the Ohio and Mississippi Railroad when the war began. His early successes in West Virginia at Rich Mountain and Carrick's Ford had made him a star. Once in charge of the Army of the Potomac, he restored morale to its defeated ranks, and did wonders with the raw recruits that came in. By the late fall of 1861, he had organized and drilled an army of 150,000 men. Yet having drilled it, he did not advance, but lay in his camp near Washington, still drilling and reviewing while weeks of good weather went by. "His policy," as one writer put it, "seems to have been to create an overwhelming force, bind the Confederate armies to the stake at Richmond, destroy them there, and end secession at a blow." But to do that he had to move. There were good and bad reasons why he didn't, even as he engaged in a dispute with Lincoln over the right battle route to take. McClellan's sense of superiority, his condescension toward the president, and his undue caution impaired his reputation, in some respects unfairly. But he dithered more than he had to, which was perhaps a given trait. It was said of him by a railway president who had employed him as a civil engineer, that he might build the best of bridges, but would never go on it himself. This state of affairs continued into the spring. Lincoln chafed at the delay, and the extremity of his frustration affected his assessment of the Western front.

In an effort to rebound from their recent defeats, the Rebels in the West had concentrated near Corinth, Mississippi, a railroad hub just across the Tennessee line. At Corinth, interconnected track linked Virginia and the Carolinas to the Mississippi River and the Gulf. As troops came in from Chattanooga, Memphis, and Mobile, Albert Sidney Johnston, P. T. G. Beauregard (one of the heroes of Bull Run), and the "fighting bishop," General Leonidas Polk, assembled upward of 40,000 men. At the same time, Grant moved up the Tennessee with his army and established it on the west bank of the river at Pittsburg Landing, where he was to await the arrival of Buell's corps, which was marching from Nashville overland. Once the armies combined, they were to advance on Corinth, where the Rebels were encamped. Sherman was now part of Grant's army. During the river war he had been stationed at Paducah, Kentucky, in charge of logistics, and exerted himself to the utmost to redeem his name. Grant was indebted to his efforts, and Sherman was moved almost to tears by the appreciation Grant expressed. When Grant set out for Pittsburg Landing, Sherman waived his seniority to become a division commander in Grant's Army of the Tennessee.

Henry Halleck, now in overall charge of Union forces in the West, didn't know how many troops Johnston had or might assemble, though more were coming up every day from Pensacola and other points south. But in several dispatches he warned Grant not to bring on a battle before all the Federals had massed. Grant did not intend to, but he also did little to prevent one from taking place. Johnston knew the Union armies were in motion and what their intentions were. Nothing had been done to disguise them. The Federal forces that had crossed the river were posted to the west of Pittsburg Landing in a curved line three and a half miles long, with its center facing the road to Corinth, along the banks.

As might have been expected, Johnston decided to attack before the Federal armies could combine. His plan was to strike the Federal center, then each of the wings on the front and flank. Once he divided and overpowered the Federals, he hoped to drive them into the Tennessee River and kill and capture the entire force. Grant was so oblivious to his peril that he took no precautions against surprise. Nor did he think it necessary to ask Buell to force his pace. As it was, Buell's army, starting from Nashville for Savannah, Tennessee, on March 16, made reasonably good time, covering 135 miles in twenty-two days. Along the way, it had to rebuild a destroyed bridge over Duck River at Columbia and ford a number of swollen streams. On April 4, William "Bull" Nelson, who commanded Buell's advance, was told by Grant "that he need not hasten his march, as he [Grant] lacked the transports to bring him over the river anyway before the following Tuesday," i.e., the 8th.

Yet Grant (and Sherman, his confederate in this) were about to be shamefully surprised, with a horrible slaughter of their men. They had placed their forces in a haphazard arrangement, with the enemy to their front and the river to their back. They had failed to entrench though told to do so by Halleck, and had made no intelligible disposition for defense. Every division and almost every brigade had been allowed to select its own encampment according to the whim or convenience of the officer in charge. Worse still, the center of the Union line had been left empty, to be filled whenever Buell's forces arrived. That left both wings in the air. No extended picket was thrown out, and no cavalry sent to feel the front and give warning of an enemy advance.

There were other mistakes, too. Buell's Army of the Ohio was composed almost entirely of veterans; Grant at Pittsburg Landing had many raw recruits. Some of these were with Sherman to the front. That meant that the greenest troops were in the most exposed positions of the line. Yet Grant and Sherman both had ample warning that danger was near. Enemy cavalry, clearly trying to test the Union lines, were continually hovering about their outposts, and boldly pushed their approaches, with skirmishing each day. Moreover, the surrounding country—rugged, thickly wooded, and traversed by streams—was favorable to the unobserved movement of troops. Beyond that, such information as could be had of the strength of Johnston's army made it out to be even larger than it was. Grant himself thought it might be upward of 80,000 men—yet no fieldworks of any kind were thrown up, nor any plan of action arranged in case of attack. "Probably there never was an army encamped in an enemy's country," wrote one military historian, "with so little regard to the manifest risks which are inseparable from such a state." Even when a squad of Ohio cavalry happened on their routine reconnaissance to catch sight of a large Confederate force, it was disregarded by Sherman as a fairy tale.

Meanwhile, the advance of Buell's army had reached Grant's headquarters at Savannah, Tennessee; Buell himself, with most of the rest of his army, was expected on the 6th.

Advancing through dense woods by two narrow roads, Johnston's army pitched its tents undetected within two miles of Sherman's division on the night of the 5th. Sherman's headquarters were at a Quaker Meeting House known as Shiloh Church. Earlier that day, two of his brigade commanders had actually seen parties of hostile cavalry hovering in the woods beyond, and, a sure sign of an advancing army, large numbers of rabbits and squirrels "scudding from the woods in front of the camps." This was all reported to Sherman, whose former paranoia seems to have been replaced by a blind trust. Indeed, that very day (Saturday) Sherman told Grant: "All is quiet along my line now. . . . The enemy has cavalry in our front, and I think there are two regiments of infantry and one battery of artillery about six miles out. . . . I have no doubt that nothing will occur to-day more than some picket-firing. . . . I do not apprehend anything like an attack." On the same day Grant wired Halleck: "I have scarcely the faintest idea of an attack (general one) being made upon us, but will be prepared should such a thing take place."

The Rebel army now came on in three great divisions—not feeling its way cautiously, but in a swift, overwhelming rush. Soon after daylight on Sunday the 6th, the token pickets were driven in, and the long roll sounded through the camps. Wholly unprepared, the Union troops were scattered about, some preparing breakfast, others sitting idly in their tents. They had hardly time to form when the compact masses of the Confederates, with their famous Rebel yell, came sweeping down in one unbroken wave. So complete was the surprise that a number of officers were bayoneted in their beds. Within minutes, Sherman's division had been overwhelmed and ran, abandoning their camp equipage and stores. Sherman himself, dashing up and down the line, tried in vain to stop their flight, but the Rebel onslaught only gained in force, as the Federals rolled backward toward the river in a great chaotic mass. A wall of bayonets closed around one Union regiment and took it prisoner; two others laid down their arms. By ten o'clock, a second Federal division had retreated. Grant, at breakfast seven miles away when the firing started, hurried up and tried to form an armed cordon to the rear. But by mid-afternoon the Federal left wing had been completely enveloped and crushed. To make matters worse, Grant's whole army was not even on the field. By a misdirected order, a division under General Lew Wallace had pitched its camp to the north. There it remained idle through the fight. Meanwhile, Grant had belatedly ordered Buell's advance up the river, but it did not reach the landing until day's end. As the great 19th-century Civil War historian John Codman Ropes wrote, Grant "at no time made any attempt to unite the disconnected portions of his army and establish a line of battle. . . . It is evident from all accounts—Grant's included—that the battle of Sunday was fought by the Union army without any directing head."

As evening fell, the Federals faced a calamitous defeat. Almost the entire front line, save one brigade, had given way, and the enemy was in full possession of several Union camps. The Federals had been driven back to within a mile of the landing—as far as the nature of the ground would permit. Upward of 5,000 soldiers also cowered in terror beneath the river bluffs. There seemed to be no alternative to surrender, or to perish in the swift torrent of the stream. At this critical moment, the advance guard of Buell's army finally appeared on the high bank opposite, and two Union gunboats, the *Lexington* and the *A. O. Tyler*, having just come up from Savannah to the mouth of Lick Creek, opened fire with their 64-pounders against the Rebel right wing. That night more of Buell's troops arrived and took up their positions in the Federal lines.

The Confederate army was now no match for its foe. The Federals had 25,000 fresh troops on the field, and a dawn attack by their newly-combined armies forced the Rebels back. Even so, the Rebels held on for eight hours before sounding a retreat. Grant's delayed pursuit, conducted by Sherman, was half-hearted at best, even though "No better opportunity than this" to destroy a Rebel army, wrote John Codman Ropes, "was ever presented to a Federal general during the war."

The Northern public, appalled by Grant's negligent generalship and high losses, implored Lincoln to remove him from command. The outcry was not just popular but echoed through the ranks. One fellow general (Lovell H. Rousseau) wrote to Secretary Chase that Grant's negligence represented a "stupendous crime." Another (James A. Garfield) more tactfully observed, "Grant seems to have been surprised at Shiloh by some criminal neglect, not yet explained." Among his own soldiers, it was said that Grant was an "imbecile" who "ought to be compelled to serve as a private for the rest of his life." Alexander McClure (the Republican power broker and publisher who had met Thomas as a colonel at Chambersburg the year before) recalled that the clamor threatened to bring down Lincoln himself. But Lincoln, to a degree some might find surprising, often made critical decisions based on parochial concerns, including state pride. That was the politician in him—in particular, the politician from Illinois. After the fall of Fort Donelson, Lincoln had remarked, as he signed the papers promoting Grant, "If Southerners think that man for man they are better than our Illinois men, or Western men generally, they will discover themselves in a grievous mistake." His extreme exasperation with the stalemate in the East (especially with McClellan's apparent inaction) also skewed his perception of events. Though the outrage against Grant was next to universal (in Congress, for example, only Elihu Washburne leapt to his defense), Lincoln resisted calls for his ouster. In a late night conference with Alexander McClure, Lincoln exclaimed: "I can't spare this man; he fights." But Lincoln had missed the point.

The Battle of Shiloh was one of the most costly of the war. The Federals lost almost 13,000 men (nearly as many as they would lose in the East at Chancellorsville and Antietam); and though no one knows for sure what the Confederate losses were, they were apparently less, though Grant claimed they were more. The battle also had a marked impact on the careers of Halleck, Thomas, Sherman, and Grant. It brought Halleck to the supreme command of the Federal armies, cast another cloud over Sherman (despite some good fighting on his part the second day), raised Thomas to army commander, and demoted and embittered Grant.

In after years, however, when Sherman and Grant did their best to rewrite to their own advantage the story of the war, Sherman claimed that the Union army had taken proper precautions and blamed Buell for not arriving sooner "to help us on the first day." In his own memoirs, Grant also glossed over his own blunders, denied he had been "surprised," or that the Confederates had shown more tactical skill. He defended his failure to entrench on the odd grounds that his men "were unused to the pick and shovel"—even though most of his troops were farm boys more familiar with such tools than with rifles or bayonets. Then he tried to bury the whole issue in a patriotic flourish. After commending the valor of both sides, he irrelevantly remarked, "The troops on both sides were American, and united they need not fear any foreign foe." The manhood of the American soldier had not been in question and was, of course, beside the point.

To close out his account, he emphasized that the Federals had been outnumbered (41,000 to 33,000); and that two of Buell's divisions (not incidentally led by generals with whom he would have a falling out) did not contribute to the win: "Thomas's [division] did not reach the field during the engagement; Wood's arrived before firing had ceased, but not in time to be of much service." Thomas, who had brought up the rear of Buell's army, did, however, arrive in time to bury the dead. His men, as one writer observed, got a good lesson thereby in what can happen to an army when its commander falls asleep.

In any case, Buell's divisions had clearly saved Grant's army, though Grant denied it to his dying day.

By their defeat at Shiloh the Confederates were thrown back upon Corinth, losing their hold on Tennessee west of the mountains, except for two or three forts on the Mississippi, which were soon wrested from their hands. A few days later Halleck arrived by steamboat from St. Louis, pitched his camp near the steamboat landing, and united the three armies of his department under his personal command. His new combined legions included Buell's Army of the Ohio, John Pope's Army of the Mississippi, and Grant's Army of the Tennessee. Together they made up a force of 120,000. At the end of April, their advance on Corinth began, but it proceeded so slowly that the Confederates had ample time to increase their own strength. The Federals covered just twenty-two miles in a month, as roads were opened, streams bridged, obstacles cleared. Every day's advance in parallels was marked by heavy fortifications that precluded any attack. As a result, the ponderous march proved a vast advantage to the Rebels, for it tied up the great Union army as completely as if it had been besieged itself.

Meanwhile, in the reorganization of his forces Halleck removed Grant from command of the Army of the Tennessee, promoted Thomas (on April 25, 1862) to major general of volunteers, and in the combined army assembled had given him command of the right wing, which included Grant's four divisions of the Army of the Tennessee plus his own 1st Division of the Army of the Ohio. Grant was made second in command, but this was really a demotion, making him a sort of adjutant general, for he had no specific body of men under him. That infuriated Grant, who was technically superior to Thomas in rank, and though Thomas had nothing to do with Grant's demotion, it became the basis of an abiding grudge on Grant's part. "Undoubtedly, here began that misunderstanding," wrote one colleague, "or lack of good understanding, between the two generals which was never cleared up . . . Grant brooded over the slights which Halleck had put upon him, and for which Thomas was made the vicarious sacrifice." Yet according to McClure, a Lincoln confidant, Grant's demotion had been arranged on the president's orders to save Grant's career. By this stratagem, he retained Grant but reassured a restive nation that, for the moment at least, Grant would have no army in his care.

P. T. G. Beauregard, who had succeeded Albert Sidney Johnston, killed at Shiloh on the battle's first day, knew he would have to give up Corinth, but Halleck made it possible for him to depart in his own capacious way. From the 20th of May on, Union scouts could hear the humming of the rails as empty cars ran into Corinth and loaded cars ran out. One soldier who joined the siege lines on the town's outskirts on the 27th recalled: "We waited for three days momentously and anxiously expecting a battle," but nothing was done to force a fight. Confederate batteries "frowned" toward the Federals in the distance, but when Halleck's troops at last marched in, they found the Rebels gone and the cannon counterfeit. Meanwhile, the Federals had captured the mouth of the Mississippi and by the end of May held the strategic river cities of New Orleans, Natchez, and Baton Rouge.

Thomas took charge of Corinth and its environs; Pope went east to command the Army of Virginia (which defended the capital); and Halleck was called to Washington as general-in-chief of the armies. In late June, Thomas asked to be relieved of the right wing and transferred with his old division back to the Army of the Ohio under Buell. This change restored Grant to his former command. Thomas was moved to this by a regard for Grant. According to Thomas B. Van Horne, chaplain of the Army of the Cumberland (which Thomas would later lead), he thought it proper to defer to Grant's seniority, though against his own interests—insofar as those interests coincided with authority and rank. Wrote Van Horne:

> In consequence of this singular request, General Thomas descended from the command of an army of five divisions and resumed his former position under General Buell in command of one. This was a long step downward for a general who was anxious to hold a large independent command, but on the score of rank it was legitimate. . . . Military history seldom records such an act of self-renunciation and generosity, and if General Thomas had not made himself prominent in history by great achievements, he would have still deserved a high place for virtues which rarely dominate the ambition and jealousies of men.

Grant, however, failed to appreciate the gesture or show any gratitude.

The departure of General Halleck without appointing a successor left the troops in his department under three independent commanders. The months of June, July, and August were consumed by the Army of the Ohio in rebuilding the Memphis & Charleston Railroad (which the capture of Fort Henry had placed in Union hands) and reestablishing the communications in northern Alabama and Middle Tennessee. On the Rebel side, after the evacuation of Corinth, Beauregard had to withdraw to Tupelo, Mississippi, where he was superseded by General Braxton Bragg.

Despite all their setbacks, the Confederates in the West were still full of fight. The deeper into Rebel territory the Northern troops advanced, the more they were exposed to guerilla operations and disruptions in their lines of communication and supply. Rebel raiders proved adept at such tactics, which tended to diminish, if not neutralize, some of the Federal gains. Moreover, by June two large Confederate armies were rapidly gearing up for a major counteroffensive into Maryland and Kentucky, the two critical remaining border states. In the East, the advance was to be led by Robert E. Lee, now in overall command; in the West, by Bragg.

Meanwhile, along the Potomac, McClellan had finally moved. He had transferred the base of his army from Washington to Fort Monroe, advanced up the peninsula toward Richmond, and fought a series of successful engagements that brought him to Seven Pines. By June 1, the Army of the Potomac was therefore on both banks of the Chickahominy River, and had come to within six miles away of Richmond, in clear view of its spires. It had come so close that soldiers in the advance could set their watches by the sound of its clocks. But that was as far as it would go. There followed a series of blind and bloody engagements in which McClellan was outmaneuvered—first by General Joseph E. Johnston, then by Robert E. Lee—and forced to withdraw. This catastrophe undid all of Lincoln's hopes. Yet McClellan's Peninsular Campaign, as it was called, might have succeeded if Lincoln had not interfered. For no sooner had McClellan begun his march than the War Department (ever in fear of the capital's safety) anxiously took 40,000 men from his army and arrayed them in the capital's defense. That made it more difficult for McClellan to outflank the Rebel wings. In anger and disappointment, he telegraphed the secretary of war, Edwin Stanton: "I know that a few thousand more men would have changed this battle from a defeat to a victory. As it is, the government must not and cannot hold me responsible for the result. . . . If I save this army now, I tell you plainly that I owe no thanks to you or to any persons in Washington." "Save your army in all events," replied

Lincoln, with self-restraint. "I feel any misfortune to you and your army quite as keenly as you feel it yourself." Stanton however, fumed: "If we gave McClellan a million men, he would sit down in the mud and yell for two."

Perhaps. Alexander K. McClure presciently remarked in 1892: "The next generation will see continued disputation as to McClellan's capabilities as a commander, and Lincoln will be censured alike for having maintained and supported McClellan as a military leader, and for having failed to appreciate and support him after having called him to responsible command." The dispute, in substance, continues to this day.

McClellan was replaced by Pope, who came to grief at the end of August at the Second Battle of Bull Run. After Pope was bested by Lee, McClellan was recalled. Lee went on the offensive, crossed the Potomac into Maryland on September 4, and on the 8th, at Frederick, issued a proclamation inviting the people of Maryland to join the Confederate States.

Meanwhile, in the West, Bragg's movements also augured well for Rebel arms. Bragg's record before the war had been outstanding. In the conflict thus far, he had managed the Gulf Coast from Pensacola to Mobile; risen from brigadier to major general; led a corps at Shiloh; and supplanted Beauregard in the Western command. He was a shrewd if cantankerous man, adroit, industrious, able, and a wizard for detail. But he lacked imagination and, some critics claimed, he was "incapable of making crucial decisions once combat was joined." Thomas and Bragg knew each other well, of course. Bragg had always admired Thomas; it is not known how Thomas regarded Bragg. But their contact cannot have been less than cordial, since Bragg's letters of recommendation on behalf of Thomas had been so strong. After Thomas "went North," however, his regard turned to hate, and the intensity of their rival allegiance would play out in their titanic struggles on the field.

By temperament, Bragg was not the best man to restore his army's morale. But he had the confidence of Jefferson Davis, who enjoyed an almost mystical reverence among Confederate troops, and they soon recovered from their late defeat. In theory, Bragg had about 85,000 men at his disposal, though only half were under his immediate command. The rest were at Knoxville and Vicksburg under Kirby Smith and Earl Van Dorn.

Bragg's principal adversary, at the outset, was Buell. Buell's record was no less sterling, but his aloof, forbidding manner and over-proud bearing put him at some distance from his men. Like Bragg, he was something of a disciplinarian and from his long stint as an adjutant general had "a fixed way of doing things." He shared McClellan's marked emphasis on drill, and at the war's start had been called to Washington to help whip new recruits into shape. In that, he had proved superb. At the same time, he was known to be ambivalent about slavery, and entertained a conservative view of the war. That was thought to be helpful for warring in a border state. Later it became grounds for impugning his devotion to the Union cause.

Had Halleck kept his huge army together, Chattanooga might have been its prize. No railroad hub was more strategic. There the Western & Atlantic and the Memphis & Charleston Railroads met. At their junction, they also formed the East Tennessee & Georgia line, which conveyed war matériel to Lee's army in the East. Just to the southwest, there was another railhead of importance, at Stevenson, Alabama, where the Nashville & Chattanooga linked up with the Memphis & Charleston line. This reticulated network, with its constant transfer of goods of all kinds, had done much to keep the Confederate war effort alive. Lincoln thought the capture of Chattanooga "fully as important as the taking and holding of Richmond." Jefferson Davis thought so, too, and was determined to see it didn't fall. But the attempt by the North was now poorly made.

In a race with Bragg, Buell set out for Chattanooga from Corinth with about 31,000 men on June 10. His progress, however, was slowed by Halleck's insistence that he rebuild and repair the Memphis & Charleston Railroad as he went. That task was largely entrusted to Thomas, who manned the line from Iuka, Mississippi, to Tuscumbia, Alabama, interspersed with bridges and depots for supplies and rolling stock. Although the track was supposed to serve as Buell's main line of communications and supply, it would have taken his whole force to fully guard it, and so this precautionary labor erased the advantage he had in getting his army in motion first. Meanwhile, the wisdom of Thomas's earlier proposal for an advance on Knoxville and Chattanooga from Kentucky, proceeding from a well-protected base, had been lost. Instead, Union troops were scattered from Helena in the west, to Cumberland Gap in the east, a distance of over 400 miles. That weakened the Federal line, leaving it open to attack at almost every point. The adverse result soon became clear.

Throughout Tennessee and Kentucky, a drought set in, rivers fell, and guerrilla warfare disrupted every other leg of Buell's march. The Northern press grew impatient with his progress, and Lincoln faulted his arduous pace. Rebel cavalry commanders captured whole garrisons, wrecked trestles, and destroyed supplies. When two of Buell's divisions finally came in sight of Chattanooga in mid-July, Bragg managed to transfer 30,000 men from Tupelo to the town by rail in the nick of time.

Andrew Johnson saw the writing on the wall and began to court Thomas behind the scenes. In early August, he wrote to tell him that he had always favored him as the leader of the East Tennessee campaign. Thomas replied that he was pleased to hear it, but would not now be inclined to lead it because in every case so far the leader of every expedition had had his hands tied. Under such circumstances, it was "entirely impossible for the most able general in the world to conduct a campaign with success."

Meanwhile, Bragg had arrived at Chattanooga on July 30, where he conferred with Kirby Smith on a joint campaign. In their plan, Smith, proceeding from Knoxville, was to turn the Union position at Cumberland Gap, while Bragg, with a feint toward Nashville, would advance into Kentucky to draw Buell's armies out of Tennessee. In Kentucky, Smith and Bragg would then unite to confront Buell. That would allow Price and Van Dorn, in a separate action, to secure West Tennessee for the South. Once Buell had been trounced, Smith would advance to Cincinnati, Bragg to Louisville, and they would prepare to carry the war north. This, in fact, had been Albert Sidney Johnston's plan, conceived before Shiloh, to follow his defeat of Grant.

In late August, Bragg decamped from Chattanooga, crossed the Tennessee River, and began marching—in his planned feint toward

Nashville—for middle Tennessee. As Bragg moved northward, Buell was obliged to give up on Chattanooga altogether and retreat through Tullahoma "to keep abreast of the Confederate move." Even so, there was now a real possibility that Bragg and Smith might unite to cut him off.

Buell, however, still had no idea what their true objective was. Thomas correctly thought Bragg's movements were aimed at the capture of Kentucky. Buell thought Nashville was Bragg's more likely goal.

In his dispatches to Buell's headquarters, Thomas indicated Bragg's practical options: if Nashville was his objective, he would come by way of Battle Creek and Stevenson or, across the mountains to McMinnville or Sparta; if Kentucky, he would cross into the Sequatchie Valley, which would also allow him to attack Nashville by another route. Buell, however, was sure that Bragg would advance toward Nashville through northern Alabama and that the best place to meet him would be somewhere along the mountain heights. Buell had twice the number of troops Bragg had, and was better equipped and supplied, but had so scattered his men that unless he chose wisely it would be difficult for him to catch and intercept Bragg with an adequate force.

Thomas went to McMinnville. There he received a dispatch from Buell: "The enemy crossed three hundred cavalry and three thousand infantry at Chattanooga yesterday. This may be for the purpose of foraging in Sequatchie Valley, but we must be prepared for more than that. Hold your command in readiness to march at the shortest notice.... You should, by means of spies and scouts, keep yourself thoroughly informed of what is going on between you and Chattanooga."

On August 22, he asked Thomas if McMinnville or Altamont (a mountain village) was better ground for a fight. Thomas replied at once: "By all means concentrate here [at McMinnville]. The enemy can not reach Nashville by any other route across the mountains unless by Sparta. Here we will have a most decided advantage, and by being here, should he march by Sparta, we can meet him either there, or at Althusford across the Caneyfork." Thomas later noted that Bragg "could not possibly have passed Sparta without fighting. He would have arrived in an exhausted condition both from fatigue and want of supplies, and in my opinion could not have fought more than one day."

Buell, however, discounted his advice. He had convinced himself that Bragg would proceed along the Alabama line, and thought Altamont was the better place to block his march. "What think you?" he wired Thomas, appealing for assent. Thomas explained that Altamont was not the right place for a stand. "We can get neither forage nor water there. It will be as difficult for us to march across the mountains to Sequatchie Valley as for the enemy" to come the other way. He also pointed out that holding Decherd (a better option) with a division would both control the road to Nashville and enable the Federals to concentrate at McMinnville as developments required.

Buell dug in his heels: "There is no possibility of our concentrating at McMinnville. We must concentrate in advance and assume the offensive, or fall back at last to Murfreesboro. I deem the former the surest, and we will act accordingly. I wish you, therefore, to move by a forced march to Altamont, there to form a junction with McCook, Crittenden, and Schoepf [Buell's other main commanders]. There must be no delay."

Thomas complied, but judged it a mistake. At Altamont, the next day, he found things as he thought. That evening, August 25, at 5 P.M., he informed Buell that water was worse than "scarce," there was "only one spring," and not even forage enough in the area to support the troops a single day. As for moving ordnance about, "the road up the mountain is almost impassable," he added. "General [Thomas J.] Wood has been [here] from six o'clock until now, and has not succeeded in getting his artillery up the road." Thomas, who had abundant experience with mountain warfare, thought it impractical to try to march a large army (Union or Confederate) across the mountains under such conditions and was sure Bragg had ruled it out. He told Buell, "I will therefore return to McMinnville and await further orders. As I mentioned in one of my dispatches, I regard McMinnville as the most important point for occupation of any. The occupation of McMinnville, Sparta, and Murfreesboro will, in my opinion, secure the Nashville and Chattanooga Railroad."

Without waiting for Buell's reply, Thomas fell back to McMinnville, as common sense required. Buell acquiesced, but sent Thomas the following dispatch: "Keep your position at McMinnville, but make nothing like a permanent establishment. Be always ready to move at a moment's notice." He thought Bragg was on his way "with a large force" and "we must be prepared to concentrate promptly. . . . The passage of so large a force across the mountains is difficult, but not as much so as you would suppose from the road you took."

Once more, Thomas was right. He had recognized that Bragg, in cutting loose from his Chattanooga base, was driven to move in light marching order, as the forage was scarce in the country through which he had to pass. If he could escape a general engagement and link up with Kirby Smith on the Ohio, all of Tennessee and much of Kentucky might fall to his arms. That would change the whole landscape of the war. He was anxious not to jeopardize his plans with a risky battle in the mountains, where Union troops might select their own defensive ground. Thomas saw all this, and while Buell remained unsure of Bragg's objectives, Thomas was never much in doubt. Indeed, had Buell followed his advice, the North would have been spared what soon transpired.

Instead, on August 30, Buell ordered his army to concentrate at Murfreesboro, Tennessee. Once the troops were in motion, he had second thoughts. On September 1, he wired Thomas: "Do any circumstances present themselves which would make a change in our movements advisable?" Thomas replied, "I think as the movement has commenced that it had better be executed." As soon as it was, Buell changed his mind again. No sooner had Thomas entered Murfreesboro than he was sent with four divisions to Nashville—in part to calm the fears of Andrew Johnson that Bragg's march had aroused. Bragg made his feint, then deflected his forces to the right. Suddenly early in September, Confederate troops, wrote one biographer of Thomas, "appeared in central Kentucky, under Kirby Smith, and Braxton Bragg's cavalry was watering its horses in the Cumberland." Just two weeks before, Smith had crossed the Cumberland Mountains and passed through Barboursville to Richmond, Kentucky, where for three days he battled and overwhelmed a hastily formed garrison of mostly raw recruits. More than 6,000 Federals were captured with all their ordnance, wagon trains, and stores. Two days later, Smith's troops fanned out, took Lexington and Frankfort, and overran Camp Dick Robinson, which they turned into a supply depot for their own campaign. Buell now faced a race for Louisville with his scattered army, and the North faced a Southern advance into its heartland only a few months after Halleck had assembled his grand army to destroy the Confederates in the West.

Meanwhile, Rebel cavalry had destroyed much of the Louisville & Nashville Railroad and blown up the tunnels near Gallatin, Tennessee. Thomas entered Nashville on September 8 just before Buell, having already pushed forward a portion of his troops, set out for Kentucky on the 9th. By then, Bragg was on his way to Glasgow to rally Rebel feeling in the state. On September 13, he issued a resounding proclamation in which he promised to help free the people of Kentucky "from the tyranny of a despotic rule" and appealed for their broad support. At the same time, he sent a brigade to Cave City, ten miles to the west, to cut the railroad leading north from Bowling Green. After slicing up the tracks, that brigade then continued on to Munfordville, where a bridge spanning the Green River was held by Union troops. There, on the 17th, Bragg forced the surrender of the entire Union garrison of over 4,000 men.

Two days later, Thomas joined Buell at Prewitt's Knob, near Cave City, where he was made second in command of the entire army. The army advanced to Munfordville, where it was expected that Bragg would make a stand. Bragg withdrew, and for several days the two armies moved nearly abreast on different roads at times almost in sight of each other, the Ohio River in their sights. Both generals scrupulously sought to avert an engagement. When Bragg veered northeast to Bardstown, the road to Louisville was left open to the Federals, who marched to the city as fast as they could. And there they arrived on September 25.

If Buell had escaped, there was little in this to give his men heart. It was not escape they wanted. In nine months of marching, they had done almost no fighting, and their mood was dark. That of Buell was darker still. "He wore a shabby hat, dusty coat, and had neither belt, sash or sword about him," wrote one eyewitness. "Though accompanied by his staff, he was not engaged in conversation with any of them, but rode silently and slowly along."

Buell found Louisville in a panic akin to a state of siege. Bragg's perceived threat to Union strongholds on the Ohio River had alarmed the whole Midwest, and the governors of Indiana, Illinois, and Ohio had taken a number of emergency measures in response to it, even as they appealed to the Federal government for help. That summer, when Bragg crossed into Kentucky, they had also, with some foresight, mounted a great enlistment drive that brought in thousands of new recruits. Their influx was timely, because after the Union debacle at Second Bull Run and Lee's invasion of Maryland, few if any troops from the East could be spared.

Both Louisville and Cincinnati across the Ohio River were expecting an attack any day and could not dig their trenches or throw up earthworks fast enough. Cincinnati's defense had been entrusted to Lew Wallace, that of Louisville to William "Bull" Nelson, a large, tempestuous man, who had been the first to cross the Tennessee River at Shiloh to reinforce Grant. At Louisville, Nelson was ready to destroy the city, if necessary, in order to save it, and had made arrangements if the Rebels took it to set it on fire and shell it from the Indiana shore. (Almost no one could stand up to his temper, but one dark day it would bring him into fatal collision with another Union general, who shot him through the heart.)

The War Department was unhappy with Buell's whole campaign. Leaving Corinth with the avowed purpose of occupying Chattanooga, his army found itself, on the 1st of October, at Louisville, 350 miles in the rear of its original destination. Kirby Smith had carried the Rebel flag to within seven miles of Cincinnati (about as near as McClellan had come to Richmond); Bragg, at Bardstown, was only thirty-five miles away. In effect, their movements had neutralized all the summer operations of the Army of the Ohio after Corinth had been taken by Union troops. Thanks to Lee's counteroffensive in the East, the South had also regained nearly all the territory it had lost since the beginning of the war.

Buell was set on going after Bragg, and now devised a strategy to drive him back. But he had not kept Thomas informed. On September 29, however, he received an order that relieved him from duty and put Thomas in his place. To the surprise of the War Department, Thomas asked that the order be suspended for both their sakes. As General Buell himself recalled the circumstances in a private, unpublished note:

> [Thomas] came to my room and stated his intention to ask the revocation of the order; that he was not prepared by information and study for the responsibility of the command. I tried to dissuade him, told him that I would give him all of my information and plans, and assured him of my confidence in his success. Finding him determined, I said that I could under no circumstances consent to his sending a dispatch which could imply that I had any wish or influence in the matter. He promised that much, went away, and after a while returned with the message that he had prepared for General Halleck. I thought that he was actuated in his course by a generous confidence in me and a modest distrust of himself with so little warning; and I considered that both motives did honor to his sterling character.

The wire Thomas sent was so self-effacing it seemed to fault himself. It read: "General Buell's preparations have been completed to move against the enemy, and I therefore respectfully ask that he may be retained in command. My position is very embarrassing, not being as well informed as I should be as the commander of this army, and on the assumption of such responsibility."

Thomas had an old-fashioned sense of seniority, and though Buell had been outmaneuvered and outmarched, he had, after all, saved the Union army at Shiloh, and, in the opinion of Thomas, should be given another chance. Thomas had also not forgotten Buell's support for his recent promotion, and his frank and proper tribute to him after his victory at Mill Springs. Moreover, Buell had already formed plans for a new campaign. To assume proper command at this juncture, Thomas thought he would need to know more about Buell's plans than he did. He also didn't want to do to Buell what had almost been done to him on the eve of his own planned East Tennessee campaign.

The order was revoked and Buell retained. But it left the impression in the War Department that Thomas was too modest or unsure of himself to take charge. Since he had previously asked to be relieved of the right wing at Corinth, allowing Grant once more to lead the Army of the Tennessee, this impression was only reinforced. But as Thomas later observed: "I am not as modest as I have been represented to be. I did not request the retention of General Buell through modesty, but because his removal and my assignment were alike unjust to him and to me. It was unjust to relieve him on the eve of a battle, and unjust to myself to impose upon me the command of an army at such a time." Nevertheless, Halleck felt rebuffed. In response to the wire suspending the order, Thomas replied: "Will await further orders but [will] go on assisting Buell in putting troops in the field. He desires placing me second in command should he be retained."

At Louisville, the Union troops refreshed themselves for a week, gained strength, and readied for a new campaign. The feared assault by Bragg had not materialized, and the legions of raw recruits that had come in to defend the port were now impatiently incorporated into the army's swelling ranks. Reinforced by several fresh volunteer brigades, Buell had about 60,000 men.

Bragg had expected Buell to take more time to get his army together and in the interim had disposed his forces in a wide strategic arc to hem him in: 22,500 troops were under Polk to the southeast at Bardstown; 10,000 more were strung through Lexington, Harrodsburg, and Frankfort. So Bragg was surprised when on October 1 Buell led his new army out of Louisville to challenge Bragg's hold on the state. Advancing southeast along a sixty-mile front—with cavalry vedettes thrown out five miles—Buell's army was divided into three corps, led by Generals Thomas L. Crittenden (brother of George Crittenden, the Southern general whom Thomas had beaten at Mill Springs); Charles C. Gilbert; and Alexander McCook. McCook commanded the left, Gilbert the center, and Crittenden, accompanied by Thomas, as a kind of supra corps commander, in this instance, the right. The weather was fair and morale once more high. The men marched out to the cheerful sound of fife and drum, their sabers and bayonets flashing and gleaming in the sun.

Bragg and Smith together had a comparable force, but they had expected it to be far larger than it was. During the early summer, John Hunt Morgan, a Rebel raider operating in Kentucky, had depicted the state as ripe for the taking, and Bragg had brought with him wagons loaded with rifles to arm some 30,000 hoped-for volunteers. But in the end, few joined. "Our prospects are not what I expected," he wrote Jefferson Davis. "Enthusiasm runs high, but exhausts itself in words." An embittered Kirby Smith more harshly disparaged Kentuckians as too attached to their thriving farms. Bragg cursed them for their "cupidity . . . love of ease and fear of pecuniary loss."

In their expectations for recruitment, both had assumed that wherever the Union armies went they created ill will by pilfering private property while living off the land. But Thomas and Buell had both forbidden such predations, and woe to anyone whom Thomas caught. Though "not easily ruffled," wrote one war correspondent, "his rage," when aroused, "was terrible." Near Bardstown one day, "Thomas was approached by a farmer whom he knew to be a good Union man, and who made complaint that one of the general's staff officers had carried off the only horse left on his farm. The general turned black with anger . . . and demanded to know who and where the offender was. The farmer pointed to a mounted infantry officer, who was attached to one of the regiments and not to the general's staff. The general rode up to him and demanded to know where he had obtained the horse which he rode. The officer replied that he had 'impressed' him. Thomas knew the man had no authority to impress horses, and, choking with rage . . . he drew his sword, and, putting the point under the shoulder-straps of the officer, ripped them off." Then he forced the man to dismount, lead the horse back to the farm, and compensate the farmer for his loss.

Bragg, meanwhile, turned to conscription. To do so "legally," he went to the state capital of Frankfort to install a pro-Confederate regime. On the morning of October 4, with considerable fanfare, he presided over the inauguration of Richard C. Hawes, an ex-official, as the new governor, under the Confederate flag. Hawes had just finished proclaiming to the assembled crowd that "the Confederate Army of the West has entered your state to help you free yourselves from the tyranny of a despotic ruler!" when a Federal division began to shell the town.

Bragg fled with Hawes, but the two Union divisions approaching were actually a feint. Buell's main army was directed toward Bardstown, expecting, ultimately, to confront Bragg there. Bragg withdrew after a slight skirmish, and tried to draw Buell toward Frankfort, where he thought the Federals could be outflanked. Instead, over the next two days both armies tried to keep track of each other as they sought more advantageous ground. Before long, however, their dispositions were deranged by a frantic search for water in the midst of the dreadful drought.

That drought had lasted all summer long and into the fall, and as the troops plodded along the chalk dirt roads, they were tormented by an unrelenting thirst. The earth was parched and blistered. Leaves had dried up on the trees, and "all the grass had withered and turned gray. The procession of men and animals stirred up blinding clouds of limestone dust, which every breeze sent whirling through the camps." Many of the creek and stream beds they came upon were dry, or had "tired-looking threads of water in them"; others had not a trace of dampness but were cracked like glaze. What water there was often was contaminated by waste. "I never saw men suffer for water as we have," wrote one soldier. "It is horrible to think what we have been compelled to drink!" One morning, soldiers found to their disgust that they had filled their canteens the night before from a pond that contained a dead mule.

Almost at the same time, the two armies approached the little hamlet of Perryville in central Kentucky, traversed by a still flowing river and laced by creeks and streams. Bragg, whose army was divided, thought the Federal force was divided, too. He did not realize that the columns converging on Perryville were three full corps. Buell's plan, in fact, had been to keep the Rebels guessing about his line of march, to prevent Bragg and Kirby Smith from linking up. And this he had done. But in other respects, the orderly style of march that had marked the Union army from Louisville to Bardstown had not been kept in this next advance. The three corps of Buell's army were not abreast, and this tempted Bragg. He hoped to beat back the corps in the lead before the others could be brought up to its relief. Bragg's rear guard under Polk was at Perryville when Gilbert, in command of the Union center, went into camp three miles away. McCook was in the rear and behind him Crittenden. The entire force had been driven to its place by a quest for water. Crittenden's force was moved far to the right to gain access to water holes.

Facing what he supposed to be Bragg's entire army, not just the 16,000 men who were there, Buell pored over area maps with his staff. He wasn't quite sure where the Rebels had drawn their line, but established his own, north to south, outside the town. Meanwhile, the Rebels occupied the town itself and disposed their forces in a roughly opposite formation, with two brigades on a ridge above a stream called Doctor's Creek to prevent the Federals from getting at the pools of water that it held. Well back from this forward position, the Rebels planted their batteries on a range of low wooded hills overlooking and completely commanding a stretch of open ground lying immediately at the foot of the range. Bragg's infantry was massed behind and around his artillery, and his cavalry ready to charge down the easy slopes and "sweep every living thing from the level ground below. This was his trap, and into this he expected the advanced positions of the Union army to fall."

On the night of the 7th, there was a heavy skirmish over Doctor's Creek, where Philip Sheridan, then a division commander, sent a brigade to seize the high ground. The next morning, as Buell waited for McCook and Crittenden to fill out their lines, he assumed that Bragg would not attempt any major action until the following day. Instead, about noon, Bragg attacked, and boldly brought all three Confederate divisions against McCook on the Union left. Two divisions of his corps—one of them composed entirely of raw recruits—bore the brunt of the assault. The unexpected withdrawal of Gilbert's corps from the right, the early death of two generals, and the slowness with which reinforcements arrived, made the contest a desperate one, and after four and half hours of heavy fighting, casualties on both sides were high. Only a lack of sheer numbers prevented the Rebels from prevailing, even in the face of fierce cannonades. "It was a life to life and death to death grapple," wrote one soldier. "The sun was poised above us, a great red ball sinking slowly in the west." As it touched the horizon, it seemed to suffuse the plain with blood.

Though the Federals had been driven back a full mile, the stout resistance of McCook's 12,000 troops against substantial odds, losing in the fight one-fourth of their number in killed and wounded, left the issue unclear. Yet this was a battle that Buell's army should have won. He had eight divisions to the Rebel three, but almost all the action of the day had taken place on the Union left. The rest of his army was so disposed that its two wings were separated by a distance of five miles. On the Union right, Crittenden, with 22,000, had been deceived by a clever deployment of Rebel cavalry into believing that a large Confederate force was in his front. Moreover, there had been no overall direction on the Union side. In fact, Buell had been strangely unaware that a great battle was taking place. For most of the morning he had been convalescing behind the lines in his tent, nursing a leg bruised by a fall. Buell had also asked his generals to report to him in person after settling into line. Thomas had declined, sending an aide instead; McCook had complied. He was just reporting to Buell that all was quiet on his front when the roar of battle broke in upon their conference. Buell sprang up from his cot. "What is the meaning of that?" he cried. "Nothing," replied McCook. "A skirmish." But the volume of fire was large. "A skirmish with such a waste of ammunition?! Go back, and put a stop to that folly," he said.

By the time Buell knew that a battle was going on it was late in the afternoon. At four a member of McCook's staff dashed in to report that the Union left was in a fight for its life. "I was astonished," Buell wrote. "Not a sound of musketry had been heard." Apparently, an "acoustic shadow" or still zone, created by a quirk of topography and wind, had "virtually deadened the sounds of battle" nearby. Indeed, it had been a confused day all around. Here and there the two armies, not always easily distinguishable by their dress, had even blurred or blended together and briefly occupied each other's lines. During all this time, Thomas had received no instructions from Buell, and had no knowledge of the horrors transpiring five miles to his left. At 4 P.M., he was told to hold one division ready to reinforce the center and to explore whether the Rebels were reinforcing their own line. But he received no orders to advance. Finally, at 6:30, after the battle was over, he learned from Buell's chief of staff that McCook's corps had been "heavily engaged," and (in a misleading synopsis of events) that part of it had "gained ground" to its front while yielding "a little" to its right.

By day's end, the Federals had lost over 4,200 men, the Confederates 3,400—a bloody toll for fighting that lasted a single afternoon. Buell hoped to redeem himself somehow by a counterattack at dawn and told Thomas and Crittenden to have their divisions ready at the left and center of the line. But Bragg now realized that the entire Federal army was to his front, and during the night fell back to Harrodsburg, where he was joined by Kirby Smith on October 10. The two withdrew across the Dix River to Camp Dick Robinson, and from there on October 12, to foil a flanking movement by Buell, abandoned Kentucky altogether and pushed back into Tennessee through the Cumberland Gap.

In his official report on the battle, Buell blamed McCook for overconfidence "which made him believe he could manage the difficulty without aid or control." But that was unconvincing, once all the reports came in. Meanwhile, in the East, McClellan fought Lee to a costly draw at the Battle of Antietam on September 17–19, 1862, but failed to exploit Lee's retreat. Yet taken together, Antietam and Perryville had arguably prevented Maryland and Kentucky from falling into Rebel hands. On September 22, Lincoln boldly issued a preliminary emancipation decree that gave warning that all slaves in the rebellious states would be freed by his military authority, by official proclamation at the start of the new year.

•   •   •

The fall of 1862 brought about a shake-up in the army's high command. Seven weeks after Antietam, McClellan was replaced by Ambrose Burnside, who had led a wing under McClellan and a brigade at First Bull Run. Burnside was surprised at the assignment and denied his fitness for the post. Lincoln ought not to have discounted his opinion. Buell was also relieved, and William Rosecrans, "the hero of Iuka and Corinth," assumed his command. The name of the army was changed to the Army of the Cumberland and the troops operating in the department were consolidated and designated as the Fourteenth Corps. These developments were attended by contention within Lincoln's cabinet, with Stanton urging Lincoln that Thomas be advanced. Thomas would have welcomed the endorsement, as he yearned for an army of his own to lead. A new campaign was in the offing, and there was no reason for him to regard himself now as ousting someone else. But Stanton's great rival, Secretary Chase, lobbied hard for Rosecrans (a fellow Ohioan), and after Lincoln considered the matter he said, "Let the Virginian wait." A member of Stanton's staff recalled that when Stanton returned from the executive mansion, "bilious with wrath at Chase's interference," his first words were: "Well, you have your choice of idiots. Now look out for frightful disaster."

That was intemperate, of course, as Stanton's outbursts often were. Rosecrans had great merit, even if Thomas deserved the command.

Born in Ohio, Rosecrans was of Pennsylvania Dutch stock and a great-grandson of Stephen Hopkins, a signer of the Declaration of Independence and colonial governor of Rhode Island before the Revolutionary War. He had entered West Point in 1837 (a year behind Thomas), roomed with A. P. Stewart and James Longstreet (two Confederate generals of subsequent renown), graduated fifth in a class of fifty-six, and as a second lieutenant in the Engineering Corps was posted to Fort Monroe in Hampton, Virginia. A man of medium height and build, erect bearing, modest, refined, polite, affable, with mild features, he had a florid complexion, and striking clear, gray eyes.

An extremely accomplished engineer, Rosecrans had helped design the formidable harbor installations for Newport, Rhode Island; the Washington Navy Yard; marine railways, sawmills, ordnance buildings, and machine shops; invented an odorless oil; and discovered a new process for the manufacture of chlorine soap. At the outbreak of the war, he was made a brigadier general of volunteers, and led a brigade under McClellan in the West Virginia campaign. Following the Battle of Bull Run, he had bested Lee at Cheat Mountain and Carnifex Ferry in 1861; routed Sterling Price at Iuka on June 19, 1862; and defeated a Rebel attempt to retake Corinth on October 3 and 4. (Grant later tried to take credit for the last two triumphs, but his claims were unjustified—which everyone seems to have known at the time.) Indeed, these two victories alone brightened the picture for the North, disheartened by a series of reversals from Virginia to Tennessee. After Corinth, Rosecrans was in a position to pursue the Rebel army and possibly destroy it, but Grant "decided that further pursuit was inadvisable and the army was recalled." Had Grant not done so, the Federals might have gone straight to Vicksburg "with but a tithe of the blood and treasure" that its surrender later cost.

By his sterling record in the war so far, Rosecrans had certainly earned preferment. But in his selection, politics and religion also mixed. A devout Catholic and the brother of the bishop of Cincinnati (a pillar of the Western church), his appointment was also meant to rally American Catholics in the North, who tended to view the conflict as a "Yankee war." In its diplomatic maneuvering, the government at once sought to exploit his prominence to bolster its position with Catholic powers abroad.

Thomas, no doubt, would have appreciated all this on its merits (had he been briefed) but the order, issued October 24, giving Rosecrans command came to him as a painful surprise. After all, he had not declined the post when it had been offered to him two months before at Louisville. He had only asked that it be suspended so Buell could execute his plans. Since he had been deemed worthy of the command then, why should it be denied to him now? He wrote to Halleck:

> Soon after coming to Kentucky, I urged upon the government to send me twenty thousand men properly equipped to take the field, that I might at least make the attempt to take Knoxville and secure East Tennessee. My suggestions were not listened to, but were even

passed by in silence. But, without boasting, I believe I have exhibited at least sufficient energy to show that, if I had been intrusted with that expedition at that time (fall of 1861), I might have conducted it successfully. Before Corinth, I was intrusted with the command of the right wing, or Army of the Tennessee. I feel confident that I did my duty patriotically, and with a reasonable amount of credit to myself. As soon as the emergency was over, I was relieved and returned to the command of my old division. . . . On the 30th of September, I received an order through your aide . . . placing me in command of the Department of the Ohio, and directing General Buell to turn over the command of his troops to me. This order came just as General Buell had by extraordinary efforts prepared his army to pursue and drive the rebels from Kentucky. Feeling that a great injustice would be done him if not permitted to carry out his plans, and that I would be placed in a situation to be disgraced, I requested that he might be retained in command. The order relieving him was suspended, but to-day I find him relieved by General Rosecrans, my junior. Although I do not claim for myself any superior ability, yet feeling conscious that no just cause exists for overslaughing me . . . I feel deeply mortified and aggrieved.

Halleck replied on November 15, 1862:

Your letter of October 30th is just at hand. I can not better state my appreciation of you than by referring you to the fact that at Pittsburg Landing I urged upon the Secretary of War to secure your appointment as major-general, in order that I might place you in command of the right wing of the army over your superiors. It was through my urgent solicitation that you were commissioned.

When it was determined to remove General Buell, another person was spoken of as his successor; and it was through my solicitation that you were appointed. You having virtually declined the command at that time, it was necessary to appoint another, and General Rosecrans was selected.

You are mistaken about General Rosecrans being your junior. But this is of little importance, for the law gives the President power to assign without regard to dates, and he has seen fit to exercise it in this case and many others.

Rest assured, General, that I fully appreciate your military capacity, and will do every thing in my power to give you an independent command when opportunity offers. It was not possible to give [you the] command after you had declined it.

That was not quite candid. But Thomas took Halleck at his word and apologized for what he deemed his own mistake. From Gallatin, Tennessee, on November 21, 1862, he replied in a conciliatory vein:

I have the honor to acknowledge the receipt of your letter of the 15th instant, and to thank you sincerely for the kindness of its tone. I should not have addressed you in the first place, if I had known that General Rosecrans' commission was dated prior to mine. The letter was written, not because I desired the command, but for being superseded by a junior in rank, when I felt that there was no good cause for so treating me. I have no objections to serving under General Rosecrans, now that I know his commission dates prior to mine, but I must confess that I should be deeply mortified should the President place a junior over me without just cause, although the law authorizes him to do so should he see fit.

When Rosecrans arrived, Thomas learned that Rosecrans was in fact his junior and that his commission as major general, originally dated August 16, 1862, had been backdated by Lincoln to March 21, 1862, to give him seniority of rank. Thomas objected strongly and told Halleck: "I have made my last protest while the war lasts. You may hereafter put a stick over me, if you choose to do so. I will take care, however, to so manage my command, whatever it may be, as not to be involved in the mistakes of the stick." By that, he seemed to be saying, with an almost insubordinate boldness, that he would act independently if he had to in order to save his men.

The whole matter had been handled poorly. Even Buell had not been informed directly that he had been dismissed. Rosecrans later recalled that when he went to see Buell at the Galt House Hotel in

Louisville, the visit "was more like that of a constable bearing a writ for the ejection of a tenant than a general coming to relieve a brother officer in command of an army."

Thomas had based his protest largely on technical grounds; but he had no personal objection to Rosecrans, whom he liked and admired. When they consulted together at Bowling Green where Rosecrans went in late October to take charge, Rosecrans told him: "You and I have been friends for many years and I shall especially need your support and advice." He added that his appointment had come to him wholly unsought, but had seemed to him all the more desirable because Thomas was the senior general in command.

In the coming months, no one would serve Rosecrans with a more loyal heart.

# 6. STONES RIVER

"In politics and war," it is said, "nothing is successful but success." For failure, scapegoats abound. In his campaign to secure East Tennessee, Buell had often confused himself, demoralized his army, and failed to achieve any of his goals. In the fall of 1862, the War Department (driven largely by Stanton's venom toward McClellan) set out to discredit everyone to whom McClellan was closely linked. In the East, General Fitz John Porter was cashiered for Pope's defeat at Second Bull Run. In the West, Buell was ordered to appear, at almost exactly the same time, before a court of inquiry assembled at Nashville to investigate his conduct of the Tennessee-Kentucky campaign.

The court included a number of generals handpicked for their hostility to Buell (including Lew Wallace and Albin Schoepf) with Major Donn Piatt as judge advocate. Piatt, the Ohio jurist and diplomat who had warned Lincoln of the inevitability of war in November 1861, had declined an officer's commission at the outbreak of hostilities to enlist as a private. When Robert Schenck, his Ohio compatriot, was made a brigadier general, however, Piatt became adjutant general on his staff. At the battle of First Bull Run, he had stood firm and tried to stop the flight of Union troops; and as a curious sidelight to that action endeared himself, by his irrepressible wit, to Rutherford B. Hayes, the future president of the United States. Hayes was then a major in Schenck's brigade, and wrote home that Piatt always had something amusing to say, even in the midst of the most trying events. On one occasion, when shells were whistling all around, Piatt told Hayes that he was striving to remember some appropriate prayer, but could only recall, "Oh Lord, for these and all thy other mercies, we desire to be thankful."

When notified that he would be judge advocate at Buell's trial,

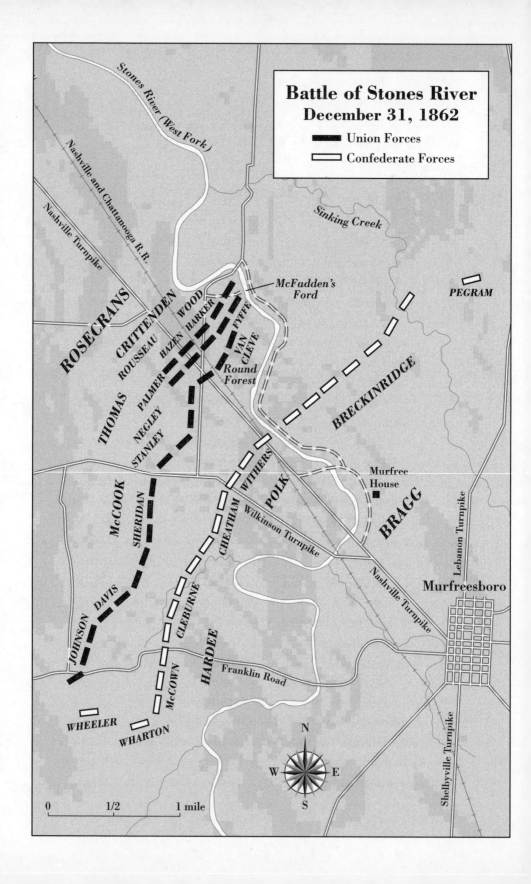

# Battle of Stones River
## December 31, 1862

■ Union Forces
□ Confederate Forces

Stones River (West Fork)

Nashville and Chattanooga R.R.

Nashville Turnpike

Sinking Creek

PEGRAM

McFadden's Ford

ROSECRANS

CRITTENDEN

WOOD

ROUSSEAU

HAZEN

HARKER

FYFFE

VAN CLEVE

Round Forest

BRECKINRIDGE

THOMAS

PALMER

NEGLEY

STANLEY

WITHERS

POLK

Murfree House

BRAGG

McCOOK

SHERIDAN

CHEATHAM

Wilkinson Turnpike

Lebanon Turnpike

Murfreesboro

JOHNSON

DAVIS

CLEBURNE

HARDEE

McCOWN

Franklin Road

Nashville Turnpike

WHEELER

WHARTON

N
W E
S

Shelbyville Turnpike

0    1/2    1 mile

Piatt went to the War Department to examine the charges but found none on file. He sought out the secretary of war, who told him, to his surprise, that none had been prepared. He was advised to ask Governors Andrew Johnson and Oliver Morton (of Tennessee and Indiana) for guidance. That told him that the court of inquiry was really a political trial.

The court convened at Cincinnati in midwinter, and at the instance of Johnson and Morton was designed to try Buell not for incapacity or misconduct, but treason. Morton claimed that Buell had been "in treasonable correspondence and even personal communication with General Bragg; and that the entire movement from Murfreesboro to the Ohio was planned and conducted for the purpose of giving both Tennessee and Kentucky" to the South. But he declined to make these unsupportable charges in any formal way. "I give you these only for your own guidance," Morton told Piatt. "Johnson and I will furnish the witnesses, and we will appear ourselves at the proper time." Stanton, in the meantime, made it clear that the members were not only to justify Buell's dismissal, but condemn every aspect of his campaign. As Piatt put it, the court had been "organized to convict."

In both open and closed hearings, marked by dozens of disputes over evidence and procedure, the court sat for six months. When the promised witnesses finally appeared, most of them knew absolutely nothing of the treason charged, while those who claimed to know were so disreputable that, recalled Piatt, "the court was ashamed to put [them] on the stand." So the trial properly devolved in the end upon Buell's judgment in command. Both sides summoned Thomas, whose character, military standing, and reputation as a court-martial judge in his own right loomed large.

Buell had conducted his own defense with considerable skill, and his intimidating presence and demeanor sometimes embarrassed and confused those who took the stand. Moreover, to show that he was not under arrest, he had "come into court in full uniform with sword on side, accompanied by two aides so well drilled and disciplined that they seemed a chorus ready at any moment to break into song." The outrageous manner in which the original charges had been brought also threatened to turn the trial into a farce.

Buell assumed Thomas would support him as a colleague, regardless of any contravening facts. "This was the situation," recalled Piatt,
when Thomas appeared. His presence was even more commanding
than that of Buell, and though he answered all questions simply and
directly, without bias, "it soon became clear to the military tribunal
that Bragg, with an inferior force, had outmaneuvered, outmarched,
and outfought Buell." The critical moment came when Thomas was
asked whether there had been any point after Bragg had crossed the
Tennessee where Buell's army could have been concentrated for a
fight. Thomas said yes, and pointed to Sparta and McMinnville on the
map. Buell was dumbstruck. The "cold, calm manner that had so far
sustained him," wrote Piatt, "vanished," and he almost writhed in his
chair.

In his cross-examination, Buell sought to cast doubt on what
Thomas had said. "Please tell the court, General," Buell demanded,
"whether that opinion has come from a study of the situation since,
or whether it suggested itself to your mind at the time?" "If you will
give me your book of telegrams," Thomas replied quietly, "I believe it
will answer better than I can." The book was produced and Thomas
"slowly turned the leaves until he came to what he was in search of,
and then returned it open to General Buell." Buell blushed as he read
the telegram aloud which showed that Thomas had advised him on
the right place for a stand.

In the end, the tribunal was just for show. It allowed Johnson and
Morton to vent their spleen, and while it acquitted Buell of any inten-
tional wrongdoing, it destroyed his career.

Stanton had expected Piatt to act as his prosecutorial agent, and
at the outset he obliged. But as the trial proceeded, his conduct of
the hearing changed. In Buell, he recognized an able general who had
simply made mistakes; in Thomas, a figure of huge potential for
the war.

Piatt remained in the War Department for a time, but his role of
dutiful servant soon came to an end. He was an ardent reformer ("If
there's any rotten apples in the barrel, he can be counted on to hook
'em out," said Lincoln, with some annoyance, who felt you had to

leave some in); and too much of an abolitionist for Lincoln's taste. Piatt had tried to push the process along in Maryland (prematurely, in Lincoln's view) and when his name came up for promotion from colonel to brigadier general, Lincoln drew his pen through it, saying, "Knows too much."

Piatt's experience with punitive military courts set up by Stanton (and Halleck), not incidentally, later led to an interesting (and amusing) exchange with Lincoln which also pointed up Piatt's grasp of some fine points of law. The time came round when Halleck wanted to put Schenck on trial. Schenck wrote Lincoln a protest and told Piatt not only to take it to the President, but to read it to him, "fearing that it would otherwise be pigeon-holed for consideration when consideration would be too late. It was late in the afternoon," wrote Piatt,

and riding to the White House, I was told the President could be found in the War Department. I met him coming out and delivered my message.

"Let me see the protest," said the President, as we walked toward the Executive Mansion.

"General Schenck ordered me, Mr. President, to read it to you."

"Well, I can read," he responded sharply, and as he was General Schenck's superior officer, I handed him the paper. He read as he strode along. Arriving at the entrance to the White House, we found the carriage awaiting to carry him to the Soldiers' Home, where he was then spending the summer, with the guard detailed to escort him drawn up in front. The President sat down on the steps of the porch and continued his study of the protest. I have him photographed in my mind, as he sat there, as a strange picture he presented. His long, slender legs were drawn up until his knees were level with his chin, while his long arms held the paper, which he studied regardless of the crowd before him. He read on to the end; then looking up said:

"Piatt, don't you think that you and Schenck are squealing, like pigs, before you're hurt?"

"No, Mr. President."

"Why, I am the Court of Appeal," he continued, "and do you think I'm going to have an injustice done to Schenck?"

"Before the appeal can be heard, a soldier's reputation will be blasted by a packed court," I responded.

"Come, now," he exclaimed, an ugly look shaking his face, "you and I are lawyers, and know the meaning of the word 'packed.' I don't want to hear it from your lips again. What's the matter with the court?"

"It is illegally organized by General Halleck."

"Halleck's act is mine."

"I beg your pardon, Mr. President, the Rules and Regulations direct that in cases of this sort you shall select the court; you cannot delegate that to a subordinate any more than you can the pardoning power," and opening the book, I pointed to the article.

"That is a point," he said, slowly rising. "Do you know, Colonel, that I have been so busy with this war I have never read the Regulations. Give me that book, and I'll study them to-night."

"I beg your pardon, Mr. President," I said, giving him the book, "but in the meantime my general will be put under arrest for disobedience, and the mischief will be done."

"That's so," he replied. "Here, give me a pencil," and tearing off a corner of the paper General Schenck had sent him, he wrote: "All proceedings before the court are suspended until further orders. A. Lincoln."

In such haphazard ways did reputations rise and fall.

After being driven out of Kentucky, Bragg had gone to Richmond, where he weathered a storm of scorn and abuse comparable to the barrage in the North that brought down Buell. "At once the dogs of detraction were let loose upon me," he wrote, "and the venal press decided I should be removed from command." But Davis had an irrepressible confidence in him that somehow survived every failure Bragg sustained. From Richmond, Bragg reentered Tennessee and arrayed his army in a great arc centered at Murfreesboro to cover all routes to Chattanooga to the south. In early November, Rosecrans moved his headquarters from Bowling Green to Nashville to plan a new campaign to evict Bragg from Tennessee.

While Bragg strengthened his new strategic line, Rosecrans found his own army in disarray. Since the Perryville campaign, some 7,000 troops had deserted, and more than 26,000 were on leave. Altogether, in mid-November, two weeks after he took charge, a total of 32,966 officers and men were absent from their commands. Of these nearly 10,000 were convalescing in the various military hospital camps that dotted the West. The army that remained was composed in about equal measure of veterans and raw recruits. The authorities in Washington wanted Rosecrans to confront Bragg almost at once, but before he could do anything arms depots had to be established, men trained and equipped, and the railroad between Nashville and Louisville (his main line of supply) secured. Nashville, moreover, had been virtually under siege for weeks and the first task of the army was to clear Rebel troops from its front. The countryside around was also swept for cavalry raiders, and Franklin (a nearby strategic town) reoccupied. In the meantime, Rosecrans subdivided his army into three grand divisions, with the right wing under Alexander McCook, a former instructor in infantry tactics at West Point; the center, under Thomas; Thomas Crittenden holding the left.

To reinspire, reorganize, clothe, and equip his men, Rosecrans "toiled terribly," night and day, scarcely taking for himself needed rest or allowing it to his officer corps. He rarely retired before two in the morning and often not before four. On most days he was up by dawn. By a special dispensation from Secretary of War Stanton, he was empowered to strip corrupt and incompetent officers of their posts. "Everywhere in the Army of the Cumberland," one soldier recalled, "the men sensed that Rosecrans was for them. The food seemed to improve; the mail and pay, both important to a soldier's life, came more on time." Even dietary luxuries, like pickles, peppers, and potatoes, suddenly appeared on their plates. The postal system was also entrusted to the direction of a police detective, who ferreted out negligence, corruption, and abuse. When an ill-equipped soldier complained he couldn't get shoes, Rosecrans demanded that pressure on this and other matters be applied up and down the line:

> Can't get shoes! Why? Go to your captain and demand what you need! Go to him every day till you get it. Bore him for it! Bore him in his quarters! Bore him at meal-time! Bore him in bed! Bore him; bore him; bore him; don't let him rest. Let the captains bore their colonels; let colonels bore their brigadiers; brigadiers their division generals; division generals their corps commanders; and let the corps commanders bore me. I'll see then if you don't get what you want. Bore, bore, bore, until you get every thing you need.

With Thomas, Rosecrans also organized an elite Engineering, or "Pioneer," Brigade, taking two skilled men from each company of every infantry regiment so that each regiment had twenty men in its specialty corps. Its members were furnished with axes, hammers, hatchets, saws, files, spikes, coils of rope, and so on, and when all brigaded together, formed a corps of about 3,000 men. In its ranks could be found military, civil, and railroad engineers, surveyors, architects, draftsmen, printers, bridge-builders, carpenters, machinists, millwrights, wheelwrights, coopers, blacksmiths, saddlers, sawyers, and woodmen. There was nothing they could not do. They repaired and constructed roads and bridges, maneuvered pontoon bridge equipment, erected fortifications, and served as sappers and miners as the army's needs required. Every railroad bridge between Gallatin and Nashville and between Nashville and Murfreesboro was built or strengthened at their hands. In and about Nashville, they completed and perfected the works of Fort Negley (the strongest inland fortress on the continent) and elsewhere constructed several massive fortifications, embankments thousands of feet high, and other defensive works.

Thomas had a large hand in all of this and was said to be the one man on whom Rosecrans constantly relied. In military matters, his in-depth knowledge extended to every aspect of an army's structure and command. General Gates P. Thruston, sometime judge advocate of the Army of the Cumberland, recalled:

When I became a member of his staff it was a matter of surprise to me to find how remarkably familiar and accomplished he was in all matters of military law and precedent, and other officers of his staff in the various departments often remarked to me that he seemed to know the usage, details and system of each department of service as thoroughly as though he had passed his entire military service in it. During two years in the judge advocate's department I devoted almost my entire time in fitting myself to the duties of the position. I sent to Europe for books, and read every thing pertaining to military law and that branch of the service; yet in the preparation of court-martial orders, or in the consideration of questions of law or precedent relating to that department, the general was always ready with useful suggestions and counsel, and seemed to have given more consideration to these subjects than any other officer in the army. . . . What was true of my department was true as to all the other branches of the service, as far as I could judge. He was master of them all.

Thomas also kept up to date with new technological developments and tried to incorporate them into his command. He was one of the first to recognize the transforming power of the repeating carbine (which made cavalry or mounted infantry into a new kind of rapid strike force); and his signal telegraph train was the most sophisticated of the war. Made up of six wagons, each containing a telegraph instrument, tool chest, axes, reels, and five miles of wire, its centerpiece was a little electric generator with a dial device that could be carried in a box by one man. The wire itself, insulated by gutta-percha, was rolled up on reels in one-mile sections, and could be mounted on poles, run out on the ground, or hung on fences or trees.

While Rosecrans labored mightily at Nashville, Thomas established his own main camp near Gallatin to keep the supply line intact. Under his aegis, some 5,000 mules were rounded up for pack trains; 3,000 repeating carbines requisitioned to equip a new cavalry division under General David S. Stanley; and five million rations sent forward from Louisville as fast as the limited capacity of the railroad would permit. Courier lines were also established between the different camps and garrisons; and new topographical surveys made of the area and incorporated into military maps. Bragg's cavalry did everything it could to disrupt the progress—attacking outposts, burning trestles, and wrecking miles of track—but by November 26 the Louisville & Nashville Railroad had been fully repaired and refurbished, and by early December most of the trains were running through.

But to Washington, all this seemed to be taking too long, and General-in-Chief Henry Halleck began to prod Rosecrans to speed things up. Some positive news was also needed on the military balance sheet. "The President is very impatient at your long stay in Nashville," Halleck wrote him on December 4. "Twice have I been asked to designate some one else to command your army. If you remain one more week I cannot prevent your removal. . . . The Government demands action, and, if you cannot respond to that demand, some one else will be tried." That was harshly imperative and utterly careless of the planned campaign. By December 5 only five days' provisions had been accumulated in reserve beyond what the army (of 70,000) consumed each day; and with so scanty a store "it would have been unwise, if not criminal," according to one contemporary official, to advance into the heart of Rebel terrain. Rosecrans replied: "I have lost no time. . . . If my superiors have lost confidence in me they had better at once put some one in my place and let the future test the propriety of the change. I have but one more word to add, which is, that I need no other stimulus to make me do my duty than the knowledge of what it is. To threats of removal or the like I must be permitted to say that I am insensible." He continued his preparations for three more weeks, held daily drills and reviews, garrisoned Nashville, and after laying up a thirty days' stock of provisions, prepared to set out with about 45,000 men.

Meanwhile, Bragg had settled into winter quarters at Murfreesboro, and thought Rosecrans had done the same at Nashville, as his army seemed arrayed for its defense. A Union campaign, in any case, was not uppermost on Bragg's mind. To ring in the holiday season, he held a number of festive parties (including a high-society wedding) in the town, and on Christmas Day sponsored a grand ball, which included a rendition of Lord Byron's "The Eve of Waterloo." As part of the party's optimistic decor, the names of Confederate generals were spelled out in evergreen, and captured Union flags adorned the walls. While their officers drank and danced, men in the ranks amused themselves with cock fights and feasted on eggs, onions, and turkeys plundered from local farms. Even the unseasonably mild weather encouraged a holiday spirit, to which the Confederate president himself seemed to give his assent. Two weeks before, Jefferson Davis had come to visit, to inspect the troops and ascertain morale. When the parade ground filled with their smartly dressed ranks, it was "a truly imposing scene" and "a time of rejoicing," as Davis and his staff rode along the lines. When Davis left for Chattanooga the next morning, he was just as convinced as Bragg that the Federals had decided to sheathe their swords till spring. Even so, Bragg sensibly established a strong perimeter guard.

By then, the War Department in Washington was frantic for good news. Sherman had exasperated the North by "floundering about" in a Mississippi bayou above Vicksburg, and was about to send his men to slaughter in a failed assault of Chickasaw Bluffs. Worse still, the very day Davis arrived in Chattanooga, the Army of the Potomac under Burnside had been mauled at Fredericksburg. Thousands of dead and dying lay heaped along a sunken road, and the night after the attack the ghostly light of the aurora borealis seemed to reflect the red gleam of their sacrifice. If, at the outset, Rosecrans had been expected to make up for the failures of Buell's late campaign, more was now hoped for, as the fortunes of the North seemed to rest largely in his hands.

Rosecrans set the time for his advance as the day after Christmas, and on Christmas night met with his general staff. As they departed, he told them, "We shall begin to skirmish as soon as we pass the outposts. Press them hard. Drive them out of their nests. Make them fight or run. Keep fighting! Good night."

December 26 dawned with a cold, dismal rain. Clouds of mist wreathed their way among the tents, and the rain ran in yellow streams along the gullies of the roads. In the dimmed first light of morning, reveille rolled like muffled thunder through the camps. By six the soldiers were up and at their breakfast; by seven, they were tramping across the rain-drenched fields. Thomas led the center, McCook the right, Crittenden the left. Stanley's cavalry swept down Nolensville Pike, driving the enemy pickets before them. Below Nashville, the army fanned out. The three corps marched down different roads, but fell in by cross roads to keep the lines tight. On either side, troops made their way through dense woods or cedar thickets interspersed with cultivated fields. Each man carried his own blanket, pup tent, rifle with 100 rounds, and three days' rations—"a pretty good load," as one soldier put it, "when the roads are good, & a big one when the rain is pouring down & the mud half knee deep." About noon, the clouds parted before a stiff northwest wind and the sun came out to brighten the winter air.

Almost at once, as Rosecrans had predicted, Rebel "nests" were uncovered and the skirmishing began. That kept the men at the ready as they toiled all day across the broken ground. That night the men bivouacked in the wide, soft fields; as they settled down, a heavy storm broke over them again and battered them in their tents. In the rainy dark, Rosecrans and his escort strayed off course in search of McCook. As they charged along among some rocks, an aide exclaimed: "General, this is hell on the horses." "That's true," he replied. "Walk." After they had moved on a way, he paused and said to his chief of staff: "Go back and tell that young man that he must not be profane." It was long after dark when McCook's camp was reached, and about one in the morning when he pitched his own tent for the night.

Over the course of the next two days, the Federal columns slowly felt their way forward through constant mist and rain. "Another division passed us in the night & were skirmishing all day yesterday," one soldier wrote on the 28th as he huddled in a field tent after a march of twenty-five miles. "They took 6 pieces of artillery. As usual it rained all day." The artillery wagons sank up to their axles in the mud; the men were drenched. At three the next morning they were roused and, teeth chattering, fell into line. Up ahead, Bragg arranged his troops for battle, and the Federals cautiously pushed through the cedar thickets toward his lines. Meanwhile, they were harried by Rebel cavalry under Joseph Wheeler, "who contested every ridge and ford."

For the past two months, the Rebel army had been scattered fairly widely through Middle Tennessee. But as soon as Rosecrans marched, Bragg called in his troops and entrenched them astride Stones River, near the Nashville Pike. His position there adjoined the Nashville & Chattanooga Railroad and sought to take advantage of the surrounding ground, which was marked by irregular outcropping of rock, with thick glades of red cedar interspersed with open farms. Most of his troops lay under the cover of the woods, but his line also extended across the river and occupied both banks. In the meantime, he sent Wheeler on a number of raids to try to sap the Union strength. In one spectacular strike, Wheeler made a complete circuit of the Union army and destroyed a supply train of over 300 wagons, capturing 800 men. "The turnpike as far as the eye could reach," recalled one Federal soldier, "was filled with burning wagons." In the darkness, flames "leapt wildly up . . . illuminating the pike's whitened surface and the somber cedar thickets by its side."

Rosecrans pushed on, and on the 29th and 30th the various Federal units halted and closed in. On the morning of the 30th Rosecrans was standing in front of his headquarters, an orderly holding his horse, when a cannon ball struck in the road a short distance off, and bounded away—a second struck still nearer, and a third with a swift, rushing sound swept past him in a line, beheading an aide in its flight. Mounting his horse to get out of range, Rosecrans rode up a slope a little way off, and halted under some trees near the road. There a shed for him was improvised by draping india rubber blankets over a lean-to of sticks and poles. With his staff, he pored over updated maps and moved his army into line.

Its left, under Crittenden, rested on Stones River and stretched across a cotton field; its right, under McCook, ranged across a wooded ridge as far as the Franklin Pike. At the foot of the ridge lay a valley covered with close cedar thickets and clumps of oak. The farthest brigade on the right was drawn back nearly at right angles to the main line, to oppose any flanking movement Bragg might try. The center, under Thomas, was posted on a rolling slope. Altogether, the Union line was three miles long. To the back of the Union position lay undulating ground, half-burned clearings, thickets, and a patchwork quilt of cornfields, woods, and swamps. Half a mile away, in a parallel array, lay the Rebel host. As the two armies came abreast, Bragg made only slight adjustments to his front. Dense cedars masked his center and good country roads radiated from his headquarters to both flanks. The armies were about the same size (roughly, 45,000 men), but Bragg was waiting for the Federals on his own chosen ground.

By an odd coincidence, both commanders had formed the same plan of attack, designed to force his opponent against the river by rolling up his right flank. Each also planned their attack for the same time. For his part, Bragg hoped to get to the Federal rear, cut it off from Nashville, and take Nashville itself. Rosecrans, with Murfreesboro in his sights, hoped to surge into the town after fording the river to take a strategic hill. Once that crest was taken, artillery, planted on its heights, would sweep the whole Rebel front. Crittenden, with a division, was to begin the Federal assault at dawn; Thomas, in the center, to follow by brigades.

As twilight darkened down to sunset, Thomas rode slowly along the lines going into camp for the night. A Union reconnaissance was in progress and heavy firing could be heard to the front and left. "What is the meaning of that, General?" an aide asked him. "It means a fight tomorrow on Stones River," he said, and calmly continued his preparations for the night.

The troops, cutting cedar boughs for beds, wrapped themselves in their blankets and lay down to sleep with the silent stars looking down. Here and there, musicians of both armies began to play patriotic songs. First came "Yankee Doodle," then, in quaint response, a spirited rendition of "Dixie," as the men tried to calm their common fears. "Every soldier on that field," wrote one officer, "knew that on the following day he would be engaged in a struggle unto death." At length, the gentle melody of "Home Sweet Home" floated mournfully up from someone's violin. Musicians North and South then took it up together, and voices from both camps joined the chorus of the song.

For the Federal attack to work, McCook had to hold his own position firmly on the right. His was the pivot on which the whole maneuver turned. That night, Rosecrans met with him in a wagon in the woods to review the next day's plans. As they talked, they sat on some rough plank boards, a single candle between them, stuck in the socket of a bayonet. The point of the bayonet had been driven into the floor. Rosecrans said to McCook: "You know the ground; you have fought over it; you know its difficulties. Can you hold your line for three hours?" McCook replied: "Yes; I think I can." Rosecrans then told him that if he had to fall back, he must do so slowly, contesting every inch of ground. He added: "I do not like your facing so much to the east. . . . If you do not think your present position the best, change it." In response, McCook, in a ruse, extended his campfires a mile beyond his line.

That turned out to be a mistake. Rosecrans had massed his reserves to turn and crush the Rebel right; Bragg had massed the larger portion of his force on his own left to crush and turn the Union right. But during the night, Bragg added still more troops to match McCook's pretended strength.

The next morning, Rosecrans rose early and, a devout Catholic, attended mass in his tent. Having thus "committed himself and his army to the God of battles," he stepped out into the cold morning air. His officers, with their overcoats on, had already gathered around newly kindled fires. Colonel Julius P. Garesché, his Catholic chief of staff, sat apart under a tree reading *The Imitation of Christ*. It was just before sunrise. As they listened for the attack to begin on their left, a strange, confused sound, like the fearful sweep of a hurricane, came suddenly from their right. At intervals, they could hear the dull, heavy roar of cannon. Then, as the noise drew nearer, the rattle of rapid rifle fire, which crackled like flames among dry brush.

Just as the Federals had begun their own attack, the Confederates had thrown themselves against the extreme right of McCook's line. Unseen, they had emerged from the cover of the cedars and were almost on top of the Federals before they knew an assault was on. Pressing rapidly forward in heavy columns, they fell upon two brigades, which crumbled to pieces as they were driven back. "In five minutes," writes historian Bruce Catton, "one of the most desperate battles of the war was in full blast. McCook's position was hopelessly swamped, hit from the flank and in front by seemingly limitless numbers. . . .

Men in reserve behind him hardly heard the crash of battle before fugitives from the front came scampering through their camps, spreading panic in their flight."

The attack came with such speed and force that a number of artillery horses were not yet harnessed, and several batteries were captured without firing a shot. After fierce fighting, three more brigades were dislodged and the Federal right taken in flank and rear. "Our comrades were falling as wheat falls before the cradling machines at harvest time," recalled one officer. "We could hear the hoarse shriek of shell . . . the impact of solid shot, the 'chug' when human forms were hit hard, the yells of pain, the cries of agony, the fearful groans. . . . Cannon balls cut down trees around and over us, which falling crushed living and dead alike."

A division under Philip Sheridan—the last stand of the Federal right wing—held out for a time and twice changed front. But at length, it ran out of ammunition, and all of its artillery fell into Rebel hands. The center under Thomas, exposed by Sheridan's retreat, was now outflanked. Rebels swept to his rear. The earth, torn, trampled, and red, lay piled with the dead and wounded. Arms and legs lay scattered on all sides. In two hours, seventeen heavy guns had been captured by the Rebels as well as 2,000 men. An aide from one of the beleaguered division commanders caught in the rush dashed up to Thomas to tell him they were trapped. Thomas told him: "Cut your way out."

Three-fifths of Bragg's army had now joined the attack, and by 10 A.M., the Confederate wheeling movement seemed about to overwhelm the Union center as McCook's entire corps was forced back to the Nashville Pike. But there, near a bend in Stones River, stood a wooded knoll known as the Round Forest—afterward as "Hell's Half Acre"—where the Federals under Thomas regrouped to make a stand. Every available brigade was called in to hold the line, drawn almost at right angles to the first, and six batteries planted on the crest. Bragg, thinking Thomas at his mercy, now mounted a relentless attack on this rise. His gunners fired up the pike and, as they got the range, waves of Rebel infantry emerged from the woods. Thomas was "everywhere along his harassed line, directing his batteries to take new positions and supervising their fire, standing in the advanced lines of his infantry as they blunted the Confederate attack. The men saw him that day wherever the fighting was." Afterward men said of Thomas: "Fighting under him was like having a stone wall in front of you or a battery to cover you." The very fact of his presence, quietly and coolly giving orders under the hottest fire, steadied his men against the storm. At risk of being flanked and overborne, Thomas stemmed the apparently resistless tide. "The scene was as grand and awful," wrote one soldier, "as anything I ever expect to witness until the Judgment Day."

Rosecrans was also valiant, and with several aides rode down to the Round Forest to join Thomas under fire. Colonel Julius Gareschê, his chief of staff, galloped by his side. As they raced across a field in the thick of the action, Gareschê was beheaded in an instant by a shell. Only a fragment of his lower jaw remained. The spouting trunk, "inclining gently from the saddle," fell forward to the earth. Rosecrans paused briefly, and exclaimed, "Brave men die in battle. Let us push on." A little later, a friend and fellow officer came upon the spot where Gareschê lay:

> I saw but a headless trunk: an eddy of crimson foam had issued where his head should be. I at once recognized his figure, it lay so naturally, his right hand across his breast. As I approached, dismounted, and bent over him, the contraction of a muscle extended the hand slowly and slightly towards me. Taking hold of it, I found it warm and lifelike. Upon one of the fingers was the class-ring, that (to me) beautiful talisman of our common school. This I removed; and, also taking from his pocket his Bible, I then parted. . . . There was no time for tears.

As the afternoon wore on, Bragg hurled up to ten brigades against the Union defenders but could not dislodge them or break their line. Emerging from the cedars with yell after yell, firing as they came, the Rebels rushed forward four lines deep each time in massed formations. But sheets of rifle fire and canister from cannon on the heights plowed long lanes through their ranks. "Men, shoot low," said Rosecrans. "Give them a blizzard at their shins." Yet again and again the Rebels rallied and came on, in four fiercely sustained charges, until one last, failed effort, as the sun was going down.

Even so, the battle overall had favored Bragg. Though he had been unable to turn the Union right completely, Rosecrans had been forced to abandon his own plan of attack, and his right had been bent back and nearly destroyed. Bragg thought Rosecrans would try to retreat to Nashville if he could, and toward evening cabled Richmond, "God has granted us a happy New Year."

Rosecrans established his headquarters that night in a log hut within artillery range of the Rebel front. Many of his generals were despondent; some (like Thomas Wood) were disabled and still bleeding from their wounds. The day had begun in disaster, and it was not yet retrieved. Many of the regiments had lost two-thirds of their officers; scarcely one had escaped without loss. Ten colonels, ten lieutenant colonels, six majors, and hundreds of line officers were gone. A fifth of the Federal artillery had also been captured. More than 7,000 men were missing from the ranks. Nearly two-thirds of the battlefield was held by the Rebels; communications cut to the rear; and some of the wagon trains destroyed. Ammunition was scarce. The soldiers were weary and hungry, and now lay shivering in the cold December air.

Rosecrans called a council of war to consider what to do. His corps commanders with their staffs crowded in. The council was full of pale, anxious faces. Rosecrans, looking grave, presided, "his old faded uniform still stiff with the blood and splattered brains of his chief of staff." Thomas, "moving in his slow, deliberate way through the throng to a corner" found a board, and, improvising a seat, leaned back and closed his eyes. A majority of the officers evidently favored a retreat. Near midnight, Rosecrans asked his surgeon general, Eben Swift, if he had wagons enough for the wounded. He said he did. Rosecrans then nudged a dozing Thomas awake to ask him if he would be able to hold his present line or cover a retreat to Overall's Creek. Starting out of his slumber, Thomas exclaimed: "This army can't retreat!"

That is one version of what Thomas said. Another eyewitness account casts him in a still more memorable light. According to Lieutenant John Yaryan, on General Wood's staff, Thomas sat apart, "as always . . . calm, stern, determined, silent and perfectly self-possessed, his hat set squarely on his head. It was a tonic to look at the man." It had begun to rain, and a grim half-hour of silence passed as raindrops continued to pelt the clapboard roof. Finally Rosecrans stood tensely erect. He put the question to each of his generals in turn: Attack or retreat? Yaryan recalled:

> From man to man Rosecrans went around the room, the answer of each, in substance, the same. Thomas was held for the last. I had watched him closely, but not a muscle moved; his eye never left the bed of coals aglow on the hearth. . . . The same set look I had seen when I came in was still there. Rosecrans hesitated when he came to him, and said, "General Thomas, what have you to say?" Without a word of reply, Thomas rose slowly to his feet, buttoned his greatcoat from bottom to top, faced his comrades, and said, "Gentlemen, I know of no better place to die than right here," and walked out of the room into the dripping night.

The rain continued all night, and at dawn was still pouring. The roads, camps, and fields were a wide expanse of mud. Military operations on any substantial scale were impossible, but the next day the Federals dug in. Provisions and ammunition were brought forward. There was only tentative contact: an artillery duel in the morning, followed by skirmishing along the line. That night, however, Rosecrans greatly improved his position when he sent a division across the river to occupy a patch of high ground. That enabled him to enfilade the Rebel right. On January 2, Bragg tried to reclaim the hill, but in a stiff fight, in which the Federals were pressed back to the stream, the Rebels were smashed by cannon massed on a nearby rise. As they fell back, a fresh Union brigade was sent forward by Thomas and rushed upon them with bayonets.

The next day Bragg and his generals took council, and resolved to retreat to avoid another fight. Soon after dusk, their rear columns moved out from their entrenchments, and in the early morning hours of Sunday, January 4, Bragg slipped away to the south, leaving his dead and wounded behind. From Tullahoma, he wired Richmond: "Unable to dislodge the enemy from his intrenchments, and learning of reinforcements to him [in fact, there were none], I withdrew from his front night before last. We have retired from Murfreesboro in perfect order. All our stores are saved."

The following morning, Thomas rode into Murfreesboro, driving the rear guard of the Rebel cavalry before him six or seven miles. McCook's and Crittenden's corps followed and encamped before the town.

Both sides had lost about a quarter of their army, between 9,000 and 10,000 men. But it was the Federals who had held. During the battle, ambulance trains had been drawn up in lines and surgeons had followed the men onto the fields. When the fighting ceased, the trains were rushed in, loaded with the wounded, and hurried away to camp hospitals in the rear. Within two hours after the battle of Friday evening, January 2, the ambulance trains had searched more than a hundred acres of ground. By eleven that night, all the dead had been interred. In Nashville, a large brick building known as the "Brickhouse Hospital" was used for amputations, several tables at once, as human limbs and pieces of flesh were cast out through the windows and the floors ran with blood. The surgeons and their attendants, in dress and appearance, "resembled butchers at work in the shambles." The dead were buried in a long sloping field to the rear.

When Lincoln learned of Bragg's retreat, he wrote Rosecrans, "God bless you, and all with you. Please tender to all, and accept for yourself, a nation's gratitude for your and their skill, endurance, and dauntless courage." From Halleck came: "All honor to the Army of the Cumberland! Thanks to the living, and tears for the lamented dead." That seemed too formulaic to be sincere. In a more proper tribute, the day after Bragg withdrew, Rosecrans attended mass in a rude log cabin on the field. It was the first clear morning after a week of storm and rain. Dead soldiers and horses were still strewn about, and burial parties engaged at their solemn task. Rosecrans, his staff and guests, assembled, communion administered, and a short address delivered by the chaplain from the text: "In Ramah was there a voice heard, lamentation, and weeping, and great mourning, Rachel weeping for her children, and would not be comforted, because they are not." (Matthew 2:18)

Later, in a tribute to the "hard-earned victory" at Stones River, Lincoln would say that "the nation could hardly have lived over" a defeat.

In Lincoln's cabinet, the battle became the subject of debate. Secretary Chase reportedly told Stanton that the outcome proved him right in having urged Lincoln to give Rosecrans the command. Stanton angrily replied that Thomas alone had saved the army from defeat. "Come now, Stanton," said Chase, "be just. We selected Rosecrans, and Rosecrans had the sagacity to select Thomas. Then, you know, there is nothing so successful as success."

In the *Annals of the Army of the Cumberland*, Thomas was called (after the wisest of the Greek warrior-counselors of the *Iliad*) the "Nestor" of the camps. But he was the last man to puff himself up— about rank, fame, or anything else. The war correspondent for *The New York Herald*, William F. G. Shanks, tells us: "He wore the uniform of a colonel for several months after he had been confirmed a brigadier general, and only donned the proper uniform when going into battle at Mill Springs. He was confirmed a major general in June, 1862, but did not mount the twin stars until after the battle of Stones River, fought on the last day of the same year—and then they found their way to his shoulders only by a trick to which his body-servant had been incited by his aides."

By their retreat, the Rebels gave up Middle Tennessee and all hope of regaining any part of the navigable waters of the Cumberland and Tennessee Rivers. Kentucky was also made secure except for raids launched through the mountain gaps. The victory at Stones River could not have been more timely, for it came during one of the darkest periods of the war. The failure of McClellan's campaign in Virginia; the defeat of Pope at Second Bull Run; the blunders at Shiloh; the slow movement of Halleck on Corinth (with the concomitant escape of the Rebels under Beauregard); the scattering of Halleck's huge force; the lost opportunity to destroy Lee's army at Antietam; the fiasco of Buell's East Tennessee–Kentucky campaign; and then, to crown it all, the ruinous assault of Ambrose Burnside against Lee's fortified heights at Fredericksburg on December 13, 1862—these, and other discouraging events, "created a doubt in the public mind that the Union could be restored." That is what Lincoln meant when he said the nation could not have "lived over" another defeat. Moreover, according to David Homer Bates, Manager of the War Department Telegraph Office, who spoke to Lincoln every day, it was the Battle of Stones River—not Antietam—that prevented France and Great Britain from recognizing the Confederate states.

The triumph at Stones River, which Rosecrans owed largely to Thomas, had kept the Union cause alive.

# 7. FROM TULLAHOMA TO CHICKAMAUGA

*"The rain descended, and the floods came and beat upon that house, and it fell not: for it was founded upon a rock."*
—MATTHEW 7:25

After the Federal army took possession of Murfreesboro, it remained for some time to recover from the carnage and exhaustion of the recent battle and refit for a new campaign. Many of the same problems that Rosecrans had confronted before his advance to Stones River confronted him once more, but on a larger scale. To help him, he now had a new chief of staff, James Garfield, a former Ohio state senator and a future president of the United States. At the outset of the war, Garfield had raised a volunteer regiment, took part in fighting in the Big Sandy Valley and at Pound's Gap, and was promoted to brigadier general. He joined Buell's march to Pittsburg Landing as head of a brigade. At Shiloh, he had taken part in the battle of the second day, participated in the subsequent advance on Corinth, and helped rebuild the bridges on the Memphis & Charleston line. Under Rosecrans, he acted as a sometimes go-between with the War Department, which, despite past tensions, seemed eager to patch things up.

When Rosecrans asked that his center and two wings be designated "army corps," as in the Army of the Potomac, Stanton replied on January 7: "The order . . . will be issued today. There is nothing within my power to grant to yourself or your heroic command that will not be cheerfully given." Under the new arrangement, the center under

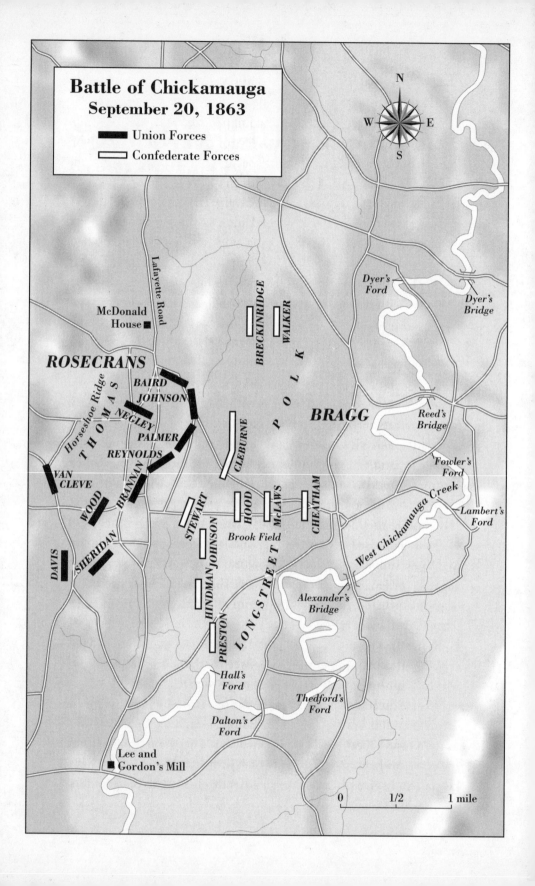

# Battle of Chickamauga
## September 20, 1863

- ▬ Union Forces
- ▭ Confederate Forces

N
W E
S

Lafayette Road

McDonald House ■

Dyer's Ford

Dyer's Bridge

**ROSECRANS**

BRECKINRIDGE  WALKER

P O L K

**BRAGG**

Reed's Bridge

BAIRD
JOHNSON
Horseshoe Ridge
NEGLEY
PALMER
T H O M A S
REYNOLDS

CLEBURNE

Fowler's Ford

VAN CLEVE
BRANNAN

West Chickamauga Creek

Lambert's Ford

WOOD

HOOD  McLAWS  CHEATHAM

STEWART

DAVIS  SHERIDAN

Brook Field

L O N G S T R E E T

HINDMAN  JOHNSON

Alexander's Bridge

PRESTON

Hall's Ford

Thedford's Ford

Dalton's Ford

Lee and Gordon's Mill ■

0    1/2    1 mile

Thomas was designated the Fourteenth Army Corps, the right wing the Twentieth, the left the Twenty-first.

As Rosecrans reorganized and equipped his army and accumulated stores, he sought a month's reserve of supplies, ammunition for at least two great battles, long and secure lines of communication, and a cavalry capable of dealing with Bragg's, which was 10,000 or 12,000 strong. Of late, Confederate cavalry (under Joseph Wheeler) had increased their raids fivefold on Union strategic sites. Most of the water stations, several depots, rolling stock, engines, and so on had been damaged; a major tunnel "filled up for . . . eight hundred feet"; and "every single bridge and trestlework on the main stem and branches, with the exception of the bridge over the Barren River and four small bridges," had been struck. Until the railroad was repaired, supplies lagged and could not be gleaned from local sources, since Rebel raiders had also scoured the countryside for miles around. Even potatoes and onions were luxuries, and scurvy threatened the ranks. The army, on half-rations, made do with meager fare. On January 25, more territory was given to Rosecrans to protect when Forts Henry, Donelson, and Heiman—in effect, the Cumberland River—were transferred from Grant's command. The very next day Wheeler boldly set out to wrest Fort Donelson from Union control. He swept past the Cumberland Iron Works to Dover, but his dreaded onslaught was thwarted when gunboats and troop transports docked at the fort on February 2. These new Union troops, under the inspired command of General Gordon Granger, called themselves the Army of Kentucky, and compelled Wheeler to withdraw. Granger then proceeded to Nashville, where he joined the built-up forces in which the Army of the Cumberland was engaged.

The army's medical facilities were also readied for battles to come. The field hospital at Murfreesboro was almost a city of tents, furnished with broad streets and alleyways with gutters on each side. Above the gutters were sidewalks made of planks. In the town itself, the largest and best-ventilated buildings were reserved for the sick and wounded. The walls were whitened, the floors thoroughly scoured, and neat cot-bedsteads ranged in exact lines through the long rooms. The mattresses were filled with fresh straw and covered with crisp new blankets, a soft pillow, and clean white sheets. Altogether the army's Medical Department boasted thirty-five general hospitals staffed by 400 surgeons and 3,000 nurses and attendants. Some 600 ambulances (in those days, horse-driven covered wagons) were kept ready to pick up the fallen on the field.

As always, Thomas kept his own corps in splendid shape. It was often said that his men saw more of him than they did of their own colonels and brigadiers. Unlike most officers of high rank, he concerned himself with every aspect of their training, and his care was epitomized by his remark to a battery commander struggling with a broken harness: "Keep everything in order. The fate of a battle may turn on a buckle or a linch-pin." In attending to his own tasks, Thomas expected no less of himself. Especially when a movement or a battle was impending, he kept everything up to date. "He made it a rule," wrote an aide, "to finish up all his work to the minutest detail.... Wherever his signature was required, even if it were only in a copy-book, he invariably signed his name himself." Every one of his aides was also selected "on account of his peculiar fitness for the particular duty required of him, and no indolent, lazy offficer ever found asylum on his staff." This was not accidental. He knew what it took to make a soldier, and what he was worth after he was made. For he looked upon the lives of his men, wrote a fellow general, "as a sacred trust, not to be carelessly imperiled. Whenever he moved to battle, it was certain that everything had been done that prudence, deliberation, thought, and cool judgment could do under surrounding circumstances to insure success commensurate with the cost of their lives." From time to time, he would visit the regimental hospitals to make sure the sick and wounded were well-cared for. In after years, many a hospital steward and company cook remembered these surprise personal inspections and how, for example, on one occasion "his face hardened into a white heat of passion when he found that a drunken commissary had neglected to provide sufficient food." Taking out his penknife, Thomas "ripped off the fellow's shoulder-straps, and said, 'Go home, Sir, by the next train. You shall not feed my soldiers.'"

In training new recruits, Thomas paid scant attention to "school-yard drill." He considered such exercises as "gotten up for show" and therefore "worse than useless"—as divorced from the imperatives of fighting as "a dancing school." He favored the real-life practice of skirmishing and reconnaissance expeditions that inured men to actual combat and dispelled some of their fears. After one such outing, in which new troops showed their mettle, Thomas said with pride:

> It is a question of nerve we have to solve and not of dexterity. It is not how to touch elbows and fire a gun; it is how to touch elbows and fire a gun under fire. We are all cowards in the presence of immediate death. This is the law of our being. It is as necessary to keep the earth inhabited as hunger. We can overcome that fear in war through familiarity. The South came into the field better equipped in this respect that the North, for at the South men were more accustomed to violence and, therefore, more familiar with death. What we have to do is to make veterans. The great error in McClellan's organization was in his avoidance in fighting. On another occasion, he explained: "McClellan made a grave mistake in not skirmishing every day of the nine months he was organizing at Washington. It was like the poor woman who warned her daughter not to go near the water yet consented to have her learn to swim."

Thomas did not discount the importance of formal discipline; but he also cherished the independent-mindedness of the American soldier as a strength. "The solution of the vexed question as to how we may have an army under a republic," he once remarked, "is solved by the French axiom, 'Soldiers on duty, comrades when off.' " In autocratic societies and states, he ventured, officers could lord it over their men at all times, and might even succeed in enhancing their own authority. But among Americans that fostered a rebellious spirit, because it contradicted their democratic ideals.

Indeed, for all his self-confessed reserve, Thomas had a splendid rapport with his troops. They found him accessible, and knew him by such affectionate and familiar epithets as "Uncle George" or "Old Pap," because of his fatherly regard for their comfort and morale. He also had "great fondness for light humor and pleasantry," and a quiet warmth of manner that won his soldiers' hearts more surely "than any momentary familiarity could do." On occasion, he would sit and visit by the campfires or listen to some of their droll anecdotes and tales. William F. G. Shanks, the war correspondent for *The New York Herald*, remembered Thomas laughing at the singing of comic Irish songs; and Colonel John Beatty, who later wrote his vivid *Memoirs of a Volunteer*, recalled a party attended by top-ranking officers of the Army of the Cumberland in which Thomas was as merry as the rest. Yet in such mingling his natural decorum imposed its own restraints. Colonel Henry Stone, long a member of his staff, tells us:

> All his personal habits marked him as a gentleman of refinement and self-control. He was extremely neat in dress and person, and free from every kind of offensiveness of speech or manner. He hated vulgarity and loudness and pretension. While not a puritan, certainly not of the type Macaulay describes, but a lover of all manly sports and exercises, with great enjoyment of jollity and good fellowship in others, he was himself abstemious and moderate in all things. He drank less whiskey than any officer I knew in the service who drank any at all, never taking it to while away an idle hour or for mere companionship, but only when tired or exhausted. Yet he always produced it when visited, and kept a staff officer who was an expert in mixing toddies. He never smoked; his private life was as pure and stainless as a saint's; he lived always in the full light of day, with no secrets to hide and no habits of which to be ashamed. He was a strong, rugged, vigorous, complete, well-rounded man, physically, mentally and morally.

> No portrait that I have ever seen of General Thomas begins to do justice to the manly strength and comeliness of his form and face. In any assembly, he would be noticeable for the grace and easy dignity of his bearing, as well as for his countenance, marked by clear intelligence, and a winning smile which lighted up all his features. His brow was very heavy and projecting, and so overshadowed his eyes—which, as General [James] Garfield well says, "were cold gray to his enemies, but warm deep blue to his friends,"—that, in sitting for a photograph, their light and expression were almost wholly lost. Such pictures wear a grim and almost forbidding look,

entirely at variance with his ordinary, every-day appearance. But, at all times, one could read in his every look the story of resistless strength, which neither time nor fate could overcome. His whole appearance expressed unconquerable power, as gentle but ineradicable as one of the elemental forces. His voice was singularly pleasant and attractive, [with] musical tones. His inherent dignity forbade undue familiarity; but with the members of his personal and military family, there was unbounded freedom of exchange. The men in the ranks never hesitated to seek him out if they wanted anything, and were sure to receive considerate attention. He once went on the bail-bond of one of his old soldiers, whom he knew only as a sentinel about his headquarters, when sued for a debt for which another was responsible, walking down to the magistrate's with him as if it were the natural thing for a major-general to do.

Such a lack of pretension allowed his sympathies the broadest scope. Thomas never rode along a road on which his men were marching, for example, kicking up dust or splattering mud in their faces, as generals in some ostentatious show of dash often did; instead, he traveled in parallel lanes, paths, and fields. His headquarters also became "a mobile humane society," with a collection of various stray creatures he picked up. General Oliver Howard tells us: "He was habitually kind and gentle, and eminently just in all the relations of life. His horse, the mules around him, and the sleek cat that followed him and lay purring at his feet, received unfailing evidence of his gentle soul." To all animals he was a friend and protector, and some of his legendary outbursts of temper were reserved for the inhumane. He once upbraided a teamster with such force for beating his mules over the head with the butt of his whip, that the man fled (as he thought) for his life into the woods. Again, when some orderlies were caught chasing a stray goose about, hoping to turn it into a meal, he flamed out so that everybody ran and hid from his wrath. After a short circling flight, the goose stopped its shrill clamor and, "quacking in diminuendo, waddled over to Thomas, and, sensing a benefactor, settled at his feet." The goose looked up, Thomas looked down, and the goose became another mascot of the camp. Some of his officers emulated his feeling and concern. "There is no suffering so intense as that of animals in their helpless and dependent state," wrote Colonel John Beatty. "A man can give vent to his sufferings, he can ask for assistance, he can find some relief either in crying, praying, or cursing; but for the poor exhausted and abandoned beast there is no help, no relief, no hope."

While Rosecrans was at Murfreesboro, Bragg had established his headquarters at Tullahoma, a small town on Rock Creek, thirty-two miles to the south. Tullahoma lay at the junction of two main lines of track, the Nashville & Chattanooga and the McMinnville & Manchester lines. It was a good defensive position as a base of operations and enabled him to move rapidly on an anterior line. It also served to draw Rosecrans from a direct movement on Chattanooga, which the Rebels had labored hard to fortify. Chattanooga was the ultimate aim of the Union advance. The rugged gateway to the South, it was the real key (as Jefferson Davis later acknowledged) to the outcome of the war. "The fate of empire," wrote Donn Piatt, "so far as the South was concerned, rested on Chattanooga and the Army of the Cumberland. . . . To conquer and hold Chattanooga was to flank the army under Lee and confine all that was left of the war to the cotton states."

Bragg held the line of railroad south, but would certainly destroy it in retreat. The wagon roads were rude and rough through the Cumberland range, and elaborate preparations had to be made to move a great army across mountains and rivers with horses, mules, wagons, compact army stores, clothing, and equipment on an interior summer campaign. That was one reason for what seemed to the War Department the army's long delay. Meanwhile, it had taken a full six months to reconstruct the Louisville & Nashville railway (the army's main line of supply) and provide it with an adequate guard. Rosecrans also hoped to avoid moving his army through the toilsome road conditions created by spring rains. From Murfreesboro south to the Cumberland Mountains, the soil was a light, sandy loam that, once drenched, became like quicksand, in which artillery and wagons sank almost to the hub. But as winter passed into spring and spring into summer, the War Department chafed.

Halleck had already indirectly prodded Rosecrans to advance with a letter, dated March 1, that he had also sent to Grant. At the time, there was a vacancy in the rank of major general in the Regular Army; and Halleck, as an enticement, offered it to the first general to gain a decisive victory in the war. Grant, then mired before Vicksburg, took the letter under advisement. Rosecrans, however, was insulted and replied on the 6th he didn't need any incentive to do his duty, felt "degraded" at the imputation, and declared that any general who would fight more for his own benefit than that of the country "would come by his commission basely" and "deserved to be despised."

Halleck was angered and abashed by this rebuke. He came from a different world. Before his misguided appointment by Lincoln, he had managed a large law practice in California centered on vast real estate deals. The incentive-based commercial world he knew was one in which people were motivated by the opportunistic prospect of large fees and commissions. He naturally thought some analogous offer within the military sphere might be as tempting to Rosecrans as it would be to himself. But the practical result of this exchange was to strengthen Halleck's military and political alliance with Grant, and shortchange the Army of the Cumberland, since Halleck thereafter turned a deaf ear to any military requests Rosecrans would make. Grant, stalled in front of Vicksburg, was concerned that troops might soon be sent from Tennessee to oppose him and began to complain of Rosecrans's failure to march against Bragg. But the risk was otherwise. Before the battle of Stones River, a division had been detached from Bragg's army for Vicksburg; since that time thousands of Confederate troops had left the bluffs above Vicksburg to strengthen Bragg's force. Rosecrans, not Grant, suffered. It was Grant's paralysis in front of Vicksburg that threatened the coordinate success of both Union army campaigns. By April 4, Grant had learned that it was Bragg who was being reinforced. However, he downplayed the fact that troops were being drawn from his front. He wired Halleck: "From information from the South by way of Corinth, I learn that the enemy in front of Rosecrans have been reinforced from Richmond, Charleston, Savannah, Mobile, and a few from Vicksburg." That "few" turned out to be several thousand men. Yet Grant tells us in his memoirs:

"After the investment of Vicksburg, Bragg's army was largely depleted to strengthen Johnston, in Mississippi, who was being reinforced to raise the siege . . . The siege of Vicksburg had drawn from Rosecrans' front so many of the enemy that his chances of victory were much greater than they would be if he waited until the siege was over, when these troops could be returned."

None of that was true.

Rosecrans, in any case, saw the strategic situation in reverse. He was convinced it was in the country's best interests to threaten Bragg from where he was, while still increasing the strength of his army. If he moved too soon and met defeat, Bragg's army would then be freed to join the fight against Grant. On the other hand, if Grant failed, and Bragg was reinforced, he could better withstand an assault if close to his base. In short, it seemed to him unwise to fight two great battles at the same time. "To show how differently things are viewed here," he wrote Halleck on June 11, "I called on my corps and division commanders and generals of cavalry for answers in writing" on these and other such questions. "Not one," he reported, thought "an advance advisable until Vicksburg's fate is determined. Admitting these officers to have a reasonable share of military sagacity, courage, and patriotism, you perceive that there are graver and stronger reasons than probably appear at Washington for the attitude of this army. I therefore counsel caution and patience at headquarters."

In the face of new harrassment, Rosecrans was so vexed that he threatened to resign. Thomas did his best to mollify him by making allowances for Washington's obtuseness. "Our government," he said, "is struggling under a heavy weight that we in the field have no knowledge of. We must take it for granted that they are doing all in their power to meet our demands." Nonetheless, Thomas thought it would be helpful if Stanton or Lincoln would send a fair-minded emissary to the army "to learn and report the actual" state of affairs. "We cannot move from our base of supplies," he noted frankly, "until this place is rendered secure." Even if, as the War Department insisted, Bragg's army was not any larger than the one Rosecrans had, Bragg's entrenched defense line gave him a formidable advantage that practically doubled the strength of his force. At Duck River, that line formed an irregular curve from Shelbyville to Wartrace, where the forced labor of some 3,000 slaves, brought up mainly from Georgia and Alabama, had created a five-mile circuit of earthworks, forts, and abatis, surpassing the famed Rebel works at Corinth, which for several weeks held a Union army of 120,000 at bay. In addition, Bragg's cavalry, posted at McMinnville on his right, was thrown out as far as Guy's Gap. Hoover's Gap and Liberty Gap were also held by troops under Bragg's ablest lieutenant, General William Hardee. Behind these, Bragg had turned Tullahoma into a great supply depot with Chattanooga to his rear. In short, Bragg's fortified line was "far better," noted Thomas, than the one he had had on Stones River "and we all know what that was."

Historians have sometimes assumed that when the government in Washington waxed impatient, it was warranted and just. But in the history of the war, from the beginning almost to the end, haste made for horrible waste, and ignorant political pressures created many mass graves. Impetuous generals were often favored by politicians as "men of action." But in the end the North gained little and lost much by its rash assaults and flawed campaigns.

In June 1863 Rosecrans began his advance. His plan was to feint toward Bragg's center-left at Shelbyville, pierce the mountain passes, turn his right, and gain his rear. By way of Manchester, he would then seize his Tullahoma base. The approaches to Bragg's front were by narrow gaps through rough country that forced the Federal columns along the straitened roads. Rosecrans, however, "declined to accept the slaughter tendered him on a line that would be fiercely fought for and conquered, if at all, at a fearful loss to himself, while leaving Bragg a line of retreat that would" make any victory null. Instead, he sought to maneuver Bragg into accepting a battlefield of his own choice. Meanwhile, the corps commanded by Thomas with three other divisions had moved out on the Manchester Pike. One division included a brigade of mounted infantry, equipped with repeating carbines, under Colonel John T. Wilder, which engaged a superior infantry force at Hoover's Gap. On the same day, Liberty Gap was attacked by a brigade under McCook. After fierce resistance, both gaps were carried, and Bragg discovered that the entire Union army was on his right flank.

Bragg's once strong position on Duck River was no longer tenable. He could either march out and fight, or fall back upon Chattanooga, which he did. Rosecrans at once pursued and took possession of the roads. That forced Bragg across Elk River and into the hills. On the morning of July 4, Rosecrans's whole force advanced to the foot of the mountains, to find the enemy in full retreat toward Chattanooga and the Georgia line.

The whole Tullahoma campaign had been a strategic tour de force. It was the first time in the war that a large army had been forced from its fortified works by flank approaches—in this case, through mountain passes the Rebels thought secure. With the loss of only 600 men killed, wounded, or missing, the Army of the Cumberland, with its nine divisions and twenty brigades, marching and wheeling through sixteen days of continuous rain (the greatest reported rainfall in the area up till that time), had maneuvered Bragg, with his seven divisions and twenty-three brigades, out of his natural and artificial strongholds, and forced him across the Tennessee River. Bragg's killed and wounded, though plainly larger, were not reported, but about 1,600 men were captured, including fifty-nine officers, along with eight field pieces, three rifled siege guns, and a large amount of ammunition and stores. Every one of Rosecrans's corps commanders, headed by Thomas, was impressed by his achievement. Washington less so, because he had seemed to take too long to get going, despite his splendid success.

Meanwhile, in the course of the Vicksburg campaign, Grant had lost thousands of men—some from frontal assaults, most from three fruitless make-work attempts to dig canals through malarial swamps. In the East, Burnside had been replaced by Joseph "Fighting Joe" Hooker, who had formed a plan for crossing the Rappahannock, cutting off Lee from Richmond, and going on the attack. But he stopped short, allowed himself to be thrown on the defensive, and was outgeneraled on May 4 at Chancellorsville. "While carrion crows darkened the horizon about the Army of the Potomac," wrote one contemporary, "and the mocking birds around Vicksburg took up and warbled the dead march in Saul that was being played continuously over the unhonored graves of brave men . . . the Army of the Cumberland was repairing railroads, opening highways, accumulating supplies, while working its way through mountain passes, over rivers, and scaling palisades, that it might carry in triumph to the front the fortunes of the [North]."

However, the masterly Tullahoma campaign "was neither appreciated at Washington nor known to the people," one writer wryly noted. "So accustomed were we to big battles and frightful slaughter that a great victory like this obtained without the useless loss of a man seemed insignificant and tame." As John Fitch, provost judge of the Army of the Cumberland, pointed out at the time, had the Army of the Cumberland stormed the ramparts of Tullahoma, spiked its seventy cannon, and driven back its Rebel defenders at the cost of 10,000 men, the victory would have been chronicled in story and song.

The irony of all this was not lost on Rosecrans. On July 7, after George Gordon Meade had replaced Hooker and bested Lee at Gettysburg, Secretary of War Stanton sent Rosecrans the following wire: "Lee's army overthrown, Grant victorious. You and your noble army now have the chance to give the finishing blow to the Rebellion. Will you neglect the chance?" Rosecrans, incensed, replied, "You do not appear to observe the fact that this noble army has driven the Rebels from Middle Tennessee. I beg on behalf of this army that the War Department may not overlook so great an event because it is not written in letters of blood." Actually, the War Department considered Meade's victory at Gettysburg incomplete. Lincoln, in particular, thought Meade had been slow to pursue Lee in retreat, and vented his frustration in a letter to him he never sent: "My dear General," Lincoln wrote, with uncharacteristic petulance,

I do not believe you appreciate the magnitude of the misfortune involved in Lee's escape. He was within your easy grasp, and to have closed upon him would, in connection with our other late successes, have ended the war. As it is, the war will be prolonged indefinitely. It would be unreasonable to expect, and I do not expect, that you can now effect much. Your golden opportunity is gone. I am distressed immeasurably because of it. I beg you will not consider this a prosecution or persecution of yourself. As you have learned that I was dissatisfied, I have thought it best to kindly tell you why.

With regard to Vicksburg, Lincoln looked past the losses and proclaimed: "The Father of Waters now rolls its waves unvexed to the sea."

Between the Army of the Cumberland and Bragg in Chattanooga lay the broad Tennessee River and the high plateau and gorges of the Cumberland range. That range, a spur of the Appalachians, stretched through Tennessee into North Georgia and was as difficult terrain as the Federals would face in the war. Its heights included Sand, Raccoon, and Pigeon Mountains, Missionary Ridge (so-called from a Catholic mission built for Indians on the bluff), and the crest of Lookout Mountain beyond the wide valley of Lookout Creek. On the top of Lookout Mountain was rolling table land; around its base, near the water's edge, the Nashville & Chattanooga Railroad had blasted out its track. In such a setting, as the struggle for Chattanooga played out between two mighty armies, it seemed to resemble "a conflict of Titans upon gigantic camping grounds." The vastness of the theater, its extremely broken and diversified nature, mountain ranges, narrow gaps, deep valleys, thick forests, rivers, and streams in snakelike and bewildering convolutions, gave an epic character to the whole scene.

Bragg considered his position at Chattanooga next to impregnable. It lay behind the left bank of the river, and where the gorge of the Tennessee broke through, it was commanded from the heights on both sides. As Rosecrans, now deep in enemy territory, began to work out the details of his new campaign, he was appalled to receive on August 4 a dispatch from Halleck saying: "Your forces must move forward without delay. You will daily report the movement of each corps till you cross the Tennessee River." Rosecrans replied: "As I have determined to cross the river as soon as practicable, and have been making all preparations and getting such information as may enable me to do so without being driven back . . . I wish to know if your order is intended to take away my discretion as to the time and manner of moving my troops." Halleck responded curtly: "The orders for the advance of your army . . . are peremptory." Rosecrans once more called all his corps commanders together to discuss their strategic options and read them his reply. He reminded Halleck of the hazards of mountain warfare and the challenge the army faced in crossing sixty miles of formidable terrain. "To obey your order literally," he said, "would be to push our troops into the mountains" at a place where Bragg would become aware of the movement and oppose it in force. That would bring the campaign to an abrupt and unhappy end. But if allowed another week or so to ready his river crossings, he could deceive Bragg completely and prevail. "If the movement which I propose can not be regarded as obedience to your order, I respectfully request a modification of it or to be relieved from the command." "That's right," Thomas reportedly exclaimed. "Stand by that and we will stand by you." The other corps leaders concurred, the telegram was sent, and Halleck drew back: "I have communicated to you the wishes of the Government," he said. "The means you are to employ and the roads you are to follow are left to your discretion."

Rosecrans took the time he needed and ten days later, on August 14, the advance on Chattanooga began. Rosecrans was too able and wise a strategist to assail Bragg in his stronghold directly when the country was open to him on either flank. He therefore spread out along the northwestern base of the Cumberland range—with camps at McMinnville, Tullahoma, Winchester, and Dechard—and advanced his army of about 60,000 on a fifty-mile front. Chattanooga lay to the southeast. His plan was to cross the Tennessee River below Chattanooga, turn the Confederate left, intercept Bragg's communications, and take the town from the rear. His three army corps were divided into seven columns (not counting the cavalry and Wilder's brigade) with Crittenden on the left, Thomas in the center, and McCook on the right. After winding their troops through steep gorges and ravines, Thomas and McCook moved their unseen columns downstream. While they advanced to their crossing points, Rosecrans built rows of campfires north across the slopes to convince Bragg he was crossing above. Troops under Crittenden also marched across open spaces exposed to view, countermarched behind the hills, and passed again and again through the same spaces, as Union drums and bugles sounded for great distances along the mountain heights. To create the impression that a bridge was being built upstream, the Federals let the ends of logs and rails and bits of lumber float down past the town. Axes, saws, and hammers could be heard vigorously at work in a feigned semblance of boat building, while fifty miles to the south where the crossing would take place train cars filled with bridge- and boat-building parts and materials were unloaded behind the woods and hills, at points entirely screened from Rebel view.

Over the course of four days, beginning on August 29, the army crossed the Tennessee River at various points, as 4,000 heavily laden wagons were bounced from the banks onto the narrow pontoon causeways and artillery vehicles rumbled over the planks. Dozens of boats of all kinds, including enormous canoes hewn out of tall poplars, and a flotilla of log rafts ferried the army across. One pontoon bridge, 1,250 feet in length, had been laid down at Caperton's Ferry, three miles from Stevenson; another, twice as long, at Bridgeport, twelve miles up. Elsewhere, Union cavalry splashed into the river, spurring their steeds into the deep water to the opposite shore. By September 4, the entire command had gained the river's south side—without the loss of a single animal or man.

His army safely across, Rosecrans pushed heavy columns through the hills. While McCook crossed Raccoon and Sand Mountains, Thomas marched fifty-one miles south from Bridgeport through deep wooded gulches and over mountain spurs to Bragg's rear. Bragg had failed to secure the gaps on his side of Lookout Mountain, which Thomas seized on September 8. "The broad Tennessee below us," wrote one Union soldier, "seemed like a ribbon of silver; beyond rose the Cumberland, which we had crossed. The valley on both sides was alive with the moving armies of the Union, while almost the entire transportation of the army filled the roads and fields along the Tennessee. . . . No one could survey the grand scene on that bright autumn day unmoved, unimpressed with its grandeur and of the meaning conveyed by the presence of that mighty host."

In just three weeks from the time the advance began, and five days from the time it crossed the Tennessee, the Army of the Cumberland had marched 300 miles from its base of supplies, crossed three mountain ranges with ridges up to 2,400 feet in height, and forded one of the mighty rivers of the West. In so doing, it had repeated the Tullahoma campaign on a still larger scale, in the face of much more formidable obstacles, again with little loss. Well might Rosecrans argue, if only with a fleeting hurrah, that he could do more with strategy than other commanders with their huge expense of lives. General M. C. Meigs, quartermaster general of the U.S. Army, who later made a close study of the campaign, pronounced it, "Not only the greatest operation in our war, but a great thing when compared with any war."

Cut off from reinforcements and supplies, Bragg evacuated Chattanooga on the 9th, and fell back to Lafayette, fifteen miles to the south. In passing down the valley in front of Thomas, Bragg endeavored to cut off some advanced Union regiments; but Thomas cautiously drew them up within the jaws of the gaps. At the same time, Crittenden crossed the main body of his troops over the Tennessee at and above Bridgeport, went over the brow of Lookout Mountain, and finding that Bragg had fled Chattanooga, took possession of the town. Had Rosecrans stopped at Chattanooga and entrenched his army strongly around it, his campaign would have been proclaimed an unblemished success. Instead, he left only one brigade to hold it, mistook Bragg's orderly withdrawal for a headlong retreat, rashly broke up his force, and ordered McCook's corps to chase Bragg south to Lafayette and Crittenden toward Ringgold. Thomas, who considered the idea of chasing Bragg imprudent, was ordered to proceed eastward through Lookout Mountain by Steven's and Cooper's Gaps. Though Bragg had been forced out of Chattanooga, now by apparent flight he lured Rosecrans on. He sent men into the Union lines with reports designed to convince him that his flight was frantic—that his army was "badly demoralized," "whipped," "short of rations," and so on, and would "not stop short of Atlanta" if pursued. That was just what Rosecrans wished to hear. Indeed, ever since the Tullahoma campaign, Rosecrans had begun to regard Bragg "as a man of little enterprise," one general wrote, whereas Thomas urged "great caution," for he "did not underestimate him" and "knew him well."

Thomas was not deceived by Bragg's ruse. He pointed out the extreme danger of scattering the troops, and knew that Bragg would detect their dispersed condition and try to attack the separated corps in detail. He also knew that by taking strong ground south of Chattanooga, Bragg could secure his own communications, and wait for reinforcements to come in. At the very moment Rosecrans was dividing his army, reinforcements were coming up by the thousands, from Charleston, Vicksburg, and Mobile. Some 8,000 Georgia state militia had also been summoned, and two divisions in ten brigades, or 14,000 men, under James Longstreet (Lee's finest corps commander) from the East. With Longstreet came Edward Porter Alexander's artillery battalion of twenty-six guns. In one week's time, Bragg's army grew from about 40,000 to upward of 80,000 men. Counting Longstreet, Robert E. Lee put the figure at 90,000 in a letter to Jefferson Davis dated September 14, 1863.

The authorities in Washington had no idea what was going on. Halleck thought part of Bragg's army had been detached to reinforce Lee (not the other way around), and that Rosecrans had occupied Chattanooga in the military sense. And so on September 11, the very day Bragg's reinforced army was gearing up to attack the scattered corps, Halleck wired Rosecrans: "After holding the mountain passes on the west and Dalton, or some point on the railroad, to prevent the return of Bragg's army, it will be decided whether your army shall move further south into Georgia and Alabama. It is reported here that a part of Bragg's army is reinforcing Lee. It is important that the truth of this should be ascertained as soon as possible." By then, Longstreet's troops had almost made their way to Bragg.

Meanwhile, General James S. Negley's division of Thomas's corps had reached Dug Gap, a mountain pass not far from Lafayette. There a Confederate officer had been captured and closely questioned on the disposition of Bragg's troops. "He was not very communicative,"

Thomas reported, "but he was generous enough to advise General Negley not to advance or he would get severely whipped." Two days later, Negley discovered "an overwhelming force" to his front and retreated to Stevens's Gap. Thomas informed Rosecrans of this on the 12th. Rosecrans thought Negley must be wrong. With a touch of condescension, he wired Thomas: "Your dispatches of 10:30 last night and of 4 this morning have been received. After maturely weighing the notes, the General commanding is induced to think that General Negley withdrew more through prudence than compulsion. He trusts his loss is not serious." Thomas replied promptly that other information (including a dispatch from McCook) confirmed that the enemy was concentrated at Lafayette in force. On his own responsibility, he ordered three divisions forward to support Negley in order to repel a possible attack. Rosecrans, who had not yet divested himself of the idea that Bragg was in retreat, was displeased with Thomas for having done this. But his confident exultation at having outflanked Bragg soon turned to bitter gloom when he realized his energetic pursuit had exposed his army to demise. After Crittenden also encountered enemy divisions gathered south of Chattanooga, Rosecrans began to see the light. He suddenly realized the grave danger his army was in and that he had to concentrate its divided columns as soon as he could. It was, as he said, now "a matter of life and death."

When Assistant Secretary of War Charles A. Dana arrived at his headquarters, Rosecrans, "burst out in angry abuse of the Government at Washington." He had not been sustained, he said; his plans had been thwarted; his requests ignored. Both Stanton and Halleck had done all they could, he declared, to prevent his success. "General Rosecrans," said Dana, somewhat nonplussed, "I have no authority to listen to complaints against the Government. I was sent here for the purpose of finding out what the Government could do to aid you, and have no right to confer with you on other matters." Rosecrans then "quieted down" and explained the straits he found himself in.

The next day, Rosecrans and Dana went up to see Thomas at Stevens's Gap. Dana watched Thomas ride up to his headquarters tent at a dignified pace—somewhat like Jehovah on horseback, massive, judicial, impassive, possessing an Olympian calm. Everything under

Thomas was found to be going well, wrote Dana. "The movements for the concentration of the three corps going forward" with the energy required. If Bragg did opt to retreat, he thought "the Army of the Cumberland had practically gained a position from which it could effectually advance upon Rome and Atlanta, and deliver there the finishing blow of the war." Though Dana's confidence in Rosecrans soon waned, he found himself in awe of the late campaign. "The difficulties of gaining this position, of crossing the Cumberland Mountains, passing the Tennessee, turning and occupying Chattanooga, traversing the mountain ridges of northern Georgia, and seizing the passes which led southward had been enormous. It was only when I came personally to examine the region that I appreciated what had been done."

Bragg's countermoves, however, threatened to turn all this on its head. After reconstituting his army, he had entrenched on a strong line fronting the slope of Lookout Mountain and the advantage was now on his side. Though McCook had been ordered to link up with Thomas, he had to take a circuitous route to do so safely, which took him four and a half days over forty-six miles. Meanwhile, Bragg had begun to march back toward Chattanooga on the 17th, to attack the Union columns before they could be joined. He had already missed two chances to effect their demise (partly through the lethargy of Leonidas Polk, one of his wing commanders); now as McCook and Crittenden converged, Bragg tried to get between the Union army and the river by seizing one of the Chattanooga roads. In the process, he had drawn his army together along the banks of a creek called Chickamauga, a Cherokee word meaning "River of Death." Bragg was on the east side of the creek, the Federals on the west, some ways back from the bank. Having passed below the point where the Union left rested, Bragg crossed the fords and bridges, in the early hours of September 19, and prepared to sweep by the Union left flank.

By an energetic night march, Thomas thrust his column between Bragg and Chattanooga, and at daylight held the line. His speed saved the day, for just two hours later, the Rebel advance came out onto the Chattanooga road. About ten o'clock that morning, Thomas told each of his division commanders, "See that the men are provided with 20 rounds of ammunition in their pockets in addition to the cartridge boxes being full." Neither army knew the exact position of the other. In this uncertain manner, battle lines formed. As Bragg prepared to assail the Union left, Thomas, feeling his way carefully through the woods to his front, struck the Southern right, where cavalry under Nathan Bedford Forrest held the advance. That brought the battle on. Forrest was forced back, but other units came forward to his aid. The Rebels were surprised to find the road occupied in their front, and followed Thomas's column back to Union lines.

The fighting spread, and as it did it drew more and more troops from both sides to that flank. Bragg gave up on his planned attack and moved to the defense of the Confederate right. Rosecrans rode among his troops as they converged to the point of heaviest fire. The shouts and yells and the roll of musketry swelled the din of battle to a roar. The fighting was fierce, without clear advantage, and as the day wore on, the Rebels tried to turn the Union left. At one point, a Rebel column came out into a clearing flanked by a deep ditch. John Wilder, and his mounted infantry brigade, equipped with their seven-shot repeater carbines, were waiting and "every shot seemed to tell." Scarcely a man escaped. The Rebels perished with such efficient slaughter that Wilder recalled afterward: "It actually seemed a pity to kill men so. They fell in heaps; and I had it in my heart to order the firing to cease, to end the awful sight. When the firing stopped, one could have walked two hundred yards down that ditch on dead Rebels, without touching the ground." After a brief interlude, to the right, the Rebels came on again and the opposing lines dueled with bayonets. The Lafayette road, along which the broken lines of each army rallied and reformed, became known as the "bloody lane."

Though it was plain that the Army of the Cumberland was contending against a much larger force, the unexpected start to the fighting had upset all of Bragg's battle plans. Some of the Virginia veterans were soon exasperated at not gaining the upper hand. They reportedly cried out, as they charged, "You're not fighting with conscripts now!" to which the Western farm boys under Thomas shouted back, "And you're not fighting Eastern clerks!" As often in the war, the woodlands prevented the hostile lines from catching sight of each other at any distance and forced firing at point-blank range. Thousands on both sides fell fighting at close quarters, their faces at times burnt by the blazing powder at the very muzzles of the guns.

The day was long and sultry, a red sun descending in the sky. The weary men were suffering from hunger and thirst, and to one Union soldier, as the battle wound down, the final fusillade of Rebel shells in the twilight seemed "like a firmament of pestilential stars." That night everything had a doleful cast. As the Union troops settled in, the ground was white with frost but no fires lit, to prevent the direction of the lines from being shown. Here and there, dimly burning candles flickered like fireflies as nurses and other medics searched for wounded along the bloody ground. All over the fields and woods lay the unburied dead, their pale faces made ghastlier by streaks of blood and clotted hair. Many had black powder stains on their lips where they had torn off the ends of cartridges with their teeth. Faint moonlight, filtering through dense foliage, added to the weird spell of the scene. "The night after a battle" wrote one Confederate general, "is dreary enough to a victorious army cheered by triumph." But to the two armies in virtual stalemate, near enough to hear the groans of the wounded and dying on each side, "the scene was indescribably oppressive and sad."

In the days leading up to the battle, Lincoln, wrote one eyewitness, had "remained in the telegraph office, sometimes for hours, waiting for the latest news. . . . The tension was very great," as Lincoln, Stanton, and Halleck "almost constantly" conferred. On the night of the 19th Rosecrans summoned Thomas and the other corps commanders to his headquarters at the Widow Glenn's house (near Lee and Gordon's Mill) for a midnight council of war. Recalled Charles Dana: "Rosecrans began by asking each of the corps commanders for a report of the condition of his troops and of the position they occupied also for his opinion of what was to be done. Each proposition was discussed by the entire council as it was made. General Thomas was so tired—he had not slept at all the night before, and he had been in battle all day—that he kept dozing off." Now and then, when he was roused for his opinion, he would say, simply, "Strengthen the left." Finally, at one in the morning, the plan for the next day's battle was set.

Thomas (with two added divisions) was to hold his present line; Mc-Cook, to form the right; Crittenden, the reserve. Thomas urged Rosecrans to draw back his right and center to the eastern slopes of Missionary Ridge and the hills behind the Lafayette road. These heights commanded every route leading to Chattanooga except the Rossville road to the north, where Gordon Granger's corps was placed. Before the council adjourned, coffee was served and McCook, who had a fine baritone voice, was called upon to sing a plaintive popular ballad called "the Hebrew Maiden's Lament."

Returning to his own campfire in the woods, Thomas lay down on the ground and studied a map that he held at an angle to the light. Near him slept two aides and other members of his staff. Soldiers round about peered intently at him out of the gloom, trying "to divine if possible from his expression . . . what the chances of the morrow's fight would be." At two that morning, Thomas received a message from one of his division commanders, General Absalom Baird, that his left did not quite extend to the road and that he could not reach it without weakening his line. Thomas went back to sleep but roused himself at six to send a note to Rosecrans asking that General Negley take position to Baird's left and rear.

"It was a night of great anxiety," wrote one chronicler,

> of constant moving of troops and shifting of positions; a night of active vigil, with little rest or sleep. The morning dawned peacefully over the quiet valley, and touched with its soft light the overhanging mountains and the upturned faces of the dead. A holy quiet filled the air; the wild flowers, freshened with the dews of night, gave forth their sweetest fragrance. The frightened birds, again seeking their nests, welcomed the morning light with songs of praise. All nature protested against the fratricidal strife; but no power, human or divine, no ties of kindred or home, or even life itself, could stay the cruel storm.

At nine o'clock, as the church bells of Chattanooga summoned its citizens to prayer, the signal guns sounding through the forests at Chickamauga called the two bleeding armies to renew the fight. Rosecrans had begun the day with Catholic rites in his tent, then rode out to inspect the lines. Discovering McCook's right to be too far back and Crittenden too far to the left, he ordered their troops to close up. He then rode to the left of the line where he found Thomas strongly protected with log breastworks and his right and left flanks bent well back toward the road.

Bragg had planned to attack at dawn. Polk, on the right, was to start it, then the rest of the army to take it up by brigades. As the sun mounted the sky, Bragg was in the saddle, surrounded by his staff. After listening in vain for the sound of Polk's guns, he at last dispatched an aide to ascertain the cause of the delay. The officer found Polk seated at a comfortable breakfast, surrounded by his own luxurious staff. When told of Bragg's peremptory order to attack, Polk replied: "Do tell General Bragg that my heart is overflowing with anxiety for the attack—overflowing with anxiety, Sir." When Bragg heard this, he swore roundly up and down and ordered his whole line to advance.

As the fighting began, Thomas and an aide were standing just behind the center of the line within range of the enemy shells. A shell passed between them "causing them to look at each other with a quiet smile. A moment afterward another shell took the same route. The general, instead of smiling this time, turned to his aide and said, 'Major, I think we had better retire a little,' and fell back a few yards to a small wood." Meanwhile, in successive and repeated charges, the whole Confederate right, brigade after brigade, assailed the Union breastworks, but was repulsed.

Rebel casualties mounted; those of the Federals were proportionately less. All went favorably, until about one in the afternoon, by the misconstruction of an order, one of the Union divisions under Thomas Wood was moved out of line. The Rebels, under Longstreet, at once poured through. The charge was tremendous, crushing Crittenden and taking both McCook and Thomas on the flank. That completely changed the nature of the fight. The Rebels came on in columns six lines deep, formed with brigade fronts, three brigades being massed behind each other, firing as they advanced. One division was rushed forward to stay the tide, but in vain. Sheridan was ordered to stand with two light brigades; but he, too, was overrun. As before at Stones River, the Rebel charge gained force and speed, and battery after battery of Union artillery was caught off guard and seized. The whole Union right seemed about to be driven from the field.

At the time, Charles Dana was napping on a plot of grass behind the lines.

I was wakened by the most infernal noise I ever heard. Never in any battle I had witnessed was there such a discharge of cannon and musketry. I sat up on the grass, and the first thing I saw was General Rosecrans crossing himself—he was a very pious Catholic. "Hello," I said to myself, "if the general is crossing himself, we are in a desperate situation." I was on my horse in a moment. But I had no sooner collected my thoughts and looked around toward the front, where all this din came from, than I saw our lines break and melt away like leaves before the wind. Then the headquarters around me disappeared. The gray-backs came through with a rush, and soon the musket balls and the cannon shot began to reach the place where we stood. The whole right of the army had apparently been routed . . . I have never seen anything so crushing to the mind as that scene.

McCook and Crittenden tried to repair the disaster in their own wings and rode about in various directions, endeavoring to collect their scattered troops. Wherever they went, they found the soldiers completely disorganized, sometimes in squads and groups, but more often singly and by twos and threes, all pushing through the thickets back toward the Chattanooga roads. Unable to reconstitute a viable command, they followed their men, and assumed all was lost. At Chattanooga itself, and along the roads going in, the wildest confusion prevailed. Fugitives, wounded, caissons, ambulances, thronged the narrow pathways. The seven brigades of McCook and Crittenden were demoralized. Rosecrans had earlier dispatched his chief of staff, General Garfield, to the front to find Thomas, while he proceeded to Chattanooga to prepare for its defense. His troops were exhausted and nearly out of rations, their ammunition low. If the Federal supply trains in the valley were cut off and destroyed, his army would starve. The safety of those trains, and the security of the fords and his pontoon bridges, was now his paramount concern. When McCook and Crittenden got to Chattanooga, separately, within a short time of each other, they looked about for Thomas, having no idea they had abandoned him to his fate. Rosecrans, for his part, concluded that his whole line had given way, and that the next stand must be made at the town itself.

Meanwhile, Dana, still at the front, looked for Sheridan in vain. "Not far away, I stumbled on a body of organized troops," he wrote,

> This was a brigade of mounted riflemen under Colonel John T. Wilder, of Indiana. "Mr. Dana," asked Colonel Wilder, "what is the situation?" "I do not know," I said, "except that this end of the army has been routed. There is still heavy fighting on the left front, and our troops seem to be holding their ground there yet." "Will you give me any orders?" he asked. "I have no authority to give orders," I replied; "but if I were in your situation, I should go to the left, where Thomas is." Then I turned my horse, and making my way over Missionary Ridge, struck the valley and rode to Chattanooga, twelve or fifteen miles away.

There he found Rosecrans so "faint and ill . . . stunned by sudden calamity" that aides had had to help him from his horse. At four o'clock, Rosecrans wired Stanton in despair, "My army is whipped and dispersed." He seemed to expect that Bragg's army would appear at any moment before the town. Dana's dispatch to Stanton also implied the worst. It began: "My report to-day is of deplorable importance. Chickamauga is as fatal a name in our history as Bull Run."

That turned out not to be so.

Under Thomas, a force of about 25,000 men had drawn itself into a horseshoe, on the crest of Snodgrass Hill (afterward known as Horseshoe Ridge) and with his artillery advantageously posted, repulsed a dozen fierce attacks on his left and center, right and rear. The stand he made was almost a reprise of that made at Stones River the year before. With bayonets and clubbed muskets the resolute Federals pierced and beat back the charging Confederates, covering the slopes of the ridge with Confederate dead. The woods caught fire from the flaming shells and scorched the bodies of the dead and dying; ammunition ran low. Still Thomas held.

Rosecrans, unaware of his heroic stand, sent word to Thomas to use his discretion in retreat. Thomas replied, "It will ruin the army to withdraw it now; this position must be held till night." From two o'clock until sunset the Rebels, in despair, hurled their entire army upon Thomas, whose forces were outnumbered by more than two or three to one. When it seemed he could hold out no longer, about 4 P.M. Gordon Granger's command, with three fresh brigades—two under General James B. Steedman—came up from the direction of Rossville, where they had formed the reserve. When Thomas first spotted their approach, he wondered for a painful moment if they were friend or foe. Then, through the clouds of smoke and dust, he caught a glimpse of the waving Stars-and-Stripes. When Steedman rode up, Thomas was standing alone in a clump of trees, with the enemy trying to turn both flanks. Pointing to the right, he exclaimed, "Take that ridge." Steedman moved at once to the attack, and, in spite of fierce resistance, took the ridge and gorge. At about the same time, Thomas sent an aide to tell one of his colonels to reinforce his right. "Where will I find you, General, when I return?" the aide inquired. Thomas thundered, "Here!"

Meanwhile, Steedman's charge had seemed "simply suicidal," wrote an eyewitness, "and I would have been less surprised if the army had made arrangements to surrender than I was to see his men charging and carrying the ridge against Longstreet's corps . . . The charge was not less of a surprise to the enemy, and the fact that it was unexpected and unaccountable under the circumstances had much to do with its success."

Some years later, a Confederate officer would remark to General Joseph Johnston (the best of the Southern generals after Lee) that Thomas "did not know when he was whipped." Johnston replied curtly, "Rather say he always knew very well when he was not." Indeed, the stand Thomas made was not just a holding action. It was such a devastating check that it put triumph itself within reach. At

8:40 on the night of the 20th, fresh from the field, Garfield wired the War Department: "General Thomas has fought a most terrific battle and has damaged the enemy badly . . . Longstreet's Virginians have got their bellies full. . . . I believe we can now crown the whole battle with victory." Charles Dana wired in turn: "Our troops were as immovable as the rocks they stood on. . . . Thomas seemed to have filled every soldier with his own unconquerable firmness." Thomas, indeed, had a remarkable hold on his men. General Steedman was once asked how Thomas was able to keep them together when, at Stones River and Chickamauga, other corps commanders failed. Steedman said: "I'll tell you. Such was the awe and veneration in which he was held that not one of his men dared leave his post. When they were in live fighting, they knew the old man was on deck, and they would rather have died than go to the rear, unless they were carried. Death was preferable to letting General Thomas see them retreating. I had the same feeling myself. I would have died before appearing to Thomas to be doing anything but my whole duty, and I would have felt myself forever disgraced." Although the Union forces had been driven from every portion of the field except the hill about the ridge itself, this heroic remnant, with its thinned ranks, reduced ammunition, and no reserves—with "everything gone but manhood and the ground they stood on"—remained. As the sun sank behind the cliffs of Lookout Mountain, the Rebels at last withdrew. In their desperate charges, they had lost many of their generals and much of their officer corps. Thomas had been the "Rock of Chickamauga" (as he was thereafter known) against which both wings of the Confederates had been hurled in vain. The military historian General Henry M. Cist wrote, "There is nothing finer in history than Thomas at Chickamauga."

In truth, his seemingly hopeless—yet successful—stand could only be compared to the ancient Greek stand against the Persians at Thermopylae.


While Thomas had held the field and kept his cool, he could not understand why the divisions of Sheridan and others did not return. He sent explicit orders by his aide-de-camp that they return by way of McFarland's Gap, which was only two and a half miles away, with no enemy force to interdict them. But the order was not obeyed. Only at nightfall, when it was too late, did they drift back. He could never understand why Sheridan chose the most roundabout route to reach him, arriving only to join the retreat.

It was not even a retreat Thomas thought he had to make.

Earlier that evening, Rosecrans had sat down at a table, and with Gordon Granger looking over his shoulder, according to one war correspondent,

> began to write the order to Thomas to fall back. Instead of making it a brief command, Rosecrans went on to detail how the retreat must be conducted, how the troops should be marshaled, this division here and another there, who should be in the van and who in the rear, and was adding that great fires must be built all along the line before the retreat began, in order to deceive the enemy into the belief that they were going to stay there . . . when Granger interrupted him: "Oh, that's all nonsense, general! Send Thomas an order to retire. He knows what he's about as well as you do."

Rosecrans tore up the order and obeyed.

After Thomas received his directive, he sent for Steedman. It was after sunset and Steedman found him in a little clearing, "sitting on a log, nervously picking off pieces of bark and biting them and throwing them away. He said: 'General Steedman, you know we must obey orders in war. I have received orders to fall back on Rossville.' As he said this he unbuttoned his coat and reached inside his breast pocket. I supposed he was going to show me the order, but he pulled out his hand and buttoned up his coat." Then they talked about the arrangements to be made.

That night, Thomas formed a new temporary line at Rossville to cover his retreat, and withdrew by the dim light of a clouded moon in perfect order with a strong rear guard. There he remained in battle line throughout the next day; sent Rosecrans a telegram "saying that his troops were in high spirits, and that he had brought off all his wounded"; and that evening posted his guns on the low range of hills to the rear and by a night march withdrew to Chattanooga five miles away. Even in his withdrawal, Thomas captured 500 Confederates and did not lose a single man.

In the horrendous battle of Chickamauga, both sides lost in killed, wounded, and missing about 17,000 men. In proportion to the numbers engaged, it was the bloodiest engagement of the war, with a casualty rate exceeding that of Gettysburg. Civil War historian John Codman Ropes linked the two in another way. "It was at Gettysburg and Chickamauga," he wrote, "that our American armies were at their best and did their best. Never were they—either before or after those memorable engagements—so strong, so well officered, so fierce, so determined to win, so resolved not to yield. . . . Never was there more resolute and obstinate and gallant fighting done, nor ever were severe losses more unshrinkingly borne."

Lincoln's own estimate of Thomas soared. On September 23, three days after the battle, Lincoln received a telegram from a political operative in New York City that questioned whether Thomas was as patriotic as he seemed. Lincoln's reply, scrawled in the telegraph office of the War Department and handed to Charles A. Tinker, the cipher clerk on duty, called that "ungracious," adding: "It is doubtful whether his heroism and skill exhibited last Sunday afternoon has ever been surpassed in the world." Then, annoyed with himself for having bothered to answer such a man, Lincoln said to Tinker, "I guess I will not send that." Tinker, however, put the reply in his pocket, and saved it. On May 27, 1867, two years after the war came to an end, he presented it to a grateful Thomas in person at Washington's famed Willard's Hotel.

The incredible calm and fortitude Thomas showed in battle under fire—"I did not think human nature was capable of it," wrote one eyewitness after Chickamauga—owed something to his sense of honor, but perhaps more to his religious faith. Though he rarely spoke of his spiritual convictions (just as he kept his private life completely private), he now and then shared a few thoughts with members of his staff. "I never was tempted to question what came to me so sweetly, and so full of consolation and comfort," he once said about his faith, "any more than I would doubt and question the love of my mother. I know that it is there, and I know that it is divine because it is good." It freed him, too, from fear: "I cannot see how a man can be an infidel and remain a brave man. Belief in God is like confidence in one's general, it holds us to the front. We feel that the power above has a wise design in making us face the deadly peril. I doubt whether any sane mind ever does positively disbelieve. One may have painful doubts, for we are brought continually face to face with mysterious and apparent contradictions, but back and above all these, we feel that there is an overruling power ever wise and ever just." When a colleague asked him if the religion he embraced was "natural" or "revealed," he at once replied: "Revealed, of course. Natural religion is so vague and uncertain; but revealed religion, that is given us in the teachings and character of Christ, is clear in all things. I never met an infidel who questioned the goodness of Christ or the purity or divinity of his teachings. Whether they will get us into heaven or not after death, there is one thing certain and that is, to obey them is to make us better and happier on earth. Accepting that, I will chance the rest."

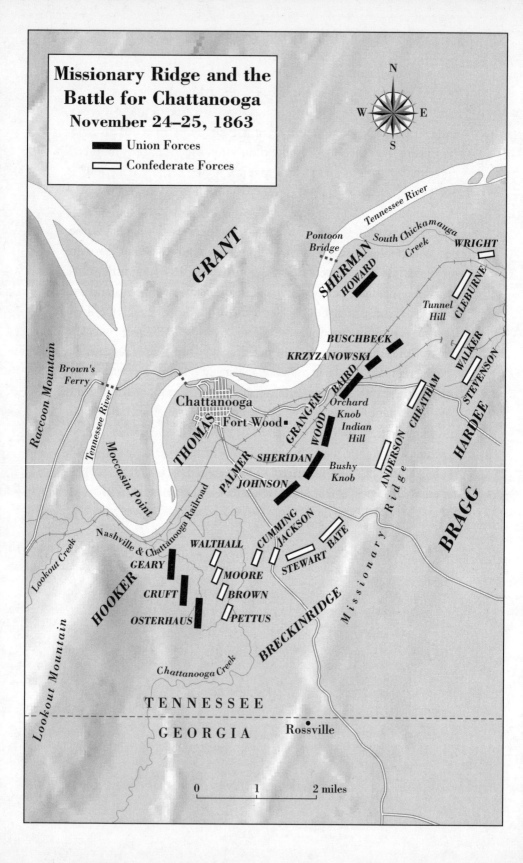

# Missionary Ridge and the Battle for Chattanooga
## November 24–25, 1863

■ Union Forces
□ Confederate Forces

GRANT

Tennessee River

Pontoon Bridge

South Chickamauga Creek

WRIGHT

SHERMAN

HOWARD

Tunnel Hill

CLEBURNE

BUSCHBECK

KRZYZANOWSKI

WALKER

STEVENSON

Brown's Ferry

Raccoon Mountain

Tennessee River

BAIRD

Orchard Knob

CHEATHAM

HARDEE

Chattanooga

THOMAS

Fort Wood

GRANGER

WOOD

Indian Hill

ANDERSON

BRAGG

Moccasin Point

SHERIDAN

Bushy Knob

PALMER

JOHNSON

M i s s i o n a r y   R i d g e

CUMMING

JACKSON

Nashville & Chattanooga Railroad

WALTHALL

BATE

GEARY

MOORE

STEWART

Lookout Creek

CRUFT

BROWN

OSTERHAUS

PETTUS

HOOKER

BRECKINRIDGE

Chattanooga Creek

Lookout Mountain

TENNESSEE

GEORGIA

Rossville

0    1    2 miles

# 8. CHATTANOOGA

Thomas, reported Charles Dana, was now the idol of the men, for he was "the man who saved them, and indeed saved us all. For my own part, I confess I share their feeling. I know no other man whose composition and character are so much like those of Washington; he is at once an elegant gentleman and a heroic soldier." By contrast, his fellow corps commanders were subjected to scorn. In the fog of war it is not easy to say whether the conduct of McCook and Crittenden had been remiss. But the impression was that it was. Secretary of War Stanton suspended both from command and ordered them to Indianapolis, Indiana, to be tried as military felons, which seemed to augur another political trial.

Until September 24, Federal troops had held the summit of Lookout Mountain, which was the key to all operations around Chattanooga. It dominated the entire scene of towering mountains and deep valleys, the tortuously winding Tennessee River, the tributary streams emptying into it, the railroads from south and west and the wagon roads. But as he hunkered down in Chattanooga and tried to prepare for its defense, Rosecrans yielded the summit (over the protests of Garfield, Granger, and others) as well as Missionary Ridge. He also gave up two Tennessee River ferries important to the Federal line of supply.

Bragg posted his army around the town, occupied all points yielded, placed his left flank along the mountain heights, held the railroads going south and even the main routes north. Altogether, his lines extended from Lookout Mountain across Chattanooga Valley to Missionary Ridge, and along its base and summit to the Tennessee

River. This left the Union army but one road, some sixty miles in length, over the mountains to Bridgeport for supplies. Even unchallenged, this road was inadequate. But it was harassed by raids, shelled off and on, awash with mud, and obstructed by hundreds of dead mules and horses who had perished hauling supplies. Bragg knew that if he could hold the river and the shorter roads to Bridgeport the surrender of the Union army was only a matter of time.

In its idyllic, natural setting, Chattanooga had once been a beautiful town. But war had turned it into a bleak, sad-looking, and semi-deserted place. Houses had been ransacked for food and clothing; its lawns and shrubbery eaten by mules; its trees felled and fences dismantled for fuel and defense works, its fields and gardens filled with tents. Just behind the town rows of crude army huts dotted the hills, and the plain in front was furrowed with riflepits. As log and earthenware breastworks and redoubts went up, the whole perimeter was fortified.

In the Federal army, rations were drastically reduced, malnutrition set in, and the men were said to be so debilitated they could hardly stand at their posts. The search for food occupied their waking hours. They followed forage wagons and picked up the grain that leaked out. They probed in the mud where the mules were fed and picked out grains of corn. Some quarreled over camp scraps and offal. The animals were almost without forage, and their very bones seemed to rattle within their drawn hides. Instead of the usual feed, they were sustained on tender cane cut from the riverbed. Over the next few weeks, thousands of draft animals would die of starvation and toil as they struggled to haul the provisions needed by the army to survive.

Through their field glasses the Rebels could watch almost every movement the Federals made. The latter in turn, wrote one colonel, "could . . . trace the intrenched lines" of the Rebels, "and note the location of their field batteries and big guns. Nearly every evening the signal torches on Lookout Mountain and on Mission Ridge were flashing messages to each other over our heads and across the valley. Our signal officers soon picked up their code. . . . Occasionally a big gun on Lookout Mountain would open out in a flash like the full moon and then we suddenly became interested in locating the fall of the shell."

Few occasions arose for levity under such dire conditions. But one morning, when Thomas and Garfield were inspecting the perimeter defenses, they heard someone shouting, "Hello, mister! you! I want to speak with you." On looking around, Thomas discovered that he was the "mister" wanted, and that the person who had hailed him was a rough backwoods soldier from East Tennessee. He stopped, and the man approached him and began, "Mister, I want to get a furlough."

"On what grounds, my man?"

"I want to go home and see my wife."

"How long since you saw your wife?"

"Ever since I enlisted—nigh on to three months."

"Three months!" exclaimed Thomas, good-naturedly. "Why, my good man, I haven't seen my wife for three years."

The East Tennesseean stopped whittling the stick he had in his hand and stared.

"Waall, you see," he said at length, with a sheepish smile, "me and my wife ain't that kind."


Rosecrans expected Bragg to try to take Chattanooga by assault, and as the Rebel shelling drew near feared a battle day and night. No attack came, and after several days, thanks to "the Herculean labors" of the army—as managed, according to Dana, mainly by Thomas—the Union defenses were made so formidable that "it was certain that [the town] could only be taken by a regular siege. . . . The strength of our forces was about forty-five thousand effective men, and we had ten days' full rations on hand. Chattanooga could hold out, but it was apparent that no offensive operations were possible until reinforcements came." These were on their way—four divisions under Sherman from Vicksburg, two corps under Hooker from Virginia—but would take time to arrive.

Besieged now by the very army he had maneuvered out, Rosecrans was in a shaken and bewildered state. Dana observed:

He dawdled with trifles in a manner which scarcely can be imagined. With plenty of zealous and energetic officers ready to do whatever needed to be done, precious time was lost because our dazed and mazy commander could not perceive the catastrophe that was close upon nor fix his mind upon the means of preventing it. I never saw anything which seemed so lamentable and hopeless. Our animals were starving, the men had starvation before them, and the enemy was bound soon to make desperate efforts to dislodge us. Yet the commanding general devoted that part of the time which was not employed in pleasant gossip to the composition of a long report to prove that the Government was to blame for his failure. . . . His mind scattered; there was no system in the use of his busy days and restless nights.

To Lincoln, Rosecrans seemed "stunned and confused, like a duck hit on the head."

Stanton had never liked Rosecrans, but after Chickamauga he "despised" him, and even called him "a damned coward," which was hardly true. "I saw him under fire at Stones River," remarked General Steedman, "and I know he was no coward. . . . But he was not the man for the tremendous events with which he was associated. They were too large for him." Before long, a consensus developed that he had to be removed. On September 28, Navy Secretary Gideon Welles noted in his diary that Lincoln considered putting an "Eastern general" in his place. But Welles told Lincoln he ought to go with Thomas for he doubted there was "any one suitable for that command or the equal of Thomas, if a change was to be made." Dana pushed hard for Thomas, too, and on September 30, Stanton agreed. "The merits of General Thomas and the debt of gratitude the nation owes to his valor and skill are fully appreciated here," he wired Dana, "and I wish you to tell him so. It is not my fault that he was not in chief command months ago." Soon thereafter, on October 4, Dana went to see Thomas and read him this telegram. "He was too much affected by it to reply immediately," wrote Dana. Thomas then said he was grateful for Stanton's confidence and wanted him to know that he had long wanted an independent command—"an army that I could myself have organized, disciplined, distributed, and combined." But, Thomas added pointedly, he did not want to take over an army where he might be "exposed to the imputation of having intrigued ... to supplant my previous commander."

The rush of events, however, was fast overriding his qualms. Dana's dispatches had so alarmed Stanton that he journeyed west to meet Grant at Indianapolis, and together they continued on to Louisville. Meanwhile, General Steedman (whose opinion was sought in Washington as an influential "War Democrat") had also gone to Washington at Lincoln's request. En route, he met with Stanton in Louisville and they talked about the crisis at Chattanooga through the night. In Washington, Steedman's audience with Lincoln lasted for three hours. Lincoln asked him directly: "Who do you think is the fittest man to command?" "There is only one man in the army fit to command it," replied Steedman. "Who is that?" asked Lincoln. "General George H. Thomas." "He grasped me by the hand, and said: 'General Steedman, I am glad to hear you say that. I have been of that opinion for the last 90 days, but nearly all the other gentlemen here have disagreed with me. I believe you are right.' "

It is not clear why Lincoln put it that way, since the opposite was clearly true. But later that day, Lincoln issued an order that placed the departments and armies of the Ohio, Tennessee, and Cumberland in the Military Division of the Mississippi under Grant; sustained Burnside as head of the Army of the Ohio; allowed Grant to replace himself with Sherman as head of the Army of the Tennessee; and gave Grant the option of giving Thomas command of the Army of the Cumberland instead of Rosecrans. Dana, who had been ordered to Louisville to meet with Stanton, was stopped en route by Grant, who told him that the new command arrangements had been made. Grant knew from various shared dispatches that Rosecrans had become untenable, and that Lincoln and Stanton both thought Thomas should take his place. Grant agreed, as expected, and wired Thomas: "Hold Chattanooga at all hazards." This unnecessary exhortation was taken by the army as an insult. Thomas replied, tersely: "I will hold the town until we starve."

The order relieving Rosecrans came to him, unannounced, at four

P.M. on October 19. At nine that evening he turned his army over to Thomas. Thomas reluctantly accepted the command—not through any false modesty as to his own capacity or fitness, but for the reasons he had given Stanton through Dana on October 4. With a concern for military order, Rosecrans asked that his farewell order be announced to the army after his departure, and at eight the next morning, October 20, just one year to the day from the time he had left his army at Corinth, Mississippi, to take command of the Army of the Cumberland, he took his leave. In his order, he commended Thomas to the men as a general of "known prudence, dauntless courage, and true patriotism," to whom they could "look with confidence" to lead them to victory ahead. But they already knew that full well.

Generals usually resent those who replace them, especially when they have proved their superiority in a subordinate role. But it was clear that Thomas had not maneuvered for the post. Rather, he had been summoned. The two generals remained friends; Rosecrans told him at the time, "You need not say anything; no misunderstanding can come between us." In a later benediction Rosecrans would describe Thomas "as near to an angel as a mortal can be"—a rather remarkable expression for an accomplished warrior to use about a peer. Yet with the changing of the guard, the army was reinspired and, recalled General W. B. Hazen, "our hopes went up with a great bound."

The first task that confronted Thomas was to feed and otherwise provision his army, and to do this he had to seize at least part of the river route. The Tennessee, sweeping north to south past Chattanooga, formed a sudden bend before flowing north again opposite the town. In so doing, it formed a peninsula with a narrow neck at a place called Brown's Ferry. For the Federals, it was essential to secure this landing and throw a pontoon bridge across the river at that point. That would greatly shorten the Union line of supply and give the Federals possession of the river from Lookout Mountain to Bridgeport on which steamers could run.

Grant, meanwhile, had set out for Chattanooga, going partway by rail. At Stevenson, he met Rosecrans, traveling west, who gave him all the information in his power. From Bridgeport, Grant proceeded by foot and horseback. The roads winding among the mountains were nearly impassable, owing to the heavy rains and freshets that poured down the mountain sides. Grant is said to have "suffered greatly during the long and tiresome ride, and to make matters worse, 'Old Jack,' his sturdy claybank horse, had slipped and fallen heavily with him, severely jamming his injured leg, just after he had crossed the Tennessee and entered the town."

Preceding Grant to Chattanooga, Colonel James H. Wilson of his staff was escorted to headquarters by Dana when he arrived early on the 23. Dana had nothing but praise for Thomas, and Wilson later recalled "I was therefore prepossessed in his favor and was ready to greet him as an able and reliable commander. . . . [But] I was not prepared to see in him so many external evidences of greatness. . . . Six feet tall, of Jovelike figure, impressive countenance and lofty bearing, he struck me at once . . . as resembling the traditional Washington in appearance, manner and character more than any man I had ever met. I found him as calm and serene as the morning. . . . He expressed a modest confidence in being able to make good his hold on Chattanooga and at once inspired me with faith in his steadiness and courage." Thomas having received them both "with every mark of consideration," then turned to Dana, and said (in a polite allusion to the latter's efforts to gain him his new command), "Mr. Dana, you have got me this time; there is nothing for a man to do in such case but to obey orders."

Wilson and Dana then called on General W. F. "Baldy" Smith (the army's chief engineer and a veteran of Antietam and Gettysburg) and General J. M. Brannan, the army's chief of artillery. "Those distinguished officers," wrote Wilson, "at once declared that under the sane and steady guidance of Thomas the danger of further disaster had not only disappeared but that order and confidence had already been established throughout the ranks. Our next duty was to ride the lines, visit the advance posts, and confer with the actual commanders of the troops. Everywhere we found short rations, little forage, and plenty of hungry soldiers and starving animals. And yet every vestige of discontentment had disappeared. Everybody seemed cheerful and hopeful. Officers and men alike had regained resolution and courage." Indeed, Thomas, in consultation with Smith, had already begun to elaborate a plan for shortening "the cracker line" (as the supply line was called) by some fifty miles.

If Union morale had been raised under Thomas, Confederate morale under Bragg had begun to sink. His army lacked confidence in him. To begin with, few gains had come under his command. He had given ground at Perryville and Stones River (both of which he might have won); and in some respects his victory at Chickamauga had been Pyrrhic, thanks to the mighty resistance Thomas had put up. Confederate general D. H. Hill, who commanded one of Bragg's corps, would later say that "after Chickamauga the élan of the Southern soldier was never seen again. He fought stoutly to the last, but after Chickamauga with the sullenness of despair and without enthusiasm or hope." Bragg also quarreled constantly with his general staff and seemed almost to hate his own men. Confederate general Edward Porter Alexander remembered an emblematic scene soon after he arrived at Chattanooga and rode out with his staff to inspect the lines:

> We came upon one of Bragg's infantry divisions forming three sides of a hollow square. Some one asked what it meant, & I answered that, according to rumor, Bragg shot a man every day, & that this three sided formation seemed to indicate that this was his hour. And, sure enough, as we rode up, an adjutant came forward & read the proceedings of a court martial, only a few days before, upon a man who had deserted from one of our Tennessee regiments & had been just captured in a Federal regiment. And then the poor wretch, who had been standing near, in charge of a guard, was led out to the side of a newly dug grave, in a wheat stubble field, & placed in front of a firing party which stood, it seemed to me, thirty yards away. Their aim, however, was true enough, for, at their fire, he sank limp as a rag—a sergeant walked up, & gave a final shot as a coup de grace, & the burial detail came forward with their shovels, & the business was quickly over.

On the evening of October 23, as the rain fell in torrents through the gloom, Grant and his escort reached Chattanooga and went at once to see Thomas, though they were wet, hungry, and covered with mud. They entered a large room in which a log fire was burning, but when Dana and Wilson arrived soon after, they found the atmosphere chill. "Grant," recalled Wilson, "was sitting on one side of the fire over a puddle of water that had run out of his clothes; Thomas, glum and silent, was sitting on the other, while [General John] Rawlins [Grant's chief of staff] and the rest were scattered about." Grant had evidently just told Thomas that his independent command was not to be as independent as he thought.

To appreciate the chagrin Thomas felt, one need only remember that Stanton had just recently assured him (through Dana) that he had long since earned an independent command. Thomas had reluctantly agreed to take charge of the army. Now he was confronted with the unpleasant fact that everything he might do was to be subject to Grant's direction and approval, and placed under his prejudiced eye. Almost everyone seems to have been aware that Grant resented Thomas—this was a "known prejudice," one officer remarked—while Thomas, in turn, distrusted Grant's military judgment and skill. "The situation was embarrassing," wrote Wilson, "but Dana and I took it in almost at a glance, and after a moment's conference with Rawlins . . . I broke in with the remark: 'General Thomas, General Grant is wet, hungry, and in pain; his wagons and camp equipage are far behind; can you not find quarters and some dry clothes for him, and direct your officers to provide the party with supper?'" That "broke the spell" and Thomas moved at once in the most hospitable manner to furnish rooms, dry clothes, and supper for his guests. "Conversation began, and it was not long till a glow of warmth and cheerfulness prevailed . . . Before the evening closed the casual observer would not have suspected that there had been the slightest lack of cordiality in the reception which had been accorded to the weary general and his staff."

Yet the incident deepened the rift between the two men. Wilson and Dana often discussed it afterward and agreed it had something to do with the fact that "Thomas's services and connections with the old army had been more creditable than Grant's," and "his rank higher," but was more deeply rooted in the Shiloh campaign, "where Grant," wrote Wilson, "nominally second in command, was really in disfavor, while Thomas, who belonged to another army, had been put in command of nearly all of Grant's troops." Indeed, Grant had arrived at Chattanooga with his old wound of a grudge still festering. Despite the renewed high spirits and élan that Dana and Wilson had both found under Thomas, Grant insisted on depicting his troops as abject, timid, and demoralized. This gave him the excuse he was looking for to assign Sherman, and Sherman's own troops, the major role in the upcoming battle for the town. Notably enough, the very night he arrived he wired Stanton: "Please approve order placing Genl Sherman in command of Dept. & army of the Tennessee with Hd. Qrs. in the field." As one officer put it, "He had scarcely begun to exercise the authority conferred upon him by his new command when his mind turned to securing advancement for Sherman."

But the broad competence of Thomas at once made itself plain. He gained Grant's approval for his plan to secure the river below Lookout Mountain to Bridgeport and sent General George T. Palmer and two brigades down the river's north bank to cooperate with General Joseph Hooker, who was to advance from Bridgeport and enter Lookout Valley while Palmer held the roads. On the night of the 27, one brigade and three batteries moved overland toward Brown's Ferry, while 1,300 men under General W. B. Hazen in flatboats manned with oars quietly drifted downstream as a slight mist veiled the full moon. Uniting opposite the ferry, all hands crossed a pontoon bridge and rushed the Rebel pickets on the opposite shore. The Federals hastily entrenched on a hill and repelled a countercharge. After artillery was brought over, the position was made secure. Meanwhile, Hooker seized another key crossing (Kelley's Ferry) at the foot of the rapids, and began marching into Lookout Valley unopposed.

Communication with Bridgeport was now secured by two routes—one, overland, by way of the little village of Wauhatchie and Brown's Ferry; the other, by river, to Kelley's Ferry, and from there by an eight-mile wagon road along the river's north bank. Prior to this time Chattanooga had been practically invested and could not have held out another week. Grant, who never gave Thomas any more credit than he had to, and often denied him the credit he deserved, acknowledged in a wire to Halleck: "Thomas's plan for securing the river and the south side road hence to Bridgeport, has proved eminently success-ful." Thomas gave the credit to Smith. Either way, instead of looking down from secure heights upon a prize which was sure to fall into his hands, Bragg found himself confronted by an enemy whose growing strength would soon exceed his own. Two steamboats were now able to run up and down part of the river and an immense wagon train ad-vanced with tens of thousands of rations between the two ferries over the land route. "We can easily subsist ourselves now, and will soon be in good condition," Thomas joyfully announced in a wire to Halleck on October 31.

On November 3, Bragg tried to create a diversion in the face of the forces assembling against him and, at the suggestion of Jefferson Davis, sent Longstreet toward Knoxville with a corps and eighty guns. At Knoxville, Ambrose Burnside had 25,000 troops on hand for his own defense, but was unnerved by Bragg's maneuver. He appealed to Washington for help, and the War Department, unnerved in turn by his pleadings, pressed Grant to do something on his behalf. Grant ac-cordingly came up with a plan for Thomas to attack Bragg's right on Missionary Ridge. This was supposed to serve as a counterdiversion to force Bragg to call Longstreet back.

It was a reckless plan. Bragg was strongly entrenched, and such an assault could not be mounted without adequate artillery support. At the time, the Federals lacked the artillery horses they needed to haul the guns. Burnside's situation was also not as urgent as Grant thought. Based on disinformation, including rumors fed to him by a deserter, Grant became convinced that Burnside was about to be overrun. So on November 7, Grant sent Thomas a peremptory order to hurl his whole army against the Ridge's northern end. "The movement should not be made one moment later than to-morrow morning," said Grant. "You having been over this country, and having a better opportunity of studying it than myself, the details are left to you."

Thomas read this order in silence. Then he sent for General Smith and told him it "meant disaster" for his army given Bragg's entrenched position on the heights. As matters stood, Bragg could mass his whole force against him, whereas if they waited for Sherman to come up they would have another wing in the attack. In the meantime, he told

Smith they had to somehow "get the order countermanded." Smith implicitly agreed and suggested to Thomas they go up and look over the ground together so they could present Grant with empirical evidence as to why the untimely plan was wrong. Accordingly, they went up to the northern end of the Ridge "as far as the mouth of Chickamauga Creek . . . From there," recalled Smith, "we made a scrutiny of the ground and the position of the right of the enemy on the ridge, as marked by their works and smokes, and it was evident that General Thomas, with his command, could not turn the right of Bragg's army without uncovering Chattanooga," i.e., exposing it to assault. "We then returned, and I went to the head-quarters of General Grant, and reported the result of the reconnaisance, and told him in my judgment, it was absolutely necessary to wait for the arrival of Sherman's army." Grant acquiesced. It can hardly be doubted that Thomas was right to resist Grant's order. General Smith would later note that Sherman with six well-equipped divisions failed eighteen days later to carry the enemy right on the Ridge "at a time when Thomas with four divisions stood threatening Bragg's center and Hooker with nearly three divisions was driving in Bragg's left."

Yet in his memoirs, Grant seized on the incident as proof that Thomas lacked the initiative to be the great offensive general Sherman was: "On the 7th, before Longstreet could possibly have reached Knoxville, I ordered Thomas peremptorily to attack the enemy's right, so as to force the return of the troops that had gone up the valley. I directed him to take mules, officers' horses, or animals wherever he could get them, to move the necessary artillery. But he persisted in the declaration that he could not move a single piece of artillery, and could not see how he could possibly comply with the order." This statement, which omitted the true circumstances under which the order was reversed, also contradicted another he had made just a few paragraphs before: "We had not at Chattanooga animals to pull a single piece of artillery, much less a supply train."

Grant's story, however, was reinforced by Adam Badeau, a journalist who joined Grant's staff as military secretary and in effect became his official historian and publicist. Badeau wrote in his authorized *Military History of U.S. Grant*: "Thomas announced that he had no horses to move his artillery, and declared himself entirely and absolutely unable to move until Sherman should arrive to co-operate. . . . Nevertheless, Thomas's delay was a great disappointment. A prompt movement on the part of that commander would undoubtedly have had the effect to recall Longstreet." In yet another twist to the tale, one early biography of Grant turned the truth on its head. There we read that Grant's "idea was to attack Missionary Ridge without delay, and of this plan he informed Burnside, telling him to hold Knoxville to the last extremity, but sober second thought, suggested by that calm prudence which is one of his best characteristics, prompted him to await the arrival of Sherman and his army, and thus by skill and carefulness to leave little to chance." In other words, the prudent delay insisted on by Thomas and condemned by Grant as timid became exemplary of the "calm prudence" that was one of the "best characteristics" Grant possessed.

Meanwhile, Sherman's Army of the Tennessee had left Vicksburg on steamers on September 27, reached Memphis October 2, but had since been delayed by heavy rains and by Halleck's order to repair the railroad as it advanced. Grant appealed to Halleck to let Sherman hurry on, but Sherman delayed his own army further "by a singular blunder" (as Dana put it in a dispatch to Stanton) according to which he sent his large wagon trains ahead of his artillery and troops. On November 14, Sherman himself finally arrived ahead of his army, conferred with Grant and Thomas, and rode out to examine the enemy's lines. Grant decided on a three-pronged attack—Sherman to advance with his divisions on the left; Hooker on the right with his two corps; Thomas, in the center with his army, against Missionary Ridge. Sherman studied the terrain, folded up his glass, and confidently exclaimed, "I can do it!" It remained for him to get his army into place by November 21, the date set by Grant for the movement to begin.

Not incidentally, when Bragg's headquarters on the crest of Missionary Ridge was pointed out, Sherman later told Garfield that Thomas lost his cool and swore, "Damn him, I'll be even with him yet." It may be doubted. Like most, if not all, of Sherman's contrived anecdotes about Thomas, the unfriendly point of it was to suggest that Thomas was "not as imperturbable" (Sherman's words) as many thought.

Despite his declaration "I can do it!" Sherman failed to get his columns to their designated place on time. Meanwhile, Grant wrongly thought Bragg might be in retreat. On the 20th, he had received a note from Bragg which read, in part: "As there may still be some noncombatants in Chattanooga, I deem it proper to notify you that prudence would dictate their early withdrawal." The object of the note, which implied an imminent attack, was to keep the Union army in their lines. Grant, however, misconstrued it completely. Howard recalled that he "smiled as he read the message, and said: 'It means that Bragg is intending to run away.'" Two days later, Grant was confirmed in his opinion by the report of an enemy deserter who was picked up near the town. Early on the morning of the 23rd, Thomas was ordered to advance some troops to ascertain if the report was true.

Two strongholds or strategic positions stood between Chattanooga and the base of Missionary Ridge. One, midway, was an earthwork called Fort Wood, which formed part of the Federal system of defenses. Between that and the rifle pits (at the base of the Ridge) was a prominent double hill called Orchard Knob. Bragg occupied this eminence as an outpost, Thomas organized an advance from the center of the Union line that called for five divisions—a force strong enough to save the advance from disaster if a general engagement ensued. "The field of operation was one well fitted for a display," recalled one officer. "The wide plain extending from the Tennessee to Lookout Mountain and Missionary Ridge formed an amphitheater that offered a fair view to not only the Confederates leaning on their guns and looking down upon our camps and lines of fortifications, but to our own army occupying various elevations from the plain."

The troops employed for the attack were under the immediate command of Gordon Granger. His division commanders included Philip Sheridan, W. B. Hazen, and Thomas Wood. Just before one o'clock the men moved out of their entrenchments, and remained in line for three-quarters of an hour in full view. Grant, Thomas, and other officers, including Dana, stood upon the ramparts of Fort Wood to observe the attack. "The spectacle," wrote Dana, "was one of singular magnificence. . . . Usually in a battle one sees only a little corner of what is going on, the movements near where you happen to be; but in the battle of Chattanooga we had the whole scene before us. At last, everything being ready, Granger gave the order to advance, and three brigades of men pushed out simultaneously. The troops advanced rapidly, with all the precision of a review." As the firing began, they swept away the pickets to their front and overran the works on Orchard Knob with such sudden force that they were taken "almost before the Confederates realized they had been attacked." Thomas, seeing the Union flag on Orchard Knob and the adjoining hills, signaled Wood: "You have gained too much to withdraw; hold your position, and I will support you." Immediately he sent two more divisions forward—one to the right, the other to the left. Even as he moved to solidify the gain, Grant ordered the men withdrawn. That made no sense to anyone, including Grant's chief of staff. He told Grant, "It will not do for them to come back," and (wrote Howard) Grant reluctantly agreed. At 3 P.M., Grant notified Halleck that the troops belonging to Thomas had "attacked the enemy's left" (in fact, they had attacked the enemy right), carried the first line of rifle pits, "running over the knoll one thousand two hundred yards in front of Wood's fort and low ridge to the right of it, taking about two hundred prisoners besides killed and wounded. Our loss small. The troops moved under fire with all the precision of veterans on parade. Thomas's troops will entrench themselves and hold their position until daylight, when Sherman will join the attack from the mouth of South Chickamauga; and a decisive battle will be fought."

Grant was clearly amazed at the cool gallantry of the troops he had so recently maligned. He had not expected, or even wanted, Thomas to gain and hold ground. His plan was for Thomas to make a junction with Sherman after Sherman had made his own successful wing attack. In his official report, however, Grant portrayed the movement as part of his original plan: "Thomas having done on the 23rd with his troops in Chattanooga Valley what was intended for the 24th, bettered and strengthened his advanced positions during the day." As Donn Piatt later wrote, "We see the first divergence from the truth that widened as it went." The junction with Sherman according to the plan explained to Halleck in a telegram of November 23 was now in fact impossible. Thomas would have had to keep most of his troops massed in Chattanooga Valley to the left. Instead, they were massed toward the center. Events were shaping themselves in accord with the better plan of battle Thomas had worked out. Everything, in fact, that subsequently happened indicates that in order to avoid failure and a useless loss of life, Thomas "managed" the great battle of Chattanooga, as one writer put it, "behind Grant's back." Perhaps he thought he had to. He did not have a high opinion of Grant's generalship. And his worst fears had already been confirmed by the first, reckless order he had received to attack Missionary Ridge. Thomas loved his army, and was loved and trusted by his men. As he had told Halleck, he was going to do the right thing by them no matter what "stick" or fool was placed over his head. He was never insubordinate; but he knew exactly what he was doing when others did not. That gave him a covert power that ultimately assured victory for the Union and spared countless lives.

That night there was a lunar eclipse. Among the Federals, some saw it as an omen of Bragg's defeat "because he was perched on the mountain top, nearest the moon." In a more obvious way, the darkness worked against him by helping to cover the progress of Sherman's troops, who were at last struggling to get into position east of the town. Yet Bragg was not idle. Awakening to the fact that the Union left overlapped his right and so endangered his supply lines, he transferred a division from the northern slope of Lookout Mountain to his extreme right on the Ridge. That gave Hooker a chance to fight one of the most celebrated actions of the war. Grant had ordered Hooker to make a demonstration against the summit of Lookout Mountain as a diversion. Hooker asked permission from Thomas to take the summit if he could. Thomas (by his 12:30 P.M. dispatch of November 24) gave his consent.

On the morning of the 24th, as a dense fog settled on the valley, Hooker crossed Lookout Creek and began his ascent. For some time, no one in the valley could see clearly how the battle was going, as the guns of both sides reverberated through the hills. Hooker's men worked their perilous way up, over boulders and jutting cliffs, clutching bushes and the branches of trees to steady their footing, as the Confederates retreated from ledge to ledge. "Up and up they went into the clouds," wrote one eyewitness, "which were settling down upon the lofty summit, until they were lost from sight, and their comrades watching anxiously in the Chattanooga valley could hear only the booming of cannon and the rattle of musketry far overhead, and catch glimpses of fire flashing from moment to moment through the dark clouds." This went on till the fog deepened into night. Then the noise died down. The Union army in the valley slept in doubt. At dawn, "cheers from sixty thousand throats went up" as the Stars-and-Stripes were seen waving from a point on the mountain known as "Pulpit Rock."

Hooker's victory, known afterward as "the Battle Above the Clouds," thrilled the nation, and wild eulogies were composed in his praise. Hooker himself was greatly heartened, for it somewhat redeemed his reputation, which had been tarnished at Chancellorsville. Grant, however, was so unhappy that he later claimed "there was no such battle, and no action worthy to be called a battle," on Lookout that day. He did not mean that literally, of course. He meant that it was vastly overblown. But even that was not so, at least by its consequence. As a bold action, it had forced Bragg to shorten his line and helped set up the tremendous victory that ensued.

Once Lookout Mountain was in his hands, Hooker marched into the valley of the Chattanooga River, worked furiously to repair the bridge across it, which the Rebels had destroyed, and, without waiting for the flooring, got a regiment across on the stringers, as soon as they were laid. Then he moved by Rossville Gap up to the crest of Missionary Ridge. Grant's battle plan was fast going awry. Sherman was three days behind schedule; Hooker (with encouragement from Thomas) had taken Lookout Mountain; Thomas had taken Orchard Knob in the advance toward Missionary Ridge.

Sherman was having a hard time of it. He had his troops north of the river concealed behind the hills, ready to attempt to cross the Tennessee to attack the east head of the Ridge on the east. The ridge appeared to be continuous, at least along the crest, but it proved otherwise. His maps were wrong. Instead of climbing directly up the slopes, he discovered himself faced by a series of fortified hills that masked the ridge itself. Each jagged knoll "had to be approached and taken like an isolated bastion." He hustled his troops through a storm of canister to take the first two, only to encounter a ravine he didn't know was there. That left him some distance short of a railroad tunnel he was supposed to occupy that day. With dusk coming on, it was too late to get his army down and up the far side. In the meantime, he had pretty much given away the Federal plan. On the heights he saw Rebels preparing for an energetic defense. Bragg, now realizing that the main attack would fall on his right, had shifted two divisions from Lookout Mountain, and began to fortify the knob north of Tunnel Hill. Flattened out and disillusioned, Sherman entrenched behind the ravine and asked to be reinforced. Two divisions were sent at once from Thomas's command.

Grant had looked eagerly to see Sherman accomplish on Bragg's right what Hooker had done on Bragg's left. When he discovered that Sherman had been repulsed with heavy loss, he reset the coordinated Union attack for the morning of the 25th. So far, everyone but Sherman had done their part. "The simple fact is," wrote General James H. Wilson, Sherman "was not the man" for the task he had been assigned. This was the situation when the unexpected transpired. The forces in the center under Thomas on Orchard Knob had till then been held in place. Thinking to draw Rebel troops away from the forces Sherman faced, Grant called on Thomas to make another demonstration and take the rifle pits connected by log and stone breastworks along the base of Missionary Ridge. On the 25th, the same four divisions that had secured Orchard Knob were ordered to advance.

In his memoirs, Grant would fault Thomas for not having made the charge sooner: "I had watched for the attack of General Thomas early in the day," Grant tells us.

Sheridan's and Wood's divisions had been lying under arms from early morning, ready to move the moment the signal was given. I now directed Thomas to order the charge at once. I watched to see the effect and became impatient at last, that there was no indication of any charge being made. The center of the line which was to make the charge was near where Thomas and I stood, but concealed from view by an intervening point. Turning to Thomas to inquire what caused the delay, I was surprised to see Thomas J. Wood, one of the division commanders, who was to make the charge, standing talking to him. I spoke to General Wood, asking why he did not charge as ordered an hour before. He replied very promptly that this was the first he had heard of it, but that he had been ready all day at a moment's notice; I told him to make the charge at once.

No one was ever found who heard Grant give Thomas that first order—even though both men were surrounded by a numerous staff. When Grant did tell Thomas to send his men forward, Thomas did so promptly, as all who witnessed the order and his response report. When the order came, wrote Howard, "the patient Thomas had been ready all day." The day before, Grant had given Thomas a general order for a morning advance, but this was only to take place in conjunction with Sherman's attack. The order read in part: "General Sherman carried Missionary Ridge as far as the tunnel with only slight skirmishing [this was wishful thinking and not true]. His right now rests at the tunnel and on top of the hill; his left at Chickamauga Creek. I have instructed General Sherman to advance as soon as it is light in the morning, and your attack, which will be simultaneous, will be in co-operation." In keeping with Grant's order, Thomas had waited for Sherman to move. Grant, too, waited all morning, and into the afternoon. He was not waiting for Thomas, but for Sherman. But Sherman could not move. He had, in fact, not carried the ridge to the tunnel (how could Grant not know this?), as Grant claimed. Grant was now in a fix. His unconscionable delay, designed to facilitate glory for Sherman, his comrade-in-arms, had reached a point where it threatened Sherman's survival and the success of the whole battle plan. Finally, Grant's chief of staff, Rawlins, confronted him and demanded that he not wait any longer. At about 3 P.M. he finally ordered the center to attack.

Sherman and Grant had both maligned the Army of the Cumberland as a demoralized and defeated force. Grant had even described it as "fixed and immovable" in a dispatch to Halleck on the 21st. For weeks, the Cumberland troops had chafed under such calumny, and out of their resentment was born a resolve. With banners waving and drums beating, the men moved out and formed in lines as if on parade. General Hazen recalled afterward that even cooks and clerks and quartermasters "found guns in some way" and joined the combat troops in their array. The day was beautifully clear and cool. Along the brow of Missionary Ridge the Rebels crowded to the front as officers rushed to their guns. For twenty minutes "there was the stillness of a cemetery," followed by a brief artillery duel between the guns on Orchard Knob and Missionary Ridge. At 3:40 P.M. a battery of six Union guns fired—the signal for the entire line to advance. Before the fifth gun had sounded the men were out of their own trenches, wheeling and marching as if on parade. Before them, the crest of Missionary Ridge rose 400 feet. Its terrain was so broken and rugged that Bragg had said "a single cordon of skirmishers could hold it against the whole Federal Army." The three divisions of Union troops facing the ridge occupied a line two miles long. Forty-two big guns pointed straight at them, while across an open space of some 600 yards lay the Rebel works. Under the circumstances, wrote one historian, "the charge of the light brigade at Balaclava seemed no more desperate than the advance of the 4th Corps of the Army of the Cumberland against Missionary Ridge."

In the rifle pits and breastworks, the Rebels "waited in grim silence" as "the long line came on with gleaming bayonets." On Orchard Knob, Grant and Thomas, each with his own staff, "soon lost sight of the combatants because of the smoke that rolled in and over" the action. Suddenly, the rifle pits were silent, and as the smoke lifted, there could be seen along the steep sides of the Ridge, from end to end, Rebels desperately clawing their way up. Right on their heels in pursuit surged the entire Union line. Once in the rifle pits, they were supposed to wait for further instructions. But to a man they understood the folly of that and continued on. As one eyewitness put it, "The situation offered them the opportunity to stand still and die, to go forward without orders, to stop the destructive fire to which they were exposed, or to retreat on the same condition to avoid it. The men in

**General George H. Thomas.** The most successful general on either side of the Civil War. He arguably won the war for the North by his generalship in several key battles. His accomplishments, however, were slighted by Sherman and Grant.

**President Abraham Lincoln.** A great statesman but a flawed war leader in the management of his command.

**General Robert Anderson.** The hero of Fort Sumter. Early in the war, he persuaded President Lincoln to appoint Thomas a brigadier general of volunteers.

**Henry W. Halleck.** Lincoln's long-time "general-in-chief."

**Andrew Johnson.** As military governor of Tennessee, he sparred with Thomas over tactics. As president, he made him the military governor of several Southern states.

**General Ulysses S. Grant.** Lincoln's ultimate choice for overall command. From the Corinth campaign on, his enmity toward Thomas was pronounced.

**William Tecumseh Sherman.** He roomed with Thomas at West Point, praised his abilities in public, but worked with Grant to limit his reputation and rank.

**General Joseph E. Johnston.** Perhaps the best of the Confederate generals after Robert E. Lee, he prevailed against McClellan in the East (before being wounded) and outwitted Sherman for much of the Atlanta campaign.

**Gideon Welles.** Lincoln's great secretary of the Navy.
He thought Thomas beyond compare and belatedly
recognized Grant's "jealous" spite.

**Edwin M. Stanton.** Lincoln's secretary of war. An able,
dedicated, but irascible man. Based on false information, he harassed
Thomas at Nashville and afterward suffered remorse.

**Salmon P. Chase.** Lincoln's secretary of the treasury.
He supported General William S. Rosecrans over Thomas
as head of the Army of the Cumberland.

**General Don Carlos Buell.** He led the Army of the Cumberland in
two unsuccessful campaigns with Thomas as second-in-command.

**General William S. Rosecrans.** An outstanding general, he was promoted over Thomas to succeed Buell.

**Charles A. Dana.** Assistant secretary of war and the "eyes" of the War Department at Chattanooga. He lobbied Stanton and others on Thomas's behalf.

**Lookout Mountain.** One of the "unassailable" heights won by the North in the battle for Chattanooga.

**General Braxton Bragg.** He led the Confederate Army of Tennessee and was decisively beaten by Thomas at Missionary Ridge.

**Grant on Missionary Ridge.** The assault on Missionary Ridge by troops under Thomas was the most spectacular and successful Union assault of the war. Grant had wanted the glory for Sherman. Here Grant (at left) surveys the ground in the battle's aftermath.

**General Oliver O. Howard.** Howard observed Thomas up close during the battle for Chattanooga and on the March to Atlanta. His memoirs helped to set the record straight. Howard University in Washington, D.C., is named after him.

**General John M. Schofield.** An ally of Grant, he tried to undermine Thomas before the Battle of Nashville by sending false information to Washington by wire.

**General James H. Wilson.** Grant's favorite cavalry commander until he served under Thomas. He led the cavalry at the Battle of Nashville and later swept through part of the South in a campaign that helped end the war.

**Colonel Arthur MacArthur.** He took a leading part in the climactic infantry assault at the Battle of Nashville.

**Fortified Bridge at Nashville.** One of several imposing efforts made by the Union to strengthen the city's defenses.

**General James B. Steedman.** A hero of the Battle of Chickamauga. He was one of many outstanding generals repelled by the efforts of Grant and Sherman to distort the story of the war.

**General John Bell Hood.** A "stand-up fighter," he succeeded Joseph Johnston as head of the Army of Tennessee. Hood was beaten by Thomas before Atlanta at Peachtree Creek and again in the Battle of Nashville, which won the war in the West.

**Colonel Nathan Bedford Forrest.** The most wily of all Confederate commanders. Thomas had to contend with him in Tennessee. After the war, Forrest became the first Grand Wizard of the Ku Klux Klan.

**General James B. Fry.** A distinguished officer who implemented Lincoln's policy on the draft, he later engaged in a public dispute with Sherman over Sherman's private doubts about Grant.

**Thomas T. Eckert.** Head of the War Telegraph Department in Washington, D.C. On his own responsibility, he held on to Grant's order relieving Thomas of command until news of the Battle of Nashville came through.

**Donn Piatt.** Army officer, judge advocate, and friend of Lincoln, he became an investigative journalist after the war. He was an important figure in attacking the corruption of the Grant administration and offered a withering critique of Grant's whole career.

**Thomas Statue, *Harper's Weekly.*** One of the finest equestrian statues on the American continent, it was cast in bronze from captured Confederate guns. It stands today at Thomas Circle in the heart of Washington, D.C.

the ranks and their immediate commanders chose to go forward," and in so doing executed the most spectacular assault of the war.

Halfway up, there was a pause. The heavy guns of the Rebels could not be lowered enough to hit their targets; the Federal guns on Fort Wood dared not continue their shelling at the risk of hitting their own men. One Union officer afterward recalled: I never felt so lonesome in my life." Then on up the men went, smashing through felled trees, halting but a moment to re-form. One soldier remembered:

> Those defending the heights became more and more desperate as our men approached the top. . . . They thrust cartridges into guns by handsfull, they lighted the fuses of shells and rolled them down, they seized huge stones and threw them, but . . . one after another the regimental flags were borne over the parapet and the ridge was ours. The finest battery . . . in the Southern army was there, the ramrods half-way down the guns when captured. These were whirled around and fired in the direction of the flying foe. . . . What yells and cheers broke from the panting, weary but triumphant ranks. They threw their haversacks in the air until it was a cloud of black spots; officers and men mingled indiscriminately in their joy.

"Who gave that order?" demanded Grant, turning to Thomas. "I know of no one giving such orders," he replied. Grant glared at Granger. "Did you order them up?" "No," said Granger, "they are going without orders. When those fellows get started, all hell can't stop them." "Well, it will be investigated," said Grant. But as he spoke, the men mounted to the summit, leaped into Bragg's entrenchments, piercing his lines in the center, doubling them to the right and left. Along the line of the ridge, at six different points, the troops belonging to Thomas could be seen pouring over the enemy breastworks and planting their flags.

Grant's fury at Thomas ("Who gave that order?") for allowing his men to go up instead of stopping at the rifle pits was next to insane. Just as Thomas had signaled his men on Orchard Knob—"You have gained too much to withdraw; hold your position, and I will support you"—so having gained the rifle pits, it made no sense not to go up. In those pits they were sitting ducks for Confederate fire. Their own common sense and initiative shamed Grant's reckless blindness to their lives. Wrote one officer, "Twenty minutes of that exposure was sufficient to annihilate the entire force. Grant said subsequently, with that charming indifference to fact so peculiar to him, that he expected the men to re-form in the captured rifle-pits and await further movement until ordered. A most appropriate place that to re-form and await orders. We know well that the forward dash was safer than a retreat." At least in the gullies, huge rocks, and trees of the slope, there was some shelter from Rebel fire.

The assault up the ridge may not have been ordered by explicit command, and begun "by an uncontrollable impulse." But, as one officer noted, the men had also been trained to execute any enterprise, however hazardous, "under a general of heroic mould." That confidence was born of a well-earned trust. For Thomas had never let them down. Indeed, "even while the shouts of victory were still filling the air," wrote one, "the shrill whistle of the first steamboat, loaded with supplies, coming up the reopened river, told the story of future plenty, after the long starvation; and added another proof, if one were needed, to the willing minds of his enthusiastic soldiers, that their commander could feed as well as fight them. It was the final test alike of his greatness in battle and his providence in their care."

Thomas rode up to the top of the hill. "I fell among some of my old soldiers, who always took liberties with me—who commenced talking and giving their views of the victory," he related. "When I attempted to compliment them for the gallant manner in which they made the assault, one man [as gaunt as a trained runner] very coolly replied: 'Why, General, we know that you have been training us for this race for the last three weeks.'" Though Grant held himself aloof from the general elation, it touched almost every other pen. "It was reserved by Providence to Thomas and his army, already four times depleted," wrote General Howard, "to storm heights more difficult than those of Gettysburg, and to capture batteries and intrenchments harder to reach than those of Vicksburg." In his dispatch to the War

Department, Dana declared the assault "one of the greatest miracles in military history . . . as awful as a visible interposition of God."

Grant's whole plan had been designed around a successful assault by Sherman near the tunnel on the northern end of Missionary Ridge. Neither Hooker's action, which swept Lookout Mountain, nor the storming of the ridge was in the plan. But in Grant's report on the 25th he tells us that the Rebel troops had massed to their right in "desperation to defeat or resist the progress of Sherman," who had not been making progress, and thereby "weaken[ed] their center on Missionary Ridge." That, Grant tells us, "determined me to order the advance at once. Thomas was accordingly directed to move forward his troops constituting our center . . . with a double line of skirmishers thrown out, followed in easy supporting distance by the whole force, and carry the rifle-pits at the foot of Missionary Ridge, and, when carried, to reform his lines with a view of carrying the top of the ridge."

Adam Badeau, in his *Military History of U.S. Grant*, expounded the same fiction: "The Rebel center, as Grant had foreseen, was weakened to save the right; and then the whole mass of the Army of the Cumberland was precipitated on the weakened point; the center was pierced, the heights carried, and the battle of Chattanooga won." Sherman's version aligned with Grant's. In his *Memoirs*, he wrote: "The object of General Hooker's and my attacks on the extreme flanks of Bragg's position was to disturb him to such an extent that he would naturally detach from his center as against us so that Thomas's army could break through his center. The whole plan succeeded admirably, but it was not until after dark that I learned the complete success of the center, and received General Grant's orders to pursue on the north side of Chickamauga Creek." An independent investigation made afterward, however, by General James Wilson revealed that this was not so—that Bragg had drawn men not from his center (on the ridge) but his left. Confederate General Edward Porter Alexander (Bragg's chief of artillery on the ridge, who would have known) also insisted no such movements from the center were made.

Night put an end to the fighting, but the victory was near-complete.

That part of Bragg's army facing the troops under Thomas had fled in a rout; that part of Bragg's army (on his right) facing Sherman retreated slowly and in order after nightfall, falling back with guns, flags, and matériel. The capture of 6,000 Rebel prisoners, several pieces of artillery, and many thousand stands of small arms was "an irreparable loss to the Confederacy," wrote Confederate general John Gordon. "In its exhausted condition these could not be replaced by new levies and new guns." By twelve o'clock all the Rebel positions around Chattanooga had been abandoned, and Bragg's disheartened army withdrew through Ringgold, Georgia, to Dalton in the greatest and most complete defeat up to that time in the war. Hooker, having rebuilt the bridge over Chattanooga Creek, pursued Bragg's army as far as Ringgold for two days. Yet Grant in his memoirs blamed Hooker for letting part of Bragg's army escape.

The fault was more with Grant. Though wont to call Thomas "slow," he had shown the very lack of initiative he was swift to decry. As William McFeely, Grant's celebrated biographer, put it: "The enemy fled, but Grant, as at Shiloh, did not move in pursuit. It was a great victory, but it had not been accomplished according to Grant's design. Sherman's Army of the Tennessee had not won the fierce battle, and Grant never forgave Thomas for the fact that the men of his Army of the Cumberland, whom Grant held in some contempt, had carried the day. The Union had won . . . but the total destruction of Bragg's army was not accomplished. . . . The splendid victory was not, finally, a complete success."

The Lincoln administration, however, portrayed the battle as perfectly fought, for its own political prestige, and Grant as the commanding genius of the fight. In that spirit, Congress praised him in a joint resolution and arranged for a gold medal to be struck in his honor "in the name of the people of the United States."

In histories of the war (as well as biographies of Grant) the course of the battle is still often portrayed as having gone as Grant planned. Grant presented it that way in his memoirs, but numerous contemporary accounts, as well as the official record, including telegrams, show that to be false.

• • •

In his own report to the War Department, Thomas remarked with exquisite tact: "It will be seen . . . that the original plan of operations was somewhat modified. . . . It is believed, however, that the original plan, had it been carried out, could not possibly have led to more successful results." Or as General Henry V. Boynton put it bluntly, "Every successful feature of the three days' battle about Chattanooga was his and not another's. Every modification of the plan of battle was his and every portion of the plan which succeeded was modified."

The successful assault on the Ridge possibly saved Burnside, too. According to Edward Porter Alexander, Longstreet had been poised to renew his attack when Burnside, "playing for time," sent in a flag of truce. "Everything was ready, & six hours might have made Burnside a prisoner. The game was worth playing for." But then Bragg suffered his calamitous defeat. Grant afterward sent Sherman, Howard, and Granger to Knoxville, racing eighty-five miles or more on separate roads. When Sherman arrived, he found Burnside safely entrenched and (though reportedly facing starvation) well fixed for supplies. Longstreet had retired to the hills. Grant proposed that Sherman chase him into South Carolina, but Sherman replied: "A stern chase is a long one," and that was that.

By the winter of 1863, the war had seemed to go on for so long, with so much carnage, that there was an impersonal largeness to it that recalled the martial epics of the Romans and Greeks. One officer, writing in his diary from Chattanooga, on Christmas Day 1863, caught something of that spirit when he wrote:

Today we picked up on the battlefield of Chickamauga the skull of a man who had been shot in the head. It was smooth, white and glossy. A little over three months ago this skull was full of life, hope and ambition. He who carried it into battle had, doubtless, mother, sisters, friends, whose happiness was to some extent dependent upon him. They mourn for him now, unless, possibly, they hope still to hear that he is safe and well. Vain hope. Sun, rain, and crows have united in the work of stripping the flesh from his bones, and while the greater part of these lay whitening where they fell, the skull has been rolling about the field, the sport and plaything of the winds. This is war.

That winter, while Grant and Sherman maneuvered for power through their patrons in the War Department and the halls of Congress, Thomas was encamped under the shadows of Lookout Mountain and Missionary Ridge. One day Howard rode over from his headquarters in Lookout Valley to Chattanooga to see him and asked him why he did not take a brief leave before the spring campaign commenced. "Oh," he said, "I cannot leave; something is sure to get out of order if I go away from my command. It was always so, even when I commanded a post. I had to stick by and attend to everything, or else affairs went wrong." Yet with Thomas there was never wasted time. While he wintered at Chattanooga, he conceived of the idea of a national cemetery for veterans laid out on the slopes of Orchard Knob. It was in this way that the system of military cemeteries was begun that became a popular source of national pride. "The general who loved his men so heartily when alive," wrote one officer, "had a religious and patriotic respect for their remains when called to their interment. They had given their courage, endurance and lives to their country, and it was fitting and seemly that their last resting places should be monuments to their sacrifice." He was not about to disgrace their memory either by perpetuating in burial the divisions of the war. When asked if the men were to be buried by state of origin, he said: "No, no, no. Mix them up. Mix them up. I'm tired of states' rights."

# 9. ATLANTA

After the battle for Chattanooga, Bragg had withdrawn to Dalton, Georgia, where he was "allowed to halt his army and intrench it," wrote the military historian Matthew Forney Steele, "within twenty-five miles of the field of his retreat." There he was soon replaced by General Joseph Johnston, who early in the war had led the Army of Northern Virginia before being severely wounded and had excelled in battles in the East. Bragg was called to Richmond to serve Jefferson Davis as chief of staff. The Richmond authorities were eager for Johnston to assume the offensive to recover Tennessee. Johnston thought that beyond his means. He told Davis it could make sense only if the Federals were first defeated when they tried to move south. Johnston reorganized his army, gave it discipline and drill, and prepared for the Federal spring campaign. He established a series of fortified works or lines extending all the way back to Atlanta, which he rendered almost impregnable. His foremost position was Buzzard's Roost Gap, with an outpost pushed as far forward as Tunnel Hill. Dalton was the "doorway" to Georgia, and Buzzard's Roost Gap was its "outer gate."

The nature of the terrain strengthened Johnston in all his plans. Between Chattanooga and Atlanta stood several mountains, gorges, valleys, and streams, including three rivers (the Oostanaula, the Etowah, and the Chattahoochee); while immediately to the front of Dalton stood Rocky Face Ridge, a bold range, with steep slopes, covered with tangled timber and loose stone, which rose in unscalable palisades of rock. There were two main routes through the thirty-mile-long ridge, one at Tunnel Hill, a railroad pass; the other, fourteen miles to the south, at Snake Creek Gap. Just south of the Etowah River the railroad broke through another palisade by way of Alla-toona Pass. Still farther to the south, in front of Marietta, stood Kene-

217

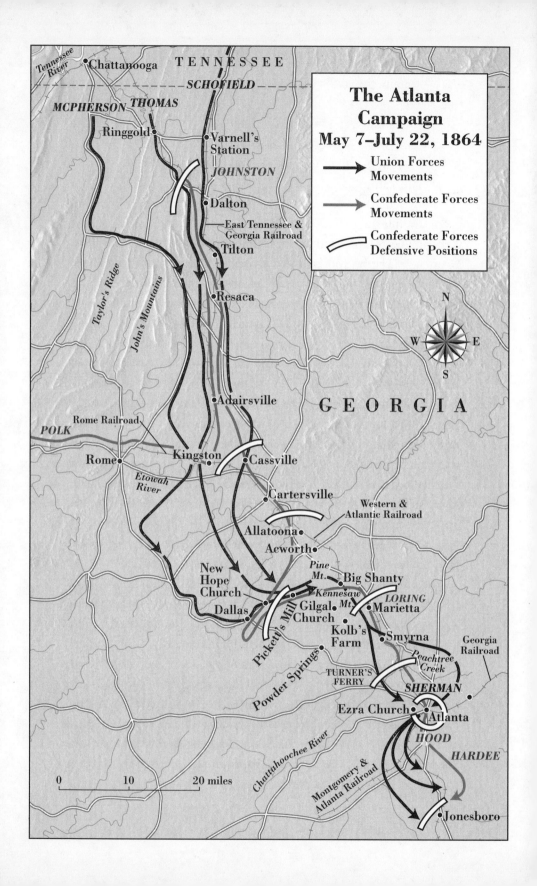

**The Atlanta Campaign May 7–July 22, 1864**

Union Forces Movements

Confederate Forces Movements

Confederate Forces Defensive Positions

Tennessee River

Chattanooga

TENNESSEE

SCHOFIELD

MCPHERSON  THOMAS

Ringgold

Varnell's Station

JOHNSTON

Dalton

East Tennessee & Georgia Railroad

Tilton

Resaca

Taylor's Ridge

John's Mountains

N W E S

Adairsville

GEORGIA

Rome Railroad

POLK

Rome

Kingston

Cassville

Etowah River

Cartersville

Western & Atlantic Railroad

Allatoona

Acworth

New Hope Church

Dallas

Pine Mt.

Big Shanty

Kennesaw Mt.

LORING

Gilgal Church

Marietta

Pickett's Mill

Kolb's Farm

Smyrna

Georgia Railroad

Powder Springs

TURNER'S FERRY

Peachtree Creek

SHERMAN

Ezra Church

Atlanta

HOOD

HARDEE

Chattahoochee River

Montgomery & Atlanta Railroad

Jonesboro

0    10    20 miles

saw Mountain, the most formidable barrier in a line of disconnected hills.

Once Chattanooga had been won, the obvious next move for the Union army was to advance. That could have been done at once before Johnston fortified. Instead, Grant sent Sherman on a trans-Mississippi campaign via Meridian to take Mobile. Jefferson Davis was surprised. After the war, he said that the loss of Chattanooga had been a terrible blow to the Confederacy, and that his only consolation was that the North seemed not to know what to do with its prize. Meanwhile, Thomas pointed out to Grant that the Confederates were strengthening their real defense line into Georgia, where the Union army would eventually have to go.

On January 19, Grant wrote Thomas that a campaign through to the Gulf at Mobile was under consideration, with Atlanta and Montgomery as intermediate points. The start was to be at the earliest possible moment in the spring. Thomas began at once to prepare for the movement, but then was ordered by Grant to make a reconnaissance in force toward Johnston's position at Dalton, and if possible to capture the place. His main motive, and Grant's, was to prevent the Confederates in Georgia from detaching some of their forces against Sherman as he moved toward Selma in the course of his Meridian raid.

The only practicable approach to Dalton from the front was through Buzzard Roost Gap, a narrow valley dominated by precipitous heights and commanded by detached ridges, which Johnston had also fortified. In addition, he had arranged to flood the whole gorge from a nearby creek should the Federals attempt to move through. At the time, about 30,000 Confederates manned these heights. Thomas, as ordered, advanced four divisions of infantry with cavalry on each flank. He reconnoitered the roads and passes to Dalton from the front; explored the gaps on the flanks, with a view to turning movements; carried Tunnel Hill, a strong range west of Rocky Face Ridge; and successfully moved through several deep valleys, forcing the heads of his columns into Buzzard Roost. That brought his lines close to the enemy's work. He was able to examine them closely, and after withdrawing to Ringgold reported to Grant that it was not possible to carry them by assault.

That was clearly true. Johnston had at least as many men as Thomas had (part of the Army of the Cumberland was then scattered among a number of posts) and more artillery, with the huge advantage of fortified heights. The surrounding landscape was also barren, with no forage for his horses and mules. Thomas had gone as far as he could go without risking entrapment, starvation, or defeat. Yet on his return to Chattanooga, he was greeted by an implied reprimand. "It is of the utmost importance that the enemy should be held in full belief that an advance into the heart of the South is intended until the fate of General Sherman is fully known," Grant told him by wire, and offered some advice as to how Thomas could keep himself supplied. "The difficulties of supplies can be overcome by keeping your trains running between Chattanooga and your position. Can't you draw teams from Bridgeport and Stevenson to send supplies to the front?" In fact, by his strong reconnaissance, Thomas had already accomplished the main thing Grant had wanted. He had forced Johnston to draw back reinforcements sent west against Sherman, and even to call for reinforcements himself. The railroad that Grant told Thomas to rely on was then in disrepair. Yet Grant in his memoirs (a sad refrain!) blithely remarks that Thomas had failed to take Dalton, as if he could. More importantly (but unmentioned by Grant), Thomas had discovered that Snake Creek Gap south of Dalton lay unguarded and offered a hidden way to Johnston's rear. This was a discovery of vast importance, and, if properly exploited, promised to save thousands of lives in a swift, smart campaign.

Thomas now proposed "a strong demonstration against Buzzard's Roost, attracting Johnston's whole attention to that point," while throwing "the main body of my infantry and cavalry through Snake Creek Gap upon his communications, which I had ascertained from scouts he had up to that time neglected to observe or guard." That (most military historians now agree) could have won the day. It was, in fact, the plan Sherman later adopted as his own, but botched. To make it work, as Thomas later recalled in his report to the congressional Joint Committee on the Conduct of the War, "I had previously asked for the return to me of Granger's troops and my cavalry from East Tennessee, and had already initiated preparations for the execution of the above movement" in the spring. As of February 28, when he proposed his brilliant flanking movement to Grant in a wire, Thomas needed only 25,000 more men to destroy Johnston's army and win Atlanta for the North. As he explained to Grant, if he had the Fourth and Fourteenth Corps in front, Howard's corps in reserve, and a strong division of cavalry in advance, he could "move along the line of the railroad and overcome all opposition to Atlanta" and beyond.

While Thomas had excelled in his assignment, Sherman had partly failed in his. Having gotten as far as Meridian (a railhead he destroyed), he had turned back without attempting to move on Selma or Mobile.

As preparations got underway for the spring campaign, Thomas had every reason to assume he would be in charge. Three weeks later, however, through an act of Congress introduced by Grant's political patron, Elihu Washburne of Illinois, and sanctioned by Lincoln, Grant assumed command of the armies of the United States as lieutenant general on March 17, 1864. One of his very first acts was to tell Thomas (who by date of his commission outranked Sherman, and whose achievements likewise had earned him priority of place) that Sherman was to take charge of the Military Division of the Mississippi and run the Atlanta campaign. Instead of being allowed to defeat Johnston as he believed he could, Thomas once more found his army subject to the direction of a general who was arguably incompetent, and almost always failed.

Yet behind the scenes, a momentous change had been briefly considered that would have affected the whole course of the war. Stanton (unhappy with Meade) had been looking for the right general to lead the Army of the Potomac, and had consulted with James Garfield about it. Garfield commended Thomas as the man. "I told him I hoped he would go no further than yourself," he wrote Thomas, "in selecting a new commander." Stanton seemed to agree. But it was Grant who ultimately received the overall command. The choice was Lincoln's, and made in part for political reasons, out of gratitude to Grant for not allowing his name to be floated as a rival presidential candidate in the upcoming campaign. Had the choice been otherwise, there might have been no Cold Harbor, no Spotsylvania, no Petersburg, to drench the last months of the war in so much needless blood.

This is not, in itself, a partisan judgment and was held by some even with a regard for Grant. Alexander K. McClure, Lincoln's friend and counselor, remarked in his celebrated memoir, *Lincoln and Men of War-Times,* that "no general was better equipped for the supreme command of all our armies" than Thomas who "would have taken Richmond with Grant's army and saved tens of thousands of gallant men from untimely death."

Almost all Civil War historians agree (however else they may differ) that when it came to picking generals, Lincoln was often flying blind. With his usual quaintness, he once said that selecting a general "was like putting one's hand in a sack to get one eel from a dozen snakes." As a politician, moreover, he often let political considerations guide, and even override, his judgment. Nor did he always follow the best evidence at hand. In this, he was not alone. No one really seems to have known what was required. Secretary of the Treasury Salmon P. Chase remarked to an army official: "I have been studying the art of war. I can find nothing in it but a calculation of chances and a quick eye for topography. Were I not so near-sighted I would be tempted to resign my place as Secretary for a command in the field." Stanton was hardly more helpful. "We have no generals," he exclaimed at one point, absurdly, "but we have men, and I will crowd them on until this rebellion is stamped out. We can lose three men to the rebels' one and win." This emotional outburst became literal military policy under Grant. It was Grant's proposition "to hammer continuously against the armed force of the enemy and his resources until, by mere attrition, if in no other way, there should be nothing left of him." And so for the duration of the war in the East, that is how it would be.

That boded ill for all in his charge. After one frightful assault (May 22) at Vicksburg, Grant was accused of having "left his dead to rot and his wounded to writhe in agony on the outer slopes of the enemy's works for three days, under the hot summer sun." Adam Badeau writes: "The hill-sides were covered with the slain and with unfortunates who lay panting in the heat, crying for water which none could bring them, and writhing in pain that might not be relieved." That seems not to have been so. The Confederates sent Grant a note under a flag of truce:

> Two days having elapsed since your dead and wounded have been lying in our front, and as yet no disposition on your part of a desire to remove them being exhibited, in the name of humanity, I have the honor to propose a cessation of hostilities for two and a half hours that you may be enabled to remove your dead and dying men. If you can not do this, on notification from you that hostilities will be suspended on your part for the time specified, I will endeavor to have the dead buried and the wounded cared for.

The Confederates, in short, were offering to look after the Union dead and wounded themselves. Grant accepted the flag of truce, but he could have arranged it three days before. He didn't because he had falsely reported to Halleck (and announced to the world) that his assault had been a success and had won the intervening ground. "Our troops were not repulsed from any point," he wired Halleck on May 24, "but simply failed to enter the works of the enemy." To ask for a truce would have shown that was not so.

Badeau endeavored to excuse Grant with the detached observation that "The wounded suffer frightfully after every battle, and the party which is repelled is always unable to bestow attention on those whom it leaves on the field." That was an interesting slip, since Grant in his dispatch to Halleck had denied that he had been repelled.

This whole sorry saga is, possibly, bound up with Grant's heavy drinking. The official story after the war was that his drinking was always under control. Lincoln inadvertently contributed to the "romance" of it by his famous remark, "Do you know where Grant buys his whiskey? I would like to present some to other generals not so successful." That was amusing but not wise. Grant's habit, insofar as it impaired his military judgment, was tragic for his men. In early June, Grant's own loyal chief of staff, General John Rawlins, wrote Grant an astonishing letter which he deemed too sensitive to entrust to a courier. From it we learn that Grant had evidently been lying about his besotted state. Rawlins thought it imperiled not only the army but, by extension, the nation itself:

BEFORE VICKSBURG, MISS., June 6, 1863, 1 o'clock A. M.

DEAR GENERAL : The great solicitude I feel for the safety of this army leads me to mention what I had hoped never again to do—the subject of your drinking. This may surprise you, for I may be (and I trust I am) doing you an injustice by unfounded suspicions, but if an error it better be on the side of his country's safety than in fear of offending a friend. I have heard that Dr. McMillan, at General Sherman's a few days ago, induced you, notwithstanding your pledge to me, to take a glass of wine, and to-day, when found a box of wine in front of your tent and proposed to move it, which I did, I was told you had forbid its being taken away, for you intended to keep it until you entered Vicksburg, that you might have it for your friends; and to-night, when you should, because of the condition of your health if nothing else, have been in bed, I find you where the wine bottle has just been emptied, in company with those who drink and urge you to do likewise, and the lack of your usual promptness of decision and clearness in expressing yourself in writing tended to confirm my suspicions.

After the Vicksburg assaults, even Washburne had second thoughts about Grant and went to see Lincoln, who reportedly put his hand on his shoulder and said: "It is a bad business, but we must try the man a little longer. He seems a pushing fellow, with all his faults."

Besides the letter above, there are a number of eyewitness accounts that contradict the claim that Grant's drinking was under control (e.g., Letter from Murat Halstead to Salmon P. Chase, February 19, 1863; Letter from John A. Rawlins to William F. Smith, June 30, 1864; Letter from William F. Smith to Solomon Foot, July 30, 1864). The overall testimony may be mixed (Charles Dana, for example, thought the rumors of Grant's drinking were false); but in these other letters, notes one scholar, we find a "drunken, stupid, foolish Grant," pledging abstinence but getting liquor on the sly. Dr. E. D. Kittoe, a member of Grant's staff, stated in the *New York Daily Tribune*, January 28, 1887, that the facts of Grant's drunkenness—at Donelson, Shiloh, Vicks-burg, and elsewhere—"are well known to every survivor of Grant's military family . . . and to many others who held intimate personal relations with him." Sherman denied it (in a manner that confirmed it) in a famous letter to Colonel John F. Tourtellotte, his former aide-de-camp, February 4, 1887: "Although we all knew at the time that General Grant would occasionally drink too much," he wrote, it never affected his judgment in the field. Of course, Sherman could not pos-sibly know this (except when he was actually with him) first-hand.

Upon Grant's promotion, Halleck was relieved at his own request of the now needless post of general-in-chief, and accepted the position of chief of staff. He remained at Washington in that capacity as mili-tary adviser to the president and the secretary of war, but really sub-ordinate to and loyally sustaining Grant. Grant left Halleck to take care of the administration of the army from the War Department in Washington, while he established his headquarters as general-in-chief near those of Meade. That also made him the de facto commander of the Army of the Potomac, with Meade (a conduit for his orders) sec-ond in command. From his headquarters in the field in Virginia, he planned to supervise the overall conduct of the war.

Meanwhile, when Grant had learned that he was to be made lieu-tenant general by a bill reviving that grade, he immediately wrote to Sherman, on March 4, 1864:

> While I have been eminently successful in this war, in at least gain-ing the confidence of the public, no one feels more than I how much of this success is due to the energy, skill, and the harmonious putting forth of that energy and skill, of those whom it has been my good fortune to have occupying subordinate positions under me.
>
> There are many officers to whom these remarks are applicable to a greater or less degree, proportionate to their ability as soldiers; but what I want is to express my thanks to you and [James B.] McPherson [who had served with Grant at Vicksburg], as the men to whom, above all others, I feel indebted for whatever I have had

of success. How far your advice and suggestions have been of assistance, you know. How far your execution of whatever has been given you to do entitles you to the reward I am receiving, you cannot know as well as I do. I feel all the gratitude this letter would express, giving it the most flattering construction.

Sherman replied on March 10 from near Memphis:

You do yourself injustice and us too much honor in assigning to us so large a share of the merits which have led to your high advancement. . . .

You are now Washington's legitimate successor, and occupy a position of almost dangerous elevation; but if you can continue as heretofore to be yourself, simple, honest, and unpretending, you will enjoy through life the respect and love of friends, and the homage of millions of human beings who will award to you a large share for securing to them and their descendants a government of law and stability. . . .

I believe you are as brave, patriotic, and just, as the great prototype Washington; as unselfish, kind-hearted, and honest, as a man should be; but the chief characteristic in your nature is the simple faith in success you have always manifested, which I can liken to nothing else than the faith a Christian has in his Saviour.

Sherman then gave Grant his opinion of his generalship: "This faith gave you victory at Shiloh and Vicksburg. Also, when you have completed your best preparations, you go into battle without hesitation, as at Chattanooga—no doubts, no reserve; and I tell you that it was this that made us act with confidence. I knew wherever I was that you thought of me, and if I got in a tight place you would come—if alive. My only points of doubt were as to your knowledge of grand strategy, and of books of science and history; but I confess your common-sense seems to have supplied all this." He went on to urge him not to stay in Washington, but "Come out West; take to yourself the whole Mississippi Valley; let us make it dead-sure, and I tell you the Atlantic slope and Pacific shores will follow its destiny as sure as the limbs of a tree live or die with the main trunk! . . . From the West, when our task is done, we will make short work of Charleston and Richmond, and the impoverished coast of the Atlantic."

On that score, Sherman was right: It was in the West where the war would be won.

But this extravagant exchange was not quite sincere. Sherman's private opinion of Grant fell short of such pronouncements, which Grant would not have been pleased to know. After Shiloh, Sherman had written to his wife, Ellen, "[Grant] is not a brilliant man"; and after Vicksburg, he told her: "We have in Grant not a great man or a Hero—but a good, plain, sensible, kindhearted fellow." Sherman considered himself smarter, with "a much quicker perception of things." Later, a deeper enmity between them would emerge.

There was no real justification for Sherman's appointment (outside of Grant's prerogative to make it) and of course it was an affront to Thomas for reasons that were clear enough. As one fellow officer noted: "He had not, at any time, lost a movement or a battle from Mill Springs to Chattanooga. The laurels of Horseshoe Ridge, and Lookout Mountain, and Missionary Ridge, were fresh on his brow. The country spoke his name with universal acclaim. He was at the head of a great army which revered him. He had personally reconnoitered the enemy's stronghold at Dalton; had made careful examination of all questions involved in a campaign, and had perfected a plan for moving forward to Atlanta." He was entitled to the command. Instead, a junior was placed over him, for the simple and obvious reason that Grant liked Sherman, didn't like Thomas, and Grant and Sherman were allied. As Sherman put it in a moment of unguarded candor: "Grant stood by me when I was crazy, and I stood by him when he was drunk."

At the time Sherman took over, Thomas's plan of campaign had not only been perfected and submitted to Grant, but even its details, such as the number of guards needed at each bridge and minor post. His Army of the Cumberland, once gathered, was 60,000 strong, well equipped and supplied, in excellent spirits, and ready to advance. The Confederate force at that time was about 50,000 of all arms. Yet almost at once a new effort to belittle Thomas got underway behind the scenes. Sherman had been trying to explain his own conduct at the Battle of Chattanooga, and to exculpate himself had blamed Thomas for his "delayed" attack on the Ridge. In a shameful letter on April 27, 1864, to his adoptive father, Thomas Ewing, Sherman went so far as to say that Thomas had been suffered to remain in charge of his army only because of his seniority and rank. "If we were to dispose of such men as Thomas summarily who would take his place? We are not masters as Napoleon was. He could make & unmake on the Spot. We must take the tools provided us, and in the order prescribed by Rank of which the Law judges."

Sherman met Grant at Nashville, accompanied him as far as Cincinnati (en route to Washington), and was briefed on Grant's plan for the spring campaign, which was to open about the first of May. In a simultaneous movement of all the armies, Grant was to go after Lee, Sherman after Johnston by way of Atlanta and push through to Savannah or the Gulf. Grant had the huge Army of the Potomac; Sherman's equally large, combined force was to consist of the Army of the Cumberland (composed of the Fourth, Fourteenth, and Twentieth Corps of Infantry and a corps of cavalry), under Thomas; the Army of the Tennessee, under James McPherson; and the Army of the Ohio, under John Schofield. Expertly trained and by far the most powerful of the three, the army under Thomas would number 61,000 men and 130 guns—two-thirds of the entire invading force—at the start of the campaign.

Grant's plan was to hammer away at Lee's army without let-up, protecting Washington by placing Lee on the defensive, while keeping him engaged so continuously that he would have little or no time to recuperate or resupply, and no freedom to dispatch troops from his own army to other theaters of the war. Whatever the toll in losses, Lee would suffer more, for he could not replace his losses, whereas Grant could. Sherman, meanwhile, was to destroy the army of Joseph Johnston, take Atlanta, and, if possible, swing into the South behind Lee, creating a rear front that could at last be attacked. Johnston's strategy was to fight only when he could inflict greater losses than he sustained; retreat slowly; destroy the railroad (Sherman's line of supply) as he withdrew; and wear out the Federal army.

Sherman's first task, and one he was particularly good at, was to secure his long supply line by way of the Cumberland River, and from Louisville to Nashville by rail. Chattanooga (his starting point) was 136 miles in front of Nashville, "and every foot of the way, especially the many bridges, trestles, and culverts, had to be strongly guarded" against the vandalism of a hostile population and enemy attacks. The tracks further south would also have to be secured as his troops advanced. Sherman wrote: "General Thomas' army . . . was best provided, and contained the best corps of engineers, railroad managers, and repair parties, as well as the best body of spies and provost-marshals. On him we were therefore compelled in a great measure to rely for these most useful branches of service." That reliance was not misplaced. In the course of the campaign, for example, the engineering branch did yeoman's work. "No matter when or where a breach was made," Sherman later wrote, "the repair train seemed on the spot, and the damage was repaired generally before I knew of the break. Bridges were built with surprising rapidity, and the locomotive whistle was heard in an advanced camp almost before the echoes of the skirmish-fire had ceased. Some of the bridges, those of the Oostanaula, the Etowah, and Chattahoochee, are fine, substantial structures, and were built in an inconceivably short time, almost out of material improvised on the spot." The trestle bridge across the Chattahoochee River near Atlanta was 780 feet in length, and 90 feet in height, and was reconstructed in four and a half days. The Potomac Creek bridge, 414 feet long and 82 feet high, was repaired in forty hours. The Aquia Creek Railroad on the Potomac, thirteen miles in length, was opened in five days after the order to begin the work was given.

Under Sherman, large quantities of provisions, munitions, and other stores were collected at Chattanooga, and all the troops destined for the new campaign (a combined army of 100,000, with 254 guns) were ordered to concentrate there on April 27. By May 6, they were in position and ready to march. If there was any ill will between Sherman and Thomas, both concealed it. On May 5, Sherman's inspector general, Willard Warner, asked him "if there was any truth in the rumor that Thomas felt aggrieved at having him (Sherman) put in command over him. He replied: 'No, not a bit! It don't make much difference which of us commands. I would obey "Tom's" orders to-morrow as cheerfully as he obeys mine today, but I think I can give an army a little more impetus [drive] than "Tom" can' . . . Their consultations were frequent, frank, and free."

Be that as it may, the strategy of advance had changed. Some weeks before, Sherman had gone to see Thomas at Chattanooga; heard and rejected his plan of turning the Rebels' position by a flanking movement through Snake Creek Gap; and wired Grant on April 24 that he planned to attack Johnston's entrenched position at Dalton instead. As Thomas later recalled, in his testimony before the Committee on the Conduct of the War:

> I proposed to General Sherman that if he would use McPherson's and Schofield's armies to demonstrate on the enemy's position at Dalton . . . I would throw my whole force through Snake Creek Gap, which I knew to be unguarded, fall upon the enemy's communications between Dalton and Resaca, thereby turning his position completely; and force him either to retreat toward the east . . . or attack me, in which latter event I felt confident that my army was sufficiently strong to beat him. . . . General Sherman objected to this plan for the reason that he desired my army to form the reserve of the united armies, and to serve as a rallying point for the two wings.

After a skirmish at Tunnel Hill, Sherman pushed up to the front of Rocky Face Ridge, split by Buzzards Roost, and into the passes that led through and over it to Dalton, where Johnston was strongly entrenched. The Union troops could not advance any farther to their front unless they scaled the heights. These were inaccessible. The passes had also been rendered extremely strong. All this had been reported by Thomas to Grant months before. Sherman had been informed of it, too, and by his own immediate reconnaissance might now have changed course. From Thomas, he knew that Snake Creek Gap, ten miles to the south, opened fifteen miles to the rear of Dalton, was wholly undefended, practical for artillery and trains, and hidden from enemy view.

Even so, Sherman went ahead with his assault. On May 7, the Armies of the Cumberland and the Ohio were flung into the fortified gorges and against the heights. For the next three days, they fought in vain up to and against stone walls and "against rocks and defiles with heavy loss. There was hand-to-hand fighting in places with clubbed muskets and "many were tumbled off the rocky palisades, falling . . . to the base of the perpendicular wall." Belatedly, McPherson with 23,000 men was sent through Snake Creek Gap with orders to push out to the railroad near Resaca and break it. His army, however, was inadequate for the task. It wasn't until the 11th that the rest of Sherman's army was made to follow, and not until the 13th that the movement was complete. But by then it was too late: Johnston had been apprised of the movement, abandoned Dalton, retired to Resaca, put down his bridges over the Oostenaula to give a safe line of retreat, and awaited Sherman's advance. There, in a position of his own choosing, he accepted battle, won a tactical victory, and safely withdrew his army to the river's south bank.

The chance to end the Atlanta campaign with a decisive early victory was thereby thrown away. From then on, the campaign would become "one big Indian fight," as Sherman later complained, with Johnston retreating from one fortified position to another, as his flanks were turned. What might have been over in early May would drag on—without a completely satisfactory result—for another four months.

In his official dispatches, Sherman implied that the assaults before Rocky Face and its adjacent ridges had only been feints, and that the move through Snake Creek Gap, which he had resisted, had been intended all along. Years later Sherman claimed in his *Memoirs* that McPherson had also been too timid to accomplish his task. He reproduced his own letters to McPherson, but claimed McPherson's ("mere notes in pencil not retained") had not survived. It later transpired that Sherman had suppressed them. When they were found in the archives of the War Department, some proved to be of great length, and showed that Sherman, not McPherson, had been the one at fault. (E.g., McPherson's letter dated May 9, 10:30 P.M.) McPherson's instructions had not been to hold the railroad but to cut it and then withdraw to Snake Creek Gap. From there, he was to strike Johnston's army in retreat. Sherman thought that with his supply line cut Johnston would have to retreat, and that McPherson would be waiting for him as Thomas and Schofield pursued.

The record, in any case, is clear. On the night of the 10th, Sherman telegraphed Halleck:

> General McPherson reached Resaca, but found the place strongly fortified and guarded.... According to his instructions, he drew back to the debouches of the gorge, where he has a strong defensive position, and guards the only pass into the valley of the Oostenaula available to us. Buzzard Roost Gap, through which the railroad passes, is naturally and artificially too strong to be attempted. I must feign on Buzzard Roost [he had already been "feigning" with his main force at great cost for several days], but pass through Snake Creek Gap, and place myself between Johnston and Resaca, when we will have to fight it out. I am making the preliminary move. Certain that Johnston can make no detachments, I will be in no hurry.

And so the plan was botched.

As it happened, when McPherson first went through, Sherman thought he had actually gained Johnston's rear. Willard Warner, of Sherman's staff, recalled:

> On the night of May 9th as we were at supper at the brick house, by the spring near Tunnel Hill Station, a letter was brought to the general. Reading it, he instantly left the table, and bade me follow him. When we had got a little way from the house, he stopped short, and, with a vehement gesture of his right hand clenched, said: "I have got Joe Johnston dead. This letter is from McPherson. At one o'clock to-day he was within one and a half mile of the railroad. He must be on it now. I want to go over and see Tom"—meaning General Thomas. On his way he said that Johnston would be compelled to abandon the railroad and most of his artillery and trains, and re-

treat to the east through the mountains . . . that we would follow the railroad, and beat Johnston to Atlanta.

Arriving at General Thomas's headquarters, we found him at supper, and General Sherman repeated to him the same expressions he used to me. General Thomas was also greatly pleased . . . Sherman and Thomas agreed that Johnston must now let go Rocky Face, and that Thomas and Schofield must push him hard in the morning to crush him and prevent his crushing McPherson. This understanding had, we returned to our headquarters, General Sherman being in high spirits.

Late that night word came from McPherson that he had failed to seize the railroad, and had fallen back to the mouth of the gap and fortified. . . . All the members of the staff will remember how disappointed and excited the general was on receipt of this news, and how cross he was the next day. . . . We all thought he might relieve McPherson of his command.

I was present when General Sherman and McPherson first met after this. . . . His first remark was, "Well, Mac, you have missed the great opportunity of your life."

After the Federals occupied Resaca on the morning of May 16, Johnston fell back to Cassville, north of the Etowah, where he prepared for another fight. When Thomas came up, Johnston retired to Allatoona across the river to the south. Sherman now decided to leave the line of the railroad and swing to the west to turn Johnston's flank at the pass. On May 23rd he marched toward Dallas (Georgia); but Johnston, quick to move, arrived in force at New Hope Church, and posted his advance at Dallas when Sherman appeared.

Two days later, near Pumpkin Vine Creek not far from the church, Thomas learned that most of Johnston's force was to his front. The rest of Sherman's army had marched off on other roads. Thomas told Captain Henry Stone of his staff "almost in a whisper" to ride back to Howard as fast as he could to hurry up the Fourth Corps. At the same time, he told Stone to walk his horse slowly, so as not to alarm the troops, until he was out of sight. No sooner had he mounted up than "there was a sudden outburst of musketry, kept up for some time, which filled me with dread." He found Howard six miles to the rear, delivered the message, and riding back to Thomas came upon Sherman, who was full of impatience and thought Thomas was advancing with too much caution since, as he wrote on the back of a note, "I don't see what they are waiting for in front now. There haven't been twenty rebels there today." He didn't know what he was talking about, as the Battle of New Hope Church, as it would soon be known, grew fierce.

After the battle, in which the Federals got the worst of it, both armies were battered by a heavy storm. Weary soldiers "doggedly made their way to the front through mud and water up to their knees or dropped exhausted by the road," where some were "trampled by the horses of bewildered staff officers" in the general confusion of the scene. Thomas calmly entrenched before the enemy to prevent panic among his men. That annoyed Sherman, who insisted that he move his headquarters back. As Thomas feared, that upset his men, and he flatly declared to a colleague (Colonel John Watts De Peyster) that "he would never do so again whatever the consequence might be to himself."

The fighting on that line went on for three more days. At length, Johnston pulled back, once more retrenched, but in such a way as to deceive Sherman about the position of his flanks. After Howard pushed through thickets and across ridges and ravines, he attacked what he believed was the end of Johnston's right. But "Johnston forestalled us," wrote Howard, "and was on hand fully prepared." Even so, Sherman ordered Howard to press ahead against the Rebel position at Pickett's Mill on May 27, where a Federal division was cut to shreds. The writer Ambrose Bierce, who took part, later called the order a "crime."

Sherman failed to mention this battle in his *Memoirs*.

The Federals finally secured the line from Allatoona to Ackworth, as Johnston, on the night of June 4, withdrew toward Kenesaw Mountain, with Marietta to his rear. Altogether, Sherman's army had now lost about 12,000 men.

Sherman spent about a week opening the railroad to Ackworth

and establishing a secondary base of supplies. On June 8, he also received 9,000 reinforcements and prepared to move on the Kenesaw line. On June 10, the whole army advanced to Big Shanty, a station six miles south of Ackworth, from where the enemy's line of fortifications on Kenesaw, Pine, and Lost Mountains could be seen. In fighting on June 15–16, Thomas broke through Johnston's works on the east side of Pine Hill. He then pushed his army across Mud Creek Valley and Nose's Creek under fire, as Kenesaw Mountain loomed up in their front. Meanwhile, it had been raining heavily since the start of June. Sherman himself described the roads as almost impassable, but blaming others for his own faltering progress sought out targets for complaint. Almost no one was spared. Thomas and his Army of the Cumberland—which had borne the brunt of the fighting—was especially maligned. In an infamous letter, Sherman slandered everyone to Grant:

*In the Field, June 18, 1864. General U. S. Grant:*

*Dear General: I have no doubt you want me to write you occasionally letters not purely official, but which will admit of a little more latitude than such documents possess. I have daily sent to Halleck telegraphs which I asked him to report to you, and which he says he has done. You, therefore, know where we are and what we have done. If our movement has been slower than you calculated I can explain the reason, though I know you believe me too earnest and impatient to be behind time. My first movement against Johnston was really fine, and now I believe I would have disposed of him at one blow if McPherson had crushed Resaca, as he might have done, for then it was garrisoned only by a small brigade, but Mc. was a little over cautious lest Johnston, still at Dalton, might move against him alone; but the truth was I got all of McPherson's army, 23,000, eighteen miles to Johnston's rear before he knew they had left Huntsville. With that single exception McPherson has done very well. Schofield also does as well as I could ask with his small force. Our cavalry is dwindling away. We can not get full forage and have to graze, so that the cavalry is always unable to attempt any thing. [Kenner] Garrard is over-cautious, and I think Stoneman [George Stoneman, one of the great cavalry officers of the war] is lazy. The former has 4,500 and the latter about 2,500. Each has had fine chances of cutting in, but were easily checked by the appearance of the enemy. [In fact, on May 18, Stoneman had saved part of Sherman's army at Cassville when he suddenly appeared with cavalry and some horse artillery off to the right of one of Johnston's corps. Stoneman "deserved special recognition from Sherman for this good work," wrote Oliver Howard.] My chief source of trouble is with the Army of the Cumberland, which is dreadfully slow. A fresh furrow in a plowed field will stop the whole column, and all begin to intrench. I have again and again tried to impress on Thomas that we must assail and not defend; we are the offensive, and yet it seems the whole Army of the Cumberland is so habituated to be on the defensive that, from its commander down to the lowest private, I cannot get it out of their heads. I came out without tents and ordered all to do likewise, yet Thomas has a headquarters camp on the style of Halleck at Corinth; every aide and orderly with a wall-tent, and a baggage-train big enough for a division. He promised to send it all back, but the truth is, every body there is allowed to do as he pleases, and they still think and act as though the railroad and all its facilities were theirs. This slowness has cost me the loss of two splendid opportunities which never recur in war. At Dallas there was a delay of four hours to get ready to advance, when we first met Johnston's head of column, and that four hours enabled him to throw up works to cover the head of his column, and he extended the works about as fast as we deployed. Also here I broke one of his lines, and had we followed it up as I ordered at daylight, there was nothing between us and the railroad back of Marietta. I ordered Thomas to move at daylight, and when I got to the point at 9.30, I found [D. S.] Stanley and [Thomas J.] Wood quarreling which should lead. I'm afraid I swore, and said what I should not, but I got them started; but, instead of reaching the Atlanta road back of Marietta, which is Johnston's center, we only got to a creek to the south of it by night, and now a heavy rain stops us and gives time to fortify a new line. Still I have all the high and commanding ground, but the one peak near Marietta, which I can turn.*

*We have had an immense quantity of rain, from June 2d to 14th, and now it is raining as though it had no intention ever to stop. The enemy's cavalry sweeps all around us, and is now to my rear somewhere. The wires are broken very often, but I have strong guards along the road which make prompt repairs. Thus far our supplies of food have been good, and forage moderate, and we have found growing wheat, rye, oats, etc. You may go on with the full assurance that I will continue to press Johnston as fast as I can overcome the natural obstacles and inspire motion into a large, ponderous, and slow (by habit) army. Of course it can not keep up with my thoughts and wishes, but no impulse can be given it that I will not guide.*

*As ever, your friend, W. T. Sherman.*

This must have been somewhat confusing to the War Department, if anyone there got wind of these complaints. Military dispatches at the time show energetic and successful work performed in the face of every kind of natural obstacle, not to mention Johnston's fortified lines. Strange to think that a fresh furrow in a plowed field would stop the whole Army of the Cumberland and set it to entrenching—the army that had stood at Horseshoe Ridge till nearly every other man was killed or wounded; that scaled Lookout Mountain and stormed Missionary Ridge. Sherman's "unsoldierly" malice knew no bounds. As General Henry V. Boynton remarked, "everybody among his subordinates was wrong, or slow, or at fault somehow; and in this long letter there was not a friendly word for anyone, or praise for anyone but himself." Oliver Howard, who later succeeded McPherson as head of the Army of the Tennessee, remembered the campaign otherwise. The march to Atlanta took over a hundred days, and on "every day but three," he wrote, "the armies of McPherson, Schofield, and Thomas were under fire. . . . Sturdy, untiring, uncomplaining, Thomas pounded Johnston's center so hard every hour of every day that Schofield and McPherson could in turn after turn play upon his flanks; and Johnston had to keep his center there to be pounded" as the march wore on.

• • •

Each army, of course, had its own character or style. No army was better managed than the army Thomas led. One fellow officer recalled: "Next to the Army of the Potomac, the Army of the Cumberland was the largest Union Army in the field. It was also the most compact, the most complete in all its departments, the most thoroughly disciplined and organized. Its esprit de corps was equaled by none. It worked like a machine, it lived like a family, it had the soul of honor. From head to foot there were neither malice, jealousies, plottings and intrigues." In short, it reflected the character of the man at its helm. As for Thomas himself, he had a thoughtful manner, which to a man of Sherman's high-strung temperament was bound to seem "slow." "His personal movements were also generally very deliberate," wrote an aide, not because he was lethargic, but because he still suffered from the spinal injury that had occurred on the eve of the war. "Hasty or violent exertion produced acute pain. He never mounted his horse without a wrench, and it was almost agony to ride fast." Even so,

on a march or a campaign, he saw every part of his army every day. On the Atlanta campaign especially, when every day brought at least a skirmish, he invariably made his way along to the head of the column. If, when he was at the rear, the sounds indicated contact with the enemy, he pushed on to the very front, where he often dismounted and walked to the outer skirmish line, to reconnoitre. Only in this way, in that obscure country, could any idea be obtained of the position of the enemy and of his own troops. It was a constant fight in the dark; but his wood-craft was almost unerring. He could make his way through the thickest forest, and come out at the spot he aimed for. When under fire his movements, whether on foot or mounted, were as deliberate as at any other time. If not indifferent to danger, he was never influenced by a sense of it. He seemed unconscious of fear; his manner in the heat of battle was the same as at any other time—always imperturbable, resolute, self-possessed, unhurried. In the crisis of an engagement he was like the great surgeon, who, in a capital operation, said he had not time enough to be in a hurry. He was never seen riding up and down his lines, waving his sword, shouting, or going through any

of those ceremonies which constitute the picturesque part of generalship. Not thus did he command the absolute confidence and
obedience of his devoted soldiers. But whenever and wherever they
saw him, they knew that all was right, and they read in his fixed
countenance the resolve that was always the harbinger of victory.
So, also, on the march nobody ever saw him, with an escort trailing
behind him, dashing past a moving column of troops, throwing up
dust or mud, and compelling them to leave the road to him. If anybody had the right of way it was they, not he. He would break
through the woods, or flounder across a swamp, rather than force
his men from the road, and so wear them out by needless fatigue.

Then there is Sherman's disparagement of Thomas for "a headquarters camp on the style of Halleck at Corinth." The extensive arrangements Thomas traveled under had a military purpose beyond
his convenience, and served as a command center not only for his
wire and intelligence service (on which Sherman constantly relied)
but to coordinate his efforts on behalf of his soldiers' needs. Thomas
had eleven Sibley tents (bell tents with a central supporting pole) for
the accommodation of himself and his staff. His adjutant general's
wagon was also the most complete in the armies of the North. In
short, his "vast mobile establishment," perfected as a command center
about the time of Stones River, was required to maintain his army "as
a fighting machine."

Though at the outset Sherman had ordered that no tents or baggage be carried en route—"only one change of clothing on our horses,
or to be carried by the men"—the order had been modified to some
degree by most of the officers, and Sherman, though in theory traveling light, also had the second largest wagon train of any Union army
in the war. Sherman himself may have had one old wall tent at the
start, in keeping with his own edicts, but he soon gave up his spartan
pretensions and began hanging around the tent town Thomas set up.
Apprised of this, Thomas kindly ordered a company of Ohio sharp-
shooters to pitch new tents for general headquarters' use, which Sherman occupied at once.

In his own personal arrangements, noted General James Garfield,

Thomas was "no anchorite . . . having perhaps a better appointed train of creature comforts than many of his companion generals. He was not abstinent but temperate, and kept a camp establishment such as Marmont prescribes for his model general 'who fulfills all the conditions of command.'" In his hospitality, he was known to set a table with "smoked fresh beef, ham and strong black coffee. At each silver plate," recalled a guest, "was a napkin of the purest white, artistically folded, a silver water goblet, a china cup, and the usual silver knives and forks. Better beef and better coffee would not have been found in the country in which the army was campaigning, while the hot rolls and potatoes, baked in the hot ashes of a neighboring fire, would have made many a French cook blush."

Yet his life of soldiering knew no rest, and he was entirely used to rough conditions in the field. The war correspondent for *The New York Herald* who accompanied the Army of the Cumberland during the Chickamauga and Atlanta campaigns, wrote that Thomas had "been confirmed by long service in the habits of camp, and appear[ed] never to be satisfied unless living" in that style. He recalled that in September 1862, when his division of Buell's army was encamped on the outskirts of Louisville, he had been asked to take rooms in the Galt Hotel near the telegraph office so he could communicate with Halleck over the proposed change in command. Late that night, "he retired to his bed. But the change from a camp-cot to clean feathers was too much for [him]. He found it impossible to sleep, and at a late hour in the night he was compelled to send Captain Jacob Brown, his provost-marshal, to his head-quarters for his camp-cot. . . . [Various events] conspired to keep the general a guest or prisoner at the hotel for a week. During all that time he slept as usual on his cot, [and] banished the chamber-maids from his room."

On the one hand, Thomas ate well and served guests in style; on the other, he was at home in the common soldier's camp. In between, he relished treats and comforts as they came. During the Atlanta campaign he was out riding one day with General Jefferson C. Davis "when they stopped to gorge themselves on some ripe blackberries growing by the road." A Confederate cavalry unit had slipped around behind them and began shooting, "their bullets slicing through the thicket" where the two generals had paused. Thomas, as always, was immune from fear. He continued eating, remarking to Davis, "This is eating blackberries under difficulties!"


Interference in military affairs by top civilian leaders—Lincoln, Stanton, Halleck—had often been counterproductive. Stanton, for example, however dedicated, wrote one critic, was "utterly ignorant of military matters . . . arrogant, impatient, irascible . . . a terror and a marplot in the conduct of the war." But then the pendulum swung the other way. On April 30, 1864, Lincoln had told Grant: "The particulars of your plans I neither know nor seek to know. You are vigilant and self-reliant; and, pleased with this, I wish not to obtrude any constraints or restraints upon you. While I am very anxious that any great disaster or the capture of our men in great numbers shall be avoided, I know these points are less likely to escape your attention than they would be mine." In so saying, he more or less ceded to Grant civilian control of the war.

That was a terrible mistake.

On May 4, Grant, with over 120,000 men, had crossed the Rapidan and plunged into the Wilderness, a broken, tangled, densely wooded region sixty-four square miles in extent where two years before, in the Battle of Chancellorsville, Hooker had come to grief. Lee quickly discovered the movement and early on the 5th the two armies began to strike at each other through the woods. Lee fought with fury and the bullets came in such a stream that some trees were actually sliced through. In many places, the woods caught fire and hundreds of wounded men were either suffocated or burned to death. In two days of battle, Grant lost almost 20,000 men. He advanced next to Spotsylvania Court House, where in a five-day battle (May 8–12) he lost 17,000 more. Grant was undeterred. "I propose to fight it out on this line if it takes all summer," he declared, grandly. He pushed on to Cold Harbor, where three weeks later in his first, blind assault he lost 7,000 men in less than half an hour. Winston Churchill, writing of this battle in his *History of the English-Speaking Peoples*, called it "unflinching butchery." Thousands of troops in Grant's army also died in the rifle pits they carved in malarial swamps. He worked his way next south of Richmond to Petersburg, Virginia, crossed the James River, and began a long siege of the town. In just one month of fighting Grant had lost over 50,000 men—more than two-thirds the number Lee had in his whole army. He had the manpower to spend, and he would spend it. Unlike Lee, he knew he could replenish what he lost. Grant's officers complained bitterly; some (including Lincoln's wife) called him "Butcher Grant." Gideon Welles, Lincoln's great secretary of the navy, remarked that Grant was "too regardless of the lives of his men." William McFeely, in his biography of Grant, charged that Grant had "produced a nightmare of inhumanity and inept military strategy that ranks with the worst such episodes in the history of warfare." By his "reckless and wasteful attacks," wrote John Codman Ropes, "Grant threw away his veterans ten thousand at a time."

"The art of war is simple enough," Grant once said. "Find out where your enemy is. Get at him as soon as you can. Strike at him hard as you can, and keep moving on." His very lack of ingenuity at times allowed the Confederates to predict his next move. Lee's chief of artillery, Edward Porter Alexander, noted that "Grant's favorite hour for attacking . . . was 4 A.M. or 4:30 A.M., & the attacks were as punctual to the minute, almost every time, as the starting of express railroad trains."

One of Grant's military maxims (coined at Donelson) was that there comes a point in every great battle when both sides are exhausted to the point of defeat. Whoever strikes first then wins. The notion that battles are slug-fests fought to exhaustion also showed his predisposition to view battles in that light.

On June 8, the Republicans nominated Abraham Lincoln for a second term as president, with Andrew Johnson, a "War Democrat," as his running mate. Later that summer, the Democrats chose General George B. McClellan as their man. McClellan repudiated part of his own party's antiwar platform and took a more militant stance. That drew toward him part of the pro-Union vote. Lincoln needed some kind of victory to prevail. The North was sick of the war and all its slaughter. The duress was in the duration. As the Atlanta campaign wore on, the stamina of the North for war steadily waned. Grant's colossal carnage in the East exacted a still greater toll. General Edward Porter Alexander noted in his memoirs: "War is sustained quite as much by the moral energy of a people as by its material resources. . . . For armies are things visible and formal, circumscribed by time and space; but the soul of war is a power unseen, bound up with the interests, convictions, passions of men." After Cold Harbor, the patience of the North had just about run out.

In histories of the war, it is common to read of the success of Grant's war of attrition. But "to the average citizen," noted Alexander,

> what was the situation? Though having odds, practically two to one in his favor, in three terrific battles within a month, he had been always thwarted, & had lost about 50,000 men. And he was no nearer Richmond at the end than his ships might have landed him at the beginning, without loss of a man. He was, indeed, consuming the Southern male population, but beside the cost of over two million dollars a day, he was paying more than man for man in Northern blood. In Georgia, Sherman, with over 100,000 men against Johnston's 45,000, had advanced as far as Kenesaw Mountain, near Marietta, but had gained no advantage over Johnston, and had fought no serious battle, Johnston's strength & position were improved as he drew near to Atlanta,

which his engineers had "wisely intrenched before hand," while Sherman's communications became more strained. "Nowhere were the Federal armies accomplishing any success of importance, &, in Virginia, it looked as if their greatest army was being wrecked."

By this incredible spectacle, the whole nation was transfixed.

One day, according to General John A. Logan of McPherson's army, Sherman happened to be reading a newspaper that described Grant's head-on assaults. He complained aloud that the "whole attention of the country was fixed on the Army of the Potomac" and that his own army was being overlooked. To get back into the headlines, it "had got to do some fighting," he said, meaning in the style of Grant. Just then

Sherman's army stood facing the heights of Kenesaw Mountain, which Johnston had fortified with every art at his command. Thomas suggested that he have McPherson sweep past and attack Marietta (the next large town) from the north. Johnston could not send an adequate force to impede him without exposing his own flank. The option was not dissimilar to that Sherman had faced at Snake Creek Gap. Instead, Sherman ordered a frontal assault. When McPherson protested, Sherman replied that "it was necessary to show the country that his troops could fight as well as Grant's." Sherman's fatal order went out on the 25th, two days before the time set. When Thomas read it, he said to William D. Whipple, his chief of staff, "This is too bad."

From June 24 to the morning of the 27th, the army prepared to give itself up to senseless carnage. Sherman called on the Army of the Cumberland to make the main thrust with support from the Army of the Tennessee up the rocky, precipitous, and thickly wooded slope. The enemy's line of works was screened by forest, and protected by slashings of timber and many entanglements. On June 26, the day before the battle, Thomas made a reconnaissance with his aide Henry Stone to select a likely point of attack, riding almost within the enemy's picket line. "During that entire search of almost half a day I did not see one place that seemed to me to afford the slightest prospect of success," Stone recalled later. "The place finally selected was chosen more because the lines were nearer each other than because the enemy's line seemed vulnerable."

The result was a predictable waste of life. The Federal assault on the 27th began at 9 A.M. with a brief but heavy bombardment. "Kenesaw smoked and blazed with fire, a volcano as grand as Etna," wrote Colonel J. F. C. Fullerton, Howard's adjutant general. "It seemed as though the whole earth was upheaving, that a grand explosion and then a downward crash would come." Four infantry brigades raced toward the Confederate salient high above them, their progress at first remarkable despite withering fire. But as they approached the breastworks, they were ripped apart. A Confederate soldier vividly recalled: "A solid line of blue came up the hill. My pen is unable to describe the scene of carnage that ensued in the next two hours. Column after column of Federal soldiers were crowded upon that line. No sooner would a regiment mount our works than they were shot down or surrendered. Yet still they came. . . . All that was necessary was to load and shoot." The troops in reserve below watched "with eager eyes, their bodies as well as their minds strained to the utmost tension," wrote Stone, who stood beside Thomas. "For an instant, as the wild cheering at the first encounter came to us it looked like success but almost as quickly the continuous cheering subsided into individual cries—and then a dread silence which told only of death and utter failure."

The dispatches between Thomas and Sherman on the 27th tell all: one brigade "advanced to within twenty paces of the enemy's breastworks," wired Thomas, "and was repulsed with canister at that range"; another brigade, likewise decimated, lost "nearly every colonel"; a third "reached near the top of the hill through very tangled brush," but was smashed. Sherman ordered a second assault. He told Thomas it would be "easier now than it will be hereafter," and in his 1:30 P.M. dispatch tried to cover his back by getting Thomas to agree: "McPherson and Schofield are at a dead-lock. Do you think you can carry any part of the enemy's line to-day? McPherson's men are up to the abatis and can't move without the direct assault. I will order the assault if you think you can succeed at any point. Schofield has one division close up on the Powder Springs road, and the other across Olley's Creek, about two miles to his right and rear." Ten minutes later, Thomas replied that his men could hold the ground they gained but didn't think direct assaults would work. He tactfully reminded Sherman that the enemy defenses were at least "six to seven feet high and nine feet thick," and pointed out that the losses thus far had been "very heavy" not only among the men but the officers corps. He suggested, instead, that the Rebel defenses be approached by saps.

Sherman didn't care for that idea. "Is there any thing in the enemy's present position," he asked at 2:25, "that if we should approach by regular saps he could not make a dozen new parapets before one sap is completed? Does the nature of the ground warrant the time . . . ?" Two more costly assaults were therefore ordered and proved just as disastrous as the first. Sherman urged a fourth, but Thomas lodged a "most earnest protest" against it, which put an end to the folly at last. At 6 P.M., Thomas tallied up the losses and sent Sherman his report. Sherman's reply (consistent with Logan's account of his motive) was: "Our loss is small compared with some of those East. It should not in the least discourage us. At times assaults are necessary and inevitable." But not in this case. When Sherman asked Thomas at 9 P.M. if he might favor a flanking movement, the usually tactful Thomas was sarcastic: "What force do you think of moving with? If with the greater part of the army, I think it decidedly better than butting against breastworks strongly abatised and twelve feet thick."

In his *Memoirs*, Sherman gives us another tall tale. He tells us that it was *he* who suggested the flanking movement to Thomas, but "General Thomas, as usual, shook his head, deeming it too risky to leave the railroad." That was made up. Since they consulted by wire, Sherman could not have known what Thomas did with his head anyway. The dispatch sent by Thomas is the record—not this exchange.

Sherman later justified the carnage by saying that "it demonstrated to General Johnston that I would assault, and that boldly." Johnston rejoiced in his boldness. Safely entrenched behind fortified works, he could wish for nothing more. Thomas meanwhile warned Sherman: "One or two more such assaults would use up this army." Indeed, no one in Sherman's army was happy about the "Kenesaw affair." Sherman's loss, compared to Johnston's, was nearly ten to one. Dissatisfaction rippled down through the army and out to the country at large. He had to find some extra-military way to explain it. The principal reason he gave—that he "had to do it" to shake up his army—was no better than the appalling motive Logan had described. Logan's story is said to be suspect, since Sherman and Logan had a falling out. But it rings true when we read Sherman's own wire to Halleck on July 9:

> The assault I made was no mistake; I had to do it. The enemy and our own army and officers had settled down into the conviction that the assault of lines formed no part of my game, and the moment the enemy was found behind any thing like a parapet, why every body would deploy, throw up counter-works, and take it easy, leaving it to the "old man" [he meant himself] to turn the position.

Had the assault been made with one-fourth more vigor, mathematically, I would have put the head of George Thomas's whole army right through Johnston's deployed lines on the best ground for go-ahead, while my entire forces were well in hand on roads converging to my then object, Marietta.

In other words, he had exposed his men to slaughter in order to teach them a lesson—and to teach Johnston, too, that he was unpredictable, and capable of unexpected things, including reckless attacks. His men, he said, were too apt to "take it easy" (though they had already lost about 15,000 of the comrades, with fighting every day), and if only they had advanced with "one-fourth more vigor, mathematically" (after clawing their way up through bristling abatis and other entanglements to within point-blank range of heavy fire), it would have all worked out.

This repellent dispatch was not the product of a crazed moment. Three days later he repeated his justification—"the enemy as well as my own army had settled down into the belief that flanking alone was my game"—in a dispatch to Grant. He added: "We lost nothing in morale by the assault."

When the flanking movement was finally made, it brought the Federals to within sight of the Chattahoochee River, just north of Atlanta. Sherman hoped to catch Johnston as he crossed, and on July 2, Thomas overtook the enemy rear guard below Marietta. Their resistance was strong and the fighting continued for two days. On July 4, Sherman rode up and impatiently told Howard: "Johnston is crossing the Chattahoochee. There is nothing in front of you but skirmishers." Howard was skeptical but advanced his line. Sherman, leaving his horse behind, followed on foot. The men sprang out, passing between the Confederate rifle pits, but "had hardly passed these outer defenses when they met, straight in their faces, an unceasing fire from a set of works that had been hitherto but dimly seen, running along the edge of the thick wood. In a few moments several batteries opened slowly from unexpected points, sending their shot and shell crosswise against our lines." Some of the shells were aimed at the very place where Sherman, Stanley, Howard, and some other officers were standing. Most of the officers took cover. "Sherman himself passed from tree to tree toward the rear"; shortly thereafter, Howard looked back and saw Sherman running the other way "making more than double-quick time down the road . . . in search of his horse."

The Federals pushed on and after crossing a wide, wooded valley gained a high bluff near Vining's Station. Across the Chattahoochee, the spires of Atlanta could at last be seen. One officer wrote home to his wife:

> Mine eyes have beheld the promised land! The "domes and minarets and spires" of Atlanta are glittering in the sunlight before us, and only 8 miles distant. On the morning of the 5th [July], . . . eagerly pressing our skirmishers forward after the rapidly retreating rebels, suddenly we came upon a high bluff overlooking the Chattahoochee, and looking southward across the river, there lay the beautiful "Gate City" in full view. . . . In a very few moments Generals Sherman and Thomas were with us (who are always with the extreme front when a sudden movement is taking place) and the two veterans, for a moment, gazed at the glittering prize in silence. I watched the two noble soldiers—Sherman stepping nervously about, his eyes sparkling and his face aglow—casting a single glance at Atlanta, another at the river, and a dozen at the surrounding valley to see where he could best cross. . . . Thomas stood there like a noble old Roman, calm, soldierly, dignified; no trace of excitement about that grand old soldier who had ruled the storm at Chickamauga. Turning quietly to my General [Absalom Baird] he said: "Send up a couple of guns and we'll throw some shells over there," pointing to some heavy timber across the river.
>
> In a moment I was off down the road, to the rear, to order up some artillery; the infantry column separated and opened the road, the artillery came thundering along through the long lines of men, and in fifteen minutes from the time our line of skirmishers reached that hill top, a Parrott shell went screaming from the high point, and burst beautifully on the south side of the Chattahoochee—the first since the war began.

This vivid snapshot of Thomas and Sherman together may be combined with another set of images from the correspondent William Franklin Gore Shanks, who compared the two men as they struck him at the time:

> One [Sherman] may be called a nervous man, and the other a man of nerve. Sherman derives his strength from the momentum resulting from the rapidity with which he moves; Thomas moves slowly, but with equally resistless power, and accomplishes his purposes by sheer strength. Sherman is naturally the dashing leader of light, flying battalions; Thomas the director of heavily-massed columns. He may be called heavy ordnance in contradistinction to Sherman, who may be likened to a whole battery of light rifle-guns; or, in the language of the prize-ring, Sherman is a light-weight and quick fighter, while Thomas is a heavy, ponderous pugilist, whose every blow is deadly. His calculations also leave a wide range for contingencies, delays, and accidents, and are not easily disturbed by untoward incidents and unexpected developments. He never goes into a campaign or battle without knowing exactly how to get out of it safely. . . . Sherman jumps at conclusions . . . [and] never takes thought of unexpected contingencies or failure. There is always a remedy for any failure of a part of Thomas's plans, or for the delinquencies of subordinates. Sherman never hesitates to answer. . . . Thomas thinks twice before speaking once; and when he speaks, his sentences are arranged so compactly, and, as it were, so economically, that they convey his idea at once.

This classic description is doubtless wedded too much to its own passion for opposites, but it caught something essential about the two men. It also reminds us that when the word "slow" was properly applied to Thomas, it was anything but a pejorative term.


Having crossed the Chattahoochee, Sherman wheeled his army to the right. Johnston withdrew to the fortifications about Atlanta while deploying his forward lines at Smyrna Station to check the Union pursuit. That placed much of his army on the south bank of Peachtree Creek. All told, Johnston's skillful holding actions had been eminently successful and "in the whole of his retreat from Dalton to Atlanta," wrote his fellow general John Gordon, he "had lost no wagons, no material of any description except four pieces of artillery, and none of the enthusiastic confidence of his officers or men, with but few killed or wounded in the almost daily skirmishes and combats . . . [He] had husbanded his army's strength and resources in this long retrograde movement so as to make it one of the most memorable in the annals of war." However, just as the cry of "On to Richmond" had prompted the North at the outset to make a number of grave mistakes, so the Confederate government now yielded to widespread cries for a decisive stand outside Atlanta with a "stand-up fight."

Jefferson Davis reportedly told the governor of Georgia, Joseph E. Brown, and Georgia senator Benjamin H. Hill, that if Johnston couldn't assure him that Atlanta would be saved, he would remove him. Davis then asked Johnston for some statement of his plans. Johnston answered, "very curtly, that being confronted by a largely superior force his plans would be governed by the enemy's movements." That was not what Davis wanted to hear. On July 12, he telegraphed Robert E. Lee: "Johnston has failed, and there are strong indications that he will abandon Atlanta. . . . It seems necessary to relieve him at once. Who should succeed him? What think you of [John Bell] Hood for the position?" Lee replied by telegram the same day: "It is a bad time to release the commander of an army situated as that of Tennessee. We may lose Atlanta and the army too. Hood is a bold fighter. I am doubtful as to other qualities necessary." Later that evening, Lee added in a note: "Hood is . . . very industrious on the battlefield, careless off. . . . I have a high opinion of his gallantry, earnestness & zeal. Genl. [William] Hardee has more experience in managing an army." Lee also confided to General John Gordon that Johnston knew how to use his army better than anyone else. Gordon in turn told Davis that "no one except General Lee himself" could take Johnston's place.

Meanwhile, behind the scenes, Hood had pressed for the command. On July 14, he told Bragg, now serving in effect as Confederate chief of staff: "During the campaign from Dalton to the Chatta-hoochee River . . . we have had several chances to strike the enemy a decisive blow. We have failed to take advantage of such opportuni-ties." Bragg in turn advised Davis that a number of Johnston's subor-dinate generals shared Hood's views. On the night of July 18, Davis relieved Johnston of command. "You have failed to arrest the advance of the enemy to the vicinity of Atlanta, far in the interior of Georgia, and express no confidence that you can defeat or repel him," Davis ex-plained to him in a wire, "and you are hereby relieved from the com-mand of the Department and Army of Tennessee, which you will immediately turn over to General Hood."

Hood was a stand-up fighter beyond all doubt and a general to be reckoned with, however rash. He had lost the use of an arm at Gettys-burg and a leg at Chickamauga. When he rode into battle he had to be strapped into the saddle of his horse. "As a division or corps com-mander, there were very few men in either army who were superior to Hood," wrote General John Gordon. But he lacked "those rare mental gifts" that made a general great. "There are crises, it is true, in battle," wrote Gordon, "when the fate of the army may demand the most dar-ing exposure of the commander-in-chief himself. It is nevertheless true that care and caution in handling an army, the forethought which thoroughly weighs the advantages and disadvantages of instant and aggressive action, are as essential in a commander as courage in his men." Gordon thought only three Southern generals in the war met this high standard—Johnston, Stonewall Jackson, and Robert E. Lee. Johnston's careful retreats preserved the strength and morale of his army. Jackson, "with all his daring and apparent relish for the fray, was one of the most cautious of men. His terrible marches were in-spired largely by his caution. Instead of hurling his troops on breast-works in front . . . he preferred to wage war by heavy marching in order to deliver his blow upon the flank. 'It is better to lose one hun-dred men in marching than a thousand in fighting,' he once declared." Of Lee, little need be said.

Hood was thirty-three at the time, and the youngest of the eight full generals of the Rebel army. No officer had had a more spectacular rise. "You are charged with a great trust," James A. Seddon, the Confederate secretary of war, told him. But no one was sure if the trust was well placed. One Rebel division commander wrote: "Hood has 'gone up like a rocket.' It is to be hoped . . . that he will not come down like a stick." When Johnston was informed of the change, he defended his tactics, adding in an obvious swipe at Hood, "Confident language by a military commander is not usually regarded as evidence of competence." Yet in transferring his command, Johnston gave Hood every help he could. As he explained his plans to him:

> First, I expected an opportunity to engage the enemy on terms of advantage while they were divided in crossing Peach-Tree Creek. . . . If successful, we had a safe place of refuge in our intrenched lines close at hand. . . . Then, I intended to man the works of Atlanta on the side toward Peach-Tree Creek . . . and, when the Federal army approached, march out with the three corps against one of its flanks. If we were successful, the enemy would be driven against the Chattahoochee where there are no fords, or to the east, away from their communications, as the attack might fall on their right or left. If unsuccessful, the Confederate army had a near and secure place of refuge in Atlanta, which it could hold forever, and so win the campaign.

Hood laid plans to attack Sherman's army at once. These were really Johnston's plans to catch some of the Federal columns as they crossed Peachtree Creek. McPherson and Schofield were engaged in railroad-destroying expeditions, and Sherman expected Hood to attack them to protect his line of supply. On the 19th, he told Thomas that he (Thomas) could probably walk to Atlanta, for nothing would be in his way. That evening, Thomas began to cross Peachtree Creek. McPherson, far to the left, was approaching Decatur; Schofield was between him and Thomas; Thomas now formed the right wing. So arranged, the flanks of the army were ten miles apart, with a separate, wide interval between Thomas's left and Schofield's right. To close this interval, Howard was ordered to the left with two divisions to link up with Schofield. This, however, created another gap of two miles. Howard was surprised at Sherman's order and asked Thomas about it. " 'We must not mind the gap between your two divisions,' said Thomas, with almost a smile. 'We must act independently.' . . . His clear head and indomitable heart never were so cool and unconquerable as in desperate straits."

Of course, he knew the disposition of troops was a mistake.

As Thomas brought the rest of his command across the stream the next day, one of his division commanders remarked that the situation to their front had "an ugly look." Hood had massed his columns, concealed by a wood and rise, in a way that placed 30,000 against some 20,000 on Thomas's left flank. As always, somehow, Thomas divined what might be in store. If he wasn't expecting an attack, he didn't discount it either. For just before the fury of Hood's onset, he had directed one of his division commanders to place two cannon on a hill guarding the extreme left wing. Hood's first assault struck that point. At 3 P.M. (two hours later than Hood had planned), the Confederates suddenly burst upon the heads of the Union columns, and the battle at once became hot. "Yelling like furies . . . like wild beasts let loose," the Rebels poured out of the woods and covered the open ground in front. The attack was made en echelon from the right to left, with orders for each division, upon reaching the creek, to sweep downstream. Wherever the Federals were found entrenched, their works were to be carried by fixed bayonets.

Thomas commanded in person within close range of enemy fire. Over the course of two hours, three Rebel assaults were thrown back. At one pivotal moment, he helped bring up a battery to thwart a rear attack, and, sitting on his horse among the guns, helped direct their fire. It was the turning point of the battle, as the Confederates were repulsed. At the height of the fighting, Thomas received a dispatch from Sherman telling him his troops should "sweep every thing before them" to Atlanta, as if not much was to their front. When at length he realized a fierce battle was going on, Sherman said, "I have been with Howard and Schofield all day and one of my staff is just back from McPherson. All report the enemy in their front so strong that I was in hopes none was left for you." But what good did that commiseration do? Thomas ("we must act independently") fought on.

At dusk, the Rebels withdrew.

The loss on both sides was heavy: the Federals about 2,000, the Confederates between 4,000 and 5,000 men in captured, wounded, or killed.

Over the next two days, Hood pulled back from Atlanta's outer works along his left and center, and thoroughly deceived Sherman into believing that he had left Atlanta behind. Early on July 22nd (as Colonel Henry Stone recalled it), "Colonel [Charles] Ewing, Sherman's brother-in-law and aide, dashed up to Thomas' tranquil headquarters frantic with excitement, swinging his cap wildly about his head and without saluting or dismounting shouted at the top of his voice: 'The rebels have gone. March right through Atlanta and go into camp on the other side,' then fiercely galloped away without a word of detail or explanation or giving a chance to ask a question. The excitement was all his own, but the order was General Sherman's." Supposing Hood at bay, Sherman had ordered an immediate pursuit. In obedience to this order, McPherson advanced, but did not get far. Riding forward to direct his line, he was killed in ambush by Hood's troops coming up from the rear. Instead of fleeing, Hood had marched east from Atlanta, made a wide detour during the night around the Union left, and without warning had fallen on its flank and rear. This attack almost succeeded, for according to General Frank P. Blair, only the position that the Sixteenth Corps had "accidentally" taken up out of line "prevented the full force of the blow from falling where it was intended to fall." Otherwise, he wrote, there would have been a "general rout." During the battle, as before at Peachtree Creek, Sherman failed to send reinforcements, so that the officers engaged (belonging to the Army of the Tennessee) "were left alone to fight Hood unaided throughout that long summer day." In justifying his failure to send help from other commands, he claimed that the Army of the Tennessee would have been "jealous" (i.e., resented it) if he had. That was a poor excuse for risking a major defeat.

Thomas, meanwhile, on his own account, had advanced with caution doubtful of Hood's flight. Shortly before noon he received a note from Sherman: "We find the enemy in force inside Atlanta. . . . I have sent word to Howard that we were mistaken in finding the enemy gone. . . . I wish you to press down from the north and use artillery freely, converging in the town. I will then throw McPherson again on your right to break the Macon road." But even as this dispatch was being sent, Hood had launched the surprise attack in which McPherson fell.

Hood next withdrew to the inner works of Atlanta, and the siege of the city began. Encircled by defense works, Atlanta was almost unassailable, and after a month in front of it, Sherman finally decided upon a turning movement, and began to extend his army to the right. He moved toward Jonesboro, but Hood moved parallel with him, building parapets as he went. Finally, at Jonesboro, on September 1, the Fourteenth Corps of the Army of the Cumberland, under Thomas, stormed Hood's works. "As his troops went into action by my side," recalled Oliver Howard, Thomas roused his old stout horse to a gallop. It was the most complete and successful assault upon formidable works of the whole campaign, and it led to the surrender of Atlanta the following day.

As the Federals sent a brigade under General Henry W. Slocum into the city, they found it being evacuated by Hood's rearguard. Sherman wired Halleck: "So Atlanta is ours and fairly won. I shall not push farther on this raid, but in a day or two will move to Atlanta and give my men some rest. Since May 5 we have been in one constant battle or skirmish." Thomas, according to Sherman (in an improbable description, designed, as one scholar, Albert Castel, put it, to make him seem "clownish") was so pleased at the fall of Atlanta that he "snapped his fingers, whistled," and "almost danced." The "news," said Sherman, "seemed to [Thomas] too good to be true." In fact, earlier that day (before the note from Slocum came to Sherman, which he said he showed Thomas) Thomas had already notified D. S. Stanley that Atlanta was in Federal hands—as he had predicted it would be in a note to Sherman the night before. So Thomas would hardly have reacted (according to this contrived vignette) in the manner described.

Meanwhile, as Hood withdrew, he split up his army. Thomas discovered this and proposed a plan to destroy the divided columns in detail. But Sherman, after a brief pursuit, let Hood go.

The fall of Atlanta created a sensation in the North. Lincoln wired his congratulations to the army and predicted that "the marches, battles, sieges, and other military operations, that have signalized the campaign, must render it famous in the annals of war." Some days before, Grant had wired Stanton: "I think it but a just reward for services already rendered that Gen. Sherman be now appointed a Maj. Gen. in the Regular Army," which of course was promptly done.

After McPherson's untimely death, Thomas had met with Sherman to select a new head for the Army of the Tennessee. John Logan has assumed command in the interim, but Thomas and Sherman settled on Oliver Howard, after Sherman rejected Joseph Hooker, who wanted the post. Hooker was furious and resigned because, as he put it, his "rank and service had been ignored." Thomas sent Hooker's resignation on to Sherman—"approved and heartily recommended," Sherman claimed—but Hooker had only praise for Thomas thereafter, while he always contended that Sherman was insane. Thomas was not part of their quarrel. When Howard assumed his new command, D. S. Stanley took his place as head of the Fourth Corps. Hooker was succeeded by Slocum, and a few days later, in another shake-up, John M. Palmer of the Fourteenth Corps resigned and was replaced by Jefferson C. Davis. Thomas incurred no ill will with these changes. Like Hooker, Palmer, a future Illinois senator and presidential candidate, had unbounded admiration for Thomas and even named a grandson after him—whereas both regarded Sherman with loathing and disgust. Hooker's opinion has often been treated with a grain of salt, because he also said Sherman would never take Atlanta. But in one sense he was probably right: left to himself, Sherman probably would have failed.

The fall of Atlanta rescued Lincoln's campaign. One thing leads to another. If Thomas had not held on at Chickamauga, the Federals would not have been able to occupy and hold Chattanooga. That would have delayed the whole Atlanta campaign, which relied on Chattanooga as a base. It is doubtful that campaign would even have been attempted. Without the good news at the end of it, with the fall of Atlanta, Lincoln might well have been defeated at the polls.

# 10. NASHVILLE, PART ONE

In the Atlanta campaign, Thomas had commanded more than three-fifths of Sherman's army and, wrote Oliver Howard, was "Sherman's wheel-horse. He bore the brunt of the skirmishes, combats, and battles"; delivered the opening battle at Buzzard's Roost and the battle at the campaign's close; in between, he had saved the army from destruction at Kenesaw Mountain by a protest that forced Sherman to change his plans; and had trounced Hood in his surprise attack at Peachtree Creek. Had he been in overall command, the campaign would likely have been won at the outset near Resaca with a strong move through Snake Creek Gap. Throughout the campaign, as one writer put it, Thomas had "approved of no movement which was a failure; he disapproved of none which was a success." "Whenever his advice was rejected, the outcome proved" that his judgment had been sound.

In taking Atlanta, Sherman said he "had not accomplished all, for Hood's army, the chief objective, had escaped." He had not accomplished half. What was left of the Confederate army was soon allowed to reconstitute itself almost before his eyes. While Sherman settled into Atlanta, expelled the inhabitants, fortified its outskirts, and turned it into a supply base to allow his men to recuperate from the late campaign, Hood's discouraged army was left unchallenged for three weeks at Lovejoy's Station, only thirty miles away.

Both Grant and Sherman had been perplexed as to how best to follow up the Atlanta march. On September 12, Grant wrote to Sherman, "What you are to do with the forces at your command I do not exactly see." Eight days later Sherman replied that he expected to neutralize Hood somehow before marching farther south. But Hood had

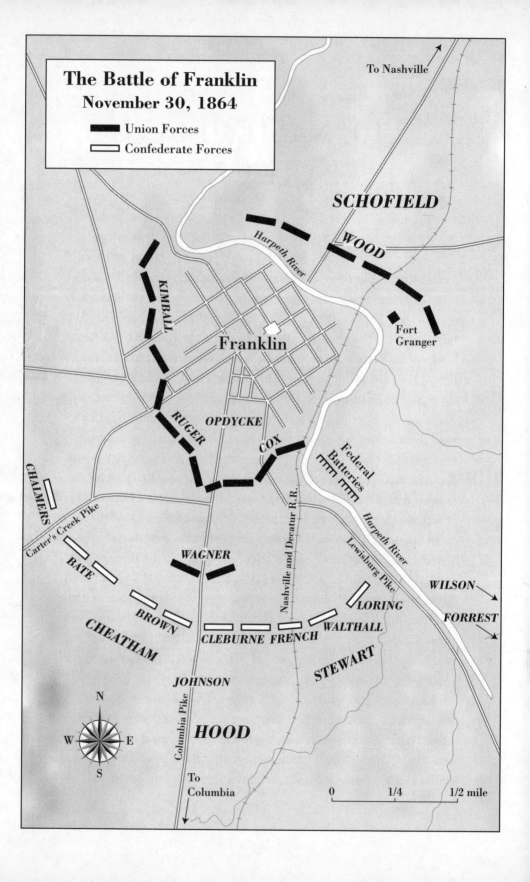

# The Battle of Franklin
## November 30, 1864

■ Union Forces
□ Confederate Forces

To Nashville

SCHOFIELD

WOOD

Harpeth River

KIMBALL

Franklin

Fort Granger

OPDYCKE

RUGER

COX

Federal Batteries

Harpeth River

CHALMERS

Carter's Creek Pike

WAGNER

BATE

Nashville and Decatur R.R.

Lewisburg Pike

WILSON

LORING

FORREST

BROWN

CLEBURNE  FRENCH

WALTHALL

CHEATHAM

STEWART

JOHNSON

Columbia Pike

HOOD

N
W        E
S

To Columbia

0        1/4        1/2 mile

no intention of waiting until Sherman had a rest. On the 20th of September—the day Sherman replied to Grant—he moved his army from Lovejoy's Station to Palmetto, southwest of Atlanta, in the first phase of a plan to cut Sherman's supply line and force him to a fight. If need be, Hood also thought he could make his way to Alabama, gather supplies and reinforcements, and fight Sherman there. He wasn't particularly afraid of Sherman. If Sherman left Atlanta, he would dog his tracks.

Sherman's logistical problems were acute. His line of communications extended all the way back to Louisville, and an arm of Hood's cavalry under Joseph Wheeler had begun to chop it up. Some reinforcements had come in, and Hood now had an effective force of about 40,000 men. Their morale had greatly improved, and he hoped by being bold and active to fully restore it. Hood moved around Sherman's right, crossed the Chattahoochee to the north, and struck the Western & Atlantic Railroad south of Chattanooga. Fighting soon developed along a broad front, with scattered detachments engaged at bridges, railroad crossings, and depots, around Marietta, Big Shanty, Decatur, and Allatoona, as new tactical advantages were sought.

When Sherman learned that Hood's army was north of the Chattahoochee and that one of his own key railway connections (the Blue Mountain–Selma) was cut, he dispatched the Fourth Corps under D. S. Stanley after him and, leaving Atlanta to be held by the Twentieth, followed with the rest of his force. From atop Kenesaw Mountain, he watched the fight for Allatoona—his chief supply depot (with a million rations)—play out. In the distance, he could see the railroad "burning for miles" to the north. Meanwhile, he had dispatched Thomas to Nashville on September 26, to take charge of the defense of Tennessee.

"The Confederate leaders in the West," as one writer put it, "had lost their cities, but they still had their army and their dream. The army was smaller, but the dream was bigger. Looking beyond the wreckage of their railroads and supply depots and surrendered cities, they believed they needed a larger concept, more expansive strategy to throw the Federals back of the Ohio River and the Potomac. At the beginning of the war they had relied on a passive defense, taking the righteous stand of a man defending his home; now, too late, they realized that the North must be defeated on its own soil before it would 'let the erring sisters go.'" That dream had become even "more fevered" after Atlanta fell.

From Decatur to Bridgeport, Thomas posted cavalry brigades to watch the river fords, but Hood veered west. Thomas wired Stanton that he hoped to interdict him, allowing Sherman to attack him from behind, but Sherman began to complain that Hood, by turning and twisting like a fox, might wear out his army in pursuit. "I cannot guess his movements as I could those of Johnston, who was a sensible man and only did sensible things." To an exasperating degree, he also found himself retracing much of the ground he had earlier won. From Allatoona on the 9th, he wired Thomas at Nashville, "We cannot defend this long line of road," and wired Grant at City Point: "It will be a physical impossibility to protect the roads, now that Hood, Forrest, Wheeler, and the whole batch of devils, are turned loose without home or habitation.... By attempting to hold the roads, we will lose a thousand men each month, and will gain no result."

For some time, he had been beguiled by the idea of marching his army through Georgia to the sea. From there he might make his way through the Carolinas to Virginia, where he could link up with Grant. He and Grant had discussed this plan, but Grant remained doubtful of its logic as long as Hood's army was intact. Sherman, however, soon grew tired of the chase, and concluded that Hood was only trying to lure him out of Georgia into Tennessee. That would undo all his own recent gains. "Let him go north, my business is down South," he exclaimed when Hood seized the Federal garrison at Dalton and tore up the tracks from Resaca to Tunnel Hill. He also wired Grant: "I can make the march and make Georgia howl." Grant worried that Hood might take advantage of his absence and reenter Tennessee. Sherman thought not, and told him Thomas could beat him if he did. He was persistent. On October 11, he appealed to Grant to let him "move through Georgia, smashing things to the sea." Hood, he added, "may turn into Tennessee and Kentucky, but I believe he will be forced to follow me. Instead of being on the defensive, I will be on the offensive.

Instead of my guessing at what he means to do, he will have to guess at my plans."

Sherman was wrong. Hood was losing interest in what Sherman planned to do. If he couldn't lure him north, he would shape his own campaign.

Meanwhile, Sherman had explained to Halleck that the proposed march would not be "purely military or strategic, but it will illustrate the vulnerability of the South. They don't know what war means, but when the rich planters . . . see their fences and corn and hogs and sheep vanish before their eyes, they will have something more than a mean opinion of the 'Yanks.' " To one cavalry commander he vowed: "I am going into the very bowels of the Confederacy, and propose to leave a trail that will be recognized fifty years hence." Grant had lingering concerns. He thought Sherman might need to create a coastal supply base in advance. Sherman replied that his troops would live off the land they passed through. Grant then wondered whether Sherman might be "bushwhacked by all the old men, little boys, and such railroad guards as are still left at home." Sherman said he would take none but "the best fighting material." Lincoln, too, had misgivings, but left the matter (as he had promised) up to Grant. In pressing Grant about his scheme, Sherman insisted his march would be "a demonstration to the world foreign and domestic, that we have a power which [Jefferson] Davis cannot resist. This is not war, but rather statesmanship." This desire to "smash things"—to bring the war home to the homesteads of the South—made a certain kind of sense, but the zest with which he undertook to do it was strange. In the end, his one great contribution to the "art of war" was to set a precedent for making war on a civilian population, which hadn't been considered proper since the Mongols. "We may well wish," as the eminent historian Stephen Z. Starr put it, "that this strategical innovation had not been thought of by an American general."

On October 17, Thomas ventured his own opinion. He advised Sherman against marching to the sea with his main force. Instead, he thought a strong cavalry movement would accomplish just as much. "I had not so much faith in cavalry as he had," wrote Sherman in his *Memoirs,* though Grant agreed with Thomas on this point.

Where did the idea of a March to the Sea originate? Sherman claimed to have come up with, but Grant later produced evidence that it was his. Thomas, it seems, had thought of it, too, but not as a campaign of devastation. According to General W. F. Smith—whose successful scheme (worked out in collaboration with Thomas) had broken the blockade at Chattanooga—Thomas had told Sherman after the fall of Atlanta: "Now you have no more use for me, let me take my little command and go eastward to the sea." Sherman told him he would have to clear it with Grant, and then heard nothing more until Sherman made it his own. But Thomas had not planned, as Sherman did, to take all, or almost all, of the best troops of the three armies that had been engaged in the Atlanta campaign. And Grant, after Sherman proposed to do the march himself, had instead wanted a cavalry force to cut its way to the coast. Either plan made more strategic sense. Instead, Sherman decided to march away from the army he couldn't beat.

Near Rome, Georgia, Hood had been joined by Wheeler and moved toward Gadsden by way of Snake Creek Gap. Sherman got his bearings and pursued, hoping to cut him off at the gap's northern end. But he failed to get there in time. At Gadsden, Hood entrenched and there on the 22nd all his troops came in. In a month's time—from September 20 when he left Lovejoy's Station until he arrived at Gadsden—Hood had drawn Sherman and his army some fifty miles back through Resaca to Gaylesville, farther and farther from his base.

That was the end of Sherman's pursuit. Unable either to catch Hood or protect his own line of supply, he tried to change the nature of the game.

By then, Hood had begun to work out his own bold plans. If possible, he would cross the Tennessee River at or near Guntersville, destroy the railway bridge at Bridgeport, cut up the Nashville and Chattanooga Railroad, and separately confront Union forces in Tennessee. If he prevailed, he would take Nashville, cross the Cumberland into Kentucky, threaten Cincinnati, and refurbish his army with new recruits from both states. Hood had already guessed that Sherman would strike for the coast. If, however, Sherman came after him, he thought he could win on even ground. Either way, he hoped in the end to either reinforce Lee in Virginia, or attack Grant from behind after marching through the Cumberland gaps. Sherman wouldn't be able to do much to check either move.

Hood now prepared to cross the Tennessee River far enough west to be beyond Sherman's reach. He sent his cavalry forward in two columns—one to threaten Huntsville, Alabama; the latter, Columbia, Tennessee—then set out himself on October 22 with his troops reinspired. They had three weeks of rations in their haversacks, and little to oppose them on their daring march. Sherman was not sorry to see Hood go. "If he'll go to the Ohio River," he remarked, "I'll give him rations." But that was exactly what Grant and others feared.

Sherman was in a hurry to get going and assured Thomas that Hood had no intention of invading Tennessee. Grant thought he would, but also failed to estimate Hood's intentions correctly. Grant guessed Chattanooga would be Hood's goal; Thomas thought Nashville, since Hood had no reason to challenge Chattanooga when he could bypass it and take a more forward base.

Grant at first withheld his consent. On November 1, 6 P.M., he wired Sherman: "Do you not think it advisable, now that Hood has gone so far north, to entirely ruin him before starting on your proposed campaign? With Hood's army destroyed, you can go where you please with impunity. I believed and still believe, if you had started south while Hood was in the neighborhood of you, he would have been forced to go after you. Now that he is far away he might look upon the chase as useless, and he will go in one direction while you are pushing in the other. If you can see a chance of destroying Hood's army, attend to that first, and make your other move secondary."

But the following day, after Hood's army suddenly reappeared in front of Decatur seventy-five miles northwest of Gadsden, far from Sherman's base, Grant acquiesced. "I really do not see that you can withdraw from where you are to follow Hood without giving up all [the territory] we have gained. I say, then, go as you propose." The government in Washington was seized with the greatest apprehension at this decision. Even Grant's own chief of staff, John Rawlins, remonstrated with the War Department about the wisdom of it behind Grant's back. Nevertheless, having assured Lincoln that the plan was sound, Grant wired Sherman on November 8: "Great good fortune attend you! I believe you will be eminently successful, and, at worst, can only make a march less fruitful of results than hoped for."

On the grand chessboard of the war, Grant was to continue to hold Lee in check at Richmond, and either capture him there or force him out of that stronghold, to capture or destroy him in the field; Sherman, with a large army, would march through Georgia and strike for the coast; Thomas, placed in temporary command of the Military Division of the Mississippi, in succession to Sherman, would hasten to Nashville to defend the Kentucky frontier. There he would also await the coming of the enemy if bold enough to follow; and, hopefully, put an end to his hopes and schemes. That looked plausible on paper, but ever less so as the days went by. The responsibility thrown on Thomas, wrote one contemporary, was "enormous. . . . To his care was committed the Military Division extending from the Ohio to the Gulf, from the Mississippi to the mountains; the task of holding Tennessee, defending the line of the Tennessee River, and the railroad lines from Chattanooga to Nashville; finally, the destruction of the Western Confederate army, the grand object of the whole war west of the Allegheny range."

Sherman, however, was elated, and in just two days managed to concentrate his forces at Kingston and Rome in preparation for his march. In mid-November, he burned Atlanta and "sallied forth to ruin Georgia," as he put it, across a sixty-mile swath with 60,000 soldiers in a march that would take him from Atlanta to the sea. Generally, his troops would loot and torch vast areas of the countryside, destroy what they did not consume, and indulge in wanton acts of violence and devastation that were unofficially condoned.

On November 12, the last telegraphic link between Thomas and Sherman was cut. "As we rode on toward Atlanta that night," wrote Sherman, "I remember the railroad-trains going to the rear with a furious speed; the engineers and the few men about the trains waving us an affectionate adieu. It surely was a strange event—two hostile armies marching in opposite directions, each in the full belief that it was achieving a final and conclusive result in a great war." Yet in marching away from the army he had been told to destroy, the whole country, from Atlanta to Nashville, was thus abandoned by Sherman to an uncertain fate. Sherman gave his enterprise a heroic cast, but British war correspondents, "disdaining the legend already being built around" him, called his march not an advance but "The Retreat to the Sea."

Sherman's announced policy of devastation was driven, in part, by motives of revenge—to inflict harm on the population of the South. Sherman's subsequent campaign into the Carolinas seems to have been wholly driven by that urge. To Grant he would write on December 18: "I do sincerely believe that the whole United States, north and south, would rejoice to have this army turned loose on South Carolina to devastate that state." And to Halleck on December 24: "We are not only fighting hostile armies but a hostile people, and must make old and young, rich and poor, feel the hard hand of war, as well as their organized armies. I know that this recent movement of mine through Georgia has had a wonderful effect in this respect. . . . The truth is, the whole army is burning with an insatiable desire to wreak vengeance upon South Carolina. I almost tremble for her, but feel that she deserves all that seems in store."

By contrast, Thomas was adamantly against such wanton violence. Of all the armies of the North, wrote Donn Piatt, the Army of the Cumberland under Thomas "left a kindly feeling in its wake among the people of the South that had experienced its rule."

Nor was Thomas sympathetic to the idea of "total war." He thought it was wrong in itself, and would make reconciliation that much more difficult when the war was done. He once reminded his soldiers: "We must remember that this is a civil war, fought to preserve the Union that is based on brotherly love and patriotic belief in the one nation. It is bad enough for us to demand that love of a restored Union at the point of the bayonet, but we can justify ourselves by claiming what we do is from a sense of duty. The thing becomes horribly grotesque, however, when from ugly feeling we visit on helpless old men, women, and children the horrors of a barbarous war. We must be as considerate and kind as possible, or we will find that in destroying the rebels we have destroyed the Union."

At the same time, Thomas held local communities responsible for the violence done in their name. After three Union soldiers on a foraging expedition were captured and executed by Rebels, Thomas issued a General Order

> that the property of all rebel citizens living within a circuit of ten miles of the place where these men were captured be assessed each in his due proportion, according to his wealth, to make up the sum of thirty thousand dollars, to be divided among the families dependent upon the murdered men for their support. . . . Should the persons assessed fail, within one week after notice has been served upon them, to pay in the amount of their tax in money, sufficient of their personal property shall be seized and sold at public sale to make up the amount. . . . The men who committed these murders, if caught, will be summarily executed, and any persons executing them will be held guiltless, and will receive the protection of this army, and all persons who are suspected of having aided, abetted, or harbored these guerillas will be immediately arrested and tried by military commission.

In putting together his army of conquest, Sherman had winnowed out the wheat from the chaff. All convalescents, the injured, those whose terms of service were about to expire—in short, all the "trash," as Sherman put it—along with damaged equipment, were sent to Thomas in the rear. He also took with him all the best cavalry mounts. While announcing his intention to live off the country, he appropriated for himself nearly the whole of the Western army's wagon train. To Thomas, on the other hand, he sent the Fourth Corps under D. S. Stanley (about 12,000 men) and the Twenty-third under John Schofield (about 10,000), along with 5,000 cavalry without mounts, and some damaged artillery. Two divisions (about 10,000 men) from the Sixteenth Corps under A. J. Smith were also to come from Missouri. Before he set out, Sherman told Thomas that Smith was well on his way, which wasn't true. When Thomas appealed to Sherman to allow him to hold on to his elite Fourteenth Corps—the first brigade of which he had organized at Camp Dick Robinson three years before—Sherman told him: "It is too compact and reliable a corps for me to leave behind"—even though he had maligned it to Grant, we may remember, as stopping at every plowed furrow in the field. Meanwhile, Thomas had a dozen cities and towns to garrison against a possible Confederate strike.

Though he had other troops within reach—for example, 5,000 at Murfreesboro under Lovell Rousseau; 4,000 under Gordon Granger at Decatur; and 5,000 at Chattanooga under James Steedman—most of these were needed where they were.

Sherman's motive in all this is pretty clear. He was bound for glory, and the way for him to get it was by a campaign he couldn't lose. Atlanta gave him the pattern. He had failed to destroy the Confederate army (the avowed purpose of the whole Atlanta march) but had thrilled the nation when Atlanta fell. Before that, in regular battle—from Louisville to Shiloh to Chickasaw Bluffs to Chattanooga—he had come up short. The capture of Savannah, however, offered him another opportunity like Atlanta. After he took Savannah, he hoped to be on hand at Petersburg or Richmond when Lee gave in.

Stanley brought the Fourth Corps to the town of Pulaski, and as soon as Schofield reached Nashville (on November 14) with the Twenty-third, he was sent on by Thomas to Pulaski to take command of the forces assembling there. Pulaski was about seventy-five miles south of Nashville, which Thomas thought Hood would try to make his ultimate prize. Schofield's mission was to delay the Confederate advance south of Duck River as long as he could.

Thomas had to buy time to build his forces up. Hood's own strong army was arranged in three corps, commanded by Generals S. D. Lee, Benjamin Cheatham, and A. P. Stewart, each containing three divisions. It numbered from 40,000 to 45,000 infantry, with a cavalry corps of from 10,000 to 15,000 men. Though Hood had not received the reinforcements he expected, his was a tightly knit, tough, and veteran force. And once more it was on the move. Thomas had 27,000 troops in the two corps at Pulaski, plus 5,000 cavalry. In Nashville, he took 5,000 men from the quartermaster's department and placed them in the city's defense line. Under Steedman, a provisional division was organized from several thousand troops returning from leave. Other manpower had to be drawn from groups of raw recruits just out of Northern training camps, untried regiments of blacks, railroad guards, the convalescents left behind, and so on to patch together a viable force. Indeed, while Hood gained momentum, Thomas lost 15,000 veteran troops by expiration of terms of service or absence on leave to vote.

While Thomas was bowed down with care, Hood was energized. He had put the disappointments of the Atlanta campaign behind him, and despite a body hobbled by wounds, had rebounded and was "ready to risk all on the casting of a die." The fact that the Federal army had divided its forces seemed to give him his chance. If he had followed Sherman through Georgia, he reasoned, he would have given up territory now under his thumb and disheartened his own troops by retreat. But if he could beat Thomas, he could undo whatever Sherman might achieve.

Thomas told Schofield to fall back toward Nashville, so as not to be trapped by flanking movements, as Hood advanced. Thomas told him: "Have everything in readiness to fight him at Pulaski . . . or cover the railroad and concentrate at Columbia. Should he attempt to turn your right flank" have the cavalry "cover the fords and ferries across Duck River and hold them" while the men at Columbia were gathered in. Meanwhile, James Wilson, formerly on Grant's staff, had been sent to Sherman, who sent him on to Thomas. On November 6, he arrived in Nashville to organize a cavalry force. Though fortified with much care, however, Nashville throughout the war had proved itself self-supporting only with the presence of a large army. As the chief city of the Mississippi Valley between the Ohio River and the ocean, however, and the center of rail, river, and telegraphic communications for the Federal forces in the West, it stood out as a great strategic prize.

Hood's movement created alarm in the North, and it was recognized at once that Thomas had better be reinforced. That would not be easy. There were only about 26,000 Federal infantry and 5,000 cavalry left in the whole area scattered from Chattanooga to the mouth of the Ohio, guarding railways and depots and the river line. Nathan Bedford Forrest had already taken advantage of this, capturing gunboats, transports, and Union posts in the western part of the state. As he made his way along the Tennessee River to Hood, he made a mess of things in his path. A single Union cavalry brigade stood between him and the Tennessee River. That could not prevent him crossing; and so he came up with Hood.

On November 19, Hood sent Forrest's cavalry forward toward Nashville, and followed with his whole army on the 21st. As his two corps under Cheatham and S. D. Lee advanced by converging roads, they almost trapped Schofield at Pulaski. By the time they caught up with Schofield at Columbia on the 26th, thirty miles to the north, Wilson had come from Nashville to take command of the Union cavalry in Schofield's front. At that point, Wilson had about 7,000 men, whom he placed along the north bank of the river to monitor whatever the Rebels did. The dilemma in which Sherman had left Thomas required everything to be done just in time. But Thomas, "whose great brain comprehended the entire movement," as one of his cavalry commanders, R. W. Johnson, put it, "directed the various parts of his command to fall back on Nashville, offering such resistance as could be made" without bringing on a fight. Meanwhile, when it became clear that Nashville was Hood's objective, Thomas ordered troops under Granger up from Decatur, Athens, and Huntsville to reinforce the garrisons at Stevenson and Murfreesboro on the Nashville & Chattanooga line.

Thomas told Schofield to hold the railway bridge at Columbia, at least until A. J. Smith's division arrived. But Schofield feared Hood would outflank him by crossing the stream above the town. On the night of the 27th he pulled back from the south bank to the north. Hood's army began to cross in turn and both armies skirmished at the fords at several points. Forrest, who had crossed in full, outfought Wilson on the Franklin Pike and tried, once more, to cut off the Union retreat.

Hood's problem was to get around Schofield, who blocked his way. On the 28th, Hood cut through the woods, crossed the river above Columbia, and marched northwest. That brought both armies to the environs of Spring Hill. Hood's advance thus far had been marked by great skill. With Wilson cut off, Schofield was left without the help of his main reconnaissance arm. So things stood on the day and night of November 29. As evening fell, Hood thought his trap was about to close. He had outflanked Schofield and held both the pike and the south side of Rutherford's Creek. At Spring Hill, the Federals had only a single division; Hood, with Cheatham and Stewart, had two full corps. Schofield remained at his mercy. All Hood needed to do was to place his troops across the road.

Schofield sent word to Thomas that his situation was "perilous," but he had no idea how perilous it was. Then something strange happened. It was as if Hood's whole army fell asleep. His troops bivouacked east of the road, and Cheatham (who had ample time to do it) failed to interdict Schofield's line of march. Almost on tiptoe—"like treading on thin ice over a smoldering volcano," as Stanley later put it—the Federal army slipped past, marching toward Franklin within the light of the Rebel fires.

About midnight Hood received a report about some passing "stragglers," but it wasn't until about 2 A.M. that this was looked into, when an aide to Cheatham rode up to the turnpike but found "everything still." To this day, no one knows how that could have been so. Colonel Henry Stone later heard that "there were queer doings" in the Rebel lines among some of Hood's officers that night. "There was music and dancing and feasting, and other gods than Mars were worshipped with sacrificing at their shrines." Others hypothesized that Hood, to alleviate his chronic physical discomforts, had taken laudanum with alcohol and was too doped up to maintain charge.

At dawn, Hood set out in frantic pursuit. He hoped to overtake Schofield at Franklin, which lay on a bend of the Harpeth River, and destroy him before he could cross. Bragg's Corps Commander A. P. Stewart took the advance. The Federals made a feint as if to give battle on the hills about four miles south, but Hood learned from captured dispatches that Schofield was told to hold Spring Hill until Franklin was secure. "Thus I knew," wrote Hood later, "that it was all important to attack Schofield before he could make himself strong."

The first Federal column reached the town's outskirts at first light on the 30th and threw up a line of earthworks in their front. As the other troops came up they prolonged the line to right and left, to incorporate three knolls, completing the work by noon. The entire line of entrenchments was about a mile and a half long. With both flanks resting on the Harpeth River, and batteries posted to repel assaults on flank and front, the line completely covered the town. A thicket of young locust trees was felled near a dwelling known as the Carter house to form an abatis; and between the pike and the railway the works were partly sheltered by a hedge. Otherwise, the ground in front was free from obstacles and every part of it in sight. Expecting Hood's attack at any time, Schofield repaired a bridge, took refuge himself on the far side of the river, and arranged his troops in a wedge. He sent one division across the river on the right; placed the Twenty-third Corps on the left and center, with a brigade behind it; and cavalry above and below the town fords. Two infantry brigades, however, were unwisely exposed far to the center front.

About this time, Thomas learned from A. J. Smith that he would not be able to get all his troops to Nashville for a few more days. Thomas wired Schofield at Franklin: "We must try to hold Hood where he now is until those troops can get up. . . . After that we will concentrate here, reorganize our cavalry and try Hood again. Do you think you can hold Hood at Franklin for three days longer? Answer giving your views and I should like to know what Wilson thinks he can do to aid you." Hood, however, arrived that afternoon and decided to try to take the place by storm.

It would prove a bloody day. Without waiting for all of his troops to come up, he launched his columns with such impetuosity that the Federals were thrown back. As the defenders swept over their own parapets in flight, they carried part of the main line with them down the turnpike toward the town. That left a wide gap in the line on each side of the road, as the Rebels, with exultant cheers, seized the earthworks and deserted guns. Two Federal batteries were turned at once on their own men. Having broken the center of Schofield's line, it looked as if Hood would force one of its wings into the stream. Stanley, however, rushed a brigade into the breach. As he led the charge, his horse was killed under him, and he was shot through the neck. Colonel Emerson Opdycke of Stanley's corps also hurled his men forward with bayonets fixed. A desperate counter-charge by Cheatham failed to oust them, and the tables were turned. Opdycke recaptured some of the guns, took hundreds of prisoners, and reestablished the line. There was also fighting on the opposite flank, where soldiers grappled along a parapet and in trenches before the Union works. It continued on into the night, the Rebels holding the ditch in front. One Rebel soldier later recalled that "blood actually ran in the ditch and in places saturated our clothing where we were lying down." At length, the Rebels drew back.

In his official report, Hood was matter-of-fact about the carnage. He had captured about 1,000 prisoners and several stand of colors, but his loss in killed, wounded, and prisoners was over 5,000, including much of his high command. The Federal loss was about half that and Hood deceived himself when he wrote that "the number of dead left by the enemy on the field indicated that his loss was equal or near our own." One of the Confederates, who beheld the field the next day, recalled that the area in front of the Federal works looked like "a slaughter-pen."

Schofield, who had stationed himself with a reserve division two miles away on the north bank of the Harpeth River, knew he had escaped by the skin of his teeth. Taking no chances, he withdrew at midnight toward Nashville, leaving his dead and many of his wounded on the field. One division, on the north bank of the river, held the bridges, Wilson's cavalry covered the flanks and rear. He had not been involved at all in directing the battle and would later be criticized by Stanley, on whom all the fighting had devolved. In his memoirs, Stanley wrote that everyone knew that Schofield would be the last man to expose himself to harm.

All that day, recalled an aide, Thomas had been noticeably "reticent and gloomy," with his military hat pulled down low over his "grave, gray eyes." But after Schofield escaped calamity, "his hat lifted, his broad brow cleared up and his strong and massive face began to shine."

Over the past two weeks, while Schofield had been making his way from Pulaski to Nashville, Thomas had done all he could to organize his detachments and complete his battle line. In every way, his task was daunting. As a railhead and turnpike crossing, Nashville had many roads of access, both in and out of town. All had to be protected. To do this, Thomas had established two lines of entrenchments, enveloping the city along the river from bank to bank. Studding these lines were earthen redoubts that he labored without rest to connect and make strong. Time was of the essence—to drill his new recruits; prepare his trains and pontoons (stripped by Sherman); and above all to fully mount and equip his cavalry troop. To play the great role Thomas had conceived for them in his battle plan, his mounted troops, with their deadly, repeating Spencer carbines, would ride to their place of battle, dismount, fight as infantry, then remount as cavalry in pursuit.

Schofield had covered the eighteen miles to Nashville as fast as he could; A. J. Smith's Sixteenth Corps of two divisions finally arrived the night of December 1 by steamer; Steedman's two black brigades from Chattanooga rumbled in on the rails. When Smith, a big bear of a man like Thomas, came striding in, Thomas literally took him in his arms and embraced him, he was so relieved to have him there. At one that morning, with Generals Smith, Schofield, and Wood looking on, Thomas explained the upcoming battle he had planned with maps spread out on the floor.

In just two weeks Thomas had made an army. Some troops were raw and uncertain; others, like Smith's veterans, famously tough. One officer encountered a group of Smith's men encamped along the river and asked them who they were. "We're A. J. Smith's guerrillas," the man replied. "We've been to Vicksburg, Red River, Missouri and about everywhere else . . . and now we're going to Hell."

Thomas placed his troops on the heights about Nashville, Smith's divisions on the right, the Fourth Corps (under Wood) in the center, and Schofield's Twenty-third Corps on the left. Steedman's troops— an assortment of convalescents, unattached units, and eight regiments of blacks—extended the left; Wilson drew up his cavalry on the extreme right. The interior line of Nashville's defense was manned largely by armed civilians. Union gunboats patrolled the Cumberland River above and below Nashville to prevent the Rebels from crossing. Wilson sent a brigade of cavalry to Gallatin to watch the north bank.

Steedman's black troops were destined for renown. Colonel

Thomas J. Morgan of the 14th USCT (United States Colored Troops) later wrote: "General George H. Thomas, though a Southerner, and a West Point graduate, was a singularly fair-minded, candid man. He asked me one day soon after my regiment was organized [November 1863], if I thought my men would fight. I replied that they would. He said he thought 'they might behind breastworks.' I said they would fight in the open field. He thought not. 'Give me a chance General,' I replied, 'and I will prove it.'" Thomas did. To his credit, he doubted the conventional wisdom of his own opinion. And then in his great battle plan, he gave them a featured role. He was, in fact, the only Union general to do so in a major battle of the war. It had been a long time coming. And after the war, blacks would point to Nashville as proof that they had earned their full citizenship rights.

Almost two years before, Lincoln's Emancipation Proclamation had led to the enlistment of blacks as Union troops. Despite resistance within the army, the policy gained ground. "So far as tested," Lincoln announced in December 1863, "it is difficult to say they are not as good soldiers as any." Five months later, Lincoln remarked that the experiment showed "no loss by it in our foreign relations, none in our home popular sentiment, none in our white military—no loss by it any how or any where." On the contrary, it added 130,000 soldiers, seamen, and laborers to the ranks.

That, however, put the best face on things. Draft riots broke out in a number of towns and cities; troops in camp grumbled and cursed; the desertion rate increased; and there was resistance even among the high command. Some generals (most notably, Sherman) refused to include black regiments in their armies, preferring instead to use blacks as laborers and railroad guards. For the most part he continued to see blacks as the South saw them, as servants, teamsters, and cooks. His prejudice went deep. He told Secretary of the Treasury Salmon Chase that "The negro should . . . not be put on any equality with the Whites," and to a friend declared: "A nigger . . . is not fit to marry, to associate, or vote with me, or mine." As for their value as soldiers, he told Halleck that a black man might be as good as a white man for stopping a bullet, but "a sand-bag is better." Lincoln reminded Sherman that the law regarding black recruitment had to be obeyed. But the leverage Sherman enjoyed as Grant's commander in the West, both before and after the capture of Atlanta, enabled him to ignore Lincoln's demand. He had refused to allow black troops to take part in the Atlanta campaign, and had stymied the government's enlistment efforts by threatening to arrest recruiters within his domain. Grant, too, had resisted using blacks in combat and only with great reluctance had stationed black troops at points along the Mississippi and the Gulf.

For his part, Thomas had long held more enlightened views. His whole disposition as a soldier and a man was to lift up the downtrodden. Wrote Oliver Howard, "You couldn't place him where he would not be a friend of the insulted, the outraged, the oppressed." As for the very idea of slavery, "His keen sense of justice revolted against the crime of unrewarded labor," according to one aide. While in Texas, he had acquired a black woman as a cook, then offered her freedom. But she was too attached to him to go. He would not sell her, and so he became her protector—before, during, and after the war. In the course of the war, Thomas was also "constantly giving black women and children protection papers," wrote Howard, "and sending them north." It is no coincidence that Howard was one of his most devoted admirers. As head of the Freedmen's Bureau, he would be the Union general most closely associated with emancipation in the postwar years.

The great black Abolitionist leader Frederick Douglass once said of Lincoln: "Viewed from the genuine abolition ground, Mr. Lincoln seemed tardy . . . but measuring him by the sentiment of his country, a sentiment he was bound as a statesman to consult, he was swift, zealous, radical, and determined." The same, as one writer noted, might be said of Thomas in the military sphere. Though not an abolitionist at the outset, he had like Lincoln become one by the war's end. He viewed black volunteers as equal to patriotic whites, and considered the army an ideal training ground for self-reliance—especially for those deprived of the chance to develop it in their lives. "In the sudden transition from slavery to freedom," Thomas wrote, "it is perhaps better for the Negro to become a soldier, and be gradually taught to depend on himself for support, than to be thrown upon the cold charities of the world without sympathy or assistance." By April 5, 1864 (before the Atlanta campaign began), he had six fully organized black regiments on duty at Chattanooga and nearby towns. Three more were being formed, and a company of blacks trained to operate a battery of guns.

Thomas Van Horne, chaplain of the Army of the Cumberland, wrote that "in accordance with his antagonism to state rights," Thomas supported the government in declaring slaves freed when they entered Union lines. He also supported the idea of "enlisting . . . [slaves] as soldiers when their freedom had been proclaimed." He sometimes brigaded black and white units together and had them fight side by side in limited engagements. In implementing that policy, he had particular confidence in two of his generals, Steedman and Granger (both heroes at Chickamauga), entrusting most of the new black troops to their care. Steedman had carried out a successful expedition against the Rebels at Dalton on September 15 (1864) with two white regiments and six companies of blacks. A month later Granger wrote Thomas proudly that his sortie with a black regiment had driven Rebels from their rifle pits up near Decatur, Alabama, and spiked their guns.

Hood, following Schofield, reached the outskirts of Nashville on December 2 and began building breastworks south of the town. On the morning of the 4th, his army marched up to within 600 yards of the Federal line, "with flags flying, deployed as if on drill," and began to entrench. His bands were brought out, trumpets blowing, drums beating, and the strains of "Dixie" could be heard from a dozen or more points along the line. Stewart's corps was on the left; S. D. Lee's in the center, astride the Franklin Pike; Cheatham's on the right. Cavalry, on the flanks, rested on the river above and below. As a diversionary tactic, Hood sent Nathan Bedford Forrest westward toward Murfreesboro to besiege the town. At the same time, Hood began to cut Nashville's communications, first with Decatur and Johnsonville, then along the Chattanooga Road. He also blockaded part of the Cumberland River by placing batteries along its shore. That left the long, exposed Louisville line of track as the city's sole source of supply.

The prospect for the Federals was anything but bright. Despite his setback at Franklin, Hood was upbeat and determined to beat Thomas at any cost. His east–west line was four miles long, and five small forts or redoubts soon covered his flanks, with breastworks to the front. Rifle pits were dug and cover given by a long stone wall. By his own count, he had at least 45,000 men of all arms. Thomas had more, but only half were regular troops. His army, if he chose to attack, was also not so large to meet the standard at the time of two or three to one for carrying entrenched works.

The recent invention of the Minié ball (a bullet that spread on impact) and rifles had transformed the whole character of war. From then on, as one military historian put it, it was imperative to entrench and deliver "an attack with such a mass of men that some at least would live to reach the enemy's parapet." Yet

> less than one out of every eight [assaults] succeeded. "One rifle in the trench was worth five in front of it," it was said. The attacking columns saw little more before them than a thin and continuous sheet of flame issuing beneath the head-log of the parapet, whilst they themselves marched uncovered against the unseen foe.... Fire was never expected to drive an enemy out of his position unless it could be followed by a bayonet charge. The defender, realizing this, often reserved his fire until the attacking line emerged at close range from its own smoke, when one volley was normally sufficient to throw it back.

Grant's men were regularly slaughtered in this way. The assaults authorized, directed, or inspired by Thomas at Lookout Mountain and Missionary Ridge, on the other hand, had won the day by skill, momentum, and surprise. Thomas was never known to favor an assault that was not apt to succeed. And none that he favored failed. Nor did he ever fail to beat back an assault on his own position—an incredible record in four years of constant fighting in the war.

Hood had no intention of attacking Nashville itself, with its imposing fortifications, but knew Thomas would be pressed to drive him off. He hoped to repulse him, and, in a counterstroke, to take the town. "Should [Thomas] attack me in position," he wrote, "I felt that I could defeat him, and thus gain possession of Nashville with abundant supplies for the army. This would give me possession of Tennessee. . . . We had captured sufficient railroad stock to use the road to Pulaski, and it was already in successful operation. Having possession of the State, we should have gained largely in recruits, and could at an early day have moved forward to the Ohio, which would have frustrated the campaign toward the Atlantic coast." For Hood, the outcome of the battle was not in doubt. He told his army chaplain: "This campaign will change very greatly the movements of both armies. There will be no more great flanking operations—the enemy will have to seek our armies & fight them where he can find them—there will be more blood spilled in 1865 than in 1864—but the losses will be on the Federal side."

At stake was everything wiser heads had feared. If Hood prevailed against Thomas or got past him, there was nothing to stop him from marching on to the Ohio River, then down into Virginia to help Lee beat Grant. In letting Sherman march away from Hood's army, Grant had blundered on a colossal scale. As Union general R. W. Johnson put it, the potential disaster threatened to "delay . . . the closing scenes of the war for years." Yet in all this, there was one note of saving grace. Once Sherman had disappeared over the horizon, Thomas, for the first time since Mill Springs, and on a far grander field, had an independent command. It was something he had sought throughout the war. "It was his grand opportunity," one contemporary officer put it, "and he seized it with great discretion and skill."

Grant, knowing that his career was at stake, had begun to second-guess the crisis from afar. On November 24, he had wired Thomas not to "let Forrest get off without punishment." Thomas replied that he lacked the cavalry to do that because Sherman had taken all the good mounts. But "the moment I can get my cavalry, I will march against Hood, and if Forrest can be reached he shall be punished," too. Horses were requisitioned throughout Kentucky and Tennessee. Every possible mount, including those of a wandering circus, were rounded up.

Not even Vice President–elect Andrew Johnson's fine stable of carriage horses was spared. Indeed, on December 1, Thomas wired Halleck that he needed just a little more time, adding: "If Hood attacks me here, he will be more seriously damaged than he was [at Franklin]. If he remains until Wilson gets equipped, I can whip him, and will move against him at once."

Halleck ought to have been reassured. Instead, he showed the telegram to Stanton, who talked with Lincoln about it. At 10:30 A.M. on December 2, Stanton wired Grant: "The President feels solicitous about the disposition of Thomas to lay in fortifications for an indefinite period, until Wilson gets equipment. This looks like the McClellan and Rosecrans strategy of do nothing, and let the enemy raid the country. The President wishes you to consider the matter." The same day Halleck wired Thomas: "If you wait till General Wilson mounts all his cavalry you will wait till doomsday, for the waste equals the supply."

These were strange wires to send. Where did Lincoln (who was known to have confidence in Thomas) get the idea that Thomas meant to "lay in fortifications for an indefinite period," if that is what Lincoln believed? Or that it would take that much longer for Wilson to get equipped? Did Stanton exaggerate the concern that Lincoln expressed? What might make him do so? And in what sense was Thomas "doing nothing," when he was toiling day and night? Grant, however, picked up the spirit of this canard and at once began to send a series of peremptory telegrams to Thomas urging him to attack. That same day he sent two. He thought that "If Hood is permitted to remain quietly about Nashville, we will lose all the roads back to Chattanooga, and possibly have to abandon the line of the Tennessee"; he thought, too, that Hood might make for the Ohio River, without taking Nashville first. Thomas, however, realized "that Hood was now tied to his wagon trains," as one writer put it, "and could make no more lightning dashes such as had carried him up from his Alabama base. In Alabama, moreover, he had been able to live off the land, but in the desolate barrens of Tennessee he had to rely on his new main base at Corinth and his lines of communication to the South."

Thomas pondered Grant's wires, and in his reply tried to explain the situation to him clearly and bring him up to date. He had "infantry enough to assume the offensive," he said, would have liked more time to mount his cavalry, but would "take the field anyhow" with what he had "in two or three days." Then he reminded Grant that his command had been "made up of the two weakest corps of General Sherman's army, and all the dismounted cavalry except one brigade, and the task of reorganizing and equipping [had] met with many delays." That implied reprimand should have made Grant blush. For it put on record that Grant had failed to manage the situation well in his new role of general-in-chief. For his part, Grant insisted that Thomas should have gone out and attacked Hood right after the Franklin fight. Few in retrospect agree. Grant was forgetting that Smith and Steedman had yet to come in, and that by going out Thomas would have left Nashville exposed, defended in the main by armed civilians and commissary troops. Hood, wrote General James H. Wilson, might have "crushed us as soon as we had marched outside our works." Moreover, Schofield had escaped at Franklin because Hood had underestimated the defenses he had hurled his troops against—the kind of mistake often made by Grant. But a field fight was different, and at the time Thomas had a much smaller army than Hood did. Old troops were also still leaving even as new troops arrived. Grant's advice, as Stephen Z. Starr put it, was "the recipe for a Union disaster that would have resounded down the years."

There now followed perhaps the most remarkable exchange of telegrams in the annals of war.

"Attack Hood at once and wait no longer for a remount of your cavalry," Grant wired Thomas on the 6th. The next day, Stanton wired Grant: "Thomas seems to be unwilling to attack because it is hazardous (as if all war was not hazardous). If he waits for Wilson to get ready, Gabriel will be blowing his last horn." This echoed Halleck's remark on the 2nd about it taking until doomsday, suggesting the tenor of the talk in the War Department at the time.

Yet as Wilson later wrote, the situation was really this:

The newspapers throughout the country . . . were filled with prognostications of disaster. Commerce and financial affairs were disturbed. Gold was falling, the War Department was demoralized, and even General Grant himself showed greater uneasiness that he had ever exhibited before. Thomas alone was calm and full of confidence. He had organized and armed eight thousand civilian employees of the supply departments and had called in all his outlying detachments except the garrison of Chattanooga. A. J. Smith, with his invincible veterans, after a month's delay, had finally joined him at Nashville, thus raising his effective force to something over sixty thousand of all arms. Nashville was now safe beyond all peradventure. Its garrison was ample for the defense of its long line of entrenchments. The cavalry alone was still in a bad way. Its horses had been worn out and many permanently disabled by hard work. It therefore required a few days' rest and many remounts before it could take the field again and properly perform the part that would surely fall to its lot. The imperturbable Thomas was the one man who fully appreciated this fact and was willing to wait until the cavalry could gather its remounds and get fairly ready to participate in the great task. . . . [Moreover] Grant had no right to assume that Thomas would have any better luck in assaulting entrenchments, even though held by inferior numbers, than he had himself in Virginia, or Hood at Franklin, or Lee at Gettysburg, or Sherman at Chickasaw Bluffs, or [Sherman] at Missionary Ridge, or throughout the Atlanta campaign, or than Grant himself on May 22, 1863, at Vicksburg. These lessons of frightful disaster had not been lost on Thomas, a soldier of sound judgment, and always a close student of the military art.

Grant then wired Halleck (December 8): "If Thomas has not struck yet, he ought to be ordered to hand over his command to Schofield. There is no better man to repel an attack than Thomas, but I fear he is too cautious to take the initiative." Halleck replied: "If you wish General Thomas relieved, give the order. No one here will, I think, interfere. The responsibility, however, will be yours, as no one here, so far as I am concerned, wishes General Thomas removed."

No one had thought Grant would go that far. In his own anxious state, Lincoln may have wanted Grant to press Thomas, but he had not expected him to try to strip him of command. Nor was he cognizant of the depths of Grant's spite.

Grant scrambled to find more reason for his haste. That night (December 8) he wired Thomas: "It looks to me evidently the enemy are trying to cross the Cumberland, and are scattered. Why not attack at once? By all means avoid the contingency of a footrace, to see which, you or Hood, can beat to the Ohio. If you think necessary, call on the Governors of States to send a force into Louisville to meet the enemy, if he should cross."

Again, Wilson provided context, as confirmed by the Official Records published in the post-war years:

> Contrary to Grant's belief, Hood was intent on hanging for the winter where he was, capturing Murfreesboro, if possible, and that he had no present design of marching to the Ohio.
>
> This assurance was made doubly sure by the further important fact that there was a fleet of iron-clads and gun-boats on the Cumberland under command of Rear Admiral S. P. Lee, patrolling the river from its mouth to Carthage, above Nashville, in cooperation with my outlying cavalry forces. All were especially on the alert to prevent Hood's crossing to the north side of the Cumberland. Upon other and stronger grounds, however, such a movement was highly improbable, if not impossible. He was already far from his base at Florence. It was winter and the roads, whenever heavily used, were soon almost impassable. The territory between the Cumberland and the Ohio had been foraged more than once by both sides. Besides, Hood was without resources with which to repair and operate the railroads, and it was beyond the waning power of the Confederacy to supply them. To use them at all he must first wrest them from our possession, and this could not be done without the defeat of Thomas's entrenched army and the capture of Nashville. That army, concentrated in comparative security behind the fortifications of Nashville, well fed, well clothed, daily growing stronger and more confident under a leader that it loved and trusted and whom it knew familiarly under the fond and expressive name of "Old Pap," was resolutely and vigorously making ready for its

spring upon the foe. Under these conditions it must be conceded that the possibility of Hood's marching around Nashville or getting away from Thomas in the effort to cross the Cumberland for a winter march into Kentucky and to the Ohio was not only reduced to a minimum, but was about the wildest and the most desperate and hopeless military undertaking possible to imagine. Here, if at any time during the war, Grant lost his head.

Thomas would not be forced. He gave Wilson two more days to ready his mounts, and that night he replied: "I can only say in further extenuation, why I have not attacked Hood, that I could not concentrate my troops, and get their transportation in order, in shorter time than it has been done, and am satisfied that I have made every effort that was possible to complete the task."

Back at City Point, Grant was beside himself. The next day (December 9), he wired Halleck: "Dispatch of 8 P.M. last evening from Nashville shows the enemy scattered for more than seventy miles down the river, and no attack yet made by Thomas. Please telegraph orders relieving him at once, and placing Schofield in command. Thomas should be ordered to turn over all orders and dispatches received since the battle of Franklin, to Schofield." Grant's order was duly prepared, but just as it was ready to be signed, an ice storm fell on the area about Nashville, and froze both armies in place. The men could hardly get their footing, even on level ground.

Meanwhile, in an act of decent forbearance for which the nation will always owe him a debt of thanks, Halleck held the order of relief throughout the day and notified Thomas of Grant's ire. Halleck then received a dispatch from Thomas in which the impossibility of attack was made clear. Halleck passed it on to Grant and asked him if he still wanted the order of relief sent through. He implied that it might be wise for him to wait.

Grant became uneasy, and wired Halleck to suspend it. He backpedaled a bit: "I am very unwilling to do injustice to an officer who has done so much good service as General Thomas has." He also wired Thomas: "Your dispatch of 1 P.M. to-day is received. I have as much confidence in your conducting the battle rightly as I have in any other officer, but it has seemed to me you have been slow, and I have had no explanation of affairs to convince me otherwise. Receiving your dispatch to Major-General Halleck of 2 P.M. before I did the first to me, I telegraphed to suspend the order relieving you until we should hear further. I hope most sincerely that there will be no necessity of repeating the order, and that the facts will show that you have been right all the time."

In the interim, an indignant Thomas had learned of Grant's order and wired Grant: "General Halleck informs me you are very much dissatisfied with my delay in attacking. I can only say that I have done all in my power to prepare, and if you should deem it necessary to relieve me, I shall submit without a murmur." He noted that he had been ready to attack the following morning, but the storm had intervened. He would therefore have to wait for it to break. In the meantime, he wasn't worried about Hood getting around Nashville, since Federal gunboats were patrolling the river above and below.

Thomas was deeply pained at the treatment he had received. On the evening of December 10, he invited all his corps commanders to his headquarters at the St. Cloud Hotel in Nashville and shared with them the exchange of telegrams. Wilson, a former member of Grant's staff (and up until that time his favorite cavalry commander), stood by Thomas completely: "No hostile action of any kind should be attempted," he said, "until a thaw had set in." Smith and Steedman emphatically concurred. Only Schofield sat silent, nursing his thoughts. When the conference came to an end, Thomas asked Wilson to stay behind. "Wilson," he said, "the Washington authorities treat me as if I were a boy. They seem to think me incapable of planning a campaign or of fighting a battle, but if they will just let me alone, I will show them what we can do."

Thomas also "could not forget that Sherman, who had taken the pick and choice of the Western troops, . . . was marching unopposed through the South, while the enemy he should have destroyed before starting on his holiday excursion had assumed the offensive and was now confronting us. He commented on this more than once," wrote Wilson, "during the so-called siege with bitterness and resentment.

But badly as he felt about it, he felt still worse in regard to Grant's impatient and inconsiderate orders to fight without further delay. . . . He . . . referred to the fact that Grant, with an army of nearly one hundred thousand men, mostly seasoned veterans, had been confronting Lee at Petersburg for seven months, while Hood had been confronting us at Nashville for only ten days. The deadlock in Virginia was far more complete than in Tennessee" with Lee showing "contempt for Grant's generalship. . . . Under the circumstances, which were well known to the entire army, it was hard for Thomas, who was conceded to be a better soldier and organizer than either Grant or Sherman, to understand why he should be censured or lectured by either of them. [Sherman's real sniping would come later.] Both were far away, as well as more or less ignorant of the actual condition of affairs in our front, and both more or less responsible for the perils we faced."

For two days rain descended, freezing as it fell. The ground became one vast sheet of ice. Movement even along level ground was hazardous and impossible up the slopes. No one was more impatient than Thomas for this to pass. "While the rain was falling and the fields and roads were ice-bound," wrote one aide, "he would sometimes sit by the window for an hour or more not speaking a word, gazing steadily out upon the forbidding prospect as if he were trying to will the storm away." Yet Grant seemed not to understand. He wired Thomas on the 11th: "If you delay the attack longer the mortifying spectacle will be witnessed of a rebel army moving for the Ohio River, and you will be forced to act, accepting such weather as you find. Let there be no further delay . . . for weather or reenforcements." It seems not to have occurred to Grant what an ice storm meant. It was hardly possible for Hood to move if Thomas could not. Nor did Grant seem to grasp the calamity of launching an offensive up sleet-covered slopes against fortified heights. Thomas replied that he would "obey the order as promptly as possible, however much I may regret it," and on the 12th, he told Halleck bluntly: "I believe an attack at this time would only result in a useless sacrifice of life." That, as one scholar put it, "should have brought the harassment to a full stop. When a commanding general of Thomas' intelligence and experience says unequivocally that an attack 'would only result in a useless sacrifice of life,' no superior with an ounce of sense would insist, from a distance of 500 miles, that the attack be made."

In his autobiography, *Under the Old Flag*, written long after the war, General James H. Wilson wrote: "Grant's telegrams of this fortnight (December 2 to 15) show that he had a good memory for injuries, real or fancied. . . . They also show a willingness, if not a settled purpose, on his part to cause Thomas' removal and downfall," provided the authorities at Washington could be induced to go along. And Thomas later told a friend: "I thought, after what I had done in the war, that I ought to be trusted to decide when the battle should be fought. I thought I knew better when it should be fought than any one could know as far off as City Point."

As generals, Grant and Thomas were opposites. "Grant was a pushing and a tenacious man—so much so," wrote one contemporary, "that on several occasions he sacrificed men to experiment. But still he went on, regardless of his partial failures. On the other hand, Thomas was cool, quiet, careful in his movements, a nice calculator of chances, but always intending to win all that could be won." In his judgment "every day increased the danger to Hood, while it improved the condition of the Union army. Why take desperate chances while a reasonable delay would render the outcome sure? Nothing was lost, much was gained."

None of this was enough to satisfy Grant. In a series of still unexplained actions, he now sent General John Logan, who happened to be at City Point, to relieve Thomas (superseding his own order placing Schofield in charge) and then started himself on the night of the 13th for Nashville by way of Washington to take command. Exactly where Logan fit into all this it is hard to say. Grant himself was confused. Grant later admitted to Logan (in a letter of February 14, 1884) that "in regard to the order for you to go to Louisville and Nashville for the purpose of relieving General Thomas, I never thought of the question of who should command the combined armies of the Cumberland and the Ohio. . . . No doubt if the order had been carried out, the question would immediately have arisen as to who was entitled to the combined command, provided General Schofield was senior in rank to you, which I do not know that he was. . . . The question, in that case, of the command of the whole would have been settled in a very few hours by the use of the telegraph between Nashville and Washington."

About this time, Lincoln himself must have expressed his own profound misgivings about Grant's judgment behind closed doors. In their intimate *Abraham Lincoln: A History*, John Nicolay and John Hay, the president's secretaries, wrote: "Thomas nowhere appears to greater advantage, not even on the hills of Chickamauga, opposing his indomitable spirit to the surging tide of disaster and defeat, than he does during this week, opposing his sense of duty to the will of his omnipotent superior, and refusing to move one hour before he thought the interests of the country permitted it, even under threat of removal and disgrace."

Captain Henry Coppee (who managed the Academy Library when Thomas taught at West Point before the war) summed up the situation as beautifully as anyone could: "A weaker man than Thomas would have yielded to the importunity and attacked before he was ready. Indeed, there seemed little discretion in the matter. He was ordered to attack at once. If he obeyed, the best interests of the country were endangered. If he did not, he was liable to the charge of 'disobedience of orders.' The firmness of General Thomas, therefore, assumes the proportions of a martyr's faith; he would die for the cause, for the honor of the profession of arms, and for his own spotless character, rather than obey" orders that would imperil the cause and doom his men.

Meanwhile, General Whipple, Thomas's chief of staff, thought there must be someone in their midst trying to bring Thomas down. Even Thomas, who had done everything right, and knew it, began to wonder, too. He asked Steedman if Andrew Johnson (then in Nashville) might be behind it. Steedman thought not, but sent an aide to the telegraph office to look into all the wires that had been sent. There he discovered a message from Schofield to Grant: "Many officers here are of the opinion," it read, "that General Thomas is certainly too slow." Since no other officer seems to have held that opinion, it sounded like a message, designed to serve as a pretext, dictated by

Grant. The aide brought it to Steedman, who brought it to Thomas, who examined it carefully and "mournfully shook his head."

Schofield had not been playing an upstanding part. Born in Gerry, New York, he had grown up in Illinois, attended West Point, saw action early in the war at the Battle of Wilson's Creek. Thereafter, he had served mostly in the training and drill of troops in Missouri's recruitment camps. He did little of note, but in Washington enjoyed the patronage of Senator Stephen Douglas, cultivated Senator John Henderson of Missouri among others, and when Sherman's march to Atlanta was arranged, won appointment as an army commander. (Much later, as secretary of war, he would award himself the Congressional Medal of Honor for undocumented valor at Wilson's Creek.) A portly man with burnside whiskers, he was altogether shrewd, allied with Grant, and "had the manner and disposition of an intriguing diplomat." Two Union generals, D. S. Stanley and Thomas Wood, then at Nashville, warned Thomas that Schofield was a Judas on his staff. They complained about his propensity for intrigue. Stanley would later write that Schofield's "fear of politicians made him play a very low, mean part in many things." At Nashville, he was second in command, and in an attempt to displace Thomas, had been sending distorted information by wire to the War Department, which Halleck and Stanton had apparently picked up.

The story is even more sordid than that. Schofield's enmity toward Thomas dated back to 1852, when Thomas had taught at West Point and Schofield had been a cadet. Schofield, an upper classman, had been assigned to help prepare a group of candidates in mathematics for the entrance exam. When three of the four applicants who failed proved to be from Schofield's group, questions were raised. It turned out that instead of helping the candidates with math, he had amused himself at their expense by asking them about their sexual and anal functions, with the help of obscene diagrams. The Academy dismissed him, but two weeks later, Senator Stephen Douglas intervened and succeeded in getting the matter reviewed. It was referred to a board of inquiry on which Thomas sat. The verdict was reversed, though Thomas and one other officer (Fitz John Porter) wanted it upheld. (Schofield later claimed, in his oft-discredited memoirs, that he did not learn how Thomas had voted until after the latter's death when, as secretary of war under Grant, he had access to the files. But no one has ever believed him.)

At length, on the 14th, a warm rain cleared away the ice. Thomas "drew a deep sigh of relief," an aide remembered, and his spirits visibly rose. General Logan by this time was just outside Cincinnati; Grant had gone to Washington and was to start for Nashville the next day. The attack was set for dawn. In his memoirs, Grant said he decided not to proceed when he saw the wire from Thomas "announcing his readiness at last to move." The oft-quoted Adam Badeau gave a similar account. Neither was true. Grant reached Washington on December 15 and went into conference at the War Department with Lincoln, Stanton, and Halleck. Grant told them of his decision to relieve Thomas and put Schofield in his place. According to David Homer Bates, manager of the War Department telegraph service in Washington, Lincoln tried to talk Grant out of it and said that Thomas on the ground was better able to judge his situation than Grant far away. Halleck and Stanton agreed. But Grant was adamant and the order was drawn up. Grant handed it to Major Thomas T. Eckert, assistant secretary of war and superintendent of military telegraphs, and then went to his hotel to prepare for his departure. But Eckert "on his own responsibility" held on to the telegram for an hour to allow for some new word from the front. That was just long enough. Suddenly, the telegraph office was overwhelmed by a flood of military dispatches from the West. "Something important" had obviously happened.

Then the news came through.

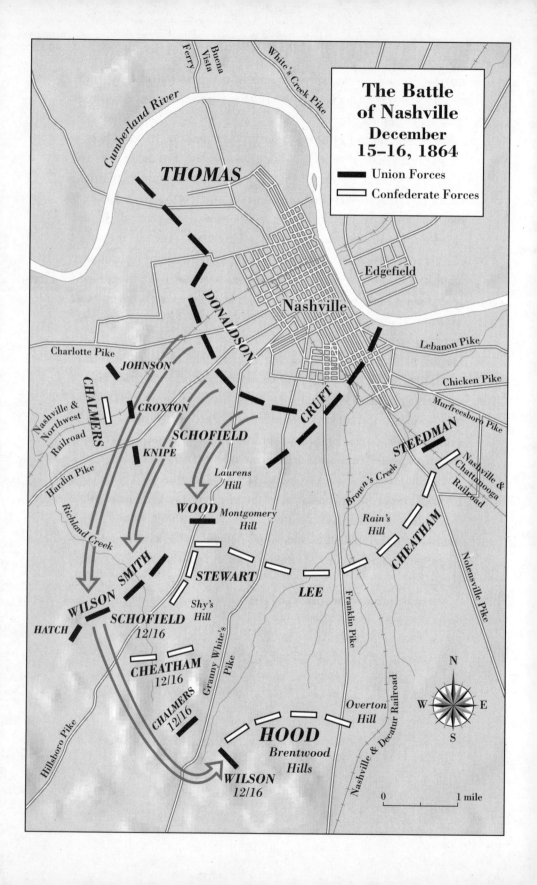

**The Battle of Nashville**
**December 15–16, 1864**

■ Union Forces
□ Confederate Forces

*Cumberland River*

THOMAS

*Buena Vista Ferry*

*White's Creek Pike*

Edgefield

Nashville

DONALDSON

*Charlotte Pike*

JOHNSON

*Lebanon Pike*

CHALMERS

CROXTON

*Nashville & Northwest Railroad*

*Chicken Pike*

CRUFT

*Murfreesboro Pike*

SCHOFIELD

KNIPE

STEEDMAN

*Hardin Pike*

*Brown's Creek*

*Nashville & Chattanooga Railroad*

*Laurens Hill*

*Richland Creek*

WOOD *Montgomery Hill*

*Rain's Hill*

CHEATHAM

STEWART

SMITH

LEE

WILSON

SCHOFIELD
12/16

*Shy's Hill*

*Franklin Pike*

HATCH

*Nolensville Pike*

CHEATHAM
12/16

*Granny White's Pike*

CHALMERS
12/16

*Overton Hill*

HOOD
Brentwood
Hills

*Nashville & Decatur Railroad*

WILSON
12/16

*Hillsboro Pike*

N
W E
S

0          1 mile

# 11. NASHVILLE, PART TWO

On the afternoon of the 14th, Thomas had called his corps commanders together once more to carefully explain the plan of attack. In Napoleonic style, his army would execute "a gigantic left wheel, with his heavy right wing swinging forward on a pivot formed by his left, which would make the first demonstrations and lead Hood to believe his right was being assailed by the main force." On the left, he placed Steedman's corps of black and white troops; Schofield in the center, to serve as the general reserve; Wood and Smith on the right. On the extreme right was Wilson's cavalry, which was to fight dismounted until the time for pursuit arrived. Thomas would shift Schofield's men to wherever needed; a provisional division would occupy the works that Steedman left; "armed civilian employees" (commissary troops and so on) would hold the rest of the interior line.

Thomas had made the most of what he had.

At dawn on the 15th, a dense fog enveloped both camps. This helped to shroud the Union formations, which were also partially concealed by the broken nature of the ground. But from the top of the southernmost salient, a clear view could be had of the country all around. The valley of Brown's Creek lay a mile to the east, that of Richland Creek two miles southwest. These two diverging streams, which fed the Cumberland River, rose within a mile of each other in the high Brentwood Hills, four or five miles to the south. Between them, the Granny White Turnpike (as it was quaintly called) ran southward along a ridge. Other pikes, too, extended south of where the winding river ran.

Hood's main line was now more than five miles long. It stretched along the hills east of the valley of Brown's Creek, from the Chatta-nooga Railway to the Franklin Pike; from there it crossed the valley and passed over the ridge of the Granny White Turnpike to a high knoll near the Hillsboro Pike, where it made a sharp turn and ran along a stone wall at its side. To the southwest, across Richland Creek, Hood had erected some detached works on hills, and halfway between his main line and the Union line on his left, he had an advanced line of skirmishers with its left posted on Montgomery Hill. Hood's line overall was strong, though too long for the number of troops he had to man it, and the general trace of the works was concave, which meant it took longer to shift men from place to place.

Thomas stood with his field glasses on a hill near the main salient in the Federal outer works east of the Hillsboro Pike. From time to time, his head swiveled slowly like a gun turret as he surveyed the undulating ground. His staff, corps commanders, and thousands of men lay in ditches and rifle pits. Along the Murfreesboro Pike, a bri-gade of black troops was poised with rifles and bayonets. The army had been in place since daybreak, waiting for the fog to lift. Federal artillery bombarded the Rebel line. Thomas made sure everything was set, then advanced his entire line to within 600 yards of the enemy's at all points. Shortly after eight the sun burned through and he turned to his chief of staff, General William Whipple, with his order for Steedman to attack the Confederate right. Up rose his men, with black troops in the forefront, and moved with such force across Brown's Creek that Hood could not afford to doubt the main attack was there.

Meanwhile, a cavalry division advanced against a Rebel battery on the Cumberland River, eight miles below Nashville, and, in conjunc-tion with Union gunboats, knocked it out. Two others, moving to Smith's right, struck the enemy along Richland Creek, drove him back, swung to the left, and captured two artillery redoubts in succes-sion and turned their guns about. Thomas swung Schofield's corps around the other two to the right, forcing Hood to prolong his lines and thin them out. One after another, Hood's detached works fell. By noon the Federals were within striking distance on the Hillsboro Pike.

Cavalry "came up fast on Hood's flank and Benjamin Cheatham's troops on the Rebel left were engaged in fighting from two sides." Thomas, as one writer put it, "was never cooler or more patient" than during these tense hours. He was so self-possessed that at one point he turned to a staff officer and told him to find out if he had drawn all of his coal allowance for the month. Remembering he had borrowed some coal for his headquarters from a neighbor, he said, "Will you please send fourteen bushels of coal to Mr. Harris?" Even at such a moment, no obligation was beneath his concern.

All this time, Steedman's troops were making progress on the Rebel right. Cheatham's corps had all it could handle. S. D. Lee's corps was immobilized in place. In this way, Thomas monopolized two-thirds of Hood's army with his provisional troops. As Hood failed to adjust his lines, Smith overran the Confederates ensconced behind the stone wall; a division under Wood carried their outpost on Montgomery Hill. The Rebels held on grimly, hoping for help to arrive.

Then the greatest cavalry movement of the war began. Under Wilson, 12,000 mounted men making a wide detour around the Rebel left dismounted and advanced, armed with seven-shot Spencer repeating carbines, and cut their way across the Granny White Turnpike to the Confederate rear. Before the short, lowering winter day closed, this force overran several redoubts, seized their artillery by dismounted infantry assaults, and sweeping over eight miles of rough terrain, stood almost facing toward the lines they had occupied when the day began. Thousands of Nashville citizens watched the battle in horror from the rooftops and adjacent hills. "No army on the continent ever played on any field to so large and so sullen an audience," one Union officer wrote. For all their hopes lay with Hood.

Evening came as a mercy to his army. Hood had been driven out of his original line of works and forced back "at all points with heavy loss"—in arms, artillery, and men. His center had been pierced, his right wing badly bruised, his left wing swept from the field.

Darkness fell: so ended the first day.

Hood withdrew south to another line of heights known as the Harpeth Hills. The Federals now occupied the Hillsboro Pike, almost at right angles to their original position, having crowded the left flank of the enemy back upon its center. Dismounted cavalry was placed in force upon the extreme right.

The night was a cold one. Hood realized with dismay that he could hardly hope to beat Thomas now, or even flank him and get into Kentucky. But perhaps he could hold the line of Duck River, repair his losses, and attempt a new advance. These were pipe dreams. Thomas had organized his army (over Grant's impatient objections) for advance, battle, and pursuit. Hood had not a moment's rest. That night he formed his new line and entrenched it. He placed his right, under S. D. Lee, on Overton's Hill, just east of the Franklin Pike; his left, with five hastily constructed log and earthen forts, under Cheatham on other hills southwest; his center under Stewart on lower ground crossed by a creek. Cavalry under J. R. Chalmers (Forrest's chief subordinate) held the rear. To protect his left, Hood sharply bent back his lines around it. That way his army covered the two main roads by which it might retreat. But his dispositions were hopeless. For they left the ground in front of Wood's Fourth Corps comparatively clear. Wood promptly pushed forward, with Steedman covering his left.

All in all, everything had gone almost exactly according to plan. As the casualty reports came in, it was apparent that Hood had lost thousands, Thomas relatively few. So many prisoners were taken that they had to be sent into the city to be housed. Black troops were assigned to do this and when some prisoners from South Carolina objected and appealed to Thomas, saying that they would rather die than enter Nashville in charge of "nigger soldiers," he replied: "Well, you may say your prayers, and get ready to die."

"So far I think we have done pretty well," Thomas remarked to an aide as he started back to Nashville to wire the War Department of the day's success. "Unless Hood decamps tonight, tomorrow Steedman will double up his right, Wood will hold his center, Smith and Schofield will again strike his left while the cavalry work away at his rear." His "only regret" was in the delay caused at the outset when a division of Smith's command crossed in front of the cavalry's line of advance. That and the early fog had cost Thomas three hours of precious daylight (on a short winter day) which might have enabled him to rout

Hood completely before dark. The heart of his dispatch at nine o'clock was inimitably succinct: "Attacked enemy's left this morning; drove it from the river, below the city, very nearly to Franklin pike, distance about eight miles." Grant, who was about to entrain for Nashville, turned back. Logan stopped at Louisville and returned to City Point. Grant was almost subdued: "I guess I will not go to Nashville," he said.

Early on the 16th, Thomas rode along the line, with Steedman, Wood, Smith, and Schofield arranged from left to right in a semicircle to the foe. Wilson's cavalry was also at its lethal posting to the rear of Hood's left flank. The Union army was thus in a very compact order—Schofield on the right toward the enemy's left flank and almost at right angles to Smith, Wood in contact with Smith, and Steedman on the left. With the infantry advancing to their front, the Federals once more attacked Hood's left obliquely, as Wilson swung his cavalry behind Hood. On the Rebel right, Wood attacked Overton's Hill, assisted by a brigade of black troops, but the going was rough. The ground they had to cross was open and exposed to view, and as soon as the men advanced, smartly, in Steedman's words, "with cool, steady bravery," they were hit by a tremendous fire of canister and grape. Twice they were driven back. Yet on they came. Wrote Steedman afterward: "I was unable to discover that color made any difference in the fighting," and Colonel Morgan (of the 12th USCT) wrote that they "fought side by side in the charge; helped each other from the field when wounded; and lay side by side in death."

By mid-afternoon, the dismounted cavalry skirmishers had entirely gained the left center rear of Hood's army. It was then about half past three. The situation for Hood's army was dire. At about this juncture, a dispatch from Hood to Chalmers was captured: "For God's sake, drive the Yankee cavalry from our left and rear or all is lost." Thomas wheeled his right into place, poised like a sledgehammer to strike the crushing blow.

The decisive moment had come. In concert with Wilson's rear assault, Smith and Schofield were now to launch a frontal attack. Suddenly, Schofield insisted on reinforcements from Smith's corps. Smith told him he couldn't spare them. Thomas dispatched his chief of staff,

General Whipple, to determine if Schofield really needed the men he claimed. Whipple sped back to Thomas to report that his request lacked merit—which sent Thomas "in person to Schofield to hasten the attack." While he listened to Schofield's protests, "Wilson appeared, after riding the long circuit around the converging battle lines." Meanwhile, General John McArthur, commanding Smith's first division, had asked permission to attack a salient point to his front. Having received no answer, he took silence for consent, and carried the point, driving the enemy back without Schofield's help.

Thomas was standing with Schofield on a small hill less than a mile from the enemy line. From that vantage point, they could see Wilson's dismounted men, their banners fluttering in the air, flanked and covered by two batteries of horse artillery, pouring over the enemy works. Wilson, incensed by the delay, appealed to Thomas. Thomas "lifted his field glasses and," wrote Wilson, "coolly scanned what I clearly showed him. It was a stirring sight, and gazing at it," he made sure that things were as they seemed. Then "he turned to Schofield and as calmly as if on parade directed him to move to the attack with his entire corps."

A blast of artillery fire opened all along the line. Then the whole line advanced and swept everything before it. The turning movement of Wilson's cavalry, which enveloped and took in reverse the Rebel line for a mile and a half, made it impossible for Hood to resist the infantry assault. At the same time, the efficiency of McArthur's charge by successive brigades—the front brigade being halfway up the hill when the second and third were put in motion—spelled Hood's doom. The whole Confederate left was "crushed in like an egg-shell." Once the arch of the Confederate line was broken, there were no reserves to restore it, and from right and left the Confederate troops peeled away from the works in wild dismay. "For the first and only time a Confederate army abandoned the field in confusion," wrote Hood himself after the war.

Roars of exultation went up from the Federal ranks. That's "the voice of the American people," said Thomas, as the cheers flowed back to where he stood. On the Union left Steedman's black troops swept up the slopes of Overton's Hill, on which they had left so many of their comrades earlier that day. This time they reached the summit and chased the Confederates down the other side. Between 3 P.M and 4 P.M. Hood's army was "effectively annihilated," as one writer put it, "its organization wrecked, its components scattered to the winds. Five thousand men threw down their rifles and surrendered in that hour."

In a theatrical sense, the denouement was so complete that "it was more like a scene in a spectacular drama," wrote a staff officer, "than a real incident in war. The hillside in front, still green, dotted with the boys in blue swarming up the slope; the dark background of high hills beyond; the lowering clouds; the waving flags; the smoke slowly rising through the leafless tree-tops and drifting across the valleys; the wonderful outburst of musketry; the ecstatic cheers; the multitude racing for life down in to the valley below—so exciting was it all that the lookers-on" (even among those rooting for the South) "instinctively clapped their hands" as at the brilliant conclusion to a play.

As the battle ended, the Rebels in full retreat, "Thomas with his staff rode to the summit of Overton's Hill, and, scanning the grounds and the results, he lifted his hat and cried, 'Oh what a grand army I have! God bless each member of it.' " Later, he came upon the bodies of black and white soldiers who had fallen together, mingled on the field. Tired of the prejudice that still afflicted Union ranks, he turned to his staff and said fiercely, "The issue is settled! Negroes will fight!"

When the black soldiers, who had played such a distinguished part in the triumph, marched out on the Franklin Pike, Thomas wheeled his horse to the side of the road to face them, and "with his head uncovered" remained in that position until they had all passed by.

Thomas was not done yet. The cavalry he had carefully assembled in spite of Grant now had its crowning task. Dismounted, it had fought with tenacity and brilliance; mounted, it sped after the fragments of Hood's army in relentless pursuit. That night, as Wilson hurried his men down the Granny White Turnpike, he heard a horseman coming up at a gallop from behind. Suddenly, Thomas himself loomed up in the darkness. " 'Is that you, Wilson?' he cried. 'Dang it to hell, Wilson, didn't I tell you we could lick 'em, didn't I tell you?' With scarcely a pause for my reply, he wheeled about. 'Follow them as far as you can tonight and resume the pursuit as early as you can tomorrow morning,' he shouted," and at a gallop disappeared into the night.

Everyone in Washington now changed their tune. "The Rock of Chickamauga," as one writer put it, had become "The Sledgehammer of Nashville." The Northern press went wild with praise. On the evening of the 15th, after Eckert had held on to Grant's infamous wire for an hour, the first of many telegrams clicked through in cipher announcing the success. According to David Homer Bates, his colleague, Eckert at once ran downstairs with two in his hand and drove in the ambulance wagon, "which was always in readiness at the door of the War Department," to Stanton's home. "Stanton appeared at the second story window and called out, 'Is that you, Major? What news?' 'Good news,' was the answer. Stanton shouted 'Hurrah,' and Eckert said he could hear Mrs. Stanton and the children also shouting 'Hurrah.'" Stanton appeared at the front door in a few moments and rode with Eckert to the White House. En route, Eckert took Grant's order relieving Thomas out of his pocket and handed it to Stanton without saying a word. The secretary asked whether it had been sent. Eckert replied no. "Mr. Secretary, I fear I have violated a military rule and have placed myself liable to be court-martialed," said Eckert. Secretary Stanton "put his arm around Eckert's shoulder and said, 'Major, if they court-martial you, they will have to court-martial me.'"

When they got to the White House, wrote Bates, "the tall ghostly form of Lincoln in his night-dress, with a lighted candle in his hand, appeared at the head of the second story landing when the two were ushered upstairs." When Stanton told him that Eckert had suppressed Grant's last order of removal, Lincoln "heartily approved." Directly after meeting with Lincoln, Stanton, at midnight on the 15th, wired Thomas: "I rejoice in tendering to you and the gallant officers and soldiers of your command the thanks of this department for the brilliant achievement of this day." From Grant, Thomas heard: "I was just on my way to Nashville, but receiving dispatch . . . detailing your splendid success of today, I shall go no farther." Then, fifteen minutes later, Grant wrote: "I congratulate you and the army." Lincoln the next morning (11:20 A.M) wrote: "Please accept for yourself, officers and men the nation's thanks for the good work of yesterday. You have made a magnificent beginning; a grand consummation is within your easy reach. Do not let it slip." It was more than a magnificent beginning, of course; by the end of the day Hood's army was no more. Before leaving the field of battle, Thomas had published these telegrams to the army in general orders, adding his own more generous words: "The major-general commanding with pride and pleasure . . . adds thereto his own thanks to the troops for the unsurpassed gallantry and good conduct displayed by them in the battle of yesterday and today." Thomas then replied to all the telegrams with: "The army thanks you for your approbation of its conduct yesterday and [wishes] to assure you that it is not misplaced."

In Washington and City Point, Thomas and his army received a 100-gun salute. Other telegrams of congratulations came in. Even Salmon Chase, now chief justice of the United States, who had previously lobbied against giving Thomas an independent command, paid him the unusually high compliment of admitting his mistake: "We all feel profoundly gratified to you and your gallant Army for the great success over Hood. I rejoice that you were in command." For his part, in his general reply to Lincoln, Stanton, and Grant, Thomas, on the 16th, gave a synopsis of the battle, then concluded: "I am happy to state that all this has been effected with but a very small loss to us. Our loss does not probably exceed three thousand, very few killed."

"Very few killed." In assaulting Hood's fortified works, Thomas had lost only about as many men as Schofield had lost in repelling Hood's attack on his own entrenched line at Franklin. Such an achievement was almost unheard of in the war. Unprecedented, too, as Colonel Henry Stone noted, was "the capture of over 10,000 prisoners—nearly one-third the enemy's whole force—with seventy-two guns . . . in an open field fight, between nearly equal numbers, and where the enemy had command of more than one line of retreat." Yet there is no evidence that Grant was truly pleased. It is not hard to guess why. Grant's manner of doing battle accepted a casualty rate more horrendous than Thomas could countenance, which meant that any success gained by Thomas with skill stood as an implied rebuke to Grant's whole style of making war.

The chase of Hood's army continued night and day in winter

weather—rain, slush, snow, and ice—over drenched fields and muddy roads through a region which the foraging parties of both armies had gleaned bare. Along the line of it, the creeks and rivers were full to overflowing; bridges down or swept away. Thomas now especially missed the exceptional pontoon train he had created, which Sherman had taken for himself. An incomplete replacement, assembled in haste in Nashville, was also delayed when an aide miswrote an order that directed it down the wrong road. It had moved out fifteen miles when, the mistake having been discovered, it slogged across fields to the Franklin Pike. Yet even under these conditions, the chase was pressed for 100 miles to the Tennessee River. In this unstinting effort, which lasted ten days, over 6,000 cavalry horses were disabled or destroyed. The pursuit finally came to an end when Hood managed to bring the broken fragments of his army across the Tennessee by a bridge at Muscle Shoals. Even then, a detachment of Union cavalry succeeded in crossing the river at Decatur, and captured the last of Hood's wagon trains. Meanwhile, Thomas had sent Steedman by rail to Decatur, Alabama, to block the river while Admiral S. P. Lee's gunboat flotilla coursed up the Tennessee.

Yet during the pursuit of Hood's army, Thomas had to contend with a new flurry of fatuous telegrams from Halleck and Grant. Both condescended to give him lessons in how to wrap things up. "Great precaution should be taken to prevent [Forrest] crossing the Cumberland or Tennessee River below Eastport," exclaimed Grant on the 18th. "After Hood is driven as far as possible to follow him, you want to reoccupy Decatur and all other abandoned points." Halleck wrote on the 21st: "Permit me, General, to urge the vast importance of a hot pursuit. . . . Every possible sacrifice should be made," and so on.

Thomas had had enough. In his reply, he set the record straight:

> General Hood's army is being pursued as rapidly and as vigorously as it is possible for one army to pursue another. We cannot control the elements, and you must remember that to resist Hood's advance into Tennessee I had to reorganize and almost thoroughly equip the force now under my command. I fought the battles of the 15th and 16th inst. with the troops but partially equipped, and not-

withstanding the inclemency of the weather and the partial equipment, have been enabled to drive the enemy beyond Duck River, crossing the two streams with my troops, and driving the enemy from position to position, without the aid of pontoons, and with but little transportation to bring up supplies and ammunition.

I am doing all in my power to crush Hood's army, and, if it be possible, will destroy it, but pursuing an enemy through an exhausted country, over mud roads, completely sogged with heavy rains, is no child's play, and cannot be accomplished as quickly as thought of. I hope, in urging me to push the enemy, the department remembers that General Sherman took with him the complete organizations of the Military Division of the Mississippi, well equipped in every respect as regards ammunition, supplies, and transportation, leaving me only two corps—partially stripped of their transportation to accommodate the force taken with him—to oppose the advance into Tennessee of that army which had resisted the advance of the army of the Military Division of the Mississippi on Atlanta from the commencement of the campaign until its close, and which is now, in addition, aided by Forrest's cavalry. Although my progress may appear slow, I feel assured that Hood's army can be driven from Tennessee, and eventually driven to the wall, by the force under my command. . . . This army is willing to submit to any sacrifice to crush Hood's army or to strike any other blow which may contribute to the destruction of the rebellion.

When Stanton saw this exchange, he was mortified. He at once wired Thomas on December 22, at 9 P.M.: "I have seen today General Halleck's despatch of yesterday and your reply. It is proper for me to assure you that this Department has the most unbounded confidence in your skill, vigor, and determination to employ to the best advantage all the means in your power to pursue and destroy the enemy. No Department could be inspired with more profound admiration and thankfulness for the great deed which you have already performed, or more confiding faith that human effort could do no more, and no more than will be done by you and the accomplished, gallant officers and soldiers of your command."

That was the whole truth. Thomas was grateful to hear it. He replied from the Headquarters Department of the Cumberland, Columbia, on December 23 at 8 P.M.: "I am profoundly thankful for the hearty expression of your confidence in my determination and desire to do all in my power to destroy the enemy and put down the Rebellion, and in the name of this army I thank you for the complimentary notice you have taken of all connected with it for the deeds of valor they have performed."

Stanton was sincere. The day before he had suggested to Grant that Thomas be promoted to major general in the Regular Army. (Thomas was still only a brigadier general in the army, though a major general of volunteers.) Grant held back: "I think Thomas has won the major-generalship, but I would wait a few days before giving it to see the extent of damage done." Lincoln thought otherwise. The next day, on Christmas Eve, Thomas heard again from Stanton: "With great pleasure I inform you, that for your skill, courage and conduct in the recent brilliant military operation under your command, the President has directed your nomination . . . as a major general in the United States Army to fill the only vacancy in that grade. No official duty has been performed by me with more satisfaction, and no commander has more justly earned promotion by devoted, disinterested and valuable services to his country."

It was a bittersweet moment of acclaim. Thomas had been passed over not once but several times—after Mill Springs, Stones River, Chickamauga, and Chattanooga—as the major general commissions had been granted, one by one, to Sherman (August 12, 1864), Meade (August 18), and Sheridan (November 8), the last a favorite of Grant's but Thomas's junior in the service by thirteen years. Sherman had been promoted during the siege of Atlanta, Meade for his overall service, Sheridan for the Battle of Cedar Creek (which had caught him offguard at Winchester twenty miles away). It had been fourteen months since Thomas had been promoted to brigadier, and now at his field headquarters at Pulaski, he sat silent and motionless with the telegram in his hand. He handed it to an aide, Chief Army Surgeon George E. Cooper, saying: "What do you think of that?"

"Thomas," said Cooper, "it is better late than never."

"I suppose it is better late than never but it is too late to be appreciated," said Thomas. "I earned this at Chickamauga."

The following day, which was Christmas, Thomas wired his thanks but, honest as ever, added: "I beg to assure the President and yourself that your approbation of my services is of more value to me than the commission itself." Thomas, in fact, remained "very sore at the rumored intentions to relieve him," wrote a friend. "It cut him to the heart." He afterward observed, rather sadly, to an aide: "There is one thing about my promotions that is exceedingly gratifying. I have never received a promotion they dared withhold."

At Nashville alone a total of 13,000 prisoners and seventy-two cannon were taken; no one knows how many Rebels were wounded and killed. But out of the 55,000 men who had set out under Hood for the invasion of Tennessee and Kentucky, only 8,000 made it back to the temporary safety of Confederate lines. After that, they were too demoralized to fight. As one fellow general put it, "Who ever heard of Hood's army again?" By the starkest contrast, the Union loss, out of 50,000 men engaged, was just 3,057. In the enduring words of the historian John Fiske, "Nashville was the most decisive victory gained by either side in the Civil War." Not only was it the most decisive, but "the most economical—a complete vindication" of Thomas's insistence that an army rightly led and prepared can win a tremendous victory without shredding its own ranks.

In the end, it would be judged one of the two most perfect battles ever fought—the other being Napoleon's victory at Austerlitz.

The victory of Nashville marked the beginning of the end. It prevented a new Southern thrust into the North, which would have prolonged the war; made good Sherman's March to the Sea; and left but one considerable Confederate army in the field, beleaguered in and around Richmond, and now doomed. Had Thomas not insisted on taking the time—and, again, it was not a long time—to remount his cavalry and properly prepare it for its great role, the Western theater would not have been won when it was; and without the great cavalry campaign that soon followed, the South would not have lost its capacity to make war. Hood's army would have survived, Lee been heartened, and Johnston (now in North Carolina) would have fought on. Grant and Sherman (whatever they may be said to have accomplished on their own) gathered up in the end the harvest Thomas had sown. Meanwhile, Sherman having taken Savannah with his army of 60,000, had let the small Rebel army defending it—10,000 to 15,000 men under William Hardee—escape. Sherman had reached the coast on December 21, "unopposed except by a few cavalry pickets," having avoided all fortified places, and had encountered no enemy in force.

Yet Grant could not praise Sherman enough: "I congratulate you and the brave officers and men under your command on the successful termination of your most brilliant campaign. I never had a doubt of the result. When apprehensions for your safety were expressed by the President, I assured him with the army you had, and you in command of it, there was no danger but you would strike bottom on saltwater some place; that I would not feel the same security, in fact would not have intrusted the expedition to any other living commander." After his own summary of the Battle of Nashville (prefaced with the remark that it had "been very hard to get Thomas to attack"), he praised Sherman's unopposed campaign as "the like of which is not read in past history."

Stanton was less impressed. He wanted to know how Sherman's large army had let Hardee's force escape. He wired Grant: "It was a sore disappointment that Hardee was able to get off his 15,000 from Sherman's 60,000. It looks like protracting the war while their armies continue to escape." Indeed, as one contemporary historian, William Swinton, put it, "The Confederacy lived in its armies, which continuing, its territory might be traversed and laid waste in vain." But no whisper of a reprimand for Sherman escaped Grant's lips. Sherman had had so little opposition on his march that on December 3, Grant sent his mail to the blockading squadron off Savannah, "to be forwarded to you as soon as heard from on the coast. Not liking to rejoice before the victory is assured, I abstain from congratulating you and those under your command, until bottom has been struck. I have never had a fear, however, for the result." Why would he? It had been a campaign mainly against livestock, crops, and inanimate objects. Railroads, mills, and cotton gins were systematically demolished; horses, cattle, hogs, poultry, corn, and stores of provisions taken or destroyed. Looting and vandalism, though officially forbidden, were indulged. "By day," wrote one historian, "the rising smoke from burning homes marked the path of destruction; by night merry campfires symbolized the helplessness of the South."

Sherman had exulted in the abundant harvest of his March. "We started with about five thousand head of cattle, and arrived with over ten thousand, of course consuming mostly turkeys, chickens, sheep, hogs, and the cattle of the country. As to our mules and horses, we left Atlanta with about twenty-five hundred wagons, many of which were drawn by mules which had not recovered from the Chattanooga starvation, all of which were replaced, the poor mules shot, and our transportation is now in superb condition. I have no doubt the State of Georgia has lost, by our operations, fifteen thousand first-rate mules. As to horses, [Hugh Judson] Kilpatrick [his cavalry commander] collected all his remounts, and it looks to me, in riding along our columns, as though every officer had three or four led horses"—quite a contrast with Thomas's plight. Not only had Sherman taken all the healthy horses for his own cavalry troop, but had collected so many more en route to Savannah that he had to shoot them by the score. This, while Thomas was faulted for taking a few desperate days to round up what horses he could.

Sherman now wrote Thomas from Savannah, December 25, 1864:

I have heard of your operations up to the 17th and I do not believe your own wife was more happy at the results than I was. Had any misfortune befallen you I should have reproached myself for taking away so large a proportion of the army and leaving you too weak to cope with Hood. But as events have turned out my judgment has been sustained, but I am nonetheless thankful to you, and to Schofield, and to all, for the very complete manner in which you have used up Hood. I only hope you will go on and pursue your advantage to the very uttermost. And if you can get far down into Alabama, don't hesitate to do so,—for my experience is that you can get plenty of forage and provisions down along the valleys of the Tombigbee and Black Warrior.

Here I am now in a magnificent house close by the old barracks. . . .

The old live oaks are as beautiful as ever, and whilst you are freezing to death in Tennessee we are basking in a warm sun, and I fear I did you personal injustice in leaving you behind whilst I made my winter excursion. But next time I will stay home and let you go it.

The offhand levity of this letter speaks for itself.

Many have held, then and since, that it was the victory by Thomas at Nashville that made good Sherman's march. That was Lincoln's view, as seen in his tactful telegram of congratulations to Sherman, which closely linked the two. He wrote to Sherman at Savannah on December 26, 1864: "When you were about leaving Atlanta for the Atlantic coast, I was anxious, if not fearful; but, feeling that you were the better judge, and remembering 'nothing risked, nothing gained,' I did not interfere . . . and, taking the work of General Thomas into account, as it should be taken, it is indeed a great success." Although Sherman's Special Field Order No. 6, of January 8, 1865, which announced the victory at Nashville, included the bizarre assertion that Thomas had "decoyed" Hood to Nashville, in his *Memoirs,* he acknowledged that Thomas's "brilliant victory" had been "necessary" to his own "to make a complete whole."

What, indeed, would have been said of Sherman's march if Thomas had failed?

The war in the West was really over. The nation itself was so stunned by the totality of it that it struggled to grasp its import. "There was something incredible in it," as one writer put it, "like the fall of an oak of a thousand years."

Yet the failure of Thomas to annihilate or capture every single man in Hood's army gave Grant a grotesque new opportunity to snipe. In his memoirs he leaned over backward to suggest that the victory was incomplete. Though the revolutionary use Thomas made of cavalry as a rapid infantry force had largely carried the day, Grant scorned their use. This is his account of the battle's denouement: "Our cavalry had fought on foot as infantry, and had not their horses with them; so that they were not ready to join in the pursuit the moment the enemy retreated. They sent back, however, for their horses, and endeavored to get to Franklin ahead of Hood's broken army by the Granny White Road, but too much time was consumed in getting started. . . . They were too late."

Grant leaves the impression that in the end Hood's army got away.

The near-universal judgment, by contrast, was voiced by Wilson, who wrote: "No other pursuit of the war had been so promptly begun nor pushed so far without pause or halt." What was the Confederate view? Hood's corps commander S. D. Lee wrote: "A more persistent effort was never made to rout the rear guard of a retiring column."

Grant's dispatch to Sherman of January 21, 1865, was also unconscionable on the same score: "[Thomas's] pursuit of Hood indicated a sluggishness that satisfied me that he would never do to conduct one of your campaigns. The command of the advance of the pursuit was left to subordinates, whilst Thomas followed far behind. When Hood had crossed the Tennessee, and those in pursuit had reached it, Thomas had not much more than half crossed the State"—as if Wilson (the greatest cavalry commander of the war, at least on the Union side) was not fit to lead the chase. As usual, there was an unpleasant double standard in all this. After the fall of Vicksburg, for example, when Sherman had begun to pursue Confederates near Jackson, Mississippi, he complained to Grant of "the intense heat, dust & fatigue." Grant replied, "Continue the pursuit as long as you have reasonable hopes of favorable results, but do not wear your men out."

Indeed, though Grant had congratulated Thomas in his letter of December 22 "for the energy with which you are pursuing Hood," he belittled the effort to Sherman, and praised Sherman to Halleck in a way that denigrated all that Thomas had done: "It is refreshing to see a commander, after a campaign of seven months' duration, ready for still further operations and without wanting any outfit or rest." How deep Grant's festering malice toward Thomas was may here be glimpsed. Sherman's March to the Sea had been an "easy" romp by Sherman's own description—so easy that it seemed to him (again by his own description) too good to be true. He also lingered untroubled at Savannah for another month.

William Franklin Gore Shanks wrote right after the war:

> I have always wondered how Sherman came to delegate the subordinate, Thomas, with the lesser half of the army, to fight the main battles and conduct the real campaign, while he, the superior officer, with the greater half of the force, made a detour in which no longer was encountered—no danger, in fact, apprehended—and which could have been better effected with half the force. . . . Hood met Thomas at Nashville, and the consequence was his annihilation. The success of Thomas made Sherman's march a success, and hence the former deserves the full credit for the latter's achievement. How great this credit is can be seen by forming in the mind an idea of the consequences which would have attended failure on Thomas' part. Had he been defeated Nashville would have fallen; Hood would have marched into Kentucky and appeared on the line of the Ohio, while Sherman, making his appearance a thousand leagues away on the South Atlantic coast, would have found himself written down a great failure instead of a great general.

In their memoirs, Grant and Sherman did all they could to save face. Sherman hugely inflated the number of troops Thomas had at his disposal; Grant's account, too, was fantastic beyond measure. The *Official Records* contradict them on every count. Even Confederate generals, who had a vested interest in inflating the size of their opponents, thought Thomas had done something amazing. The Confederate general D. H. Maury remarked that the patchwork army "with which Thomas gained his victory . . . largely made up of forces detached for the occasion from other armies, of new levies" had been on its face "ill-fitted to cope with the veteran army of Hood." Grant's whole aim, of course, was to depict Thomas as having had ample strength to attack at any time. That alone could justify his infamous telegrams. But in a private letter to Wilson (not published until 1906)

Assistant Secretary of War Charles Dana admitted that it was "indisputable that Sherman left Thomas with insufficient forces" for his task.

The other theme Grant sought to develop was that Thomas was "slow." With Sherman, it had become his favorite theme. "To me his delay was unaccountable," Grant wrote in his memoirs, "sitting there and permitting himself to be invested, so that, in the end, to raise the siege he would have to fight the enemy strongly posted behind fortifications. It is true the weather was very bad. The rain was falling and freezing as it fell, so that the ground was covered with a sheet of ice, that made it very difficult to move. But I was afraid that the enemy would find means of moving, elude Thomas and manage to get north of the Cumberland River." And so on. But as D. H. Maury remarked, "I never heard anyone in Hood's army say that Thomas was slow." In truth, if he moved slowly, remarked one Federal officer appalled at the canard, "he moved with irresistible power; and if he ground slowly, it was like the mills of the gods."

In Grant's official *Military History* written by Badeau, and later in his memoirs, Grant suppressed all the dispatches that incriminated his judgment. He reproduced only his own dispatches to Thomas, omitting Thomas's replies. He also omitted the dispatches Thomas sent to Halleck—much as Sherman, in his account of the Atlanta campaign, omitted McPherson's end of the correspondence about the movement through Snake Creek Gap. It wasn't until the 1890s that a nearly full record of the war was compiled. But by then the Grant-Sherman legend had been established, and the tenor of most Civil War history writing set.

Yet Grant and Sherman had much to be grateful for. Had fortune's needle shifted but one degree, even Thomas might not have been able to save the day. If Hood had not paused at Florence for three weeks to await reinforcements and supplies, but had sped straight to Nashville, he would have arrived with an army whose numbers had not been reduced by the Franklin fight, with twice as many troops as Thomas had.

That and many other fortuitous events saved Grant and Sherman from disgrace.

# 12. "THE NOBLEST FIGURE"

After crushing Hood's army, Thomas had planned to give his forces some rest (but not a long one) and then to assemble and thoroughly equip an army of cavalry under Wilson to sweep through the South. On December 30, he therefore sent his troops into winter quarters to recuperate for the spring campaign. But Grant had other plans. The very next day, Thomas received a wire from Halleck: "Lieutenant General U.S. Grant directs all your available forces not essential to hold your communications, to be collected on the Tennessee river,—say at Eastport and Tuscumbia, and be made ready for such movements as may be ordered. . . . General Grant does not intend that your army shall go into winter quarters. It must be made ready for active operations in the field."

Bitter weather forestalled Grant's plans, but in letters to Sherman and Halleck, Grant continued his campaign against Thomas behind the scenes. Sherman picked up the notion that Thomas had been "slow" at Nashville, while Grant expanded on the theme. On January 15, in a letter to Halleck, he wrote that Thomas was "too ponderous in his preparations and equipments to move through a country rapidly enough to live off it," and did not believe Thomas would ever get to Selma or Montgomery—objectives of the next campaign. To make sure of it, he broke up his army, to prevent more laurels from adorning his brow. Wilson complained after the war that Grant had "scattered the infantry around as well as the splendid body of cavalry I had got together with so much pain."

Thomas and Wilson at once began to assemble an entire new cavalry force—first at Huntsville, in northern Alabama, then in cantonments extending about twelve miles from Gravelly Springs to Waterloo Landing along the north bank of the Tennessee. Supplies in abundance came down the river. By the first week of March, 27,000 cavalrymen had been assembled in the camps. Of these, 20,000 were mounted, and 15,000 equipped with the Spencer repeating carbine. It was, as Wilson described it, "the largest body of cavalry ever collected" on American soil. Though it had taken them only nine weeks in midwinter, from the 1st of January to the 1st of March, to complete their preparations, Grant began once more to harass Thomas from his own "inactive" camp. Intent on breaking up the new army, too, he ordered Thomas to send one division of 5,000 from Wilson's corps to General Edward Canby, operating against Mobile, and wanted Wilson himself to go with 5,000 more to make a demonstration against Tuscaloosa and Selma. That made no sense to Thomas, so instead he went to Waterloo Landing by steamer to confer with Wilson about the right use of their force. Wilson came on board and told Thomas that if allowed, he thought he could take not only Tuscaloosa and Selma but all the major remaining arsenals and production centers in the South.

Thomas approved this plan, wired Grant for clearance, and obtained it, on condition that Wilson enjoy "all the latitude of an independent command." Meanwhile, Grant had written Sherman: "Ever since you started on the last campaign [this was Sherman's new march of devastation north through the Carolinas] . . . I have been attempting to get something done in the West, both to cooperate with you and to take advantage of the enemy's weakness there—to accomplish results favorable to us. Knowing Thomas to be slow beyond excuse, I depleted his army to reinforce Canby," adding, however, that he couldn't get Thomas to get Wilson or Stoneman going "in time to do much good."

Grant himself remained motionless before the Confederate forces at Petersburg. He had earlier told a delegation of Philadelphians who came to protest his inaction: "Just as soon as I hear that Sherman is at some one of the points designated on the seacoast, I will take Richmond. Were I to move now without advices from Sherman, Lee would evacuate Richmond, taking his army somewhere South, and I would have to follow him." But Grant, in fact, lingered at City Point for three months after Sherman reached the coast; and not until Goldsboro had fallen, in the interior of North Carolina, did he make his move. Meanwhile, Wilson had crossed the Tennessee River on March 18 and began a spectacular rampage through rural and industrial Alabama, taking Tuscaloosa, and defeating Forrest outside Selma, with its great arsenal of furnaces, foundries, and its cache of arms. Canby in turn moved against Mobile on the Alabama coast; and Stoneman (whom Sherman had dismissed as "lazy") swept through southwest Virginia, blocking Lee's line of communication and diminishing his already scant supplies. He then turned into North Carolina, captured the prison pen of Salisbury, and interrupted Lee's railroad links through that state. "It was a large factor in the pinching situation which was fast forcing the abandonment of Richmond," General Henry V. Boynton noted, though Grant failed to properly acknowledge it in his summary of the last days of the war. "Most of these expeditions," Grant wrote in his memoirs, "got off finally, but too late to render any service in the direction for which they were designed. . . . The war was practically over before their victories were gained."

That was hardly so. The sequence of events was this: The war began to draw to a close with Canby marching into Alabama, Wilson taking Selma and Montgomery, and Stoneman advancing through Virginia and western North Carolina, in a diversion in favor of Sherman's northward march. With a cavalry force 10,000 strong, Stoneman reached Jonesboro on March 24; on the 27th, he crossed over the Blue Ridge Mountains to Salem, Virginia; then divided his force for separate raids. Stations, depots, bridges, and miles of track fell to his men. Meanwhile, Wilson had started on March 22 from Chickasaw and after taking Selma in early April, had moved on to Montgomery, which surrendered on the 12th. In tandem with these developments, Lee had left the Petersburg trenches in an attempt to unite with the Confederate forces in North Carolina—a move that Thomas effectively blocked by sending Stoneman there. Grant now followed, eventually surrounding Lee near Appomattox Court House and receiving his surrender just before Montgomery fell. Wilson's path of conquest then took him to Columbus, Georgia, thence to Macon, which he captured on April 21 before the armistice between Joseph Johnston and Sherman was confirmed. On May 10, a troop of Wilson's men also captured Jefferson Davis at Irwinsville, Georgia, disguised as an old woman in a bonnet and a dress.

Thomas had kept a very close eye on the details of all these cavalry movements, as a constant flurry of wires reveals. Though in theory their commanders were "independent," they all reported to Thomas, whom they considered in charge. Indeed, after Lee surrendered at Appomattox, Thomas directed his various subordinate generals (George Stoneman, James Wilson, James Steedman, Lovell Rousseau, Cadwallader Washburn, I. N. Palmer, John T. Croxton, Gordon Granger, Edward Hatch, and so on) within his jurisdiction in Alabama, Kentucky, Mississippi, and Tennessee to call upon Rebels in their area to surrender "upon the same terms as Lee surrendered to Grant." On May 1, he had also informed Grant (now at Washington) that he was hot in pursuit of Jefferson Davis, with Stoneman, Wilson, and others dispatching scouts to ascertain his whereabouts. (At that point, he knew that Davis was trying to make his way across North Georgia to the Mississippi, where he might try to cross between Vicksburg and Memphis.) Stoneman was at Knoxville, Steedman at Resaca, Washburn at Memphis, Hatch at Eastport, Granger at Decatur. As the dragnet tightened, it was Thomas who pulled the strings. He dispatched Stoneman down the east side of the Savannah River toward Augusta; Croxton up along the Alabama-Mississippi line; and had Wilson establish a cordon of troops at various transit points that extended for 350 miles. "I think," Thomas told Grant, "it will be impossible for Davis to escape," adding wryly: "If Davis escapes . . . he will prove himself a better general than any of his subordinates." Wilson closed in, scooped him up, and sent him under a strong guard to Thomas at Nashville. Thomas wired Grant to ask where he wished him to go from there. Meanwhile, Thomas directed the generals in charge at Louisville, Chattanooga, and Cincinnati to handle Davis as he passed through with courtesy, discretion, and care.

The capture of Davis was obviously momentous but Grant failed to respond in a timely fashion to Thomas's wire. So on May 15, Thomas decided to take matters into his own hands. He wired Grant: "Wishing to forward Jeff. Davis and party without delay and having received no instructions to govern me, I have directed that he be placed on board a steamer at this place, forwarded to Parkersville, Virginia, thence by rail to Washington to be turned over to the Provost Marshal General U.S.A. This arrangement appears to me to be not only the safest but most expeditious. He will be under an ample and efficient guard." Without delay, he put Davis on the steamer *Shamrock*, which carried him from Nashville to Louisville to Parkersville, and from there to Washington on a special train.

Meanwhile, in the agreement Sherman had signed with Johnston for the surrender of Johnston's army, he made political arrangements he had no authority to make. Among other things, they allowed for the recognition of current state governments in the South (subject to their oath of allegiance to the United States) and guaranteed current rights of person and property to Confederate soldiers returning home. This was viewed, plausibly enough, as reinstating the property right of slavery and confirming Rebel governments in place. Sherman was accused of treason by Stanton and others and Grant had to hurry off to Sherman's camp to arrange an annulment of the terms.

The last Confederate army was surrendered by General Kirby Smith, west of the Mississippi, on May 26.

By then, Lincoln was dead. On Good Friday, April 14, General Robert Anderson had once more raised the Union flag over Fort Sumter, Lincoln met with his cabinet for the last time, and that evening attended Ford's Theatre with his wife, where John Wilkes Booth shot him in the back of the head. According to Secretary of the Navy Gideon Welles, Grant's animus toward Thomas intruded even into the president's last hours. In the cabinet meeting of the 14th, which Grant attended, Lincoln spoke of a recurrent dream he had which had preceded "every great and important event of the war. Generally the news had been favorable . . . and the dream itself was always the same." In it, Lincoln dreamed that "he seemed to be in some singular, indescribable vessel, and that he was moving with great rapidity towards an indefinite shore." He said he had had that dream before a number of successful battles, including Stones River. Grant rudely interrupted Lincoln's poignant speech (often viewed as a premonition of his death) to say that "Stones River was no victory—that a few such fights would have ruined us. The President," wrote Welles in his diary, "looked at Grant curiously and inquiringly; said they might differ on that point, and at all events his dream had preceded it." Welles, on this occasion, was forcefully struck by "Grant's jealous nature. In turning it over in my mind at a later period, I remembered that . . . there was jealousy manifested towards General Thomas and others who were not satellites."

Even as Thomas was wrapping things up in the West, he was trying to attend to the humanitarian needs of the population of the captured states. He was—if anyone was—the practical manifestation of Lincoln's noble pronouncement in his Second Inaugural Address: "with malice toward none, with charity toward all." On May 2, he had wired Stanton that the sorry plight of the inhabitants of North Georgia and Alabama had them on "the verge of despair." He urged that civil law be restored and that a military governor be appointed at once to oversee elections. He volunteered to serve in that role, and asked that General Steedman be allowed to go to Washington as his representative "to explain fully" the situation as he saw it at the time. Stanton insisted that Thomas come himself. "I . . . want to see and know personally," wrote Stanton, "so good and great a soldier that has served his country so well." When Thomas went to see him, Stanton said, "I have always had great confidence in you." Thomas replied: "Mr. Stanton, I am sorry to hear you make this statement," which he knew was knowingly false. Stanton seems to have accepted the rebuke. He afterward remarked to General Robert Schenck: "I feel before him as if I were in the presence of George Washington."

A remarkable number of contemporaries, in fact, thought Washington was the only man of stature to whom Thomas could be compared. Generals Wilson, Garfield, and Rosecrans, as well as Assistant Secretary of War Charles Dana, had voiced that opinion; others concurred. Garfield, in a famous tribute, singled out "the gravity and dignity of his character, the solidity of his judgment, the careful accuracy of all his transactions, his incorruptible integrity, and his extreme but unaffected modesty." General Willard Warner, inspector general on

Sherman's staff, spoke of his "Washington greatness," and General Oliver Howard thought Thomas not only greater than Stonewall Jackson and Robert E. Lee, but Washington's equal: "With less opportunity, his achievements put him by Washington's side." By that he meant that Thomas had accomplished all he had without the advantage of being in supreme command. In Garfield's opinion, the military genius of Thomas equaled that displayed by Washington, Zachary Taylor, and the Duke of Wellington, which was quite a triumvirate. When Gideon Welles finally met Thomas after the war, he thought him "intellectually and as a civilian, as well as a military man," beyond compare.

His innate majesty, indeed, seemed to evoke something like religious awe. At Nashville, Thomas had rented a house where his wife joined him in the spring. Most of his neighbors were civil, but on one side of him lived a man "who had been known as a rebel, but who did not have the courage to fight for the principles which he pretended to hold so dear. Every evening he came out onto his verandah," we are told, "within handshaking distance of Thomas, whom he pretended not to see. Thomas ignored the slight, but one evening, after six months or so had passed, this Southern aristocrat advanced in a very patronizing manner to shake hands. Thomas waved him back: 'Too late, too late, sir; you have sinned away your day of grace.'" The man recoiled as if the Last Judgment had been pronounced upon him, and was evidently so mortified, he never showed his face again.

With the establishment of military government at the close of the war, Thomas learned that he alone of the six major generals of the Regular Army would not be assigned to command a military division—but only a subdivision or department. Halleck was to have the Pacific Coast; Sheridan, the territory west of the Mississippi; Sherman, the Midwest and South; and Meade, the Atlantic Coast down to Georgia. For Thomas, only a department within Sherman's Military Division of the Mississippi was shown. He was understandably displeased, and "folding up the map and placing his fist upon it," asked his friend and colleague General John F. Miller, the Nashville commander, to go to Washington and speak to President Andrew Johnson about setting this right. Thomas told him: "I wish you to take the first train for Washington, and tell President Johnson that during the war I permitted the National authorities to do what they pleased with me; they put my juniors over me, and I served under them; the life of the Nation was then at stake, and it was not then proper to press questions of rank, but now that the war is over and the Nation saved, I demand a command suited to my rank, or I do not want any."

Miller met with the president and urged him to give Thomas charge of reconstruction in the various states in which he had served. Johnson agreed and took a pencil and on the map Miller brought with him outlined a sixth military division consisting of the states of Kentucky, Tennessee, Mississippi, Alabama, and Georgia for Thomas to command. "You know my appreciation of General Thomas," Johnson said. Sherman was not happy about this and insisted that his own diminished dominion be extended to the Rocky Mountains to make up the loss. Sheridan in turn received the Gulf states of Florida, Louisiana, and Texas. Even so, more Southern states were assigned to Thomas than to any other man.

A way had now to be found for the Southern states to resume their normal place, send representatives to Washington, participate in presidential elections, enjoy their share of Federal appointments, and restore law and order within their domains. That was the moderate Reconstruction policy on which Lincoln had hoped to embark. But there were two main questions to be settled—the emancipation of blacks, and the reannexation to the Union of the conquered states. Lincoln's Emancipation Proclamation had only freed slaves in the states with which the North was at war (but not in Maryland, Kentucky, Delaware, and Missouri—slave states that had remained in the Union). In his second campaign for president, Lincoln had proposed an emancipation amendment to the Constitution abolishing slavery in every state. But emancipation was not the same as the right to vote. Lincoln had also offered a general amnesty to Rebels who would lay down their arms and renew their oath of allegiance. But Congress insisted that the new state governments could not include anyone who had belonged to the Confederate establishment and had "voluntarily" borne arms against the United States. This tended, in practice, to eliminate those with local stature, who were needed to make Reconstruction work.

The provisional state governments did not cooperate, and tried, indirectly at first, to re-create the oppressive system of the prewar years. Though blacks were given limited civil rights, "Black Codes" were also enacted by legislatures dominated by men obsessed by racial fears. The ire of the North was aroused. Senator Charles Sumner of Massachusetts declared: "It is essential to complete Emancipation [so that] all shall be equal before the law." By two amendments to the Constitution (the Thirteenth and Fourteenth), slavery was universally and forever abolished, and blacks invested with full citizenship rights and powers.

In the midst of all this turmoil, Thomas proved firm but fair, and managed his military rule with ability and tact. In Tennessee, clashes were frequent between returned Confederate soldiers and "loyal citizens," and the sea of troubles was sometimes made more stormy by the use of black soldiers to enforce the law. Thomas thought the blacks were doing their job extremely well, and assured President Johnson on September 5, 1865, that they were "under good discipline. . . . I believe in the majority of cases of collision between whites and negro soldiers that the white man has attempted to bully the negro, for it is exceedingly repugnant to Southerners to have negro soldiers in their midst & some are so foolish as to vent their anger upon the negro because he is a soldier."

On a number of occasions, Thomas also testified before the congressional Joint Committee on Reconstruction and proved an exceptionally reliable voice. Though optimistic at first, he was hard to fool, and well attuned to the undertow of sedition and violence that remained. He warned Washington about "secret organizations being formed" to resuscitate Confederate doctrine, and was the first to sound the alarm about the Ku Klux Klan. The Klan claimed to recognize the Constitution and its laws, but Thomas saw through its mask. In memorable words, he described it as "a species of political cant, whereby the crime of treason might be covered with a counterfeit varnish of patriotism, so that the precipitators of the rebellion might go down in history, hand-in-hand with the defenders of the Government, thus wiping out with their own hands their own stains." Correctly convinced that the Klan would soon evolve into an armed organization designed to control Southern elections through violence and intimidation, Thomas warned Washington of the peril of its rise. Washington failed to act, and before long, local police departments (soon made up largely of Klan members) became agents of its schemes. By 1868, the Klan was fully organized on a semimilitary basis as a terror organization with Nathan Bedford Forrest as its first Grand Wizard or head. White sheets—said to represent the ghosts of dead Rebel soldiers—became its familiar garb.

Aside from having his eyes on the KKK, with his clear grasp of its broad strategy and intentions, Thomas was vigilant overall in guarding the polls, and exposing attempts to reinstitutionalize bigotry by legislation and new laws. In the interests of orderly government, he understood that it was important for the South to reestablish its legal system, but insisted on the elimination of all laws that in any shape or form treated blacks as inferior to whites.

One by one, Southern states were readmitted to the Union as their legislatures ratified the Fourteenth Amendment, which guaranteed citizenship rights to all regardless of race, color, or previous condition of servitude. In Tennessee, however, the legislature almost broke up over the issue and ratification came only after the military government under Thomas had two absent legislators arrested to ensure a quorum for the vote. This action followed scattered violence and a race riot in Memphis in which forty blacks lost their lives. Thomas wanted the whites held fully accountable; to his dismay, a grand jury "failed to take any notice whatever of the offenders," as he complained sharply to Grant.

Ratification of the Fourteenth Amendment was also resisted in Kentucky. And when some citizens of Rome, Georgia, marked the anniversary of Georgia's secession by bold displays of the Confederate flag, Thomas wrote: "With too many of the people of the South, the late civil war is called a revolution, rebels are called 'Confederates,' loyalists to the whole country are called damned Yankees and traitors, and over the whole great crime, with its accursed record of slaughtered heroes, patriots murdered because of their true-hearted love of country, widowed wives and orphaned children, and prisoners of war slain . . . they are trying to throw the gloss of respectability. . . . Everywhere in the States lately in rebellion, treason is respectable and loyalty odious."

With respect to emancipation, Thomas believed that the degradation of slavery—"the terrible ordeal," he called it, "to which [the black] has been subjected"—could not be eradicated overnight, and that a process of personal reconstruction would take some time. But for Thomas this process of transformation was urgent, and as far as it lay within his power, he tried to move it along. He knew that ex-slaves would be adrift, even lost and hopeless when they first tasted freedom. Where possible, he settled blacks on the estates of former slaveowners who had fled, but in each case (being meticulous about the law) Thomas saw to it that the lands were legally acquired. Each former slave was also given equipment and a chance to prove he could earn his own livelihood. Few abolitionists did as much practical good as Thomas in this respect. For he set his sights not on revenge against Southern whites, but on giving blacks the true dignity in practice they deserved.

At the same time, whenever former Confederate officers, such as Richard Ewell and James Longstreet, showed a change of heart, he was gracious and tried to help them if he could. Even John Bell Hood came to see him for a heart-to-heart talk. Soon after Thomas transferred his headquarters from Nashville to Louisville in 1866, Hood went to Louisville on a business trip and through an intermediary asked Thomas if they could meet. They had not seen each other since serving together in the 2nd Cavalry in Texas before the war. As Hood clattered down the corridor on his crutches, Thomas opened his door, threw his arm about him and helped him to a chair. The two spoke for about an hour, and Hood emerged with tears in his eyes. Upon returning to his room, he said to the lady who had arranged the talk, "Thomas is a grand man; he should have remained with us, where he would have been appreciated and loved."

That was a sentimental thought. Thomas, who had begun the war as a Constitutional Unionist, had emerged from it "inclined to the radicals" (as Gideon Welles put it) with little patience for anyone who refused to acknowledge that the Confederacy was dead. He toured Mississippi, Alabama, and Georgia during the fall of 1865; encouraged progress where he found it; but when he learned that the Right Reverend Richard Hooker Wilmer, the bishop of Alabama, had told his clergy to omit the prescribed prayer for those in civil authority, he suspended Wilmer's right to preach and closed the churches in his diocese. In his general order against him, Thomas described Wilmer as "a pretended Bishop" who had forgotten "his mission to preach peace on earth and good will," being "animated with the same spirit [i.e., rebellion against authority] which through temptation beguiled the mother of men to the commission of the first sin."

Honors came his way. On March 3, 1865, Thomas received the thanks of Congress in a formal resolution; on November 2, 1865, the Tennessee state legislature followed suit. The latter also arranged to have his portrait painted, to hang in the State Library, and in commemoration of his Tennessee service ordered that a gold medal be struck. That medal, presented to Thomas on the second anniversary of the Battle of Nashville, featured his bust with the motto made famous at Chattanooga, "I will hold the town till we starve." Thomas was somewhat abashed by these and other tributes, accepted a jeweled badge of the Army of the Cumberland from his staff, but when other generals were accepting munificent gifts from a grateful public— "when it was not considered wrong to accept them," as one noted— Thomas emphatically refused the gift of a house in Cincinnati and an engraved service of silver plate, offered by a group of officers and friends. To his aide Colonel Alfred Hough he explained that he was "satisfied with his pay, and could live on it." "Whatever my services were," he added, "they were rendered to the country itself." When admirers raised money for him in recognition of his achievements, he asked that it be given to the widows and orphans of the war.

In that spirit, while on a visit to Washington in 1866, he reluctantly agreed to appear before the House of Representatives, at the behest of his friends. Escorted to the speaker's stand, Thomas was greeted by a tremendous ovation. It was almost too much for him. Overcome by modesty and embarrassment, his hand—ever steady in battle—trembled and he blushed.

From time to time, there were military reunions, and among the soldiers of the West, he was always the star. At one in Chicago (held in December 1868), he sat on the platform between Grant and Sherman, but the raucous roar of toasting and feasting drowned out most of the speeches made. Sherman introduced a number of generals and congressmen, but almost no one paid attention to what they said. According to one eyewitness, it was like watching a "dumb show." Some of the guests gave up on speaking at all and handed out transcripts of their remarks to the press. However, when Thomas was introduced as the "determined soldier . . . the beloved commander . . . true to his trust wherever found . . . the Rock of Chickamauga," the troops leapt to their feet and rocked the huge hall with cheering and applause.

Not surprisingly, when the Society of the Army of the Cumberland was formed in Cincinnati, it elected Thomas its first president by acclamation. Speeches, reminiscences, eulogies, and feasting occupied two full days. At a banquet that ended the session, Thomas was asked to speak in response to a toast made with "the audience rising . . . in the wildest excitement." Though he disliked public speaking, and shunned it when he could, when obliged to, he had a succinct, winning way with words. He now stood and recalled the battle for Chattanooga and the success of his troops at Missionary Ridge. In the course of it, he gave Sherman (who sat nearby) the benefit of every doubt. Then he said: "Now, gentlemen, my time is very nearly up. I will close by touching on one subject which no gentleman has touched upon tonight. It is this: the civilizing influences of discipline. . . . The discipline of the Army of the Cumberland alone has civilized two hundred thousand valuable patriots and citizens. I have traveled a little since the war was over. Wherever I have been . . . I have either seen [them] on the steamboat . . . in the fields, along the railroads, engaged in peacefully following the plough, and setting an example of industry worthy to be followed by all."

In 1867, an attempt was made to draft Thomas as a candidate for president of the United States. In Ohio and Tennessee especially, strong organizations were formed on his behalf, but he told one ad-mirer: "I am a soldier, and I know my duty; as a politician I would be lost. No, sir . . . I want to die with a fair record, and this I will do if I keep out of the sea of politics." Besides, as he told General Henry Cist, he was utterly unsuited by temperament to political life. The whole idea of having "to induce people to do their duty by persuasive mea-sures," as he put it, was "repugnant" to him. Even so, politicians in the North eagerly put forth his name. Not only was he strong in the mid-Atlantic states, but "throughout the Southwest . . . he was unques-tionably the favorite." As a candidate, "there is little doubt that he would have swept the country," if some of his advocates may be be-lieved. In truth, his temperament was probably ideal for the chal-lenges ahead. But "he underrated his qualifications," wrote a colleague, which shone forth during his postwar term of military rule. "An infi-nite number and variety of questions came up for adjudication," but despite his autocratic power,

> his orders always were based on broad grounds of law and justice. . . . One looks in vain for any trace of bitterness or hostility toward the people of the South, though of all men living, he might be par-doned for entertaining and expressing such feeling. This judicial habit of mind also raised him above all political considerations in his dealing with men and events. He never was swayed in the slight-est by any thought as to the influence his action might have upon his own personal fortunes. Indeed, he more than once, by his insis-tence on what he deemed right and just, stood in the way of his own advancement.

Such high-minded detachment applied even to the fame of what he had done. In a talk before a scientific club in Washington after the war, he insisted that he had made a mistake at the Battle of Nashville in not having fully arranged for the possibility of a panic rout. Had he done so, he might have sent at the end of the first day a strong force to the rear of the enemy to cut off its retreat. Yet just before the rout, Hood had planned to attack the very flank with which Thomas would have made the movement. It was therefore only a theoretical "mistake" because things turned out as they did. Thomas, however, was so modest in his discussion of the matter that one U.S. senator, who happened to be present, remarked: "Had we not known that he was the commanding general, and that every movement was the result of the action of his mind, we should never have imagined it . . . When it came to noting mistakes, he threw the blame entirely on himself."

This was not some theatrical affectation. Alexander McClure recalled that "It required exhaustive ingenuity to induce Thomas to speak about any military movements in which he was a prominent participant. Anyone might have been in daily intercourse with him for years and never learned from him that he had won great victories in the field."

Thomas also declined to allow President Andrew Johnson to use him in a political gambit against Grant. In an attempt to curb Grant's political aspirations, Johnson tried to get rid of him by making Thomas lieutenant general in his place. On February 21, 1868, he sent Thomas's name to the Senate. But in his own letter to Senate President Benjamin Wade of Ohio, Thomas asked that his name be withdrawn. "For the battle of Nashville, I was appointed a Major-General in the United States Army," he explained. "My services since the war do not merit so high a compliment; and it is too late to be regarded as a compliment, if conferred for services during the war." In so doing, he declined to take advantage of an opportunity to humiliate Grant.

In the fall of 1868, Thomas was summoned to Washington to preside over the court of inquiry convened to investigate the conduct of General Alexander B. Dyer, chief of ordnance during the latter part of the war. Dishonest contractors and disgruntled inventors had besieged Congress with complaints about him, but after a six-month investigation Dyer was cleared. About this time, Thomas also wrote a touching letter to General Fitz John Porter, who in 1862 had been cashiered for failing to obey a misguided order at Second Bull Run. The trial, as noted earlier, was a political one, with the government looking to save face for the defeat. John Pope, the Union general in charge, had singled out Porter's actions as the reason he had failed. After Porter was convicted, he spent the rest of his life trying to clear his name.

His case would later be judged one of the great miscarriages of military justice during the war.

In 1868, Porter sought to reopen his case, and sent Thomas a copy of his appeal to Grant, now president-elect. Thomas wrote to support his appeal and told him that no one he knew had ever thought "for one moment" his conviction had been just. "It was universally believed," he said, that the court had been "misled by evidence which we had not seen reported in the papers during the progress of the trial." That was the kindest thing he could have said—that Porter's reputation was intact among his peers. Grant, however, rejected the appeal. (In 1878, the verdict was finally overturned.)

As president-elect, Grant named Sherman to succeed himself as general of the army and raised Sheridan to lieutenant general in Sherman's place. Thomas had been favored over Sheridan by many of their colleagues, but there was no doubt whom Grant would choose. As General W. W. Averell, a cavalry officer who had served with Sheridan, noted in a letter to a colleague. "I think his [Grant's] . . . meager praise of Thomas which he takes some pains to discount afterwards is rather curious when contrasted with his constant and unconditional praise of Sheridan. How difficult it is to believe in any History after seeing a page or two of our own made!" Thomas for his part remarked to a former aide that he always expected Grant to "exercise the right to appoint his friend to an office in preference to another whom he did not particularly like." Then he added, sharply: "I much prefer to deserve the place and not have it than to get it without having deserved it. . . . But enough said about Grant's administration."

Yet Thomas continued to suffer humiliations at Grant's hands. Nor does it speak well for Grant as a person that he lost no chance to rub salt in the wounds.

As a rule, Thomas had managed, with considerable conscious effort, to keep personal affronts at a distance, and in a telling incident once told a fellow officer who had complained about being passed over for promotion: "Colonel, I have taken great pains to educate myself not to feel." He did not mean feel for others, of course, which he never failed to do, but to take insults too much to heart. Yet in the end he did come to feel some wounds acutely, despite efforts to let them go.

At about this time, Thomas had set his sights on a suitable military post and hoped to be given command of the Military Division of the East—nearer, that is, to home—as he had served almost entirely in the West, before, during, and after the war. But that post had been promised to General Meade. Most of his peers had also been assigned divisions, while his own command in Louisville had been reduced. According to Colonel Alfred Hough, Thomas's longtime aide, soon after Grant's election in November 1868, Thomas was summoned to Grant's home late one evening and shown into the library, where the president-elect, Mrs. Grant, and her father were present. Grant brought up the matter of changes in command, saying,

> "Thomas, there has got to be a change on the Pacific Coast, and either you or Sheridan will have to go there. How would you like it?" "As for myself," Thomas replied, "I would have no objection to serving there, but on Mrs. Thomas' account I would not want to take her any farther away from her friends in the East." Mrs. Grant interjected: "Your having a wife is one reason you should go there instead of Sheridan, as he ought to stay here, where he can get one." This was said laughingly, and caused a smile from the others, and immediately the conversation was changed by General Grant, not another word being spoken on the subject.

But Thomas saw at once that the joke was a cover for a decision that had already been made. On the way home, he remarked to Hough, "We are going to California, that was settled tonight."

Thomas accepted command of the Military Division of the Pacific and on March 16, 1869, he was ordered to relieve Henry Halleck, then in charge. In late March, however, he learned that Grant had changed his mind and that Schofield would get the post instead. Thomas told Sherman that if the change were made "he would publicly protest against it." Sherman advised Grant to yield, but the whole episode, according to a friend, left Thomas feeling "humiliated and heartsore." In effect, Grant tried to make Thomas plead for a post that he had not wanted in the first place, and should not have had to take.

Though Thomas had not favored the Pacific command, he planned to make the most of it, and his family—meaning his wife and her sister—got into the spirit of it, for as he wrote to Fitz John Porter, "my ladies anticipate enjoying a pleasant sojourn [there] for the next three or four years." En route to San Francisco by rail, Thomas stopped at Chicago, Omaha, and Promontory Point, Utah, where the east–west railroad lines now almost met. An old friend from his Florida days, General Erasmus Darwin Keyes, met the party, and was shocked to see how worn-out Thomas was. "White lines bordered his lips," wrote Keyes, "and his eyes had lost their wonted fires. . . . He made no complaint but applied himself with customary strictness to duty." Indeed, he gave it his all. He traveled from one remote post to another, with a second trip across the continent and back. In seeing to his affairs, Thomas logged some 14,000 miles in one year. Setting out on June 15, 1869, he visited forts in Nevada, Arizona, Southern California, Idaho, and the Washington Territory; explored the coast of Alaska and its islands; and returning to headquarters on September 16, complained to Sherman about the random killing in Alaska of fur seals, sea otters, and other animals by bored troops. He also presciently warned that a gold rush would destroy the native communities and the cultures of the peoples on their lands. "There will be a rush of adventurers to the Territory and the usual depredations will soon follow. . . . The Aleutians are a civilized race, very industrious, docile & amiable [but] they have a weakness for whiskey, and already the whiskey dealers have demoralized all to whom they have access."

Sherman wasn't concerned. He regarded Native Americans as "an enemy to our race and civilization" (meaning the White one), and wrote later to Sheridan in support of his harsh tactics against Indians out West: "Go ahead in your own way and I will back you with my whole authority. . . . I will say nothing and do nothing to restrain our troops . . . and will allow no mere vague general charges of cruelty and inhumanity to tie their hands."

Thomas returned to the East to report to the War Office before once more taking up his post in San Francisco, this time with his wife at his side. But there were aggravations of all kinds, some connected to his past service in the war. For example, unreconstructed members of the Tennessee House of Representatives wanted to sell the portrait of him that hung in the State Library. He offered to buy it back at its original cost, and wrote the speaker on December 31, 1869, that he would return the gold medal, too, as soon as he could. In the end, the legislature let the portrait stand. Not surprisingly, Southern newspapers questioned his motives for choosing the North, and the story was repeated that he fought for the Union only because he had been refused a commission in the Confederate high command. There were also unsupported allegations (made only after his death) that he had wavered in his decision to support the Union cause.

Nashville also came to haunt his thoughts. At a banquet in San Francisco that Halleck arranged in his honor, Thomas learned for the first time of Grant's suspended order at Nashville placing Schofield in command. Thomas knew, of course, that Logan had been on his way to relieve him, which was contained in a general order. But he did not know of the other order Halleck had prepared. At the same time, he had known about Schofield's machinations. Now it all fell into place. "I am now satisfied," he told Colonel Hough, "that what I have suspected for some time is true, that General Schofield intrigued for my removal, to enable him to get my command."

Then on March 12, he received a still graver wound. An anonymous letter appeared on the front page of the *New York Tribune* that disparaged his military achievements and ascribed to Schofield the success of the Nashville campaign. The letter was signed, "One Who Fought at Nashville." Thomas thought Schofield had either written the letter himself or put someone up to it. The author turned out to be Jacob D. Cox, who had led a division in Schofield's Twenty-third Corps, and was now a member of Grant's cabinet (having been appointed interior secretary in 1868). But Schofield had known about the letter and approved it in advance. If Schofield had his own obvious motives for doing so, Grant may have had a hand in the matter, too. Thomas's formidable name had just been floated again as a presidential candidate, and some think Grant and his political allies had moved at once to tarnish his image and preemptively sweep him from the scene. (In fact, Grant had nothing to fear. Thomas had just written to John Tyler, Jr., one of his promoters, and President John Tyler's son—dismissing a presidential bid.)

A week later the *New York Tribune* published a second letter, in answer to the first, signed by "Another Man Who Fought at Nashville," which leapt to Thomas's defense. It noted that Schofield's Battle of Franklin had been successful, but almost accidentally so, since it had been fought from necessity, not design; and that the battle of Nashville, by contrast, was an acknowledged masterpiece and was already being taught as one of "the great battles of history" at West Point.

On the morning of March 28, 1870, Thomas went to his office at 204 Sutter Street, and told his aide, Colonel Hough, that he had decided to write a letter himself to the *Tribune* in answer to the first. He said he wanted to do a complete job of it. It would probably have been better if he had let the matter go. On this occasion, as he wrote, it would seem his temper rose. He tried to explain all the circumstances of the battle, which, as he recalled them, strained his strength. Aside from his own account, he appealed to the recollections of Thomas Wood, D. S. Stanley, and others—for example, that the cavalry allowed him by Sherman had all been dismounted, that the new regiments he got were unequipped, and so on. As for his use of Schofield's corps—which the letter said Thomas had not employed to best effect—they had been held in reserve for reinforcing Steedman, if he proved unable to hold his ground. But Steedman had held firm, so the reserve supported Smith against the enemy left, where the main thrust was. As Smith advanced, he left an interval between himself and the cavalry to his right. Schofield was sent to fill that gap. "It is therefore left to candid minds to judge," wrote Thomas wryly, "whether the 10,000 men were advantageously posted originally and afterwards used to advantage, or not."

The letter had also accused Thomas of not being prompt in pursuit of Hood's army—which, he noted, no one but the benighted author of the letter would say. (Another would say it, of course, later in his memoirs—Grant.)

Fair and just to the end, Thomas had just given due credit to Schofield for the Battle of Franklin as the prelude to his own triumph when a blood vessel burst in his brain. "A few blurred and disconnected lines followed," wrote an aide, "as the Angel of Death hovered near." At 1:30 P.M., Thomas staggered to the outer door of his office, opened it, and called out, "I want air," then fell unconscious to the floor. Three doctors were called and administered stimulants, which revived him. But it soon became apparent that he had suffered a massive stroke. His wife, her sister, and several staff officers were summoned as he was stretched out on a couch. Everyone left the room except his wife and Colonel Hough. Hough wrote afterward: "I observed he was speaking, and putting my ear down, heard him say he was feeling easier and had no pain. He looked up to Mrs. Thomas, who leaned down." He whispered something to her, struggled briefly, convulsed, tried to rise, lost consciousness, and twenty-five minutes past seven that evening died. His long, unfinished letter to the *Tribune* was found on his desk.

General Sherman, now general-in-chief, announced his death to the army on March 29. In his tribute, he remarked that he had known Thomas well "since they sat as boys on the same bench," and saluted "his complete and entire devotion to duty. . . . In battle he never wavered," and "never sought advancement of rank or honor at the expense of any one. Whatever he earned of these were his own, and" (sounding a rather defensive note) "no one disputes his fame." He was, said Sherman, "The very impersonation of honesty, integrity, and honor . . . the *beau ideal* of the soldier and gentleman. Though he leaves no child to bear his name, the old Army of the Cumberland, numbered by tens of thousands, called him father, and will weep for him many tears of grief."

Public buildings were covered with funeral emblems. At all military posts guns were fired in salute and the flag placed at half-staff.

As his body returned east by rail to be deposited in his wife's family vault at Troy, New York, mourning crowds gathered at every station. His remains arrived in Troy on April 7 and were taken to St. Paul's Episcopal Church, where the casket, draped with flags and trimmed with evergreens, was placed on view. President Grant, members of his cabinet, representatives from both houses of Congress, and the governors of several states, were in attendance. Generals Meade,

Rosecrans, Hazen, Granger, John Newton (a former division commander under Howard), and Hooker were among the pallbearers. Schofield was among them, too, because of his rank as a major general and former secretary of war. On April 8, the funeral ceremonies took place, and as the cortege moved through the streets it passed along lanes of silent thousands to Oakwood Cemetery, where the military escort raised its rifles in a last salute.

America's greatest soldier-patriot since George Washington was laid to rest.

Grant's shadow still lies across his grave. Thomas's wife believed that Grant's aggressive efforts to demean him had contributed substantially to her husband's death. "I will say that it preyed upon and affected his health," she wrote, "which General Schofield's base attack on his military reputation added to, and which was the cause of the fatal attack on March 28, 1870." The modern scholar Stephen Z. Starr goes so far as to say that "Thomas was killed by the Nashville affair just as surely as if Grant had shot him," which is a doleful charge. Unfortunately, there is enough truth to it to make one gasp.

Before he died, Thomas let it be known that he did not want his private papers made public. "All I did for my Government," he said, "are matters of history. But my private life is my own, and I will not have it hawked about in print for the amusement of the curious." His aide, Colonel Hough, winnowed out his private correspondence, and bundled up the letters for his wife to do with as she wished. "This sad duty occupied me three days. Of course many of the papers were deeply interesting, but all of them only confirmed the strength and beauty of his character; not a paper was destroyed, and not one need ever be by Mrs. Thomas." In 1879, she made an effort to collect his official papers for safekeeping, but his personal papers have disappeared and were presumably destroyed.

Though it has generally been assumed that Thomas and his wife had a rather formal relationship—since he was away on duty for much of their married life—that seems not to have been so. They had made a radiant couple at the outset at West Point; he had been eager to have her with him in Texas; and he had brought her to Nashville (before he had to send her out of danger) in the fall of 1864. There she joined him again after the battle was fought. Recently, a letter turned up in the West Point archives dated March 4, 1865, in which he confided to a friend that they had been "very happy in one another" and had been sustained by their "mutual love and confidence" during the years they were apart.

This gives us a touching glimpse of what his lost correspondence might have held.

The relationship he had with his own family remains something of a riddle. So far as is known, he had almost no contact with them from the moment the war began. This is all the more poignant since his early surviving letters suggest that they were affectionate and close. His oldest brother, John, vanished without a trace; Benjamin, who apparently lived in Vicksburg, maintained some connection with him after the war and offered to help him buy back the official portrait that had been repudiated by the legislature of Tennessee. His sisters may or may not have disowned him. The evidence for that is written in disappearing ink. Dr. W. D. Barham, a family physician, reported that his sisters (Judith and Fanny) were appalled by the story that they had turned his picture to the wall. But when Oliver Howard was later asked to write a brief sketch of his life and wrote to Judith for any information she or her sister could provide, she curtly returned his letter and wrote on the back: "General Howard: In answer to your inquiry respecting the character of the late General Thomas, I can only inform you that he was as all other boys are who are wellborn and well-reared." That was all.

In April 1870, there was a memorial service in Cleveland, Ohio, where Sherman spoke again, as well as General Garfield and Chief Justice Salmon Chase. Garfield described the death of Thomas as "a national calamity and an irreparable loss." He was not alone. Most of the tributes to Thomas were on an epic scale. Joseph Hooker called him "the ablest, the most just, and the most beloved man I ever knew. I never shall know his equal. I never supposed a man of his merit could live." He went on to say, "There is on record the name of but one man who was his equal." He meant George Washington. General Joseph S. Fullerton called him "a faultless soldier, an irreproachable man," noting that his record as a general was "perfect." This was not an exceptional judgment. General Henry Boynton said: "Of him, and of him alone, among all our great and honored captains, can it be truthfully said that he never lost a movement or a battle." General James Steedman went further: "He was the grandest character of the war; the noblest figure of the great Rebellion; the most accomplished soldier America ever produced."

The clique—and it was a clique—of Grant, Sherman, Sheridan, and Schofield demurred, almost alone.

The Society of the Army of the Cumberland commissioned an equestrian statue in his memory, cast in bronze from captured Confederate guns. It was completed a decade later and stands today at Thomas Circle in the heart of Washington, D.C. At its unveiling, before a great throng of admirers on November 20, 1879, there was an outpouring of poignant remembrance. It also brought forth the last letter Joseph Hooker wrote before his death, in which he called Thomas "the most gifted soldier" America had ever known. General McClellan (now governor of New Jersey) wrote from Trenton, and seized the occasion to take a swipe at Halleck, Stanton, and Grant. In a reference to Nashville, he praised "the magnificent self-possession with which [Thomas] disregarded the attempts of men ignorant of the circumstances, or incapable of appreciating them, to force him to give battle prematurely" but waited till "the proper moment arrived." Though McClellan may not have been the ideal voice for it, the feeling persisted throughout the army that Sherman and Grant had belittled Thomas in order to steal his fame.

Sherman was on hand and spoke in a personal vein. But as always a certain guilty ambivalence showed through: "The relations between Thomas and myself were more of a social character than that of the commander and commanded," he said. "You remember that our acquaintance began in boyhood [i.e., at West Point], and it was very hard, after growing up side by side with him, afterwards to believe him to be a hero. But I know that General Thomas had noble qualities." That was muted, to be sure. He claimed to love him all the more for having known him so long personally, and predicted that however much sectional animus might still cloud his reputation among Southerners, he would one day become "the idol of the South." Sherman went on to remind the audience that Thomas was "indebted for his first commission as brigadier-general to Robert Anderson, and to him alone" (though five years later, in his *Memoirs*, he claimed that distinction for himself), and ended his speech rather strangely: "I wish that I could have a few hours' talk with you, and I could explain to you a great many things which you don't understand."

He would have had much to explain. Thomas always gave Sherman the benefit of the doubt. From the time he had protected Sherman as a plebe from West Point bullies, he had trusted in their friendship, which Sherman privately demeaned though publicly professed; and even after the Battle of Nashville (as we know from a recovered letter, today in the West Point archives, to Mrs. Hamilton Draper) Thomas retained affection for Sherman's youthful, enthusiastic ways. He never knew of the deceitful communiqués Sherman sent Grant, Halleck, and others behind his back. And we may be thankful—for it would have been too much for him to bear. He died before the publication of the *Official Records* brought the falseness of Sherman's friendship to light.

Grant and Sherman in their memoirs covered one another with glory and ignored Thomas as best they could. Gamaliel Bradford noted in *Union Portraits* that "Grant was apt to couple Thomas' name with some innuendo, as was Sherman," to their own peculiar shame. Sherman never publicly admitted a mistake. When Grant composed his memoirs, he disguised his own failures, slighted the achievements of Thomas and others, and took credit for achievements that were not his own. But toward the end of the writing, he tried to work in a tribute to Thomas that he knew history would applaud. In summing up, he wrote:

As my official letters on file in the War Department as well as remarks in this book reflect on General Thomas by dwelling somewhat upon his tardiness, it is due to myself, as well as to him, that I give my estimate of him as a soldier. I had been at West Point with Thomas one year and had known him later in the old army. He was a man of commanding appearance, slow and deliberate in speech and action; sensible, honest and brave. He possessed valuable soldierly qualities in an eminent degree.

He gained the confidence of all who served under him, and almost their love. This implies a very valuable quality. It is a quality which calls out the most efficient services of the troops serving under the commander possessing it.

Thomas' dispositions were deliberately made and always good. He was not as good, however, in pursuit as in action. I do not believe that he could ever have conducted Sherman's army from Chattanooga to Atlanta against the defenses and the commander guarding that line in 1864. On the other hand, if it had been given him to hold the line which Johnston tried to hold, neither that general nor Sherman, nor any other officer could have done it better.

Most Civil War historians have accepted this appraisal on its face. Those more familiar with the record have known it to be half-true in its praise. Bruce Catton said of Thomas, "What a general could do, Thomas did; no more dependable soldier for a moment of crisis existed on the North American continent, or ever did exist." As for Thomas being a "defensive general" (a description calculated to excuse Grant's harassment of him at Chattanooga and Nashville), Catton wrote: "Thomas comes down in history as the Rock of Chickamauga, the great defensive fighter, the man who could never be driven away.... That may be a correct appraisal. Yet it may also be worth making note that just twice in all the war was a major Confederate army driven away from a prepared position in complete rout—at Chattanooga and at Nashville. Each time the blow that routed it was launched by Thomas." Catton ultimately confessed before he died to a "haunting feeling" that Thomas was perhaps "the best [general] of them all," and that the history of the Civil War would have to be "upgraded" to give him his rightful place. "There was nothing slow about Thomas," he added, or "primarily defensive ... Grant was wrong."

One great unanswered question (in the light of Schofield's false telegrams, which read as if they had been dictated by Grant) is whether Grant and Schofield had conspired from the outset to bring Thomas down. In his memoirs, Schofield disparaged Thomas for lacking just those qualities he possessed: "I believe it must now be fully known to all who are qualified to judge," he wrote, "and have had by personal association or by study of history full opportunities to learn the truth, that General Thomas did not possess in a high degree the activity of mind necessary to foresee and provide for all the exigencies of military operations, nor the mathematical talent required to estimate 'the relations of time, space, motion, and force' involved in great problems of war." Schofield once more sought to take credit for the Battle of Nashville, but too many were still alive to let that stand. "Robbing a grave of a body is a light crime," wrote General Steedman, compared with what Schofield tried to do. He thought some of Schofield's claims so "absurd" that they made "the self-lauding fictions written by General Sherman [whose own *Memoirs* had recently been published] a modest production." In his own autobiography, General D. S. Stanley wrote that he could "pick to pieces" most of Schofield's battle accounts. He implied, too, that Schofield had lied about his handling of the events leading up to and including the Franklin fight. Schofield "assumes a grand superiority and wisdom, in each case at variance with the facts," he wrote, "and appropriates circumstances entirely accidental and the run of luck in our favor as a result of his wise foresight."

Questions about the competence of Grant and Sherman have long lingered as a subtext of Civil War studies and force themselves to the forefront whenever the documentary record is examined with care. The quality of Grant's generalship has always been in doubt. Few, if any, have seen fit to compare him to Lee, and "the chief source of his illusory glamor as a soldier," as Stephen Z. Starr put it, "may be traced to the iconic image of his manly acceptance of Lee's surrender at Appomattox Courthouse, which more or less closed the war." But that is just an image. In the light of his whole career, its catastrophic mistakes, deceptions, and cruel machinations, we may well agree with Starr that "as a strategist, as a commander of armies, and above all, as a human being, Grant had shortcomings so fundamental as to negate his right to occupy the very high place his modern-day admirers have sought to award him."

The first draft of history is always written by those in power. The military clique of Grant, Sherman, Sheridan, and Schofield constituted a dynasty of command that lasted for more than twenty years. During this period of "unprecedented military control," as one writer put it, Sherman succeeded Grant as commander of the army in 1869; Sheridan succeeded Sherman as commander in 1884; and Schofield succeeded Sheridan in 1888. The trend of Civil War history—largely shaped by their memoirs, but also by the official control their postwar prominence gave them over the public understanding of events—long enjoyed the stature of tradition, as fixed in the popular mind. This has been unfortunate for the national memory, and for the true story of the war. *The Official Records of the War of the Rebellion*, as they are called, were substantially compiled, collated, and published between 1880 and 1900, with supplementary volumes appearing in later years. Sherman's *Memoirs* were first published in 1875; Grant's a decade later, in 1885. The veracity of both were challenged from the start, and often contradicted by the record that emerged.

What is urgently needed today in Civil War studies are heavily annotated critical editions of the memoirs and letters both men wrote. That would be a start, and benefit their biographers immensely. "The unexamined life is not worth living." It is also not worth writing about.

As early as 1893, in his speech before the Society of the Army of the Cumberland, General Joseph Fullerton (former chief of staff to D. S. Stanley), lamented the serious errors that had become part of the popular account of the war. He noted that the truth had often been suppressed, and that many had not spoken up because they knew they would have been "stoned to political and social death." As a result, "the names of some of our greatest soldiers and heroes are lusterless, and almost unknown to the generation that has come on since, because credit for the deeds of those great but modest men was unjustly assumed by or awarded to some hero of the hour." Then he drove the point home: "You, men of the Army of the Cumberland, know of such a soldier; you have seen him; you remember him well. Now is the time, while your memories are yet fresh, your minds active, your spirits strong, to see that his star be properly set in the galaxy of the great generals of the world."

The risks of speaking up were real. Henry Adams wrote that Grant's administration not only "outraged every rule of ordinary decency, but scores of promising men . . . were ruined in saying so." Donn Piatt, who became an investigative journalist after the war, was almost killed as a result when Grant's son Frederick and brother-in-law James J. Casey broke into his Washington home armed with clubs. (Piatt happened to be away, but his family was terrorized.) As editor of the prominent Washington weekly *The Capital*, Piatt had diligently exposed the corruption of the Grant administration without respect for rank or power. He never ceased to remind his audience that Grant had a shady past, had exposed his men to reckless slaughter, had taken credit for the achievements of others as a soldier, and as president indulged in shocking cover-ups. (In connection with the Whiskey Ring, for example, Grant even perjured himself before the chief justice of the United States.)

After Sherman's *Memoirs* appeared, General Henry Boynton published a book entitled *Sherman's Historical Raid: The Memoirs in the Light of the Record*, in which he exposed a number of Sherman's canards. He insisted that Sherman claimed honors for himself belonging to others, blamed others for his own mistakes, was "unreliable," "erratic," "cruelly unjust to nearly all his distinguished associates," and "thrust his pen recklessly through reputations as dear to the country as his own." This was strong stuff, but Boynton cited the *Official Records* (then being organized and published) to prove his claims.

Boynton was no ordinary soldier. As a young officer he had played a critical role in the stand Thomas made at Chickamauga, and received the Congressional Medal of Honor for his heroic part in the storming of Missionary Ridge. In that action he was severely wounded, retired from the army, became the Washington correspondent for the *Cincinnati Gazette*, and a quarter-century later in 1893 (upon the insistence of his fellow officers, for whom the memory of his valor still lived) was also awarded the Bronze Star. In 1898, he would be called back into service as a brigadier general of volunteers for the Spanish-

American War; served as Chief Marshal at the State Funeral for President William McKinley in 1901; and enjoyed the esteem of Theodore Roosevelt, who as president attended Boynton's own funeral in 1905. He is buried in Arlington National Cemetery.

In 1880, however, Sherman had tried to destroy him. After Boynton published his critique, Sherman prompted his brother-in-law, C. W. Moulton (then assistant quartermaster of the army), to write a rebuttal based on Sherman's own interlined copy of Boynton's book. That rebuttal floundered on the merits, so Sherman in 1880, in his official capacity as general of the army, denounced Boynton as "entirely without character. . . . Nobody . . . wishes to dirty their hands with such a creature. . . . Why, for $1,000 he would slander his own mother!" That was Sherman's response. Boynton, understandably appalled, preferred charges against him for "conduct unbecoming an officer and a gentleman" under the 83rd Article of War. Sherman escaped trial; but in 1902, a bundle of old autograph letters, some of them by Sherman, all unpublished, turned up in a Third Avenue secondhand bookshop in New York. In one to Moulton, dated November 9, 1875, Sherman admitted to having described Thomas as "slow" but half-excused himself by claiming that "Gen. Grant . . . knows well that it was he and not me who first used that expression." However, he had been willing to take the heat for it, he said, for Grant's sake.

In the same letter, Sherman also cast aspersions on Boynton, who was still alive in 1902. He was asked by *The New York Times* to comment, and said that when Sherman's *Memoirs* were first published in 1875, even Grant had been offended, for he felt that he had not received his due.

Before *Sherman's Historical Raid* was published, Grant had taken "a personal interest in the progress" of the work, recalled Boynton, "and had his records in the White House searched for materials he wished to have used in contradiction of some of Sherman's claims." Boynton sent the manuscript to Grant to examine, to make sure the official records would sustain all its "material points." The manuscript was returned by Grant's private secretary, "with the statement," recalled Boynton, "that none of its points" had been contravened by the record and "none would be." Grant, however, later denied any connection to the book.

Boynton's bitter dissection of Sherman's *Memoirs* has never been refuted. On the contrary. One hundred years later, the able Civil War historian Albert Castel subjected them to the light of modern scholarship and confirmed them in a now classic essay, "Prevaricating Through Georgia." Castel concluded from the *Official Records* that in case after case Sherman's account was packed with "omissions and distortions of fact and with deliberate and sometimes malicious prevarications, fabrications, and falsifications" throughout. He was especially shocked at Sherman's "malicious and slanderous" treatment of Thomas, which had done so much to injure his name. Even Sherman's outstanding biographer at the time, John F. Marszalek, was obliged to admit the truth of Castel's critique. Colonel Henry Stone's memorable verdict on Sherman's account of the Atlanta campaign after all proved right. It was, said Stone, "often widely at variance with the Official Record, and with anyone's recollections except his own."

Sherman's official attack on Boynton was not an isolated case. He also tried to destroy the career of another distinguished officer, General James B. Fry. Fry had entered West Point the year Grant left; served as chief of staff to both General Irvin McDowell and Don Carlos Buell; and was in almost daily contact with Lincoln as Provost-Marshal-General of the Army from March 1863. In that capacity, he had the all-important duty of catching deserters, recruiting volunteers, and implementing the draft—in short, keeping the army intact. In December 1885, Fry published an article entitled "An Acquaintance with Grant," in the *North American Review* in which he wrote: "The time has not come for a final judgment of Grant. He had great abilities and great opportunities. Chance is undoubtedly an important factor in the race for glory, and perhaps it favored Grant in the war of rebellion. General Sherman goes so far as to have said since Grant's death, that, 'had [General] C.F. Smith lived, Grant would have disappeared to history after Donelson.'" (It may be remembered that Smith would have been in charge at Shiloh had he not suddenly died.) Sherman, stunned, challenged Fry to reveal his source. Fry declined, but noted that Sherman did not deny making the statement. Sherman wrote that it was "impossible" he could have made it and claimed that Fry had "invented the quotation." In a letter to R. C. Drum, the Adjutant-General of the Army, he also demanded that Fry be disciplined by the Secretary of War, thereby threatening Fry's career. Finally, on December 16, Sherman asked the editor of the *North American Review* (Allen Thorndike Rice) to print "my denial of the literal truth of Fry's quotation" and predicted that Fry "when cornered" would "dodge the issue," implying cowardice. For Fry, that was the last straw. He had offered Sherman a way out by tactfully suggesting he drop the whole issue. He now promptly produced a lithographic facsimile (the late 19th century version of a xerox) of a letter Sherman had written on September 6, 1885 to Colonel R. N. Scott, the Custodian of the War Records in Washington, D.C. It turned out that Fry had quoted Sherman exactly, word for word. The relevant paragraph read: "Now as to Halleck-Grant—I had the highest possible opinion of Halleck's knowledge and power, and never blamed him for mistrusting Grant's ability. Had C. F. Smith lived, Grant would have disappeared to history after Donelson." That was even more damning. Not only did it single out chance as the pivotal factor in Grant's rise, but cast doubt on Grant's innate generalship and skill.

Sherman, having cornered himself, was forced to acknowledge his authorship.

All this casts a rather curious light on the "friendship" between Grant and Sherman, who gained power through their military and political alliance, promoted each other in public, and to some degree (despite some divergence) in their official versions of key events. Yet Grant covertly tried to expose some of Sherman's fabrications (those, that is, that might diminish his own reputation); while Sherman covertly implied that Grant was not the general people thought he was. He also blamed him for starting the story that Thomas was "slow."

This was all grotesquely shabby. When we turn to Thomas, it is like throwing open a window to let in fresh air.

It cannot be denied that Grant and Sherman falsified the record and gave critical events their own mendacious "spin." They did so toward the end of the war, in backbiting correspondence; in its aftermath, when they used their political authority to suppress damaging material and facts; and ultimately in their memoirs, in which they endeavored to reinforce each other's version of events. Neither can be relied on even for some fundamental facts. Some recent books on Grant, Sherman, the Army of the Tennessee, and the Civil War in general also show an unhappy inclination to repeat information long since disproved. That is a sad thing. The whole slander about Thomas being "slow" was always unseemly on its face. That respectable historians should ever have given any credit to it is strange. The only ascertainable time Thomas was ever "slow" was in withdrawing under fire. Not only did he win every battle he ever fought (proving that his deliberate preparations were sound, not "slow"), but he rose to meet every occasion, however unforeseen. He *never* failed, which shows how really quick he was. Only a razorlike judgment combined with an incredibly sure and prompt capacity for action could have rescued the Union army from calamity at Stones River, Chickamauga, and Peachtree Creek. There is absolutely nothing in the careers of either Grant or Sherman that remotely compares to it. So then, what remains? Nashville. And there we see he was not slow but wise.

Either Thomas was overcautious and deliberate—to the hasty, "slow"—or, quite simply, the greatest Union general of the war. Thomas himself, however, gave the credit to his troops. General Garfield once asked him to what he ascribed his success. "To my men," he replied at once. "I made my army and my army made me." The deliberate suppression of his fame by the two best-known soldiers of the Union, Sherman and Grant, is a continuing national tragedy that must be set right.

"Justice never dies."

# ACKNOWLEDGMENTS

In the course of its creation, this book received valuable help from: the War Department Files, National Archives, Washington, D.C.; the Library of Congress; John Rhodehamel, Norris Foundation Curator, American Historical Manuscripts, the Huntington Library; Susan Lintelmann, Manuscripts Curator, the U.S. Military Academy Library at West Point; John Tofanelli, Anglo-American Literature and History Librarian, Butler Library, Columbia University; Jeffrey T. Ruggles, Associate Curator for Prints and Photographs, the Virginia Historical Society; Ron Westphal and Darla Brock, Tennessee State Library and Archives; Frances W. Kunstling, Archives and Manuscripts Unit, Technical Services Section, Tennessee State Library and Archives; the Kansas City Public Library; the U.S. Army Military History Institute; Bentley Historical Library, University of Michigan; the Georgia Department of Archives and History; Duke University Library; the New York Public Library; the Southern Historical Society; the Massachusetts Historical Society; the Chicago Historical Society; the Illinois State Historical Library; the Ohio Historical Society; Brooks Memorial Library; Timothy Hughes, Rare and Early Newspapers; and the Library of Congress Photoduplication Service.

My thanks to Wiley Sword for permission to quote from a letter in his possession that Thomas wrote as a cadet. In a more general sense, I am much indebted to a number of previous books and articles on Thomas that formed a firm foundation to my own. As always, I also relied on family, friends, and colleagues for encouragement and advice, including: my wife, Hilary, James Bobrick, Peter Bobrick, Anne Bloom, Marvin and Evelyn Farbman, Edy Rees, Mark Katz, Robin Brownstein, Peter Guttmacher, Anthony Chiappelloni, Carolyn Gregory, Danielle Woerner, Peter Murkett, Hagop Merjian, Debbie Jacobs, Svetlana Gorokhova, Emily McGrath, Stephen Minkin, Arlene Distler,

Tori Wiecher, and Rich Garant. I also want to thank the folks at Amy's Bakery Arts Cafe (Amy Comerchero, Leslie Myette, Matthew and Megan Rink, and Rebecca Pedersen) and at Mocha Joe's (Anders Burrows and Ginger Murawski), who often allowed me to work in their cafés past closing time.

As ever, my peerless agent, Russell Galen, and my superb editor, Bob Bender, proved good shepherds to my grazing flock of words. Bob's ever reliable assistant, Johanna Li, made sure they were herded to the proper gates.

Finally, no word of thanks would be sufficient without a tribute to the companionship of our beloved pets—Jasper, Zuzu, Chelsea, and Shiloh; the unseen black bear that bounds from time to time past our house; the coyote den just beyond the margins of the woods; the ruby-throated hummingbirds that thrum about our deck; and the occasional resident possum, skunk, and bat. God bless!

# NOTES

## EPIGRAPHS

xi  "Time and history": Van Horne, *The Life of Major General George H. Thomas*, p. v.

xi  "It takes time for jealousy": Howard, "A Sketch of the Life of General George H. Thomas," Military Order of the Loyal Legion of the United States, October 1890, Commandery, State of New York, *War Papers*, p. 296.


## 1. AN END TO INNOCENCE

**Page**

1  "each portion wheeling": *Harper's Weekly*, April 23, 1870, p. 1.

3  "The figure of Thomas": Swinton, *The Twelve Decisive Battles of the War*, p. 273.

3  "The incidents of his life": Johnson, *Memoir of Major General George H. Thomas*, p. 5.

3  "He stood by me": Shanks, *Personal Recollections of Distinguished Generals*, p. 36.

3  "The peer of any": Longacre, *Grant's Cavalryman*, p. 289.

3  "Grant felt uneasy" Piatt and Boynton, *General George H. Thomas*, p. 485.

4  "a prosperous farmer," etc.: O'Connor, *Thomas*, p. 53.

5  "potent enough": Oates, *The Fires of Jubilee*, p. 1.

5  "the gently rolling": Johnson, *The Nat Turner Slave Insurrection*, p. 12.

5  "minefields of submerged": Parramore, *Southampton County, Virginia*, p. 54.

5  "a smoky cluster": Oates, *Fires*, p. 1

6  "seducing [the slave], if possible": Link, *Roots of Secession*, p. 5.

6  I saw a Virginian: Olmsted, *The Cotton Kingdom*, p. 38.

7  "full half": Ibid.

7  "pretense of dignity": Ibid., p. 34.

7  "at least as much vice": Ibid., p. 39.

7 "George was playful," etc.: Howard, "Sketch," p. 287.

8 "poured the stories": Dwight, ed., *Critical Sketches of Some of the Federal and Confederate Commanders*, Papers of the Military Historical Society of Massachusetts, Vol. 10, p. 165.

8 "three or four," etc.: Johnson, *Nat Turner*, p. 230.

9 "grew to manhood": Oates, *Fires*, p. 26.

9 "Seek ye the Kingdom": Johnson, *Nat Turner*, pp. 231–32.

10 "The Spirit appeared to me": Ibid., p. 233.

10 "a mind capable": Ibid., p. 244.

10 "struggled through the damp": Oates, *Fires*, p. 32.

10 "white spirits and black": Johnson, *Nat Turner*, pp. 233–34.

10 "as much as he could," etc.: Ibid.

11 "And they believed": Oates, *Fires*, p. 27.

11 "having soon discovered": Johnson, *Nat Turner*, p. 231.

11 "For as the blood": Ibid., p. 234.

12 "arise and prepare": Ibid., p. 235.

12 "pored over": Oates, *Fires*, p. 54.

12 "it could be looked at directly": Ibid.

12 "like a black hand": Ibid., p. 55.

12 "the absurd predictions": Parramore, *Southampton County, Virginia*, p. 75.

12 "in the glare": Oates, *Fires*, p. 67.

13 "an advanced guard": Foner, ed., *Nat Turner*, p. 133.

13 "rode into the yard": Cleaves, *Rock of Chickamauga*, p. 6.

13 "in and out of gloomy": Furguson, "Catching Up with Old Slow Trot," p. 11.

13 "Alone with the fox's bark": Foner, *Nat Turner*, p. 135.

13 "a more than Indian adroitness": Ibid., p. 136.

14 "Was not Christ crucified?": Johnson, *Nat Turner*, p. 235.

14 "The seals are broken": Foner, *Nat Turner*, p. 8.

14 "in terms of blood": O'Connor, *Thomas*, p. 56.

14 "intolerable to the enslaved": Ibid.

14 "a private school": Howard, "Sketch," p. 288.

15 "Having done": Parramore, *Southampton County*, p. 156.

15 "No cadet": Dwight, ed., "Critical Sketches," p. 167.

15 "reticent and introspective": Society of the Army of the Cumberland, 1879 Reunion, *Report*, p. 173.

16 "bore a remarkable": Ibid.

16 "Sherman, Thomas and I": Coppee, *General Thomas*, p. 323.

16 "If anybody could bring": Howard, "Sketch," p. 289.

16 "We then march": U.S. Military Academy Bulletin, No. 1, "Cadet Life Before the Mexican War," p. 12.

17  "It was heads up": French, *Two Wars*, p. 11.

17  "a dull speck": Cleaves, *Rock*, p. 10.

17  "We stole boiled potatoes": O'Connor, *Thomas*, p. 65.

17  "usually had a grease spot": Ibid.

17  "the best hash maker": Ibid.

17  "We had glorious times": "Cadet Life Before the Mexican War," p. 22.

18  "he stored away in the recesses": Johnson, *Memoir of Major General George H. Thomas*, p. 15.

19  "never allowed any thing": Ridpath, *The Life and Work of General James A. Garfield*, p. 251.

19  "never forgot anything": Johnson, *Memoir*, p. 15.

19  "A furlough," etc.: George H. Thomas, Letter of March 28, 1838, U.S. Military Academy Library Archives.

20  "A strong southern feeling": Morrison, *Best School*, p. 131.

20  "the hotbed": Ibid.

20  The principle of representation: Rawle, *A View of the Constitution of the United States of America*, pp. 296–97.

20  "If it had not been": O'Connor, *Thomas*, p. 67.

20  'Supposing that arrangements': Ibid., p. 118.


## 2. A WIDER WORLD

**Page**

23  "a swampy land": Coppee, *Thomas*, p. 7.

23  "traced ancient Indian," etc: Cleaves, *Rock*, 14.

24  "the last drop": "Wars and Battles," Second Seminole War, U.S. History .com.

24  "The white man shall not": Wikipedia, "Second Seminole War."

25  a cluster of weather-beaten: Cleaves, *Rock*, p. 17.

25  "semifluid rancid": Keyes, *Fifty Years' Observation of Men and Events*, pp. 163–64.

25  "discovered he could stretch": Cleaves, *Rock*, p. 17.

26  "Floating in the water": Williams, *The Territory of Florida*, p. 65.

26  "valuable and efficient aid": Johnson, *Memoir*, p. 21.

26  "for gallantry": Ibid.

27  "the pile-built": Cleaves, *Rock*, p. 21.

27  "bowers of roses": Johnson, *Memoir*, p. 23.

27  "won his spurs": Ibid.

27  "a patrician": Keyes, *Fifty Years'*, p. 175.

27  "received and gave": Ibid.

28 "of a family": George H. Thomas, Letter to Mrs. Hamilton Draper, March 4, 1865, U.S. Military Academy Library Archives.

28 "argued bitterly": O'Connor, *Thomas*, p. 73.

28 "many delicately": French, *Two Wars*, p. 26.

29 "to defend Texas": Steele, *American Campaigns*, Vol. 1, p. 83.

30 "The mortality": Stephenson, *Texas and the Mexican War*, p. 198.

31 "making the ground": Giddings, *Sketches of the Campaign in Northern Mexico*, pp. 168–69.

31 "determined that not": Ibid.

31 "interspersed sacred music": Cleaves, *Rock*, p. 34.

31 "its corridors": Meade, *The Life and Letters of General George Gordon Meade*, Vol. 1, p. 145.

32 "the highest praise": Dwight, ed., *Critical Sketches*, p. 170.

32 "for the bold advance": O'Connor, *Thomas*, p. 89.

32 "found the expedition": French, *Two Wars*, pp. 69–70.

33 "of every color": Cleaves, *Rock*, p. 39.

33 "in gorgeous tassels": Ibid.

33 "I wish to save you": Carleton, *The Battle of Buena Vista*, pp. 36–37.

33 "without infantry to support it": Steele, *American Campaigns*, Vol. 1, p. 95.

34 "was always in action": Dyer, *Zachary Taylor*, p. 237.

34 "we would not have maintained": Van Horne, *Thomas*, p. 6.

34 "Thomas more than sustained": Ibid.

34 "A little more grape": in Coppee, *Thomas*, pp. 16–17.

34 "American troops had seldom": Steele, *American Campaigns*, Vol. 1, p. 100.

35 "Vera Cruz must be taken": Ibid., p. 101.

35 "Scott is lost": Ibid.

37 "and have the thing": George H. Thomas, Letter to John W. Thomas, October 25, 1848, Shands Papers.

37 "to lead a lonely life," etc.: Ibid.

37 "paralleled those": Parramore, *Southampton County*, p. 153.

38 "The vacancy, I think": Braxton Bragg, Letter to John Y. Mason, November 17, 1848.

38 "tall, perfectly," etc.: Howard, "Sketch," p. 292.

38 "a warm and winning smile": Ibid., p. 301.

38 "his words and confidence": Ibid.

39 "the deep and sonorous": Coppee, *Thomas*, 183.

39 "caught every eye": Howard, "Sketch," p. 292.

40 "no more capable officer": McKinney, *Education in Violence*, p. 57.

41   "the six days": George H. Thomas, Letter to Major E. D. Townsend, July 14, 1854, War Department Files, National Archives.

41   "dwindled to a sluggish brick-red": Robinson, *Story of Arizona*, p. 110.

41   "The hills around": Johnson, *Memoir*, p. 28.

41   "felt like a hot": www.militarymuseum.org./Ft.Yuma.html.

42   "his skin dry": McKinney, *Education*, p. 62.

42   "gambled, drank": Redman, "Major-General George H. Thomas, Practitioner of Emancipation," www.aotc.net/Thomashome.htm.

42   "a mounted force": Cleaves, *Rock*, p. 55.

42   "a solid, sound": Ibid., p. 54.

43   "kept a watchful eye": O'Connor, *Thomas*, p. 88.

43   "gleamed with shining brass": Col. M. L. Cummins, "Major George H. Thomas in Texas," p. 78.

44   "had a marked": Rister, *Robert E. Lee in Texas*, p. 61.

44   "Neither Major": Ibid., p. 67.

45   "waffles, eggs": Ibid., p. 80.

45   "The Major can fare": Jones, *Life and Letters of Robert E. Lee*, p. 86.

46   "to stay at Fort Belknap": Rister, *Lee in Texas*, p. 141.

46   "recognized his rights": Ibid.

46   "I have been waiting": McKinney, *Education*, p. 77.

47   "one old Comanche": O'Connor, *Thomas*, p. 97.

## 3. "A HOUSE DIVIDED"

**Page**

50   "It elected Presidents": Smith, *The United States*, p. 228.

51   "the people in the North": Ibid., p. 228.

52   "While the Union lasts": Bobrick, *Testament*, p. 13.

53   "A house divided against itself": Thomas, Isaac, ed. *The Words of Abraham Lincoln*, pp. 27–28.

54   "The love of Union": Sherman, *Recollections*, Vol. 1, p. 245.

54   "men will be cutting": Wellborn, *The Growth of American Nationality*, p. 811.

54   "There is no crisis": Stephenson, *Abraham Lincoln and the Union*, p. 99.

54   "There is nothing": Ibid.

55   "the countryside would soon": Bridges, "Donn Piatt, Diplomat and Gadfly."

56   "Bound to the Federal": Johnson, *Memoir*, p. 37.

56   "A nation divided against itself": "Sam Houston," www.forttumbleweed.net.

56 "rushed madly onward": Johnson, *Memoir*, p. 37.

57 "marched the men north": Torrance, *General George H. Thomas*, Minnesota Commandery of the Military Order of the Loyal Legion of the United States, March 9, 1897.

57 "despondent over": Coppee, *Thomas*, p. 36.

57 "what salary": Ibid.

57 "Superintendent": McKinney, *Education*, p. 87.

57 "it is not my wish": George H. Thomas, Letter to Letcher, March 12, 1861, Calendar of Virginia State Papers, Vol. 9, p. 106.

57 "strong and bitter": Society of the Army of the Cumberland, 1870 Reunion, *Report*, p. 67.

57 "he denounced the idea": Ibid.

58 "I shall never bear arms": Freeman, *Robert E. Lee*, Vol. 1, p. 425.

58 "Justice and Truth": Parramore, *Southampton County*, p. 157.

59 "There glowed": Ibid.

59 "had fallen into disuse" etc.: Sherman, *John Sherman's Recollections*, Vol. 1, p. 55.

59 "There was treason": Upton, *The Military Policy of the United States*, p. 238.

60 "pale, sad, and nervous": Abbott, *The History of the Civil War in America*, p. 86.

60 "In your hands": Foote, *The Civil War*, Vol. 1, pp. 39–40.

60 "I guess we will manage": Sherman, *Recollections*, Vol. 1, p. 242.

60 "I found the nation": Abbott, *History*, p. 92.

61 "I have spent": Ibid.

61 "a useless waste of life": Annual Report, American Historical Association, 1913, p. 181.

62 "flung to the breeze": Headley, *The Great Rebellion*, Vol. 1, p. 55.

62 "It was a mild": Ibid.

63 "Sixty years": Fuller, *The Generalship of Ulysses S. Grant*, p. 16.

63 "glanced off like marbles": Abbott, *History*, p. 90.

63 "stood, with palpitating heart": Ibid., p. 91.

64 "to repossess": Upton, *Military Policy*, p. 227.

65 "appalled to silence": McClure, *Lincoln and Men in War-Times*, p. 70.

65 "Whichever way": Coppee, *Thomas*, p. 36.

65 "which had gone up": Ibid., p. 29.

65 an entire fabrication: Piatt and Boynton, *Thomas*, pp. 84–85.

67 "virtually Secretary of War": Sherman, *Recollections*, Vol. 1, p. 243.

67 "I know that promotion": Ibid., p. 244.

67 "You can't avoid taking": Ibid., p. 245

67 "he was very conservative": Ibid., p. 234.

68 "I will bide my time": Ibid., p. 244.

69 "webbed feet": Robertson, *Concise Illustrated History of the Civil War*, p. 60.

71 "two armed mobs": Fuller, *Generalship*, p. 16.

71 "I had been fishing": Gordy, *Heroes and Leaders in American History*, p. 5.

71 "the trained soldiers": Steele, *American Campaigns*, Vol. 1, p. 144.

71 "No citizen soldier": Ibid.

72 "Lincoln sent for me": Joyner, "Robert Cumming Schenck, First Citizen and Statesman, Ohio History," *The Scholarly Journal of the Ohio Historical Society*, July 1949, p. 293.

72 Among the early arrivals: Sherman, *John Sherman's Recollections*, Vol. 1, p. 317.

73 "I don't care": Johnson, *Memoir*, p. 38.

73 Thomas, with that modesty: McClure, *Lincoln and Men of War-Times*, p. 341.

74 "never leaped a grade": Ridpath, *The Life and Work of James A. Garfield*, p. 88.

74 "not a man of iron": Ibid., pp. 250–51.

74 "reserve power": Van Horne, *Thomas*, p. 19.

74 "My experience teaches me": George H. Thomas, Letter of April 4, 1856, quoted in McKinney, *Education*, p. 67.

75 "In the last resort": Johnson, *Memoir*, p. 41.

75 "I knocked in": Ibid.

76 "the only man": Steele, *American Campaigns*, Vol. 1, p. 250.

76 "I have thought it all over": Torrance, *General George H. Thomas*, p. 8.

76 "They got out a big map": Sherman, *John Sherman's Recollections*, Vol. 1, p. 250.

77 "watched the cavalry": McKinney, *Education*, p. 100.

77 "without stopping": *Military Service Institution Journal*, Vol. 56, p. 40.

78 I had no opportunity: Upton, *Military Policy*, p. 243.

79 "had refused to remain": Headley, *Great Rebellion*, Vol. 1, p. 123.

79 "I have always believed": George H. Thomas, Letter to Robert Patterson, August 8, 1864, quoted in Piatt and Boynton, *Thomas*, pp. 101–2.

80 "everywhere": Sherman, *Recollections*, Vol. 1, pp. 260–61.

81 I notice that: Van Horne, *Thomas*, p. 37.

81 "Mr. President, Old Tom": O'Connor, *Thomas*, p. 130.

81 "because so many": Sherman, *Memoirs*, p. 178.

82 "At the request": Abraham Lincoln to Simon Cameron, August 19, 1861, Dearborn Collection.

82 "Yes, I will guarantee it": Howard, "Sketch," p. 295.

82 "the greatest pleasure": George H. Thomas, Letter to Robert Anderson, August 26, 1861, U.S. Military Academy Library Archive.

82 "I may be mistaken": George H. Thomas, Letter to Henry Stone, August 31, 1861, U.S. Military Academy Library Archives.

## 4. MILL SPRINGS

**Page**

83 "Kentucky gone": McDonough, *War in Kentucky*, p. 61.

83 "denounced secession": Coppee, *Thomas*, p. 41.

86 "Damn this speech-making": McKinney, *Education*, p. 110.

86 "as step by step": Ibid.

86 "I am beginning": George H. Thomas to Captain O. D. Green, September 21, 1861, Johnson Papers, 13:2889.

87 "Wherever and whenever": Piatt and Boynton, *Thomas*, p. 335.

88 "since the Secretary of War": Van Horne, *Thomas*, pp. 43–44.

88 "to have the execution": Ibid., p. 44.

88 "the necessity": McKinney, *Education*, p. 115.

89 "You are authorized": Coppee, *Thomas*, p. 49.

89 "not be allowed": Sherman Papers, 9:1603.

89 "miracles": Sherman, *Memoirs*, p. 188.

90 Louisville, Kentucky: *War of the Rebellion: A Compilation of the Official Records of the Union and Confederate Armies*, 1st Series, Vol. 4, p. 339.

90 "With four more": Ibid.

91 "the country never has": Sherman, *Memoirs*, p. 191.

91 "I have done all": Johnson, *Memoir*, p. 52.

91 Our enemies have a terrible: Sherman, *Memoirs*, p. 190.

92 "Answer": Flood, *Grant and Sherman*, p. 60.

92 "I am sorry": Ibid.

92 "Have you heard": Piatt and Boynton, *Thomas*, p. 117.

92 "culpable": Ibid., p. 118.

92 "discontented persons": Ibid., p. 117.

92 "I am sure": Cleaves, *Rock*, p. 90.

93 "the disheartened": Ibid., p. 91.

93 "We must have passed": Ibid.

93 "absurd": Ibid.

93 "I know not whether": O'Connor, *Thomas*, p. 143.

93 "crazy": Sherman, *Memoirs*, p. 198.

93 "with suspicion": Ibid.

93 "askance": Ibid.

94   "Have arms gone": *War of the Rebellion, Official Records*, 1st Series, Vol. 7, p. 530.

94   "like pulling plows": www.civilwarhome.com/darkandbloodyground .html.

94   "cheerful fires": Bishop, *The Story of a Regiment*, p. 35.

95   "The usual method," etc.: O'Connor, *Thomas*, p. 148.

95   "ready," etc.: Shanks, *Personal Recollections*, p. 66.

96   "Trees were flecked": Bishop, *Story*, p. 42.

96   "We must not shoot": Johnston, *Albert Sidney Johnston*, p. 402.

96   "We were doing pretty well": www.civilwar.org/historyclassroom/hc_mill springshist.html.

97   "whose homes": O'Connor, *Thomas*, p. 154.

97   "marked by an expression": Cleaves, *Rock*, p. 99.

97   "no tactical mistakes": McKinney, *Education*, p. 129.

98   Up to this time: Coppee, *Thomas*, p. 62.

98   "brilliant victory": Dwight, ed., *Critical Sketches*, p. 178.

98   "the military and personal": Ibid.

99   "he would have outranked," etc.: O'Connor, *Thomas*, p. 156.

99   "If my right is thus broken": Dwight, ed., *Critical Sketches*, p. 177.

100   I state my general idea: Steele, *American Campaigns*, Vol, 1, p. 153.

100   "If, . . . it is a wise maxim": Van Horne, *Thomas*, p. 61.

101   "ranked near the bottom": Wellborn, *The Growth of American Nationality*, p. 849.

101   "came to him": Stoddard, *Grant*, p. 20.

103   "congregations were dismissed," etc.: Johnson, *Memoir*, p. 65.

## 5. FROM SHILOH TO PERRYVILLE

**Page**

107   "Nothing of interest": Schmucker, *A History of the Civil War in the United States*, p. 163.

107   "His policy": Smith, *The United States*, p. 263.

109   "that he need not hasten": Steele, *American Campaigns*, Vol. 1, p. 181.

109   "Probably there never was": Ibid., 173.

110   "scudding from the woods": Ibid., p. 174.

110   "All is quiet along": Ibid., p. 179.

110   "I have scarcely": Ibid.

111   "at no time made any attempt": John Codman Ropes, quoted in Fuller, *Generalship*, p. 108.

111   "No better opportunity": Ibid., p. 111.

112   "stupendous crime": Engle, *Don Carlos Buell*, p. 236.

112   "Grant seems to have been": James A. Garfield, quoted in ibid.

112   "imbecile": Engle, *Don Carlos Buell*, p. 236.

112   "If Southerners think": Flood, *Grant and Sherman*, p. 89.

112   "to help us on the first day": O'Connor, *Thomas*, p. 169.

113   "were unused to": Grant, *Personal Memoirs*, p. 192.

113   "The troops on both sides": Ibid.

113   "Thomas's [division]": Ibid.

114   "Undoubtedly, here began": Dwight, ed., *Critical Sketches*, p. 178.

114   "We waited for three days": Bobrick, *Testament*, p. 76.

115   "In consequence of this": Van Horne, *Thomas*, p. 65.

116   "I know that a few thousand": Gordy, *Heroes and Leaders*, p. 171.

116   "Save your army": Ibid.

117   "If we gave": Ibid.

117   "incapable of making": Miles, *Piercing the Heartland*, p. 85.

118   "a fixed way": Ibid., p. 82.

118   "fully as important": Office of the Chief of Military History, United States Army, *American Military History*, www.army.mil.htm.

119   "entirely impossible": George H. Thomas to Andrew Johnson, August 16, 1862, Thomas Papers, Henry E. Huntington Library.

120   "to keep abreast": Miles, *Piercing*, p. 73.

120   "The enemy crossed three hundred": Piatt and Boynton, *Thomas*, p. 162.

120   "By all means concentrate": Ibid., p. 163.

121   "could not possibly": Beatty, *Memoirs of a Volunteer*, p. 117.

121   "What think you?": Piatt and Boynton, *Thomas*, p. 163.

121   "We can get neither forage": Ibid.

121   "There is no possibility": Ibid.

121   "scarce," etc.: Ibid., p. 164.

121   "I will therefore": Ibid.

122   "Keep your position,": etc. Ibid.

122   "Do any circumstances": Ibid., p. 166.

122   "I think as the movement": Ibid.

122   "appeared in central Kentucky": O'Connor, *Thomas*, p. 181.

123   "from the tyranny": McDonough, *War in Kentucky*, p. 155.

124   "He wore a shabby hat": Engle, *Buell*, p. 293.

125   [Thomas] came to my room: Johnson, *Memoir*, p. 300.

125   "General Buell's preparations": Ibid.

126   "I am not as modest": Piatt and Boynton, *Thomas*, p. 171.

126   "Will await further orders": Cleaves, *Rock*, p. 113.

127   "Our prospects are not": Miles, *Piercing*, p. 74.

127   "cupidity . . . love of ease": Catton, *This Hallowed Ground*, p. 200.

127 "not easily ruffled," etc.: Shanks, *Personal Recollections*, pp. 64–66.

128 "the Confederate Army of the West": O'Connor, *Thomas*, p. 186.

128 "all the grass had withered": Bobrick, *Testament*, p. 99.

128 "tired-looking threads"; Miles, *Piercing*, p. 82.

128 "I never saw men suffer": McDonough, *War in Kentucky*, p. 210.

129 "sweep every living thing": Bobrick, *Testament*, p. 100.

130 "It was a life to life": Ibid., p. 276.

130 "What is the meaning of that," etc.: Piatt and Boynton, *Thomas*, p. 174.

130 "I was astonished": Miles, *Piercing*, p. 82.

131 "heavily engaged": Van Horne, *Thomas*, p. 82.

131 "which made him believe": *Battles and Leaders of the Civil War* Vol. 3, pp. 48–49.

132 "Let the Virginian wait": Piatt and Boynton, *Thomas*, p. 199.

132 "bilious with wrath": Ibid., pp. 198–99.

133 "decided that further pursuit": Fitch, *Annals of the Army of the Cumberland*, p. 33.

133 "with but a tithe": Ibid., p. 34.

133 Soon after coming to Kentucky: Piatt and Boynton, *Thomas*, pp. 199–200.

134 Your letter of October 30th: Ibid., p. 200.

135 I have the honor: Ibid., p. 202.

135 "I have made my last protest": Van Horne, *Thomas*, p. 88.

136 "was more like that": Military Order of the Loyal Legion of the United States, District of Columbia Commandery, *War Papers*, Vol. 68, pp. 5–6.

136 "You and I have been friends": Society of the Army of the Cumberland, 1887 Reunion, *Report*, p. 48.


## 6. STONES RIVER

**Page**

137 "In politics and war": McClure, *Lincoln and Men*, p. 355.

137 "Oh Lord, for these": www.heritagepursuit.com/Logan/LoganLate/htm.

139 "in treasonable correspondence": Piatt and Boynton, *Thomas*, p. 178.

139 "I give you these only": Ibid.

139 "organized to convict": Engle, *Buell*, p. 325.

139 "the court was ashamed": Piatt and Boynton, *Thomas*, p. 179.

139 "come into court": Ibid., p. 180.

140 "This was the situation": Ibid.

140 "it soon became clear": Ibid.

140 "cold, calm manner": Ibid.

140 "Please tell the court": Ibid., p. 181.

140 "If you will give me": Ibid.

140 "slowly turned the leaves": Ibid., p. 199.

140 "If there's any rotten apples": Logan County, Ohio, History, 584—Biographical Sketches, on-line article.

141 "Knows too much": Ibid.

141 "fearing that it would": Brugger, *Maryland: A Middle Temperament*, p. 293.

142 "At once the dogs": McWhiney, *Braxton Bragg and the Confederate Defeat*, p. 235.

143 "toiled terribly": Fitch, *Annals*, p. 371.

143 "Everywhere in the Army": Hicken, *Illinois in the Civil War*, p. 100.

144 Can't get shoes: Abbott, *History*, p. 359.

145 When I became a member: Piatt and Boynton, *Thomas*, p. 506.

146 "The President is very impatient": Steele, *American Campaigns*, Vol. 1, p. 325.

146 "it would have been unwise": Fitch, *Annals*, p. 382.

146 "I have lost no time": Steele, *American Campaigns*, Vol. 1, p. 325.

147 "a truly imposing scene": Cozzens, *No Better Place to Die*, p. 38.

147 "floundering about": Ibid.

147 "We shall begin to skirmish": Headley, *Great Rebellion*, Vol. 2, p. 130.

148 "a pretty good load": Bobrick, *Testament*, p. 124.

148 "General, this is hell": Headley, *Great Rebellion*, Vol. 2, p. 130.

148 "Go back and tell": Ibid.

148 "Another division passed": Bobrick, *Testament*, p. 124

148 "who contested every ridge": Haskew, "Winter Fury Unleashed," p. 5.

149 "The turnpike as far": Fitch, *Annals*, p. 317.

149 "leapt wildly up": Ibid.

150 "What is the meaning": Piatt and Boynton, *Thomas*, p. 205.

150 "Every soldier on that field": Cist, *The Army of the Cumberland*, p. 105.

151 "You know the ground": Fitch, *Annals*, p. 688; Abbott, *History*, p. 366.

151 "committed himself": Headley, *Great Rebellion*, Vol. 2, p. 134.

151 "In five minutes": Catton, *Hallowed Ground*, p. 193.

152 "Our comrades were falling": Haynie, *The Nineteenth Illinois*, pp. 186–87.

152 "Cut your way out": Cleaves, *Rock of Chickamauga*, p. 127.

152 "everywhere along his harassed": O'Connor, *Thomas*, p. 210.

153 "Fighting under him": *Ibid.*, p. 211.

153 "The scene was as grand": Abbott, *History*, p. 371.

153 "inclining gently": Fitch, *Annals*, p. 36.

153 "Brave men die": Ibid.

153 "I saw but a headless trunk": Ibid, p. 249.

153 "Men, shoot low": Swinton, *Twelve Decisive Battles*, p. 211.

154 "God has granted us": Haskew, "Winter Fury Unleashed," p. 7.

154 "his old faded": Piatt and Boynton, *Thomas*, p. 211.

154 "moving in his slow": Ibid.

154 "This army can't retreat!": Coppee, *Thomas*, pp. 100–101.

155 "as always," etc.: Military Order of the Loyal Legion of the United States, Indiana Commandery, *War Papers*, Vol 1., p. 174.

156 "Unable to dislodge": Abbott, *History*, p. 378.

156 "resembled butchers": Fitch, *Annals*, p. 292.

156 "God bless you": Ibid., p. 411; Abbott, *History*, p. 378.

156 "All honor to the Army": Fitch, *Annals*, p. 292.

157 "hard-earned victory": Williams, *Lincoln and His Generals*, pp. 208–9.

157 "Come now, Stanton": Piatt and Boynton, *Thomas*, p. 214.

157 "Nestor": Fitch, *Annals*, p. 262.

157 "He wore the uniform": Shanks, *Recollections*, p. 63.

158 "created a doubt": Sherman, *Recollections*, Vol. 1, p. 329.

## 7. FROM TULLAHOMA TO CHICKAMAUGA

**Page**

159 "The order": Abbott, *History*, p. 306.

161 "filled up for": Cist, *Army*, p. 138.

162 "Keep everything in order": Society of the Army of the Cumberland, 1870 Reunion, *Report*, pp. 80–81.

162 "He made it a rule": Dwight, ed., *Critical Sketches*, p. 199.

162 "on account of his": Johnson, *Memoir*, p. 116.

162 "as a sacred trust": Boynton, *Was General Thomas Slow at Nashville?*, p. 4.

162 "his face hardened": *Harper's Weekly*, April 23, 1870, Vol. 14, No. 695, Front Page.

162 "schoolyard drill": Piatt and Boynton, *Thomas*, p. 342.

162 "gotten up for show": Ibid.

163 "a dancing school": Ibid.

163 It is a question of nerve: Ibid., pp. 347–48.

163 "McClellan made a grave": Ibid., p. 343.

163 "The solution of the vexed": Ibid., p. 349.

163 "great fondness": Ibid., p. 197.

163 "than any momentary": Shanks, *Personal Recollections*, p. 80.

164 All his personal habits: Dwight, ed, *Critical Sketches*, p. 200.

165 "a mobile humane society": O'Connor, *Thomas*, p. 202.

165 "He was habitually kind": Howard, "Sketch," p. 301.

165    "quacking in diminuendo": O'Connor, *Thomas*, p. 203.

166    "There is no suffering": Beatty, *Memoirs of a Volunteer*, p. 267.

166    "The fate of empire": Piatt and Boynton, *Thomas*, p. 329.

167    "degraded," etc.: Cist, *Army*, p. 218.

167    "From information from": Piatt and Boynton, *Thomas*, p. 254.

167    "After the investment": Grant, *Personal Memoirs*, p. 325.

168    "To show how differently": Coppee, *Thomas*, p. 123.

168    "Our government": Piatt and Boynton, *Thomas*, p. 329.

168    "to learn and report": Ibid., p. 330.

168    "We cannot move": Ibid.

169    "far better": Ibid.

169    "declined to accept": Ibid., p. 331.

170    "While carrion crows": Piatt and Boynton, *Thomas*, p. 426.

171    "was neither appreciated": Ibid., p. 356.

171    "Lee's army overthrown": Korn, *The Fight for Chattanooga*, p. 30.

171    "You do not appear": Ibid., p. 18.

171    "My dear General": Gordy, *Heroes and Leaders*, p. 201.

172    "The Father of Waters": Piatt and Boynton, *Thomas*, p. 375.

172    "a conflict of Titans": Coppee, *Thomas*, p. 120.

172    "Your forces must move": Ibid., p. 371.

172    "As I have determined": Ibid.

173    "The orders for the advance": Ibid.

173    "To obey your order": Society of the Army of the Cumberland, 1879 Reunion, *Report*, p. 175.

173    "That's right": Ibid.

173    "I have communicated": *The Campaign for Chattanooga* p. 13.

174    "The broad Tennessee": Hicken, *Illinois in the Civil War*, p. 195.

175    "Not only the greatest": Piatt and Boynton, *Thomas*, p. 379.

175    "badly demoralized," etc.: *War of the Rebellion, Official Records*, 1st Series, Vol. 30, Part 3, p. 481.

176    "as a man of little": Johnson, *Memoir*, p. 85.

176    "great caution": Ibid.

176    "After holding": www.aotc.net/Rosecrans_home.htm.

176    "He was not very": *War of the Rebellion, Official Records*, 1st Series, Vol. 30, Part 3, p. 510.

177    "an overwhelming force": Ibid., p. 564.

177    "Your dispatches": Ibid., pp. 564–65.

177    "a matter of life and death": Villard, *Memoirs*, Vol. 2, p. 97.

177    "burst out": Dana, *Recollections of the Civil War*, p. 109.

177    "General Rosecrans": Dana, *Recollections of the Civil War*, p. 109.

178    "The movements for": Ibid., p. 10.

178 "The difficulties of gaining": Ibid.

178 "See that the men": *War of the Rebellion, Official Records,* 1st Series, Vol. 30, Part 1, p. 111.

179 "every shot seemed to tell": Abbott, *History,* p. 423.

179 "It actually seemed": Ibid.

179 "bloody lane": Gordon, *Reminiscences of the Civil War,* p. 203.

179 "You're not fighting": Fitch, *Annals,* p. 467.

180 "like a firmament": *United Service Journal,* September 1896, p. 223.

180 "the night after a battle": Gordon, *Reminiscences of the Civil War,* p. 205.

180 "remained in the telegraph office": Bates, *Lincoln in the Telegraph Office,* p. 158.

180 "Rosecrans began": Dana, *Recollections of the Civil War,* p. 113.

181 "the Hebrew Maiden's Lament": Wilson, *Life of Charles A. Dana,* p. 260.

181 "to divine if possible": Military Order of the Loyal Legion of the United States, District of Columbia Commandery, *War Papers,* Vol. 2, p. 18.

181 "It was a night": Torrance, *Thomas,* p. 13.

182 "causing them to look": Shanks, *Personal Recollections,* p. 70.

183 I was wakened: Dana, *Recollections,* p. 115; Wilson, *Dana,* p. 264.

184 not far away: Ibid.

184 "faint and ill": Cox, *Military Reminiscences of the Civil War,* Vol. 2, p. 10.

184 "My army is whipped": Stanton, quoted in "Talk with General Steedman," *The New York Times,* November 24, 1879, p. 2.

184 "My report to-day": O'Connor, *Thomas,* p. 43.

185 "It will ruin the army": Ibid., p. 152.

185 "Take that ridge!", etc.: Ibid., p. 151.

185 "simply suicidal": Shanks, *Personal Recollections,* p. 285.

185 "did not know": Torrance, *Thomas,* p. 15.

186 "General Thomas has fought": Dwight, ed., *Critical Sketches,* p. 181.

186 "Our troops were as immovable": Ibid.

186 "I'll tell you": "Talk with General Steedman," *The New York Times,* November 24, 1879, p. 2.

186 "everything gone": Dwight, ed., *Critical Sketches,* p. 182.

186 "There is nothing finer": O'Connor, *Thomas,* p. 47.

187 began to write: Shanks, *Personal Recollections,* p. 273.

187 "sitting on a log": "Talk with General Steedman," *The New York Times,* November 24, 1879, p. 2.

187 "saying that his troops": Dana, *Recollections,* p. 117.

188 "It was at Gettysburg": Dwight, ed., *Critical Sketches,* p. 266.

188 "ungracious," etc.: Bates, *Lincoln in the Telegraph Office,* p. 170.

188 "I did not think": Shanks, *Personal Recollections,* p. 67.

189 "I never was tempted": Piatt and Boynton, *Thomas,* p. 335.

189 "I cannot see how": Ibid.

189 "natural," etc.: Ibid., pp. 359–60.


## 8. CHATTANOOGA

**Page**

191 "the man who saved them": Wilson, *Dana*, p. 265.

192 "could . . . trace": Bishop, *Story of a Regiment*, p. 17.

193 "Hello, mister!": Shanks, *Personal Recollections*, pp. 72–73.

193 "the Herculean labors": Dana, *Recollections*, p. 121.

194 He dawdled: Dana, *Recollections*, p. 128.

194 "stunned and confused": Williams, *Lincoln and His Generals*, p. 285.

194 "a damned coward": "Talk with General Steedman," *The New York Times*, November 24, 1879.

194 "I saw him under fire": Ibid.

194 "Eastern general": Welles, *The Diary of Gideon Welles*, Vol. 1, p. 447.

194 "any one suitable": Ibid.

194 "The merits": Coppee, *Thomas*, p. 162.

194 "He was too much affected," etc.: Dana, *Recollections*, p. 125.

195 "Who do you think," etc.: "Talk with General Steedman," *The New York Times*, November 24, 1879, p. 2.

195 "Hold Chattanooga": Van Horne, *Thomas*, p. 156; Wilson, *Dana*, p. 277.

195 "I will hold the town": Ibid.

196 "look with confidence": Fitch, *Annals*, p. 481.

196 "you need not": Society of the Army of the Cumberland, 1869 Reunion, *Report*, pp. 77–78; 1879 Reunion, *Report*, p. 176.

196 "as near to an angel": Address of John Watts, New York Historical Society, January 5, 1875.

196 "our hopes went up": Hazen, *A Narrative of Military Service*, p. 100.

197 "suffered greatly": Wilson, *Under the Old Flag*, Vol. 2, p. 272.

197 "I was therefore prepossessed": Wilson, *Under the Old Flag*, Vol. 1, p. 272.

197 "with every mark": Wilson, *Dana*, p. 286.

197 "Mr. Dana, you have got me": Ibid.

197 "Those distinguished officers": Ibid., p. 280.

198 "after Chickamauga": O'Connor, p. 219.

198 We came upon: Alexander, *Fighting for the Confederacy*, p. 307.

199 "Grant . . . was sitting": Wilson, *Dana*, p. 281.

199 "known prejudice": Dwight, ed., *Critical Sketches*, p. 186.

199 "The situation was embarrassing," etc.: Wilson, *Dana*, p. 281.

199 "Thomas's services": Ibid., p. 283.

200 "Please approve order": Flood, *Grant and Sherman*, p. 203.

200 "He had scarcely begun": Ibid.

200 "Thomas's plan for securing": Howard, "Sketch," p. 299.

201 "We can easily subsist": *War of the Rebellion, Official Records*, 1st Series, Vol. 30, Part 1, p. 41.

201 "the movement should not be made": Piatt and Boynton, *Thomas*, p. 462.

201 "meant disaster": Ibid.

202 "get the order countermanded": Ibid.

202 "as far as the mouth," etc.: Ibid., p. 462.

202 "at a time when Thomas": *Battles and Leaders*, Vol. 3, p. 715.

202 "On the 7th": Grant, *Personal Memoirs*, p. 341.

202 "We had not at Chattanooga": Ibid.

202 "Thomas announced": Badeau, *Military History of U.S. Grant*, Vol. 1, pp. 463–64.

203 "idea was to attack": Piatt and Boynton, *Thomas*, p. 463.

203 "by a singular blunder": Dana, *Recollections*, p. 143.

203 "I can do it": Lewis, *Sherman*, p. 317.

203 "Damn him": William T. Sherman to James A. Garfield, July 28, 1870, Sherman Papers; *North American Review*, April 1887, p. 377.

204 "not as imperturbable": Lewis, *Sherman*, p. 318.

204 "As there may still": Grant, *Personal Memoirs*, p. 349.

204 "smiled as he read": Howard, *Autobiography*, Vol. 1, p. 477.

204 "The field of operation": Piatt and Boynton, *Thomas*, p. 476.

204 "The spectacle": Dana, *Recollections*, p. 145.

205 "almost before the Confederates": Ibid.

205 "You have gained too much": Van Horne, *Thomas*, p. 174.

205 "It will not do": Howard, *Autobiography*, Vol. 1, p. 479.

205 "attacked the enemy's left": Piatt and Boynton, *Thomas*, p. 477.

205 "Thomas having done": Ibid., p. 479.

205 "We see the first divergence": Ibid.

206 "managed . . . behind Grant's back": Redman, "Thomas: Practitioner of Emancipation."

206 "because he was perched": Illinois State Historical Library, *Publications*, Vol. 35, p. 299.

207 "Up and up they went": Flood, *Grant and Sherman*, p. 212.

207 "cheers from sixty thousand": Piatt and Boynton, *Thomas*, p. 479.

207 "there was no such battle": Young, *Around the World with General Grant*, Vol. 1, p. 100.

208 "had to be approached": Howard, *Autobiography*, Vol. 1, p. 483.

208 "The simple fact is": Wilson, *Under the Old Flag*, Vol. 2, p. 296.

208 "I had watched for": Sherman, *Memoirs*, p. 348.

209 "the patient Thomas": Howard, *Autobiography*, Vol. 1, p. 485.

209 "General Sherman carried": Piatt and Boynton, *Thomas*, p. 490.

210 "fixed and immovable": Ibid., p. 462.

210 "found guns": O'Connor *Thomas*, p. 249.

210 "there was the stillness": Piatt and Boynton, *Thomas*, p. 481.

210 "a single cordon": O'Connor, *Thomas*, p. 249.

210 "the charge of": Ibid.

210 "waited in grim": Piatt and Boynton, *Thomas*, p. 481.

210 "soon lost sight of": Ibid.

210 "The situation offered them": Van Horne, *Thomas*, p. 192.

211 "I never felt so lonesome": Military Order of the Loyal Legion of the United States, District of Columbia Commandery, *War Papers*, Vol. 54, p. 11.

211 Those defending the heights: Bennett, *History of the 36th Illinois Volunteer Regiment*, p. 529.

211 "Who gave that order": Piatt and Boynton, *Thomas*, p. 481.

212 "Twenty minutes of that exposure": Ibid., p. 483.

212 "by an uncontrollable impulse": Dwight, ed., *Critical Sketches*, p. 198.

212 "under a general": Ibid.

212 "even while the shouts": Ibid.

212 "I fell among some": Van Horne, *Thomas*, p. 426.

212 "It was reserved by Providence": Howard, *Autobiography*, Vol. 1, p. 484.

213 "one of the greatest miracles": Dana, *Recollections*, p. 151.

213 "desperation to defeat": Piatt and Boynton, *Thomas*, p. 485.

213 "determined me to order": Ibid.

213 "The Rebel center": Badeau, *Military History*, Vol. 1, pp. 525.

213 "The object of General Hooker's": Sherman, *Memoirs*, p. 335.

214 "an irreparable loss": Gordon, *Reminiscences*, p. 224.

214 "The enemy fled": McFeely, *Grant*, p. 262.

214 "in the name": Flood, *Grant and Sherman*, p. 225.

215 "It will be seen": O'Connor, *Thomas*, p. 255.

215 "Every successful feature": Wilbur Thomas, *Thomas*, pp. 28–29.

215 "playing for time": Alexander, *Fighting for the Confederacy*, p. 328.

215 "Everything was ready": Ibid.

215 "A stern chase": Lewis, *Sherman*, p. 328.

215 Today we picked up: O'Connor, *Thomas*, p. 256.

216 "Oh, . . . I cannot leave": Howard, *Autobiography*, Vol. 1, p. 479.

216 "The general who loved": Van Horne, *Thomas*, p. 213.

216 "No, no, no": Ibid.

## 9. ATLANTA

**Page**

217 "allowed to halt": Steele, *American Campaigns*, p. 535.

217 "doorway," . . . "outer gate": Howard, *Autobiography*, Vol. 1, p. 493.

220 "It is of the utmost importance": *War of the Rebellion, Official Records*, 1st Series, Vol. 32, Part 2, pp. 480–81.

220 "a strong demonstration": Joint Committee on the Conduct of the War, *Supplemental Report*, Vol. 1, p. 198.

220 "I had previously asked": Ibid.

221 "move along the line": Ibid., p. 197.

221 "I told him": O'Connor, *Thomas*, p. 262.

222 "no general was better": McClure, *Lincoln*, p. 363.

222 "was like putting": Piatt and Boynton, *Thomas*, p. 268.

222 "I have been studying": Ibid., p. 442.

222 "We have no generals": Ibid., p. 511.

222 "to hammer continuously": Ibid.

222 "left his dead to rot": Reed, *The Vicksburg Campaign*, p. 116.

222 "The hill-sides were covered": Ibid.

223 "Two days having elapsed": Ibid., p. 117.

223 "Our troops were not repulsed": Reed, *The Vicksburg Campaign*, p. 116.

223 "The wounded suffer": Reed, Vicksburg, p. 117.

223 "Do you know where": Quoted by W. T. Sherman, Letter to Colonel John E. Tourtellate, February 4, 1887.

224 "BEFORE VICKSBURG": Piatt and Boynton, *Thomas*, p. 319.

224 "It is a bad business": Ibid., p. 234.

224 "drunken, stupid": Fingerson, "A William Tecumseh Sherman Letter."

225 "Although we all knew": Ibid.

225 While I have been eminently: Sherman, *Memoirs*, p. 369.

226 You do yourself injustice: Ibid.

226 "This faith gave you": Ibid., p. 370.

227 "[Grant] is not a brilliant man": Flood, *Grant and Sherman*, p. 195.

227 "We have in Grant": Ibid.

227 "He had not, at any time": Piatt and Boynton, *Thomas*, p. 519.

227 "Grant stood by me": Shanks, *Personal Recollections*, p. 36.

228 "If we were to dispose": Redman, "Thomas: Practitioner of Emancipation."

229 "and every foot": Sherman, *Memoirs*, p. 381.

229 "General Thomas' army": Ibid., p. 382.

229 "No matter": Smith, *The United States*, p. 279.

229 "if there was": Sherman, *Personal Memoirs*, 4th ed., Vol. 2, Appendix, p. 545.

230 I proposed to General Sherman: Piatt and Boynton, *Thomas*, p. 525.

231 "against rocks and defiles": Fullerton, quoted in Hedley, *Marching Through Georgia*, p. 86.

231 "many were tumbled off": Ibid.

231 "one big Indian fight": Bailey, *Battles for Atlanta*, p. 75.

231 "mere notes in pencil": Piatt and Boynton, *Thomas*, p. 527.

232 General McPherson reached Resaca: Ibid., p. 530.

232 On the night of May 9th: Sherman, *Personal Memoirs*, 4th ed., Vol. 2, Appendix, p. 539.

233 "almost in a whisper": Military Historical Society of Massachusetts, *Papers*, Vol. 8, p. 409.

234 "there was a sudden": Ibid.

234 "I don't see": Ibid.

234 "doggedly made their way": Dwight, ed., *Critical Sketches*, p. 410.

234 "trampled by the horses": Ibid.

234 "he would never do so again": Cleaves, *Rock of Chickamauga*, p. 216.

234 "Johnston forestalled us": Howard, *Autobiography*, Vol. 1, p. 593.

234 "crime": Castel, *Winning and Losing in the Civil War*, p. 97.

235 *In the Field, June 18, 1864*: Piatt and Boynton, *Thomas*, pp. 534–35.

236 *"deserved special"*: Howard, *Autobiography*, Vol. 1, p. 595.

237 "everybody among his subordinates": Ibid., p. 530.

237 "every day but three": Howard, "Sketch," p. 299.

238 "Next to the Army of the Potomac": Thomas, *General George H. Thomas*, p. 27.

238 "His personal movements," etc.: Dwight, ed., *Critical Sketches*, p. 199.

239 "vast mobile establishment": O'Connor, *Thomas*, p. 295.

239 "as a fighting machine": Ibid.

239 "only one change": Lewis, *Sherman*, p. 354.

240 "no anchorite": Coppee, *Thomas*, p. 306.

240 "smoked fresh beef": Shanks, *Personal Recollections*, p. 76.

240 "been confirmed by long service," etc.: Ibid., pp. 62–63.

240 "when they stopped": O'Connor, *Thomas*, p. 289.

241 "utterly ignorant": Fuller, *Generalship*, p. 39.

241 "The particulars of your plans": Stoddard, *Ulysses S. Grant*, p. 224.

241 "I propose to fight it out": Ibid., p. 229.

241 "unflinching butchery": Churchill, *A History of the English-Speaking Peoples*, p. 252.

242 "Butcher Grant": Wellborn, *Growth of American Nationality*, p. 919.

242 "too regardless of the lives of his men": Welles, *Diary*, Vol. 2, p. 276.

242  "produced a nightmare": McFeely, *Grant*, p. 165

242  "reckless and wasteful": John Codman Ropes in Dwight, *Critical Sketches*, p. 208.

242  "The art of war is simple enough": Robertson Jr., *The Civil War*, p. 54.

242  "Grant's favorite hour": Alexander, *Fighting for the Confederacy*, p. 290.

243  "War is sustained": Alexander, *Fighting for the Confederacy*, p. 416.

243  "to the average citizen": Ibid.

243  "whole attention": Piatt and Boynton, *Thomas*, pp. 542–43.

244  "it was necessary": Lewis, *Sherman*, p. 375.

244  "This is too bad": Society of the Army of the Cumberland, 1893 Reunion, *Report*, p. 118.

244  "During that entire search": Military Historical Society of Massachusetts, *Papers*, Vol. 8, p. 480.

244  "Kenesaw smoked and blazed": Society of the Army of the Cumberland, 1893 Reunion, *Report*, p. 119.

244  "A solid line of blue": Flood, *Grant and Sherman*, p. 255.

245  "with eager eyes": Military Historical Society of Massachusetts, *Papers*, Vol. 8, p. 480.

245  "advanced to within," etc.: Piatt and Boynton, *Thomas*, pp. 544–46.

246  "General Thomas, as usual": Sherman, *Memoirs*, p. 435.

246  "it demonstrated": *War of the Rebellion, Official Records*, 1st Series, Vol. 38, Part 4, p. 60.

246  "One or two more such": O'Connor, *Thomas*, p. 276.

246  The assault I made: Piatt and Boynton, *Thomas*, p. 547.

247  "take it easy": O'Connor, *Thomas*, p. 277.

247  "the enemy as well as": Piatt and Boynton, *Thomas*, p. 548.

247  "Johnston is crossing": Society of the Army of the Cumberland, 1898 Reunion, *Report*, p. 123.

247  "had hardly passed": Howard, *Autobiography*, Vol. 1, p. 597.

248  "Sherman himself passed": Ibid.

248  Mine eyes have beheld: Connolly, *Three Years in the Army of the Cumberland*, pp. 234–35.

249  One [Sherman] may be called: Shanks, *Personal Recollections*, pp. 61–62, 78.

250  "in the whole of his retreat": Gordon, *Reminiscences*, p. 136.

250  "very curtly": Alexander, *Fighting for the Confederacy*, p. 468.

250  "Johnston has failed": McMurry, *John Bell Hood*, p. 117.

250  "It is a bad time": Ibid.

250  "Hood is . . . very industrious": Ibid.

250  "no one except General Lee": Gordon, *Reminiscences*, p. 133.

251  "During the campaign": McMurry, *Hood*, p. 118.

251 "You have failed": Ibid., p. 121.

251 "As a division or corps commander," etc.: Gordon, *Reminiscences*, p. 129.

252 "You are charged": McMurry, *Hood*, p. 123.

252 "Hood has 'gone up' ": Ibid., p. 124.

252 "Confident language": Johnston, *A Narrative of Military Operations and Recollections*, p. 349.

252 First, I expected: Ibid., p. 350.

253 " 'We must not mind' ": Howard, *Autobiography*, Vol. 1, p. 607.

253 "an ugly look": John Newton, quoted in Cleaves, *Rock*, p. 229.

253 "Yelling like furies": Society of the Army of the Cumberland, 1893 Reunion, *Report*, p. 130.

253 "sweep every thing before them": Piatt and Boynton, *Thomas*, p. 550.

253 "I have been with Howard": *War of the Rebellion, Official Records*, 1st Series, Vol. 38, Part 4, p. 196.

254 "Colonel [Charles] Ewing": Military Historical Society of Massachusetts, *Papers*, Vol. 8, p. 444.

254 "accidentally": Hood, *Advance and Retreat*, p. 189.

254 "were left alone": Piatt and Boynton, *Thomas*, p. 551.

254 "jealous": Ibid.

254 "We find the enemy in force": *War of the Rebellion, Official Records*, 1st Series, Vol. 38, Part 3, p. 323.

255 "As his troops went": Howard, "Sketch," p. 299.

255 "So Atlanta is ours": O'Connor, *Thomas*, p. 287.

255 "clownish": Castel, *Winning and Losing*, p. 109.

255 "snapped his fingers," etc.: Sherman, *Memoirs*, p. 477.

255 "the marches, battles, sieges": Sherman, *Memoirs*, p. 478.

256 "I think it but a just reward": Flood, *Sherman and Grant*, p. 257.

256 "rank and service": Sherman, *Personal Memoirs*, Vol. 2, p. 86.

256 "approved and heartily recommended": Ibid.

## 10. NASHVILLE, PART ONE

**Page**

257 "Sherman's wheel-horse": Howard, "Sketch," p. 299.

257 "approved of no movement": Coppee, *Thomas*, p. 227.

257 "had not accomplished all": Steele, *American Campaigns*, Vol. 1, p. 555.

257 "What you are to do": Ibid., p. 556.

259 "burning for miles": Grant, *Personal Memoirs*, p. 524.

259 "The Confederate leaders": O'Connor, *Thomas*, p. 293.

260 "I cannot guess": William T. Sherman, Letter to George H. Thomas, October 20, 1864, Dearborn Collection.

260 "We cannot defend": Sherman, *Memoirs*, p. 519.

260 "It will be a physical": Ibid., p. 514.

260 "Let him go north": Ibid., p. 430.

260 "I can make the march": Ibid., p. 429.

260 "move through Georgia": Sherman, *Memoirs*, p. 520.

261 "purely military or strategic": McDonough, *Nashville*, p. 8.

261 "I am going into the very": Ibid.

261 "bushwhacked by all the old men": Ibid., p. 9.

261 "the best fighting material": Ibid.

261 "a demonstration to the world": O'Connor, *Thomas*, p. 297.

261 "We may well wish": Starr, "Grant and Thomas: A Classic Case of Micro-Management—Bad for Business, Deadly for Armies," fn. 15.

261 "I had not so much faith": Sherman, *Memoirs*, p. 526.

262 "Now you have no more use": O'Connor, *Thomas*, p. 295.

263 "If he'll go to the Ohio River": Lewis, *Sherman*, p. 430.

263 "Do you not think it": Sherman, *Memoirs*, p. 530.

263 "I really do not see": O'Connor, *Thomas*, p. 298.

264 "Great good fortune": McDonough, *Nashville*, p. 10.

264 "enormous . . . To his care": Swinton, *Twelve Decisive Battles*, p. 440.

264 "sallied forth to ruin Georgia": *War of the Rebellion, Official Records*, 1st Series, Vol. 39, Part 3, p. 359.

264 "As we rode on toward": Sherman, *Memoirs*, p. 335.

265 "disdaining the legend": O'Connor, *Thomas*, p. 303.

265 "I do sincerely believe": Ibid.

265 "We are not only fighting": Ibid., p. 504.

265 "left a kindly feeling": Ibid., p. 501.

266 that the property: Ibid., p. 501.

266 "trash": Sherman, *Memoirs*, p. 525.

267 "It is too compact": Van Horne, *Thomas*, p. 261.

268 "ready to risk all": Coppee, *Thomas*, pp. 238–39.

268 "Have everything in readiness": O'Connor, *Thomas*, p. 300.

269 "whose great brain": Johnson, *Memoir*, p. 179.

270 "perilous": Steele, *American Campaigns*, Vol. 2, p. 568.

270 "like treading on thin ice": Stanley, *Personal Memoirs of Major-General D. S. Stanley*, p. 204.

270 "stragglers": Steele, *American Campaigns*, Vol. 1, p. 567.

270 "everything still": Ibid.

270 "there were queer doings": McDonough, *Nashville*, p. 75.

270 "Thus I knew": Ibid.

271 "We must try to hold": Thomas Papers, Henry Huntington Library, wire of November 30, 1864.

272  "blood actually ran": McMurry, *Hood*, p. 176.

272  "the number of dead left": *Tennessee Historical Quarterly*, Vol. 64, No. 3, p. 190.

272  "a slaughter-pen": Ibid.

272  "reticent and gloomy": Rusling, *Men and Things I Saw in Civil War Days*, p. 86.

272  "his hat lifted": Ibid.

273  "We're A. J. Smith's guerrillas": Ibid.

274  "General George H. Thomas, though": McPherson, ed., *The Negro's Civil War*, p. 235.

274  "So far as tested": Smith, *The United States*, p. 63.

274  "no loss by it": Ibid.

274  "The negro should": Flood, *Grant and Sherman*, p. 273.

274  "A nigger . . . is not fit": Ibid.

274  "a sand-bag is better": Bailey, *The Chessboard of War*, p. 231.

275  "You couldn't place him": Howard, "Sketch," p. 289.

275  "His keen sense of justice": Dwight, ed., *Critical Sketches*, p. 199.

275  "constantly giving": Howard, "Sketch," p. 301.

275  "Viewed from the genuine": Douglass, *The Life and Times of Frederick Douglass*, p. 489.

275  "In the sudden transition": Cleaves, *Rock*, p. 204.

276  "in accordance with his antagonism": Van Horne, *Thomas*, p. 214.

276  "enlisting . . . [slaves] as soldiers": Ibid.

276  "with flags flying": Steele, *American Campaigns*, p. 583.

277  "an attack": Fuller, *Generalship*, p. 58.

278  "Should [Thomas] attack me": *Tennessee Historical Quarterly*, Vol. 54, No. 3, p. 190.

278  "This campaign will change": McMurry, *Hood*, p. 178.

278  "delay . . . the closing scenes": Johnson, *Memoir*, pp. 180–81.

278  "It was his grand opportunity": Coppee, *Thomas*, p. 241.

278  "let Forrest get off": Piatt and Boynton, *Thomas*, p. 652.

278  "the moment I can get": Ibid.

279  "If Hood attacks me": Van Horne, *Thomas*, p. 300.

279  "The President feels solicitous": *War of the Rebellion, Official Records*, 1st Series, Vol. 45, Part 2, pp. 15–16.

279  "If you wait till General Wilson": Johnson, *Memoir*, p. 188.

279  "If Hood is permitted": *War of the Rebellion, Official Records*, 1st Series, Vol. 45, Part 2, p. 17.

279  "that Hood was now tied": O'Connor, *Thomas*, p. 307.

280  "infantry enough": *War of the Rebellion, Official Records*, 1st Series, Vol. 45, Part 2, p. 18.

280 "crushed us as soon": Wilson, *Under the Old Flag*, Vol. 2, p. 59.

280 "the recipe": Starr, "Grant and Thomas."

280 "Attack Hood at once": Ibid., p. 55.

280 "Thomas seems to be unwilling": Ibid., p. 84.

280 "The newspapers throughout": Wilson, *Under the Old Flag*, Vol. 2, pp. 62–63, 96.

281 "If Thomas has not struck yet": Ibid., p. 96.

281 "If you wish General Thomas relieved": Ibid.

282 "It looks to me evidently": *War of the Rebellion, Official Records*, 1st Series, Vol. 45, Part 2, p. 97.

282 "Contrary to Grant's belief": Ibid., pp. 64–65.

283 "I can only say": *War of the Rebellion, Official Records*, 1st Series, Vol. 45, Part 2, p. 97.

283 "Dispatch of 8 P.M.": Ibid., p. 115.

283 "I am very unwilling": Ibid.

283 "Your dispatch of 1 P.M. to-day": Ibid.

284 "General Halleck informs me": Ibid.

284 "No hostile action": Cleaves, *Rock*, p. 258.

284 "Wilson, . . . the Washington authorities": Wilson, *Under the Old Flag*, Vol. 2, p. 102.

284 "could not forget that": Ibid., pp. 104–106.

285 "While the rain was falling": Stone, "Hood's Invasion of Tennessee," p. 609.

285 "If you delay the attack": *War of the Rebellion, Official Records*, 1st Series, Vol. 45, Part 2, p. 143.

285 "obey the order as promptly": Van Horne, *Thomas*, p. 306.

285 "I believe an attack": War of the Rebellion, Official Records, 1st Series, Vol. 45, Part 2, p. 155.

285 "should have brought": Starr, "Grant and Thomas."

286 "Grant's telegrams": Wilson, *Under the Old Flag*, Vol. 2, pp. 68–69.

286 "I thought, after what": Van Horne, *Thomas*, p. 313.

286 "Grant was a pushing": Coppee, *Thomas*, p. 265.

286 "every day increased": Ibid.

286 "in regard to the order": Schofield, *Forty-six Years in the Army*, p. 240.

287 "Thomas nowhere appears": Nicolay and Hay, *Abraham Lincoln: A History*, Vol. 10, p. 28.

287 "A weaker man than Thomas": Coppee, *Thomas*, p. 262.

287 "Many officers here": Cleaves, *Rock*, p. 259.

288 "mournfully shook his head": Ibid., p. 260.

288 "had the manner and disposition": McDonough, *Nashville*, p. 16.

288 "fear of politicians": O'Connor, *Thomas*, p. 301.

289  "drew a deep sigh": *Century Magazine*, August 1887, p. 609.

289  "announcing his readiness": Starr, "Grant and Thomas," fn. 82.

289  "on his own responsibility": Wilson, *Under the Old Flag*, Vol. 2, p. 94.

289  "Something important": O'Connor, *Thomas*, p. 315.


## 11. NASHVILLE, PART TWO

**Page**

291  "a gigantic left wheel": O'Connor, *Thomas*, p. 316.

291  "armed civilian employees": Steele, *American Campaigns*, Vol. 2, p. 573.

293  "came up fast": Ibid.

293  "was never cooler": Ibid.

293  "Will you please send": Van Horne, *Thomas*, p. 346.

293  "No army on the continent": Zimmerman, *Guide to Civil War Nashville*, p. 52.

293  "at all points with heavy loss": O'Connor, *Thomas*, p. 320.

294  "nigger soldiers": Johnson, *Memoir*, p. 197.

294  "So far I think": Rusling, *Men and Things*, p. 96.

294  "only regret": Wilson, *Under the Old Flag*, Vol. 2, p. 113.

295  "Attacked enemy's left": Johnson, *Memoir*, p. 198.

295  "I guess I will not go": Wilson, *Under the Old Flag*, Vol. 2, p. 95.

295  "with cool, steady bravery": Steedman's official report, "Battle of Nashville," www.civilwarhome.com/steedmannash.htm.

295  "I was unable to discover": Smith, ed., *Black Soldiers in Blue*, p. 63.

295  "fought side by side": Trudeau, *Like Men of War*, p. 344, fn. 17.

295  "For God's sake": *Tennessee Historical Quarterly*, Vol. 54, No. 3, p. 258; Wilson, *Under the Old Flag*, Vol. 2, p. 115.

296  "in person": O'Connor, *Thomas*, p. 321.

296  "Wilson appeared": Ibid.

296  "lifted his field glasses": Wilson, *Under the Old Flag*, Vol. 2, p. 116.

296  "crushed in like an egg-shell": Steele, *American Campaigns*, Vol. 1, p. 576.

296  "For the first and only time": Hood, *Advance and Retreat*, p. 302.

296  "the voice of the American people": Rusling, *Men and Things*, p. 101.

297  "effectively annihilated": O'Connor, *Thomas*, p. 322.

297  "it was more like a scene": *Battles and Leaders*, Vol. 4, p. 464.

297  "Thomas with his staff": Johnson, *Memoir*, p. 195.

297  "The issue is settled": Trudeau, *Like Men of War*, p. 349, fn. 32.

297  "with his head uncovered": Torrance, "Thomas," p. 22.

297  " 'Is that you, Wilson?' ": Wilson, *Under the Old Flag*, Vol. 2, p. 126.

297  "The Rock of Chickamauga": O'Connor, *Thomas*, p. 323.

298 "which was always," etc.: Bates, *Lincoln in the Telegraph Office*, pp. 317–18.

298 "I rejoice in tendering": Johnson, *Memoir*, p. 198.

298 "I was just on my way": Bates, *Lincoln*, p. 318.

298 "I congratulate you": Ibid., pp. 318–19; Johnson, *Memoir*, p. 198.

298 "Please accept for yourself": Ibid., pp. 197–98.

299 "The major-general commanding": *War of the Rebellion, Official Records*, 1st Series, Vol. 45, Part 1, p. 50.

299 "The army thanks you": Ibid., Part 2, p. 210.

299 "We all feel profoundly": Cleaves, *Rock*, p. 269.

299 "I am happy to state": Johnson, *Memoir*, p. 200.

299 "the capture of over 10,000": Dwight, ed., *Critical Sketches*, p. 192.

300 "Great precaution": Johnson, *Memoir*, p. 200.

300 "Permit me, General": *War of the Rebellion, Official Records*, Vol. 45, Part 2, p. 295.

300 General Hood's army: Ibid., pp. 295–96.

301 "I have seen today": Ibid., p. 307.

302 "I am profoundly thankful": Ibid., pp. 203–4.

302 "I think Thomas has won": Piatt and Boynton, *Thomas*, p. 575.

302 "With great pleasure": Van Horne, *Thomas*, p. 371.

302 "What do you think": Rusling, *Men and Things*, p. 104.

303 "I beg to assure": Piatt and Boynton, *Thomas*, p. 377.

303 "very sore": *War of the Rebellion, Official Records*, 1st Series, Vol. 45, Part 2, p. 461.

303 "There is one thing": O'Connor, *Thomas*, p. 327.

303 "Nashville was the most": Fiske, *The Mississippi Valley in the Civil War*, p. 355.

303 "the most economical": O'Connor, *Thomas*, p. 324.

304 "unopposed except by": Alexander, *Fighting for the Confederacy*, p. 496.

304 "I congratulate you," etc.: Piatt and Boynton, *Thomas*, p. 577.

304 "It was a sore disappointment": Ibid.

304 "The Confederacy lived": Swinton, *Twelve Decisive Battles*, p. 470.

304 "to be forwarded": Sherman, *Memoirs*, p. 566.

305 "By day": Wellborn, *Growth of American Nationality*, p. 917.

305 I have heard of your: O'Connor, *Thomas*, p. 324.

306 "When you were about leaving": Sherman, *Memoirs*, p. 532.

306 "brilliant victory": Ibid., p. 580.

306 "There was something incredible": O'Connor, *Thomas*, p. 325.

307 "Our cavalry had fought": Grant, *Personal Memoirs*, p. 542.

307 "No other pursuit": Wilson, *Under the Old Flag*, Vol. 2, p. 125.

307 "A more persistent": *War of the Rebellion, Official Records*, 1st Series, Vol. 45, Part 1, p. 690.

307  Thomas's pursuit of Hood: Ibid., p. 553.

307  "The intense heat": Flood, *Grant and Sherman*, p. 191.

307  "Continue the pursuit": Ibid.

307  "for the energy": O'Connor, *Thomas*, p. 326.

307  "It is refreshing": *War of the Rebellion, Official Records*, 1st Series, Vol. 45, Part 2, p. 264.

308  "easy": Flood, *Grant and Sherman*, p. 278.

308  I have always wondered: Shanks, *Personal Recollections*, p. 86.

308  "with which Thomas gained": O'Connor, *Thomas*, p. 349.

309  "indisputable that Sherman": Wilson, *Dana*, p. 351.

309  "To me his delay": Grant, *Personal Memoirs*, p. 538.

309  "I never heard anyone": Van Horne, *Thomas*, p. 367.

309  "he moved with irresistible": Torrance, "Thomas", p. 20.

## 12. "THE NOBLEST FIGURE"

**Page**

311  "Lieutenant General U. S. Grant": O'Connor, *Thomas*, p. 330.

311  "too ponderous": Ibid., p. 331.

311  "scattered the infantry": Wilson, *Under the Old Flag*, Vol. 2, p. 180.

312  "the largest body of cavalry": Ibid., p. 165.

312  "inactive": Piatt and Boynton, *Thomas*, p. 597.

312  "all the latitude": Wilson, *Under the Old Flag*, Vol. 2, p. 180.

312  "Ever since you started": Sherman, *Memoirs*, p. 666.

312  "Just as soon as I hear": Lewis, *Sherman*, p. 458.

313  "It was a large factor": Piatt and Boynton, *Thomas*, p. 580.

313  "Most of these expeditions": Grant, *Personal Memoirs*, p. 620.

314  "upon the same terms": Thomas Papers, Henry Huntington Library, Letter of May 1, 1865.

314  "I think . . . it will be impossible": Ibid.

314  "If Davis escapes": Longacre, *Grant's Cavalryman*, p. 222.

314  "Wishing to forward Jeff. Davis": Thomas Papers, Henry Huntington Library, Letter of May 15, 1865.

315  "every great and important event," etc.: Welles, *Diary*, Vol. 2, pp. 282–83.

316  "the verge of despair": Thomas Papers, Henry Huntington Library, Letter of May 2, 1865.

316  "to explain fully": Ibid.

316  "I . . . want to see": *War of the Rebellion, Official Records*, 1st Series, Vol. 49, Part 2, p. 514.

316  "I have always had": Ibid., p. 548.

316 "Mr. Stanton, I am sorry": Ibid.

316 "I feel before him": Piatt and Boynton, *Thomas*, p. 438.

316 "the gravity and dignity": Ridpath, *Garfield*, p. 253.

317 "Washington greatness": Sherman, *Personal Memoirs*, 4th ed., Appendix, p. 540.

317 "With less opportunity": Howard, "Sketch," p. 302.

317 "intellectually and as a civilian": Welles, *Diary*, Vol. 2, p. 382.

317 "who had been known": Johnson, *Memoir*, pp. 232–33.

317 "folding up the map": Van Horne, *Thomas*, p. 395.

317 "I wish you to take": Ibid., p. 396.

318 "You know my appreciation": Ibid.

319 "It is essential": Smith, *The United States*, p. 300.

319 "under good discipline": Johnson Papers, 76:6701.

319 "secret organizations": Cleaves, *Rock of Chickamauga*, p. 294.

319 "a species of political cant": Van Horne, *Thomas*, p. 405.

320 "failed to take any notice": Cleaves, *Rock*, p. 291.

320 "With too many of the people": *Army and Navy Journal*, March 2, 1867.

321 "the terrible ordeal": O'Connor, *Thomas*, p. 352.

321 "Thomas is a grand man": Van Horne, *Thomas*, p. 406.

321 "inclined to the radicals": Welles, *Diary*, Vol. 2, p. 212.

322 "a pretended Bishop": Van Horne, *Thomas*, pp. 409–10.

322 "when it was not considered wrong": Coppee, *Thomas*, p. 307.

322 "satisfied with his pay": Ibid., p. 308.

322 "Whatever my services were": O'Connor, *Thomas*, p. 340.

323 "dumb show": Military Historical Society of Massachusetts, *Papers*, Vol. 10, p. 198.

323 "the audience rising": Van Horne, *Thomas*, pp. 425–26.

323 "Now, gentlemen": Johnson, *Memoir*, p. 242.

324 "I am a soldier," etc.: Van Horne, *Thomas*, p. 422.

324 "throughout the Southwest": Coppee, *Thomas*, p. 295.

324 "there is little doubt": Ibid.

324 "he underrated his qualifications," etc.: Dwight, ed., *Critical Sketches*, p. 203.

325 "Had we not known": O'Connor, *Thomas*, p. 348.

325 "It required exhaustive": McClure, *Lincoln & Men of War-Times*, p. 370.

325 "For the battle of Nashville": Dwight, ed., *Critical Sketches*, p. 203.

326 "for one moment": Thomas Papers, Henry Huntington Library, Letter of March 22, 1869, to Col. R. H. Ramsey.

326 "I think his": Cleaves, *Rock*, pp. 301–2.

326 "exercise the right": Thomas Papers, Henry Huntington Library, Letter of March 22, 1869.

326 "Colonel, I have taken": Johnson, *Memoir*, p. 134; Shanks, *Personal Recollections*, pp. 70–71; Bradford, *Union Portraits*, p. 129.

327 "Thomas, there has got to be": Van Horne, *Thomas*, pp. 433–34.

327 "We are going to California": Ibid.

327 "he would publicly": Ibid., p. 434.

327 "humiliated and heartsore": McClure, *Lincoln and Men*, p. 371.

328 "my ladies anticipate": Thomas Papers, Henry Huntington Library, Letter of October 18, 1869, to Fitz John Porter.

328 "White lines bordered": Keyes, *Fifty Years'*, p. 167.

328 "There will be a rush": George H. Thomas, Letter, September 21, 1869, War Department Files, National Archives.

328 "an enemy to our race": "William Tecumseh Sherman," on-line biography.

328 "Go ahead in your own way": www.aotc.net/Grant.htm.

329 "I am now satisfied": O'Connor, *Thomas*, p. 360.

330 "the great battles of history": Ibid., p. 362.

330 "It is therefore left to candid": Thomas, *Thomas*, p. 624.

331 "A few blurred": Van Horne, *Thomas*, p. 455.

331 "I want air": Ibid., p. 442.

331 "I observed he was speaking": Ibid.

331 "since they sat as boys": Johnson, *Memoir*, pp. 258–59.

332 "I will say that it preyed": John N. Hough Papers, quoted in Thomas, *Thomas*, p. 617.

332 "Thomas was killed": Starr, *Grant and Thomas*.

332 "All I did for my Government": Piatt and Boynton, *Thomas*, p. 50.

332 "This sad duty": Van Horne, *Thomas*, p. 444.

333 "very happy in one another": Thomas Papers, Henry Huntington Library, Letter of March 4, 1865, to Mrs. Hamilton Draper.

333 "General Howard: In answer": Howard, "Sketch," p. 287.

333 "a national calamity": Johnson, *Memoir*, p. 264.

333 "the ablest, the most just": Society of the Army of the Cumberland, *Yearbook*, 1871, p. 71.

334 "a faultless soldier": Wilbur Thomas, *Thomas*, p. 27.

334 "Of him, and of him alone": Piatt and Boynton, *Thomas*, pp. 76–77.

334 "He was the grandest character": "Talk with General Steedman," *The New York Times*, November 24, 1879, p. 2.

334 "the most gifted soldier": O'Connor, *Thomas*, p. 367.

334 "the magnificent self-possession": Johnson, *Memoir*, p. 279.

334 "The relations between Thomas," etc.: Ibid., pp. 286–88.

335 "Grant was apt": Bradford, *Union Portraits*, p. 130.

335  As my official letters: Grant, *Personal Memoirs*, p. 624.

336  "What a general could do": Catton, *Hallowed Ground*, p. 283.

336  "Thomas comes down in history": Ibid., p. 369.

336  "haunting feeling": Catton, "Rock of Chickamauga."

337  "I believe it must now": Schofield, *Forty-six Years*, pp. 241–42.

337  "Robbing a grave": O'Connor, *Thomas*, p. 376.

337  "pick to pieces": McDonough, *Nashville*, p. 17.

337  "assumes a grand": Ibid.

337  "the chief source": Starr, "Grant and Thomas."

337  "as a strategist": Ibid.

338  "unprecedented military control": Wilbur Thomas, *Thomas*, p. 33.

338  "stoned to political": Society of the Army of the Cumberland, *Yearbook*, 1893, p. 60.

339  "outraged every rule": Bridges, "Donn Piatt, Diplomat and Gadfly."

339  "unreliable," etc.: *The New York Times*, January 31, 1880.

340  "entirely without character": Ibid.

340  "conduct unbecoming": Ibid.

340  "Gen. Grant . . . knows well": "New Sherman Letters—General Boynton's Reply," *The New York Times*, August 24, 1902, p. 21.

340  "a personal interest": Ibid.

340  "material points": Ibid.

340  "with the statement": Ibid.

341  "omissions and distortions": Castel, *Winning and Losing*, p. 92.

341  "often widely at variance": Ibid., p. 111.

341  "The time has not come": "An Autographic Justification of Gen. Fry's Assertions," *The New York Times*, January 30, 1886, p. 10.

342  "impossible": Quoted in ibid.

342  "invented the quotation": Quoted in ibid.

342  "my denial": Quoted in ibid.

342  "when cornered": Quoted in ibid.

342  "dodge the issue": Quoted in ibid.

343  "To my men": O'Connor, *Thomas*, p. 197.

# BIBLIOGRAPHY

## MANUSCRIPTS AND PAPERS

Reports of General Officers in the Old Records Division of the Adjutant General's Office, War Department; War Department Files, National Archives, Washington, D.C.; R. S. Ewell Papers, R. W. Johnson Papers, Fitz John Porter Papers, W. T. Sherman Papers, and Edwin M. Stanton Papers, Library of Congress, Washington, D.C.; Don Carlos Buell Papers, Rice University, Houston, Texas; George H. Thomas Papers, Henry E. Huntington Library, San Marino, California; John N. Hough Papers, University of Colorado, Boulder, Archives; Mattie R. Tyler Papers, Office of the Clerk, Southampton County, Courtland, Virginia; Miscellaneous Papers, Chicago Historical Society Library; California State Library, Sacramento; Pennsylvania Historical Society Library, Philadelphia; Tennessee State Library and Archives, Nashville; Virginia Historical Society, Richmond; Duke University Library, Durham, North Carolina; United States Military Academy Library, West Point.

## PERIODICALS

*American Heritage*, April 1959.

Anderson, Colonel Thomas M. "General George H. Thomas." *Military Service Institution Journal* 56 (January–February, 1915), 37–42.

*Army and Navy Journal*, March 1867.

"An Autographic Justification of Gen. Fry's Assertions." *The New York Times*, January 30, 1886, p. 10 (Online archive).

Bowers, John. "The Rock of Chickamauga." *Military History Quarterly* 3 (Winter 1991), 50–59.

Byers, S. H. M. "Some More War Letters." *North American Review* 144 (April 1887), 374–80.

"Cadet Life Before the Mexican War." *U.S. Military Academy Bulletin*, No. 1, pp. 12–24.

*Century Magazine*, August 1887.

"The Charge and Specifications (Gen. Boynton vs. Gen. Sherman)." *The New York Times*, January 31, 1880, p. 8 (online archive).

Crane, R. C. "Major George H. Thomas on the Trail of Indians in 1860." *West Texas Historical Association Year Book* 20 (October 1944), 77–84.

Cummins, Colonel M. L. "An Episode in the Texas Career of General David E. Twiggs." *Southwestern Historical Quarterly* 41 (October 1937), 167–73.

———. "Major George H. Thomas in Texas." *West Historical Association Year Book* 14 (October 1938), 73–81.

Davis, Steve. "John Bell Hood's 'Addictions' in Civil War Literature." *Blue & Gray Magazine* (October 1998), 10–21.

"Fitz John Porter's Trial." *The New York Times*, January 4, 1879, p. 10 (online archive).

"Funeral of General Boynton." *The New York Times*, June 8, 1905, p. 9 (online archive).

Furguson, E. B. "Catching Up with Old 'Slow Trot.'" *Smithsonian Magazine* (March 2007), 11–17.

"General H. V. Boynton Receives the Five Pointed Star." *The New York Times*, November 10, 1893, p. 10 (online archive).

"George H. Thomas. One of the General's Last Letters." *The New York Times*, March 14, 1872, p. 2.

Gist, W. W. "The Battle of Franklin." *Tennessee Historical Magazine* 6 (October 1920), 213–65.

Hay, Thomas R. "The Battle of Spring Hill." *Tennessee Historical Magazine*, 7 (April 1921), 74–91.

Horn, Stanley F. "Nashville During the Civil War." *Tennessee Historical Quarterly* 4 (March 1945), 3–22.

"Isle of Wight County Records." *William and Mary Quarterly* 7, no. 4 (April 1899), 205–316.

Johnson, Lewis. "General Thomas's First Victory." *United Service Journal*, 13 (October 1895), 385–99.

Johnston, General Joseph E. "Opposing Sherman's Advance to Atlanta." *Century Magazine* 12 (August 1887), 584–96.

Joyner, Fred B. "Robert Cumming Schenck, First Citizen and Statesman, Ohio History," *The Scholarly Journal of the Ohio Historical Society*, July 1949, 22–32.

MacDonnell, Francis. "The Confederate Spin on Winfield Scott and George Thomas." *Civil War History* 34 (December 1998), 255–66.

"New Sherman Letters—General Boynton's Reply." *The New York Times*, August 24, 1902, p. 21 (online archive).

*North American Review*, December 1885, January 1886.

"Notes & Queries." *Southern Historical Papers*, 10 (November 1882), 524–25; 12 (December 1884), 568.

Piatt, Donn. "The General Who Heard Mass Before Battle." *The Collector* (January–February 1942), 33–36, 49–52.

Sherman, General W. T. "Old Shady, with a Moral." *North American Review* 147 (October 1888), 361–68.

Stone, Colonel Henry. "Hood's Invasion of Tennessee." *Century Magazine* 12 (August 1887), 597–616.

"Talk with General Steedman." *The New York Times*, November 24, 1879, p. 2 (online archive).

*Tennessee Historical Quarterly* 64, no. 3 (Fall 2005).

*Troy Times*, April 6, 1870.

*Virginia Magazine of History and Biography* 40, (October 1932), 331, 69 (January 1961) 5–6.

Wells, Colonel E. T. "The Campaign of Chickamauga." *United Service Journal* 16, (September 1896), 217–27.

## GENERAL SOURCES

Abbott, J. S. C. *The History of the Civil War in America*. 3 vols. New York: Henry Bill, 1867.

Alexander, Edward Porter. *Fighting for the Confederacy*. Chapel Hill: University of North Carolina Press, 1989.

Ambrose, Stephen E. *Upton and the Army*. Baton Rouge: Louisiana State University Press, 1964.

Anderson, Charles C. *Fighting by Southern Federals*. New York: Neale, 1912.

Andrews, Peter. "The Rock of Chickamauga." In *The Civil War: The Best of American Heritage*. New York: Houghton Mifflin, 1991.

Angle, Paul M. *Lincoln's Speeches and Letters*. New York: E. P. Dutton, 1957.

*Annual Report of the American Historical Association for the Year 1913*. Vol. 1. Washington, D.C.: U.S. Government Printing Office, 1915.

Badeau, Adam. *Military History of U. S. Grant*. 3 vols. New York: Appleton, 1881.

Bailey, Anne J. *The Chessboard of War. Sherman and Hood in the Autumn Campaigns of 1864*. Lincoln: University of Nebraska Press, 2000.

Bailey, Ronald H. *Battles for Atlanta: Sherman Moves East*. New York: Time-Life Books, 1985.

Baird, Charles W. *History of the Huguenot Emigration to America*. 2 vols. New York: Dodd, Mead, 1885.

Banks, R. W. *Battle of Franklin*. Dayton, OH: Morningside, 1982.

Bates, David Homer. *Lincoln in the Telegraph Office*. New York: Century, 1907.

*Battles and Leaders of the Civil War*. Ed. R. U. Johnson and C. C. Buel. 4 vols. New York: Century, 1887–88.

Baumgartner, Richard A., and Larry M. Strayer. *Echoes of Battle: The Struggle for Chattanooga*. Huntington, WV: Blue Acorn, 1996.

Beale, Howard K. *The Critical Year: A Study of Andrew Johnson and Reconstruction*. New York: Frederick Ungar, 1958.

———, ed. *The Diary of Edward Bates, 1859–1866. Annual Report of the American Historical Association*. 4 vols. Washington, D.C., 1930.

Beatty, John. *Memoirs of a Volunteer*. New York: W. W. Norton, 1946.

Bennett, L. G. *History of the 36th Illinois Volunteer Regiment*. Phoenix: Prairie State Press, 2009.

Berlin, Ira, Joseph P. Reidy, and Leslie S. Rowland, eds. *Freedom's Soldiers: The Black Military Experience in the Civil War*. New York: Cambridge University Press, 1998.

Berry, Thomas. *Four Years with Morgan and Forrest*. Oklahoma City, Harlow-Ratliff, 1914.

Bickham, W. D. *Rosecrans' Campaign with the Fourteenth Army Corps*. Cincinnati: Moore, Wilstach, Keys, 1863.

*Biographical Sketches, Union Army*. 8 vols. Madison: Federal Publishing Co., 1908.

Bishop, Judson W. *The Story of a Regiment*. St. Cloud, MN: North Star, 2000.

Boatner, Mark M. III. *The Civil War Dictionary*. New York: David McKay, 1988.

Bobrick, Benson. *Testament: A Soldier's Story of the Civil War*. New York: Simon & Schuster, 2003.

Bowman, John S., ed. *Encyclopedia of the Civil War*. North Dighton, MA: J. G. Press, 2001.

Boynton, Edward C. *A History of West Point*. New York: Ayer, 1963.

Boynton, H. V. The *Chickamauga and Chattanooga National Military Park*. Washington, D.C.: Government Printing Office, 1896.

———. *Sherman's Historical Raid: The Memoirs in the Light of the Record*. Cincinnati: Wilstach, Baldwin, 1875.

———. *Was General Thomas Slow at Nashville? With a Description of the Greatest Cavalry Movement of the War and General James H. Wilson's Cavalry Operations in Tennessee, Alabama and Georgia*. New York: F. P. Harper, 1896.

Bradford, Gamaliel. *Union Portraits*. Boston: Houghton Mifflin, 1916.

Bradley, Michael, R. *Tullahoma—The 1863 Campaign for the Control of Middle Tennessee*. Shippensburg, PA: White Mane, 1999.

Bridges, Peter. "Donn Piatt, Diplomat and Gadfly." http://www.unc.edu/depts/diplomat/item/2007/0103/life/bridges_piatt.htm.

Brock, W. R. *The Character of American History*. New York: St. Martin's, 1960.

Brockett, L. P. *Our Great Captains: Grant, Sherman, Thomas, Sheridan, and Farragut*. New York: C. B. Richardson, 1865.

Brugger, Robert J. *Maryland: A Middle Temperament 1634–1980*. Baltimore: The Johns Hopkins University Press, 1996.

Buckeridge, J. O. *Lincoln's Choice*. Harrisburg: Stackpole, 1956.

Buell, Thomas B. *Warrior Generals: Combat Leadership in the Civil War*. New York: Three Rivers, 1997.

*The Campaign for Chattanooga*. Chickamauga and Chattanooga National Park Commission, 1896.

Canfield, S. S. *History of the 21st Regiment, Ohio Volunteer Infantry*. Toledo: Higginson Book Co., 1893.

Carleton, James H. *The Battle of Buena Vista*. New York: Harper & Brothers, 1848.

Castel, Albert. *Decision in the West: The Atlanta Campaign of 1864*. Lawrence: University Press of Kansas, 1992.

———. *Winning and Losing in the Civil War*. Columbia: University of South Carolina Press, 1996.

*Catalogue of the Library of the U.S. Military Academy, West Point, N.Y.* New York: John F. Trow, 1852.

Catton, Bruce. *The Civil War*. Boston: Houghton Mifflin, 1960.

———. "Rock of Chickamauga." Review of F. F. McKinney's *Education in Violence*, http://home.earthlink.net/~oneplez/majorgeneralgeorgehthomas blogsite/id35.html.

———. *This Hallowed Ground*. Garden City: Doubleday, 1956.

Chittenden, L. E. *Recollections of President Lincoln and His Administration*. New York: Harper & Brothers, 1891.

Churchill, Winston. *A History of the English-Speaking Peoples*. New York: Dodd Mead, 1983.

Cist, Henry M. *The Army of the Cumberland*. New York: Blue & Gray Press, n.d.

Cleaves, Freeman. *Rock of Chickamauga: The Life of General George H. Thomas*. Norman: University of Oklahoma Press, 1949.

Coffin, Charles C. *The Drum Beat of the Nation*. New York: Harper & Brothers, 1887.

Connolly, James A. *Three Years in the Army of the Cumberland*. Bloomington: Indiana University Press, 1959.

Conyngham, David P. *Sherman's March Through the South*. New York: Sheldon & Co., 1865.

Coolidge, L. A. *Ulysses S. Grant*. Boston: Houghton Mifflin, 1917.

Coppee, Henry. *General Thomas*. New York: Appleton, 1897.

Coulter, E. Merton. *Civil War and Readjustment in Kentucky*. Chapel Hill,: University of North Carolina, 1926.

Cox, Jacob D. *Atlanta*. New York: Charles Scribner's Sons, 1882.

———. *Battle of Franklin*. Dayton, OH: Morningside, 1983.

———. *The March to the Sea*. New York: Charles Scribner's Sons, 1882.

———. *Military Reminiscences of the Civil War*. 2 vols. New York: Charles Scribner's Sons, 1900.

Cozzens, Peter. *No Better Place to Die: The Battle of Stones River*. Urbana: University of Illinois Press, 1990.

———. *The Shipwreck of Their Hopes: The Battles of Chattanooga*. Chicago: University of Illinois Press, 1994.

———. *This Terrible Sound, The Battle of Chickamauga*. Chicago: University of Illinois Press, 1992.

Cullum, George W. *Biographical Register of Officers and Cadets of the U.S. Military Academy*. Vols. 1–3. Chicago: R. R. Donnelley, 1930.

Dana, Charles A. *Recollections of the Civil War*. Lincoln: University of Nebraska Press, 1996.

Daniel, Larry J. *Shiloh—The Battle That Changed the Civil War*. New York: Simon & Schuster, 1997.

Davis, Jefferson. *Rise and Fall of the Confederate Government*. 2 vols. New York: D. Appleton, 1881.

Davis, William C. *Stand in the Day of Battle*. New York: Doubleday, 1983.

Day, L. W. *The Story of a Regiment. The One Hundred and First Ohio*. Cleveland: W. M. Bayne, 1894.

Deaterick, J. B. *The Truth About Shiloh*. Memphis: S. C. Toof, 1942.

*Dedication of the Chickamauga and Chattanooga National Military Park*. Washington, D.C.: U.S. Government Printing Office, 1896.

De Leon, T. C. *Belles, Beaux and Brains of the Sixties*. New York: G. W. Dillingham, 1909.

DeVoto, Bernard. *The Year of Decision, 1846*. Boston: Little, Brown, 1943.

*Dictionary of American Biography*. 3 vols. New York: Scribner's, 1971.

Donald, David Herbert. *Lincoln*. New York: Simon & Schuster, 1995.

"Donn Piatt." *Biographical Sketches*. Logan County, Ohio History, www.heritagepursuit.com/LoganLate.htm.

Douglass, Frederick. *The Life and Times of Frederick Douglass*. Whitefish, MT: Kessinger Publishing House 2004.

Dowdey, Clifford. *Experiment in Rebellion*. New York: Doubleday, 1946.

Drewry, William Sidney. *The Southampton Insurrection*. Washington, D.C.: Neale, 1900.

Dwight, Theodore, ed. *Critical Sketches of Some of the Federal and Confederate Commanders.* Papers of the Military Historical Society of Massachusetts. Vol. 10. Boston: Houghton Mifflin, 1895.

Dyer, Brainerd. *Zachary Taylor.* Baton Rouge: Louisiana State University Press, 1946.

Dyer, Frederick H., ed. *A Compendium of the War of the Rebellion.* New York: Thomas Yoseloff, 1959.

Dyer, John P. *From Shiloh to San Juan: The Life of "Fightin' Joe" Wheeler.* Baton Rouge: Louisiana State University Press, 1992.

Eicher, David J. *The Longest Night: A Military History of the Civil War.* New York: Simon & Schuster, 2001.

Einolf, Christopher J. *George Thomas: Virginian for the Union.* Norman, OK: University of Oklahoma Press, 2007.

Eisenschiml, Otto. *The Celebrated Case of Fitz John Porter: An American Dreyfus Affair.* Indianapolis: Bobbs-Merrill, 1950.

Eisenschiml, Otto, and Ralph Newman. *The American Iliad.* Indianapolis: Bobbs-Merrill, 1947.

*Encyclopaedia Britannica.* 15th ed. 29 vols. Chicago, 1988.

*Encyclopedia Americana.* 30 vols. New York: American Book-Stratford Press, 1954.

Engle, Stephen D. *Don Carlos Buell.* Chapel Hill: University of North Carolina Press, 1999.

Farley, J. P. *West Point in the Early '60's.* Troy, NY: William H. Young, 1902.

Fellman, Michael. *Citizen Sherman: A Life of William Tecumseh Sherman.* New York: Random House, 1995.

Fingerson, Ronald L. "A William Tecumseh Sherman Letter." *Books at Iowa 3* (November 1965) (online archive).

Fiske, John. *Essays Historical and Literary.* Vol. 1. New York: Macmillan, 1903.

———. *The Mississippi Valley in the Civil War.* Boston: Houghton Mifflin, 1900.

Fitch, John. *Annals of the Army of the Cumberland.* Philadelphia: J. B. Lippincott, 1864.

Fitch, Michael Hendrick. *Echoes of the Civil War.* New York: R. F. Renno, 1905.

Flood, Charles Bracelen. *Grant and Sherman. The Friendship That Won the Civil War.* New York: Farrar, Straus & Giroux, 2005.

Foner, Eric. *Nat Turner.* Englewood Cliffs, NJ.: Prentice Hall, 1971.

Foote, Shelby. *The Civil War: A Narrative.* 3 vols. New York: Vintage, 1986.

Force, M. F. *Campaigns of the Civil War—From Fort Henry to Corinth.* New York: Noble Offset Printers, n.d.

———. *General Sherman.* New York: D. Appleton, 1899.

Forman, Sidney. *Cadet Life Before the Mexican War.* West Point: United States Military Academy Printing Office, 1946.

Fox, William F. *Regimental Losses in the Civil War*. Albany, NY: Albany Publishing Co., 1889.

Frantz, Mabel Goode. *Full Many a Name*. Jackson, TN: McCowat-Mercer, 1961.

Freeman, Douglas Southall. *Lee's Lieutenants: A Study in Command*. 3 vols. New York: Charles Scribner's Sons, 1942–1944.

———. *Robert E. Lee*. 4 vols. New York: Charles Scribner's Sons, 1935.

Freeman, Douglas Southall. Ed. *Lee's Dispatches*. Baton Rouge: Louisiana State University Press, 1957.

Freemon, Frank R. *Gangrene and Glory: Medical Care During the Civil War*. Chicago: University of Illinois Press, 2001.

French, Samuel G. *Two Wars*. Huntington, WV: Blue Acorn, 1999.

Fry, James B. *Operations of the Army Under Buell*. New York: D. Van Nostrand, 1884.

Fuller, J. F. C. *The Generalship of Ulysses S. Grant*. New York: Dodd, Mead, 1929.

Garfield, James A. *Oration on the Life and Character of General George H. Thomas. Delivered Before the Society of the Army of the Cumberland, Cleveland, November 25, 1870*. Cincinnati: Robert Clarke & Co., 1871.

———. *The Wild Life of the Army: Civil War Letters of James A. Garfield*. Ed., F. D. Williams. East Lansing. Michigan State University Press, 1964.

Geer, Walter. *Campaigns of the Civil War*. Old Saybrook, CT: Konecky & Konecky, 1926.

Giddings, L. *Sketches of the Campaign in Northern Mexico*. New York: G. P. Putnam, 1853.

Glatthaar, Joseph T. *Forged in Battle: The Civil War Alliance of Black Soldiers and White Officers*. New York: Free Press, 1990.

Gordon, John B. *Reminiscences of the Civil War*. New York: Charles Scribner's Sons, 1905.

Gordy, Wilbur F. *Heroes and Leaders of American History*. Boston: Charles Scribner's Sons, 1917.

Govan, Gilbert, and James Livingwood. *A Different Valor: Joseph E. Johnston*. New York: Konecky & Konecky, 1956.

Gracie, Archibald. *The Truth About Chickamauga*. Boston: Houghton Mifflin, 1911.

Grant, U. S. *Personal Memoirs*. New York: Penguin, 2001.

Gray, Thomas R. *The Confession, Trial, and Execution of Nat Turner*. Baltimore, 1831. Appended to F. Roy Johnson, *The Nat Turner Insurrection*, pp. 225–248.

Groom, Winston. *Shrouds of Glory—From Atlanta to Nashville*. New York: Atlantic Monthly Press, 1995.

Hafendorfer, Kenneth A. *Perryville*. Owensboro, KY: McDowell, 1981.

Hall, Clifton R. *Andrew Johnson: Military Governor of Tennessee*. Princeton: Princeton University Press, 1916.

Hamilton, Holman. *Zachary Taylor*. 2 vols. Norwalk, CT: Easton Press, 1989.

Hart, H. Liddell. *Sherman: Soldier, Realist, American*. New York: Frederick A. Praeger, 1958.

Haskew, Michael E. "Winter Fury Unleashed," America's Civil War, www.the history.net.

Hattaway, Herman, and Archer Jones. *How the North Won: A Military History of the Civil War*. Urbana: University of Illinois Press, 1991.

Hay, Thomas R. *Hood's Tennessee Campaign*. New York: Walter Neale, 1925.

Haynie, J. H. *The Nineteenth Illinois*. Whitefish, MT: Kessinger, 2001.

Hazen, William B. *A Narrative of Military Service*. Boston: Ticknor, 1885.

Headley, J. T. *The Great Rebellion*. 2 vols. Washington, D.C.: National Tribune, 1898.

Hebert, Walter A. *"Fighting Joe" Hooker*. Indianapolis: Bobbs-Merrill, 1944.

Hedley, F. Y. *Marching Through Georgia*. Chicago: R. R. Donnelly, 1887.

Heitman, Francis B. *Historical Register and Dictionary of the U.S. Army*. 2 vols. Washington, D.C.: U.S. Government Printing Office, 1903.

Henry, Robert Selph. *"First with the Most" Forrest*. Indianapolis: Bobbs-Merrill, 1944.

———. *The Story of Reconstruction*. New York: Grosset & Dunlap, 1938.

———. *The Story of the Confederacy*. Indianapolis: Bobbs-Merrill, 1936.

———. *The Story of the Mexican War*. New York: Frederick Ungar, 1961.

Henry, W. S. *Campaign Sketches of the War With Mexico*. New York: Harper & Brothers, 1847.

"Henry W. Halleck." *Mr. Lincoln's White House* (online archive).

Hergesheimer, Joseph. *Sheridan*. Boston: Houghton Mifflin, 1931.

Hicken, Victor. *Illinois in the Civil War*. Urbana: University of Illinois Press, 1966.

Hill, D. H. *Chickamauga*. New York: Century Magazine, 1887.

Hirshson, Stanley P. *The White Tecumseh: A Biography of William T. Sherman*. New York: Wiley & Sons, 1997.

*The History of Our Country*. 8 vols. Philadelphia: History Co., 1899.

Hitchcock, Henry. *Marching with Sherman*. New Haven: Yale University Press, 1927.

Hood, John B. *Advance and Retreat*. New Orleans: Hood Orphan Memorial Fund, 1880.

Hopkins, Timothy. *The Kelloggs in the Old World and the New*. 3 vols. San Francisco: Sunset Press and Photo Engraving Co., 1903.

Horn, Stanley F. *The Army of Tennessee*. Indianapolis: Bobbs-Merrill, 1941.

————. *The Decisive Battle of Nashville*. Baton Rouge: Louisiana State University Press, 1957.

Howard, Oliver Otis. *Autobiography*. 2 vols. New York: Baker & Taylor, 1908.

*Indiana at Chickamauga*. Indianapolis: Sentinel, 1900.

"James B. Fry." *Mr. Lincoln's White House* (online archive).

Johnson, F. Roy. *The Nat Turner Slave Insurrection*. Murfreesboro, NC: Johnson, 1966.

Johnson, Richard W. *Memoir of Major General George H. Thomas*. Philadelphia: J. B. Lippincott, 1881.

————. *A Soldier's Reminiscences*. Philadelphia: J. B. Lippincott, 1886.

Johnson, Rossiter. *Fight for the Republic*. New York: G. P. Putnam's Sons, 1917.

Johnston, Joseph E. *A Narrative of Military Operations and Recollections*. New York: Da Capo, 1959.

Johnston, W. Preston. *Albert Sidney Johnston*. New York: D. Appleton, 1878.

*Joint Committee on the Conduct of the War Report*. 9 vols. Wilmington, NC: Broadfoot, 1998.

*Joint Committee on the Conduct of the War. Supplemental Report, 1866*. 2 vols. Lansing: University of Michigan Library, 2001.

Jones, John William. *Life and Letters of Robert E. Lee*. New York: Neale, 1906.

Jordan, Thomas, and J. P. Pryor. *The Campaigns of General Nathan Bedford Forrest and of Forrest's Cavalry*. New York: Da Capo, 1996.

Kenly, John R. *Memoirs of a Maryland Volunteer: War with Mexico*. Philadelphia: J. B. Lippincott, 1873.

Kennett, Lee. *Sherman: A Soldier's Life*. New York: HarperCollins, 2001.

Keyes, Erasmus D. *Fifty Years' Observation of Men and Events*. New York: Scribner, 1885.

King, Charles. *The Rock of Chickamauga*. New York: Dillingham, 1907.

————. *The True Ulysses S. Grant*. Philadelphia: J. B. Lippincott, 1914.

Kniffin, Gilbert C. *The Life and Services of Major General George H. Thomas*. Washington, D.C.: Judd & Detweiler, 1887.

Korn, Jerry. *The Fight for Chattanooga: Chickamauga to Missionary Ridge*. New York: Time Life Books, 1985.

Lambert, William H. *George Henry Thomas: Oration Before the Society of the Army of the Cumberland, at Rochester N.Y., September 17, 1884*. Cincinnati: Robert Clarke, 1885.

Lamers, William M. *The Edge of Glory: A Biography of General William S. Rosecrans*. Baton Rouge: Louisiana State University Press, 1999.

Lee, Robert E., Jr. *Recollections and Letters of General Robert E. Lee*. Garden City: Garden City Publishing, 1926.

Leech, Margaret. *Reveille in Washington*. New York: Harper & Brothers, 1941.

Lewis, Lloyd. *Sherman: Fighting Prophet*. New York: Harcourt, Brace, 1932.

Link, William A. *Roots of Secession. Slavery and Politics in Antebellum Virginia.* Chapel Hill: University of North Carolina Press, 2003.

Logan County, Ohio History, 584. "Biographical Sketches," http://www.heritagepursuit.com/LoganLate.html.

Long, E. B. *The Civil War Day by Day.* New York: Doubleday, 1971.

Longacre, Edward G. *Grant's Cavalryman: The Life and War of General James H. Wilson.* Mechanicsburg, PA: Stackpole, 1996.

Longstreet, James. *From Manassas to Appomattox.* Philadelphia: J. B. Lippincott, 1896.

Lyman, Theodore. *Meade's Headquarters, 1863–1865.* Boston: Atlantic Monthly Press, 1922.

Macartney, Clarence E. *Grant and His Generals.* New York: McBride, 1953.

———. *Highways and Byways of the Civil War.* Pittsburgh: Gibson, 1938.

Marszalek, John F. *Sherman: A Soldier's Passion for Order.* New York: Free Press, 1993.

McClure, Alexander K. *Lincoln and Men of War-Times.* Philadelphia: Times Publishing Co., 1892.

McDonough, James Lee. *Nashville: The Western Confederacy's Final Gamble.* Knoxville: University of Tennessee Press, 2004.

———. *War in Kentucky: From Shiloh to Perryville.* Knoxville: University of Tennessee Press, 1994.

McElroy, John. *Life of Maj.-General George H. Thomas.* Washington, D.C.: National Tribune, 1896.

McFeely, William S. *Grant: A Biography.* New York: W. W. Norton, 1981.

McKinney, Francis F. *Education in Violence: The Life of George H. Thomas and the History of the Cumberland.* Chicago: Americana House, 1991.

McMurry, Richard M. *John Bell Hood.* Lexington: University of Kentucky Press, 1982.

McPherson, James M. *Battle Cry of Freedom.* New York: Oxford University Press, 1988.

McPherson, James M., Ed. *Battle Chronicles of the Civil War, 1862.* New York: Macmillan, 1989.

———, Ed. *The Negro's Civil War.* New York: Vintage, 1965.

McPherson, James M., and Bruce Catton, Eds. *New American Heritage History of the Civil War.* New York: Simon & Schuster, 2001.

McWhiney, Grady. *Braxton Bragg and Confederate Defeat.* Vol. 1. Tuscaloosa: University of Alabama Press, 1969.

Meade, George Gordon. *The Life and Letters of General George Gordon Meade.* 2 vols. New York: Charles Scribner's Sons, 1913.

Miles, Jim. *Piercing the Heartland: A History and Tour Guide of the Tennessee and Kentucky Campaigns.* Nashville: Rutledge Hill, 1991.

"Military Conditions at the Outbreak of the Civil War." Instructions for cadets. West Point Museum, n.d.

Military Historical Society of Massachusetts Papers. Vol. 7, *Campaigns in Kentucky and Tennessee, 1862–64* (1908); Vol. 8, *The Mississippi Valley, Tennessee, Georgia, Alabama, 1861–64* (1910); Vol. 10, *Critical Sketches of Some Federal and Confederate Commanders* (1895).

Military Order of the Loyal Legion of the United States. *Papers, 1887–1915*. 70 vols. Wilmington, NC: Broadfoot, 1991–1997.

Miller, Marion Mills. *American Debate*. New York: G. P. Putnam's Sons, 1916.

Milton, George F. *The Age of Hate: Andrew Johnson and the Radicals*. New York: MacManus, 1930.

Monaghan, Jay. *Civil War on the Western Border, 1854–1865*. New York: Bonanza, 1955.

Moore, Frank, ed. *The Rebellion Record: A Diary of American Events, 1860–1862*. New York: G. P. Putnam, 1862.

Morrison, James L., Jr. *The Best School, West Point, 1833–1866*. Kent: Kent State University Press, 1986.

Moulton, C. W. *The Review of General Sherman's Memoirs Examined, Chiefly in the Light of Its Own Evidence*. Cincinnati: R. Clarke, 1875.

National Park Service. Pamphlets on battles and memorial parks.

Nevins, Allan. *The War for the Union: The Improvised War, 1861–1862*. New York: Charles Scribner's Sons, 1959.

———. *The War for the Union: War Becomes Revolution, 1862–1863*. New York: Charles Scribner's Sons, 1960.

Nicolay, John G., and John Hay. *Abraham Lincoln: A History*. 10 vols. New York: Century, 1909.

Noe, Kenneth. *Perryville: This Grand Havoc of Battle*. Lexington: University of Kentucky Press, 2001.

Oates, Stephen B. *The Fires of Jubilee*. New York: Harper & Row, 1975.

O'Connor, Richard. *Thomas: Rock of Chickamauga*. New York: Prentice Hall, 1948.

Olmsted, Frederick Law. *The Cotton Kingdom. A Traveller's Observations on Cotton and Slavery in the American Slave States*. New York: Da Capo, 1996.

Palmer, George T. *A Conscientious Turncoat*. Cambridge: Oxford University Press, 1941.

Palmer, John M. *Personal Recollections*. Cincinnati: Robert Clarke, 1901.

Palumbo, Frank A. *George Henry Thomas, Major General, U.S.A.: The Dependable General, Supreme in Tactics of Strategy and Command*. Dayton, OH: Morningside, 1983.

*Papers of the Military Historical Society of Massachusetts*. 15 vols. Wilmington, NC: Broadfoot, 2000.

Park, Roswell. *A Sketch of the History and Topography of West Point*. Philadelphia: Henry Perkins, 1840.

Parramore, Thomas C. *Southampton County, Virginia*. Charlottesville: University Press of Virginia, 1978.

Parrington, Vernon L. *The Beginnings of Critical Realism in America, 1860–1920*. New York: Harcourt, Brace, 1930.

Patton, James Welch. *Unionism and Reconstruction in Tennessee*. Chapel Hill. University of North Carolina Press, 1934.

Peckham, Howard H. *The War for Independence: A Military History*. Chicago: University of Chicago Press, 1959.

*Photographic History of the Civil War*. 10 vols. New York: Thomas Yoseloff, 1957.

Piatt, Donn, and H. V. Boynton. *General George H. Thomas: A Critical Biography*. Cincinnati: Robert Clarke, 1893.

———. *Memories of the Men Who Saved the Union*. New York: Belford, Clarke, 1887.

Porter, Horace. *Campaigning with Grant*. New York: Century, 1897.

Pratt, Fletcher. *The Civil War on Western Waters*. New York: Henry Holt, 1956.

———. *Eleven Generals: Studies in American Command*. New York: William Sloane, 1949.

———. *Stanton: Lincoln's Secretary of War*. New York: W. W. Norton, 1953.

Quarles, Benjamin. *The Negro in the Civil War*. New York: Da Capo, 1983.

Rawle, William. *A View of the Constitution of the United States of America*. Philadelphia: Philip H. Nicklin, 1829.

Redman, Bob. "Major-General George H. Thomas, Practitioner of Emancipation." www.aotc.net/article5.htm.

Reed, Samuel Rockwell. *The Vicksburg Campaign and the Battles About Chattanooga Under the Command of General U.S. Grant in 1862–1863*. Cincinnati: Robert Clarke & Co., 1882.

Reid, Samuel C. *Scouting Expedition of McCulloch's Texas Rangers*. Philadelphia: G. B. Zieber, 1848.

Reid, Whitelaw. *Ohio in the Civil War*. 2 vols. Columbus, OH: Eclectic Publishing Co., 1893.

Rhodes, James Ford. *History of the American Civil War, 1861–1865*. New York: Macmillan, 1923.

Richardson, Albert D. *The Secret Service*. Hartford: American Publishing Co., 1865.

Richardson, Rupert N. *The Comanche Barrier to the South Plains Settlement*. Austin: Eakin, 1996.

Ridpath, John Clark. *The Life and Work of General James A. Garfield*. Cincinnati: J. Q. Williams, 1881.

Ripley, Roswell S. *The War with Mexico*. 2 vols. New York: D. Appleton, 1849.

Rister, Carl C. *Robert E. Lee in Texas*. Norman: University of Oklahoma Press, 1946.

Robertson, James I., Jr., *The Civil War*. Washington, D.C.: U.S. Civil War Centennial Commission, 1963.

———. *Concise Illustrated History of the Civil War*. Gettysburg: National Historical Society, 1971.

Robertson, James I., Jr., ed. *Medical and Surgical History of the Civil War*. 15 vols. Wilmington, NC: Broadfoot, 1997.

Robinson, Fayette. *An Account of the Organization of the Army of the United States*. 2 vols. Philadelphia: E. H. Butler, 1848.

Robinson, Will H. *Story of Arizona*. Whitefish, MT: Kessinger, 2004.

Rodenbough, Theodore F., and William L. Haskin, eds. *The Army of the United States: Historical Sketches of Staff and Line with Portraits of Generals-in-Chief*. New York: Argonaut, 1966.

Rogers, Augustus C. *Sketches of Representative Men North and South*. New York: Atlantic, 1873.

Rusling, James F. *Men and Things I Saw in Civil War Days*. New York: Eaton & Mans, 1899.

Sandburg, Carl. *Abraham Lincoln: The War Years*. 4 vols. New York: Harcourt Brace, 1939.

Scaife, William R. *The Campaign for Atlanta*. Atlanta: Published by the author, 1985.

Schaff, Morris. *The Battle of the Wilderness*. Boston: Houghton Mifflin, 1910.

Schmucker, Samuel M. *A History of the Civil War in the United States*. Cincinnati: Bradley, 1863.

Schofield, John M. *Forty-six Years in the Army*. New York: Century, 1897.

"Schofield and Thomas: Blind Ambition at Nashville," on-line article. http://home.alt.net./~dmercado/Schofield and Thomas.htm

Seitz, Don C. *Braxton Bragg*. Columbia, SC: State Co., 1924.

Shanks, W. F. G. *Personal Recollections of Distinguished Generals*. New York: Harper & Brothers, 1866.

Shannon, Fred A. *The Organization and Administration of the U.S. Army, 1861–65*. 2 vols. Cleveland: Arthur H. Clarke, 1928.

Sheridan, Philip H. *Personal Memoirs*. 2 vols. New York: Charles L. Webster, 1888.

Sherman, John. *John Sherman's Recollections of Forty Years in the U.S. Senate, House and Cabinet*. Chicago: Werner, 1893.

Sherman, William T. *Memoirs*. New York: Penguin, 2000.

———. *Personal Memoirs*. 4th Edition. 2 vols. New York: Charles L. Webster, 1891.

———. *The Sherman Letters*. Ed. R. S. Thorndike. New York: Charles Scribner's Sons, 1894.

Sherwood, Isaac R. *Memories of the War*. Toledo: Chittenden, 1923.

Simon, John Y., and David L. Wilson, eds. *Ulysses S. Grant: Essays, Documents*. Carbondale: Southern Illinois University Press, 1981.

Simpson, Brooks D., and Jean V. Berlin, eds. *Sherman's Civil War: Selected Correspondence of William T. Sherman, 1860–1865*. Chapel Hill: University of North Carolina Press, 1999.

Smith, Goldwin. *The United States. An Outline of Political History, 1492–1871*. New York: Macmillan, 1901.

Smith, Jean Edward. *Grant*. New York: Simon & Schuster, 2001.

Smith, John David, ed. *Black Soldiers in Blue: African American Troops in the Civil War Era*. Chapel Hill: University of North Carolina Press, 2002.

Smith, Justin H. *The War with Mexico*. 2 vols. New York: Macmillan, 1919.

Society of the Army of the Cumberland. Reunion *Reports*. 30 vols. Cincinnati: Robert Clarke, 1868–1910.

———. *Yearbooks*, 1871, 1879, and 1893.

Sorrel, G. Moxley. *Recollections of a Confederate Staff Officer*. New York: Neale, 1905.

*Southern Historical Society Papers*. 55 vols. Wilmington, NC: Broadfoot, 1999.

Sprague, John T. *The Florida War*. New York: D. Appleton, 1847.

Squires, W. H. T. *The Days of Yesteryear*. Portsmouth, VA.: Printcraft, 1928.

———. *The Land of Decision*. Portsmouth, VA.: Printcraft, 1931.

Stanley, D. S. *Personal Memoirs of Major-General D. S. Stanley*. Cambridge: Little, Brown, 1917.

Starr, Stephen Z. "Grant and Thomas: December, 1864," *A Cincinnati Civil War Round Table Presentation*, 2002.

———. *The Union Cavalry in the Civil War*. 3 vols. Baton Rouge: Louisiana State University Press, 2007.

Steele, Matthew F. *American Campaigns*. 2 vols. Washington, D.C.: U.S. Infantry Association, 1931.

Stephenson, Nathaniel W. *Abraham Lincoln and the Union*. New Haven: Yale University Press, 1918.

———. *Texas and the Mexican War*. New Haven: Yale University Press, 1921.

Stevenson, Alexander F. *The Battle of Stone's River*. Boston: J. R. Osgood, 1884.

Stockdale, Paul H. *The Death of an Army: The Battle of Nashville & Hood's Retreat*. Murfreesboro, TN: Southern Heritage Press, 1992.

Stoddard, William O. *Ulysses S. Grant*. New York: Frederick A. Stokes, 1886.

Stone, Henry. *Some Federal and Confederate Commanders*. Boston: Houghton Mifflin, 1895.

Sunderland, Glenn W. *Lightning at Hoover's Gap: Wilder's Brigade in the Civil War*. New Jersey: Thomas Yoseloff, 1969.

Swiggett, Howard. *The Rebel Raider: A Life of John Hunt Morgan*. Garden City: Garden City Publishing, 1937.

Swinton, William. *Campaigns of the Army of the Potomac*. New York: Charles B. Richardson, 1866.

———. *The Twelve Decisive Battles of the War*. New York: Dick & Fitzgerald, 1867.

Sword, Wiley. *The Confederacy's Last Hurrah: Spring Hill, Franklin, and Nashville*. Lawrence: Kansas University Press, 1993.

———. *Mountains Touched with Fire: Chattanooga Besieged, 1863*. New York: St. Martin's, 1995.

Taylor, Benjamin F. *Mission Ridge and Lookout Mountain*. New York: D. Appleton, 1872.

Temple, Oliver P. *East Tennessee and the Civil War*. Freeport, NY: Books for Libraries Press, 1971.

———. *Notable Men of Tennessee*. New York: Cosmopolitan, 1912.

Thomas, Isaac, ed. *The Words of Abraham Lincoln*. Chicago: Western Publishing House, 1898.

Thomas, Wilbur. *General George H. Thomas: The Indomitable Warrior: A Critical Biography*. New York: Expository, 1964.

Torrance, Ell. *General George H. Thomas*. Address to the Minnesota Commandery of the Military Order of the Loyal Legion of the United States, March 9, 1897. Pamphlet.

Trudeau, Noah Andre. *Like Men of War: Black Troops in the Civil War, 1862–1865*. Boston: Little, Brown, 1998.

Tucker, Glenn. *Chickamauga: Bloody Battle in the West*. Dayton, OH: Morningside, 1984.

Turchin, John B. *Chickamauga*. Chicago: Fergus, 1888.

Upton, Emory. *The Military Policy of the United States*. Washington, D.C.: U.S. Government Printing Office, 1917.

U.S. Congress. Joint Committee on the Conduct of the War. *Report of Major General George H. Thomas*. Milwood, NY: Kraus Reprint, 1977.

U.S. Quartermaster General. *Organization of the Army of the Cumberland at the Battle of Chickamauga*. Washington, D.C.: U.S. Government Printing Office, 1932.

Vance, Wilson J. *Stone's River*. New York: Neale, 1914.

Van Horne, Thomas B. *History of the Army of the Cumberland*. 3 vols. Cincinnati: Robert Clarke, 1875.

———. *The Life of Major General George H. Thomas*. New York: Charles Scribner's Sons, 1882.

Villard, Henry. *Memoirs*. 2 vols. Boston: Houghton Mifflin, 1904.

*Virginia: A Guide to the Old Dominion*. New York: Oxford University Press, 1940–41.

Wakefield, John F., ed. *The Battle of Nashville*. Florence, AL: Honors Press, 2001.

Warner, Ezra J. *Generals in Blue*. Baton Rough: Louisiana State University Press, 1959.

———. *Generals in Gray*. Baton Rouge: Louisiana State University Press, 1959.

*War of the Rebellion: A Compilation of the Official Records of the Union and Confederate Armies*. 128 vols. Washington, D.C.: U.S. Government Printing Office, 1880–1901. *Supplement to the Official Records*. 100 vols. Wilmington, NC: Broadfoot, 1999.

Weigley, Russell F. *A Great Civil War: A Military and Political History, 1861–1865*. Bloomington: Indiana University Press, 2000.

Weise, A. J. *History of the City of Troy*. Troy, NY: William H. Young, 1876.

Wellborn, Fred W. *The Growth of American Nationality, 1492–1865*. New York: Macmillan, 1943.

Welles, Gideon. *The Diary of Gideon Welles*. 3 vols. Boston: Houghton Mifflin, 1911.

Werner, Edgar A. *Historical Sketch of the War of the Rebellion, 1861–1865*. 2 vols. Albany, NY: Weed, Parsons, 1890.

*West Point Atlas of American Wars*. Vol. 1., 1689–1900. New York: Frederick Praeger, 1959.

Westrate, Edwin V. *Those Fatal Generals*. Whitefish, MT: Kessinger, 2005.

Wheeler, Richard. *Voices of the Civil War*. New York: Thomas Y. Crowell, 1976.

Whitridge, Arnold. *No Compromise*. New York: Farrar, Straus & Cudahy, 1960.

Wilcox, Cadmus M. *History of the Mexican War*. Washington, D.C.: Church News Publishing, 1892.

Wiley, Bell Irvin. *The Common Soldier in the Civil War*. New York: Grosset & Dunlap, 1952.

"William Tecumseh Sherman," on-line biography. http://www.aotc.net/grant.htm

Williams, John Lee. *The Territory of Florida*. Facsimile of 1837 edition. Gainesville: University of Florida Press, 1962.

Williams, T. Harry. *Lincoln and His Generals*. New York: Alfred A. Knopf, 1952.

Wilmer, Richard H. *The Recent Past*. New York: Thomas Whittaker, 1887.

Wilson, James H. *Heroes of the Great Conflict: Life and Services of William F. Smith*. Wilmington, DE: J. M. Rogers, 1904.

———. *Life of Charles A. Dana*. New York: Harper & Brothers, 1907.

———. *Life of John A. Rawlins*. New York: Neale, 1916.

———. *Under the Old Flag*. 2 vols. New York: D. Appleton, 1911.

Wilson, William B. *A Few Acts and Actors in the Tragedy of the Civil War*. Philadelphia: Published by the author, 1892.

Winston, Robert W. *Robert E. Lee*. New York: Grosset and Dunlap, 1934.

Woods, Joseph T. *Steedman and His Men at Chickamauga*. Toledo: Blade Printing & Paper Co, 1876.

Woodworth, Steven E. *Nothing but Victory: The Army of the Tennessee, 1861–1865*. New York: Alfred A. Knopf, 2005.

Wyeth, John A. *Life of General Nathan Bedford Forrest*. New York: Harper & Brothers, 1899.

Young, John Russell. *Around the World with General Grant*. 2 vols. Whitefish, MT: Kessinger, 2006.

Zimmerman, Mark. *Guide to Civil War Nashville*. Nashville: Battle of Nashville Preservation Society, 2004.


## WEB SITES

http://home.att.net/%7Edmercado/

http://homepages.dsu.edu/jankej/civilwar/civilwar.htm

http://www.aotc.net (Army of the Cumberland)

http://www.civilwarhome.net

http://www.cwipremium.com/

http://www.perryville.net

http://www.thehistory.net

http://sunsite.utk.edu/civil-war/

http://tinyurl.com/2rkzy

http://www.link archive.engine

http://www.home.att.net/~dmercado/Schofield_and_Thomas.htm

http://www.civilhome.com/CMHnashville.htm

http://www.civilwarhome.com/coxnashville.htm

# INDEX

Page numbers in *italics* refer to maps.